Herr Sabin

GERMAN READING GRAMMAR

Revised Edition

BY

STANLEY L. SHARP

Chairman, Department of Language Arts
College of San Mateo

AND

FRIEDRICH WILHELM STROTHMANN

Executive Head, Department of Germanic
and Romanic Languages
Stanford University

Blaisdell Publishing Company

A Division of Ginn and Company

NEW YORK · TORONTO · LONDON

Ninth Printing, 1964

Printed in the United States of America

TO THE STUDENT

You were uppermost in our minds when we first wrote this reading grammar, and it was for you and with students like you that we have written this revision. Here is a book which will, we believe, enable you to learn German efficiently and pleasantly.

In the relatively short time our academic pattern and your crowded schedule permit, you can reach the primary goal we have set: the ability to read German. From actual experience we know that if you can read the average English freshman composition reader, you will be able to learn to read the language of Goethe, Schiller, Heine, Kant, Hegel, and Beethoven—to name only a few of the great men whose native tongue was German. Grammar is but a means to this end; the number of artificial "grammar sentences" has been restricted, therefore, to the absolute minimum necessary to insure your competence before you proceed to the mature, interesting reading material which composes the major portion of the book. In other words, you do not just learn about the language; you actually learn to read German, and with enjoyment.

A mastery of this book will require the acquisition of an active vocabulary of only 1050 words, although there are more than 33,000 running words of reading material. We have systematically provided you with as much repetition as we could, using 800 of the 1050 words in five or more lessons and 400 in ten or more lessons. Finally, we have explained grammatical principles as clearly and as simply as we could; we have made every effort to be helpful to you and to save you time.

May we make three suggestions?

1. Develop regular study habits. Countless college students have failed to graduate from college because they did not develop regular study habits. Systematic study of German can help you to develop such habits, and you can profit by them in other courses

also. Regular study habits go far toward insuring success in college.

2. Do not look upon language as you look upon a physical science, for it is neither so precise nor so uniform. For example, we say one goes to jail but to *the* penitentiary, to college but to *the* university, to church but to *the* theater. German uses the definite article with similar irregularity, and for "in the far distance" says "in far distance," for "on the broad sea" says "on broad sea," and for "in life" says "in the life."

3. Do not be afraid of overlearning. You will discover, if you have not already found out, that studying can be enjoyable. If you "overlearn," you will derive added pleasure from it.

Work with your instructor, attend class regularly, and apply yourself consistently, and you will be pleased with and proud of your accomplishments. We wish you every success.

THE AUTHORS

TO THE TEACHER

The aim of this grammar is to enable the student of German by the end of his first year of study to read, with the exclusive aid of a dictionary, an average German text, even of a scientific nature, without having to wrestle with perfectly normal syntactical patterns which are either still entirely new to him or not yet assimilated.

From the outset, reading is emphasized; every feature of the book has been designed with the achievement of reading ability in view.

In our effort to help the average American college student to reach the reading goal, we decided it was necessary

1. To introduce early essential grammatical elements of high frequency, particularly necessary syntactical patterns, and to use them often.

2. To explain and use freely such elements as anticipative pronouns, participial phrases, flavoring particles, and the like, usually not found in first-year grammars.

3. To restrict the vocabulary to the starred stems (1018 in number) of the Minimum Standard German Vocabulary (and about 30 other words in the same collection).

4. To capitalize on the word-family principle of German, which we consider to be the best possible way of building a working vocabulary. Thus there are numerous paragraphs dealing with word formation, exercises on compounds and derivatives, and sections called "Building a Passive Vocabulary."

5. To give the student lively and interesting reading of a nature which will appeal to him and give him the incentive to do more reading.

Since the vocabulary is relatively small, the student can devote much more time and attention to syntactical difficulties. Hence it was possible to offer as nearly normal and average German as one might ever expect to find in a first-year text.

While the active vocabulary is restricted, the attention given to word formation and the word-family principle enables the student to acquire a passive vocabulary of between 2000 and 3000 words. This result is accomplished through paragraphs on prefixes, suffixes, verb-noun pairs, compounds, and the like, and through abundant exercises.

Although the *German Reading Grammar* in revised form is basically the same book as the original, it will be considerably easier to teach. We have taken less student ability for granted and know that the changes will enable students to learn faster and more easily. The major alterations are as follows:

1. Many grammatical explanations have been improved upon, several having been completely reworked. We have proceeded from the known to the unknown and from the simple to the complex.

2. Changes have been made in the German text to simplify or clarify. They range from single words to entire selections. We did not sacrifice our ideal of providing a grammar which leaves as small a gap as possible between "textbook" German and ordinary German; on the contrary, we believe the revised version will speed up considerably the acquisition of a reading knowledge. Text B of Lessons IV and VI and Text A of several lessons were completely rewritten. The new Texts A provide many more examples of the grammar introduced in the respective lessons. In Text B we have tried to eliminate all grammatical forms or syntactical patterns which had not previously been explained, and we have striven for more clarity and easier comprehension.

3. The apparatus is now more complete. The section on pronunciation has been greatly changed and improved. Translations are provided for German sentences which illustrate points of grammar. The vocabularies have been thoroughly checked and are more nearly complete. Tables have been added. The Appendix has been enriched by a section containing translations of the most difficult compounds and derivatives in Exercise V, beginning with Lesson VIII, and four complete vocabulary lists of words introduced through Lessons III, V, VIII, and XII in

the hope that they may prove useful to students for review and to faculty in devising examinations. The Index has been revised to include both page and paragraph numbers.

4. All known errors have been corrected, and several gaps have been filled. We have given careful consideration to every suggestion that has been made to us.

5. In this edition the first six lessons are printed in Roman letters, as are the German-English and English-German vocabularies at the back of the book. When we used multigraphed copies of the early lessons experimentally, in class, and then transferred to the textbook, we found that students learn word patterns that way much more easily and can subsequently shift to the German letters with less difficulty. The hazard of mislearning letters is also reduced thereby.

It is quite impossible for us to express our appreciation here to all who have helped us. In giving the names of only four we are doing an injustice to large numbers, for many have helped us. Nevertheless, we cannot refrain from thanking publicly Professor John L. Kind and Professor William I. Schreiber, who wrote reviews of our book which have proved invaluable in the revision, Professor B. Q. Morgan, who agreed to our using the first edition in mimeographed form in our classrooms for three years and who read and criticized our original manuscript, and Mrs. Adelaide M. Budde, editor, who was appointed by our publishers to serve as critic of the revision, and proved to be of great help. We are deeply grateful to these four and thank them and all who have rendered assistance. We also wish to make acknowledgment for permission to use an adaptation (page 217) of a drawing in the Oxford University Press edition of *Psyche*, which was edited by Eiserhardt and Pettengill.

STANLEY L. SHARP
F. W. STROTHMANN

CONTENTS

CONTENTS

GERMAN READING GRAMMAR

REVISED EDITION

PRONUNCIATION*

ACCENT

German words are usually accented on the first syllable: **Váter** *father*, **Mútter** *mother*, **Brúder** *brother*, **Schwéster** *sister*. (Only in dictionaries and grammars, i.e., for instructional purposes, are accents indicated in print.)

Loan words usually do not follow this rule: **Atóm, Generál, Charákter, Muséum, Públikum.** Your instructor will give you the correct pronunciation of such words.

When two words are compounded, the first component receives the accent: **Gróßvater** *grandfather*, **Húndehaus** *doghouse*, **Háus-hund** *house dog*.

The following six prefixes are never accented: **be-, ent-, er-, ge-, ver-, zer-: beríchten** *report*, **entdécken** *discover*, **erfáhren** *find out*, **gewínnen** *win*, **verstéhen** *understand*, **zerbréchen** *smash*.

Accented vowels are long:

when double: (**aa, ee, oo**): **das Haar** *the hair*, **das Heer** *the army*, **das Boot** *the boat*, **die Seele** *the soul*;

when followed by an **h** belonging to the same syllable: **das Jahr** *the year*, **mehr** *more*, **das Ohr** *the ear*;

when followed by a single consonant: **der Tag** *the day*, **der Vater** *the father*.

VOWEL QUALITY

Some German sounds differ from English sounds. Correct pronunciation can be learned only through the ear and by imitation. The following comparisons are only approximations given for

---

*In order to provide a complete table of reference, both Roman and German type-faces have been used in the explanation of the pronunciation of German sounds. However, since German type is not introduced into the text until Lesson VII, the use of German type has been limited here to those explanations where reference to German letter-forms and usages seems requisite.

reference use. (Note that German vowels may be either long or short.)

a (a) when long resembles the *a* in *father*: **Haar, Bahn, Tag;**
when short resembles the *a* in *artistic*: **dann, alt, das.**

e (e) when long resembles the first vowel sound in *payer*: **See, mehr, geben;**
when short resembles the *e* in *debt*: **Bett, kennen, hell;**
when unaccented resembles the last two vowels in *Hélena*: **Écke, Klásse, frágen, Váter.**

i (i) when long resembles the *ie* in *niece* and *piece*: **viel, ihm;** (Long **i** is never doubled; **e** is used as the lengthening sign instead.)
when short resembles the *i* in *wit*: **mit, hinter, bis.**

o (o) when long resembles the first vowel sound in *mower*: **wo, wohnen, oder;**
when short resembles the *o* in *forty*: **hoffen, wollen, kommen.**

u (u) when long resembles the *oo* in *pool*: **tun, rufen, Schuh;**
when short resembles the *u* in *put*: **unter, und, Mutter.**

VOWELS WITH UMLAUT

ä (ä) when long resembles the *ai* in *fair*: **fährt, erklären, Mädchen;** (Many Germans pronounce long **ä** like German long **e**.)
when short is like German short *e* (**Bett**): **Männer, Kälte, Gäste.**

ö (ö) when long is formed by pronouncing German long **e** (**mehr**) with lips rounded: **mögen, Röte, hören;**
when short is formed by pronouncing German short **e** (*debt*) with lips rounded: **können, Köln.**

ü (ü) when long is formed by pronouncing German long **i** (**ihm**) with lips rounded: **über, natürlich, Frühling;**
when short is formed by pronouncing German short **i** (*wit*) with lips rounded: **Gründe, dünn, fünf.**

DIPHTHONGS

ai (ai) resembles the *ei* in *height*: **Kaiser.**
au (au) resembles *ou* in *house*: **kaum, auf, Haus.**
äu (äu) resembles the *oy* in *boy*: **Fräulein.**
ei (ei) the same as **ai**: **ein, allein.**
eu (eu) the same as **äu**: **heute, Europa.**

CONSONANTS

b (b) initial and medial between vowels is like English *b*: **bei, aber;** at the end of a word or syllable **b** is pronounced like English *p*: **ob, lebte.**
c (c) is usually like English *k*: **Stück.**
ch (ch) has two sounds: following **a, o, u,** and **au** it is a back sound formed by expelling the air between the back of the tongue and the soft palate, as in the Scottish word *loch*: **acht, hoch, Buch, auch;** in all other cases it is a front sound and can best be formed by pronouncing *hew* with a loud or sharp whisper: **ich, dicht, mancher.**
chs (chſ, chs) is pronounced like English *ks* or *x* as in *wax*: **wachsen** (wachſen), **sechs** (ſechs). (Note that the German trigraph chs is used in final position and compounds: Wachstum.)
ck (ck) is like English *ck*: **Stück, Blick.**
d (d) initial or medial is like English *d*: **danken, finden;** when final, **d** has the *t*-sound of English *d* in certain past participles such as *stopped*: **Feld, Wand.**
f (f) is like English *f*: **finden, hoffen.**
g (g) initial or between vowels is like English *g* in *good*: **gut, fragen.** When final or before voiceless consonants like **t, st,** it is like English *k*: **weg, Tag, fragt.** However, in the suffix **-ig** it is pronounced like the German front **ch**: **auswendig, durstig.** In many parts of Germany final **g** is pronounced like **ch: Tag, Krieg.**

h (𝔥) initial is like English *h*: **halten, Herr.** It maintains this pronunciation after prefixes and in compounds: **behalten, Hausherr.** In words where **h** follows the stem vowel it is silent and indicates that the preceding vowel is long: **mehr, ehrlich, erfahren, gehen.**

j (𝔧) is like *y* in *yes*: **Jahr, jung, ja.**

k (𝔨) is like English *k* but is never silent: **kaufen, kein, Knabe.**

l (𝔩) resembles English *l* but is pronounced farther forward. The tip of the tongue touches the back of the upper teeth: **lieben, leben, glauben, holen.**

m (𝔪) is like English *m*: **Mutter, kaum.**

n (𝔫) is like English *n*: **neben, neu.**

ng (𝔫𝔤) is pronounced like English *ng* in *ring, sing,* not like *ng* in *finger*: **Ring, lang, Finger.**

p (𝔭) is like English *p*: **Preis, Papier.** Note **pf** in **Pfund, Pfennig.**

q (𝔮) occurs rarely, and then only in the combination **qu.** It is then pronounced like English *kv*: **Quantität.**

r (𝔯) has two equally acceptable pronunciations: trilled and uvular. The trilled **r** is usually easier to learn; it is produced by the vibration of the tip of the tongue against the upper gums: **rot, Herr, brauchen.**

s (ſ, 𝔰) is either voiced like the *s* in *capitalism* or voiceless like the *s* in sea. It is voiced initially before vowels, between vowels, and also between **m, n, l, r** and a vowel: **so** (ſo), **dieser** (dieſer), **Hänsel** (Hänſel), **Else** (Elſe); in all other positions it is voiceless: **Erbse** (Erbſe), **liest** (lieſt), **Lust** (Luſt). The capital form of ſ is 𝔖: 𝔖and. When voiceless **s** stands at the end of a word or at the end of the first element of a compound or derivative, the 𝔰-form is used in German type: **das** (da𝔰), **was** (wa𝔰), **Häuschen** (Häu𝔰chen). But note: Da𝔰 Hau𝔰, *nom.*, de𝔰 Hauſe𝔰, *gen.*)

sch (ſch) is like English *sh*, but pronounced with the lips more protruded: **schlafen** (ſchlafen), **Schnee** (Schnee).

sp (ſp) when initial is pronounced like English *shp*: **spät, spielen.**

ss (ſſ) is always voiceless. In German type the digraph ſſ ap-
ß (ß) pears when **ss** occurs between two vowels, the first of which is short: **Wasser** (Waſſer), **müssen** (müſſen), **lassen** (laſſen); when **ss** occurs between two vowels, the first of which is long, after a short vowel when no other vowel follows, and in final position, the digraph **ß** (ß) is used (always in German, optional in Roman type): **mußt** or **musst** (mußt)—from **müssen** (müſſen), **Faß** or **Fass** (Faß).

st (ſt) when initial is pronounced like English *sht*: **still, Stück.**

t (t) is like English *t*: **Tag, hinter, rot.**

tz (tz) is like English *ts* in *fits*: **sitzen** (ſitzen), **Katze** (Katze).

v (v) is like English *f*: **Vater, vergessen, viel.** However, in words of foreign origin the pronunciation varies between English *f* and *v*; *f* in **Eva** and **Dativ,** *v* in **November** and **Venus.** Your instructor will give you the correct pronunciation of such words.

w (w) is like English *v*: **wann, Wasser** (Waſſer), **wie.**

x (x) occurs rarely. It is pronounced like English *x* in *tax*.

y (y) occurs rarely. It is pronounced like German **ü**.

z (z) is like English *ts* in *fits*: **zu, zwischen** (zwiſchen), **Zeit.**

GLOTTAL STOP

Before an initial accented vowel the glottis is closed and suddenly reopened. The sound thus produced is called the glottal stop. It can best be heard in a whispered sentence such as:

Eine alte Eule sitzt unter einer alten Ulme.

CAPITALIZATION

All nouns and words used as nouns are capitalized. In letters the pronouns **du** and **ihr** and their corresponding possessive adjectives are capitalized.

PUNCTUATION

All German dependent clauses are set off by commas. Independent clauses may be set off by a comma, semicolon, or period. A colon precedes quotations.

SYLLABICATION

A single consonant (including **ch** and **sch**) is carried over to the next line: **mei-nen, ge-ben;** so is **st: be-ste.** Only the last of two or more consonants goes to the following line: **fin-den, hungrig, bekom-men.** Compounds are divided into their component parts: **Haus-herr, aus-arbeiten.**

PRONUNCIATION EXERCISE

Pronounce the following word pairs very carefully until you can pronounce long and short **ü** and long and short **ö** well:

Biene, Bühne	**Binde, Bünde**	**heben, höben**
dienen, Dünen	**Bitte, Bütte**	**Werther,* Wörter**
miete, mühte	**Beete, böte**	**Becken, Böcken**
missen, müssen	**sehnen, Söhnen**	**kennen, können**

Pronounce the following words:

frisch	**Held**	**essen**	**Fräulein**	**dicht**	**ehrlich**
liegen	**immer**	**ohne**	**gehen**	**doch**	**Erbse**
Wand	**jeder**	**schlafen**	**heute**	**über**	**etwas**
wach	**alt**	**wissen**	**Preis**	**Bühne**	**zeigen**
viel	**Deutsch**	**Woche**	**recht**	**Hälfte**	**Zeit**
Gesicht	**dünn**	**Frau**	**auch**	**Ecke**	**zu**

German Type

Small Letters: 𝔞, 𝔟, 𝔠, 𝔡, 𝔢, 𝔣, 𝔤, 𝔥, 𝔦, 𝔧, 𝔨, 𝔩, 𝔪, 𝔫, 𝔬, 𝔭, 𝔮, 𝔯, 𝔰 (ſ ß), 𝔱, 𝔲, 𝔳, 𝔴, 𝔵, 𝔶, 𝔷.

Capital Letters: 𝔄, 𝔅, ℭ, 𝔇, 𝔈, 𝔉, 𝔊, ℌ, ℑ†, ℑ†, 𝔎, 𝔏, 𝔐, 𝔑, 𝔒, 𝔓, 𝔔, ℜ, 𝔖, 𝔗, 𝔘, 𝔙, 𝔚, 𝔛, 𝔜, ℨ.

---

*__th__ is pronounced like **t**. The English *th* sound does not occur in German.

†The capital letter-forms **I** and **J** are usually not distinguished in German type. ℑ is read **J** before vowels, since it then functions as a consonant.

INTRODUCTION TO LESSON I

GRAMMAR §§ 1–2

1. Infinitive, Stem, and Present Tense. Since the verb is the most important element in a sentence, the logical starting point in the learning of a language is the verb. Moreover, since the present tense is more frequently used than any other, the present tense of the verb properly marks the best point of departure.

English verbs show few changes in form in the conjugation of the present tense, *e.g.*, *I hope, you hope, he hopes; I do, you do, he does; I have, you have, he has.* German verbs show more such changes, but the patterns can be learned readily.

Most German infinitives end in **-en**; a few end in **-n.** The stem of a verb is the infinitive minus the ending **-en** or **-n.** The present tense is formed by adding for each person the proper ending to the stem. Thus hundreds of German verbs which are regular in the present tense are conjugated as follows:

hoffen to hope

ich hoffe	I hope	**wir hoffen**	we hope
du hoffst	you hope	**ihr hofft**	you hope
er / **sie** / **es** } **hofft**	he / she / it } hopes	**sie hoffen**	they hope
		Sie hoffen	you hope

denken to think

ich denke	I think	**wir denken**	we think
du denkst	you think	**ihr denkt**	you think
er / **sie** / **es** } **denkt**	he / she / it } thinks	**sie denken**	they think
		Sie denken	you think

2. Haben, sein. The three most frequently used German verbs are irregular; they are:

haben to have   **sein** to be   **werden** to become

In the present tense **haben** and **sein** are conjugated as follows:

haben to have

ich habe	I have	**wir haben**	we have
du hast	you have	**ihr habt**	you have
er / sie / es hat	he / she / it has	**sie haben**	they have
		Sie haben	you have

sein to be

ich bin	I am	**wir sind**	we are
du bist	you are	**ihr seid**	you are
er / sie / es ist	he / she / it is	**sie sind**	they are
		Sie sind	you are

3. "You" in German (Pronouns of Address). German has three ways of expressing English *you*: **du, ihr,** and **Sie. Du** (*singular*) and **ihr** (*plural*) are used in addressing relatives, intimate friends, and young children; **Sie** is used in addressing adults who are not relatives or intimate friends. This so-called "polite" form **Sie** is both singular and plural. It is always capitalized and always takes the verb form of the third person plural.

EXERCISE

Conjugate in the present tense:

lachen	to laugh	**hören**	to hear
sagen	to say	**verstehen**	to understand
fragen	to ask	**zeigen**	to show
schreiben	to write	**gehen**	to go, walk

LESSON I

TEXT A*

Frank hat Papier.—Frank schreibt auf Papier.—Ich habe kein Papier.—Wer hat das Papier?—Hat Frank Papier?—Ich höre, Frank ist nicht alt.—Das Fräulein ist nicht alt.—Alt ist das Fräulein nicht.—Mehr sage ich natürlich nicht.—Das Mädchen ist schön.—Herr Jones versteht das Mädchen nicht.—Wer ist Herr Meyer?—Verstehst du das Fräulein? 5

Natürlich hört er nun nichts.—Du verstehst das Mädchen nicht.—Dann verstehst du das Mädchen nicht.—Nun lacht das Mädchen.—Wer lacht?—Neben Frank sitzt Anna.—Das ist kein Wunder.—Haben sie ein[1] Stück Papier[1]?—Haben Sie Papier?—Versteht Herr Schmidt das Mädchen?—Sitzt Anna neben Frank? 10

„Anna ist einfach schön", meint Frank. „Einfach und schön, sagst du?" fragt Hans. „Einfach schön, nicht einfach und schön", sagt Frank.

NOTE. 1. **ein Stück Papier** supply "of": a piece of paper.

VOCABULARY†

aber but, however
alle *all*‡
alles everything
alt *old*
auch also, too; either; even
auf on, upon; *up*
beobachten to observe, watch
berichten to report
dann *then*
das the; *that*
denken to *think*
Deutsch German
ein a, *an*; one
einfach simple, simply
finden to *find*
fragen to ask
Fräulein Miss
  das Fräulein the young lady

---

*Sentences in Text A in the early lessons are generally disconnected in thought.

†All accents have been intentionally omitted in the vocabulary which forms a part of each lesson. Accents are indicated in the main vocabulary at the end of the book. The student should try from the start to imitate the pronunciation of the teacher, who will read the new words aloud in class.

‡English cognates, i.e., words related in origin to German words, are printed in italics.

gehen to *go*; walk
haben to *have*
Herr Mr.
  der Herr the gentleman
hoffen to *hope*
hören to *hear*
kein no, not any
lachen to *laugh*
das Mädchen the girl
mehr *more*
meinen to think; say; *mean*
natürlich *naturally*
neben next to, beside
nicht *not*
nichts nothing
nun *now*
oder *or*
das Papier the *paper*
sagen to *say*; tell
schön beautiful, handsome; fine
schreiben to write (*scribe*)
schwer difficult, hard; heavy
sein to be
sitzen to *sit*
so *so*; as; thus
das Stück the piece
und *and*
verstehen to understand
wer who
wie as; like; how
wieder again
das Wunder the *wonder*
zeigen *to* show
zu *to*; too; at; for

TEXT B*

John und Nancy

John[1] sitzt neben Nancy.[1] Professor Jones sagt natürlich nicht John und Nancy, er sagt Herr Miller und Fräulein Wells. Aber wir sagen einfach John und Nancy und berichten: Nancy sitzt neben John. Sie haben „Abnormal Psychology". John versteht nichts. Kein Wunder, er ist normal. Er beobachtet Nancy und denkt: „Das Mädchen versteht alles. Ist sie intelligent, oder ist sie nicht normal?" Auch Nancy versteht nichts, aber sie zeigt es nicht. Kein Wunder, sie ist ein Mädchen.

Dann gehen Nancy und John zu Professor Schmidt. Sie haben nun Deutsch, und wieder sitzt John neben Nancy. „Ich hoffe, Deutsch ist nicht so schwer wie Psychologie", meint John. „Schwer?" fragt Nancy. „Wie meinen Sie das? Ich finde, Psychologie ist nicht schwer." John sagt nichts mehr.

„Fräulein Wells", fragt Professor Schmidt, „wie sagen Sie ‚i'?" — „I, i, i", sagt Nancy. „Nun machen[2] Sie den Mund rund[2] und sagen Sie

*The superior figures in Text B refer to the notes following.

wieder ‚i'!"—„Ü, ü, ü", sagt Nancy nun. John lacht, aber dann sagt er auch „i" und „ü". „Hm", denkt er, „ich sage ‚i', und es klingt[3] wie[3] ‚ü'. Ich bin nicht normal!"

Alle sagen „i" und „ü". John hört es nicht, er beobachtet wieder Nancy. „Das Mädchen ist schön", denkt er. „Ich hoffe, ich bin so alt wie sie." „Wie alt sind Sie?" schreibt er auf ein Stück Papier. „Ich bin achtzehn (18)", schreibt Nancy. „Das ist schön", schreibt John, „ich bin auch achtzehn." 5

NOTES. 1. The names *John* and *Nancy* are used because the action takes place in America. 2. **machen . . . rund** round your lips (make the mouth round). 3. **klingt wie** sounds like.

GRAMMAR

4. English Progressive and Emphatic Forms. German has no progressive form. Both *I am laughing* and *I laugh* are expressed by **ich lache**; *he is writing* and *he writes* by **er schreibt**. The emphatic form is also lacking; *I do hope* is simply **ich hoffe.** Thus, **ich lache** may mean *I laugh*, *I am laughing*, and *I do laugh.*

5. Connecting e. If the stem of a verb ends in **d** or **t**, the endings **st** and **t** are changed to **est** and **et** to make them audible.*

du findest	**du beobachtest**
er findet	**er beobachtet**
ihr findet	**ihr beobachtet**

6. Verb-Second Position. In statements the inflected verb (that is, the form that indicates person and number: *I* ***eat***, *he* ***eats***, *I* ***have*** *eaten*, *he* ***has*** *eaten*) is the second element of the sentence. The first element may be a single word or any group of words (such as a prepositional phrase or dependent clause) which constitutes one unit. This first unit is usually, but by no means always, the subject with its modifiers. (If the subject does not come first, it usually comes third.)

---

*There are very few exceptions to this rule. The important ones will be taken up later.

Compare:

Frank *hat* das Papier.	Frank has the paper.
Das Papier *hat* Frank.	Frank has the paper.
Nun *lacht* Anna.	Now Anna is laughing.
Wenn du „ü" sagst, *lache* ich.	When you say "*ü*," I laugh.

As in English, the co-ordinating conjunctions **und, aber, oder,** etc. (*and, but, or,* etc.) are simply links joining two sentences or main clauses. They are not integral parts of the following clause and are not, therefore, considered to be the first element. Exclamatory expressions such as **Kein Wunder** (*No wonder*) and the adverbs **ja** (*yes*) and **nein** (*no*) are regarded as sentences in themselves, are set off by commas, and do not alter the word order of the following sentence.

In questions introduced by interrogative pronouns the inflected verb is the second element in both English and German. Examples:

Wer *hat* das Papier?	Who *has* the paper?
Wer *versteht* nichts?	Who *does*n't understand anything? (Who *understands* nothing?)

7. Verb-First Position. In all types of questions where the *inflected* verb comes first in English the *inflected* verb also comes first in German. Examples:

***Hat* er Papier?**	*Has* he paper? (*Does* he have paper?)
***Ist* Nancy schön?**	*Is* Nancy beautiful?
***Beobachtest* du das Mädchen?**	*Are* you watching the girl?

8. Unaccented Prefixes. The prefixes **be-, ent-, er-, ge-, ver-,** and **zer-,** which form the first syllable of many verbs, are never accented; instead the second syllable is accented. Compare **beobachten, berichten,** and **verstehen.**

EXERCISES

I

Answer in German the following questions, following Text B as closely as possible: **1. Wer sitzt neben Nancy? 2. Sagt Professor**

Jones Fräulein Wells und Herr Miller? Ja (yes), **Professor Jones . . . 3. Was haben John und Nancy? 4. Wer versteht nichts? 5. Wer ist normal? 6. Wer versteht auch nichts? 7. Wer geht zu Professor Schmidt? 8. Was haben John und Nancy nun? 9. Wer sagt nichts mehr? 10. Wer sagt „i"? 11. Wer sagt „ü"? 12. Wer lacht? 13. Sagen alle „i" und „ü"? Ja, alle . . . 14. Wer beobachtet Nancy? 15. Ist Nancy schön? Ja, . . . 16. Wie alt ist Nancy?**

II

Translate into German: 1. Nancy is a girl. 2. She is a girl. 3. Nancy is beautiful. 4. John is eighteen. 5. He hears the girl. 6. He is watching the girl. 7. Who is writing? 8. She observes John again. 9. She now has German. 10. Now he has German. 11. Nancy says German is not hard. 12. No wonder, she is a girl. 13. Now Karl is laughing. 14. Who has the paper? 15. Nancy does not understand anything (understands nothing).* 16. What do they have now?

III

Conjugate in the present tense:

sein	**denken**	**finden**
haben	**beobachten**	**meinen**
lachen	**verstehen**	**sagen**

IV

Supply the missing endings:

du geh ____	**sie** (they) **sag** ____	**er beobacht** ____
ihr schreib ____	**sie** (she) **mein** ____	**du denk** ____
wir sitz ____	**Sie** (you) **hoff** ____	**ihr beobacht** ____

---

*Words in parentheses are to be used in translation.

LESSON II

TEXT A

Anna fährt allein nach Berlin.—Warum fährst du nicht allein nach Hamburg?—Herr Meyer wird alt.—Du wirst wieder jung.—Ich bin nicht mehr so jung wie du.—Schläfst du schon? Oder schläfst du noch? —Bist du nun wach?—Warum atmest du so schwer?—Meyer liest die Zeitung.—Warum liest du das Buch?—Hier hast du das Buch.—Der Bleistift ist rot.—Auch das Buch ist rot.

Es ist natürlich alt.—Frank rechnet gut.—Er sieht nichts.—Er läuft gut.—Ich habe kein Geld.—Hat er noch so viel Geld?—Frank denkt nur an Anna.—Wer ist zufrieden?

VOCABULARY

allein *alone*
an *on*; at; near
atmen to breathe
bleiben to stay, remain
der Bleistift the pencil
brauchen to need; use
bringen to *bring*; take
das Buch the *book*
dicht *thick*; close
fahren (ä) to ride, drive, go
die Frau the woman; wife
  Frau Mrs.
für *for* (*prep.*)
das Geld the money
das Glas the *glass*
gut *good*; well
das Haar the *hair*
hier *here*
holen to fetch, bring; get
die Jugend (state of) youth
jung *young*
lang (lange) *long*
laufen (äu) to run
legen to *lay*, place
leise soft(ly), gentle, gently
lesen (ie) to read
man one (*impers. pron.*)
die Mark* the *mark* (coin)
nach to; toward; after; according to
noch still, yet
nur only
rechnen to figure, *reckon*
reisen to travel, journey
  die Reise the trip
rot *red*

---

*__die Mark.__ Nouns denoting a unit of measure, such as **Mark, Kilogramm, Zentimeter** (centimeter), and **Pfund** (pound), rarely form a plural. (Cf. English: three head of cattle.)

schlafen (ä) to *sleep*
schon already
sehen (ie) to *see*; look
tun to *do* (**ich tue, du tust, er tut**)
über *over*; above; about
das Urteil the judgment, opinion*
versuchen to try, attempt
viel much
viele many
wach *awake*
warum why
was *what*
das Wasser the *water*
werden (i) to become; get
zahlen to pay
die Zeitung the newspaper
zufrieden satisfied, contented
zurück back
zwar to be sure; granted

IDIOMS

denken an to think of
nicht mehr no longer

TEXT B

Herr und Frau Meyer

Gustav Meyer ist zufrieden. Natürlich! Warum nicht? Seine[1] Zahnbürste[2] wird nicht rot, sein[1] Haar ist noch dicht, und auch sein Auto läuft noch gut. Außerdem[3] raucht er eine Zigarre[3] und liest die Zeitung. Mehr braucht er nicht, um[4] zufrieden zu[4] sein.

„Siehst du, Frau", sagt Meyer, „hier hast du es! ‚Nach Berlin für nur achtzehn (18) Mark!' " Aber Frau Meyer schläft schon, sie atmet schwer, und Meyer fährt allein nach Berlin. Er bleibt nicht lange. Frau Meyer wird wieder wach und holt Gustav zurück. „Fünfhundert (500) Mark", liest Meyer nun, „fünfhundert Mark zahlen wir für ein Urteil über die weltbekannte[5] Zahnpasta[5] Odontoschein."[6] „Hm", sagt Frau Meyer, „fünfhundert Mark? Das ist viel Geld." Sie rechnet. „Gustav, das ist das Geld für die Reise nach Neuyork." „Hm", sagt auch Herr Meyer, holt Bleistift und Papier und schreibt. Zwar braucht er kein Odontoschein. Er hat ein Gebiß,[7] und das legt er abends[8] in ein Glas Wasser. Aber für fünfhundert Mark tut man viel. Meyer denkt, er schreibt, verbessert,[9] schreibt, verbessert wieder. Dann liest er zufrieden:

„Bist du jung?—Odontoschein bewahrt[10] die Jugend.
Bist du alt?—Odontoschein bringt sie[11] zurück."

**Slogan* as used in Text B.

„Bringt sie zurück", sagt leise Frau Meyer und denkt zurück an ihre[12] Jugend. „Gustav", meint sie, „Gustav, d i e[13] Zahnpasta versuche ich auch."

NOTES. 1. **sein, seine** his. 2. **Zahnbürste** toothbrush. 3. **Außerdem . . . Zigarre** Besides, he is smoking a cigar. 4. **um . . . zu** in order to. 5. **weltbekannte Zahnpasta** world-renowned toothpaste. 6. A fictitious name. 7. **Gebiß** a set of false teeth. 8. **abends** in the evening. 9. **verbessert** corrects. 10. **bewahrt** preserves. 11. **sie** it. 12. **ihre** her. 13. **d i e Zahnpasta** *that* toothpaste. (German printers leave spaces between letters to indicate emphasis.)

GRAMMAR

9. Gender of Nouns. German nouns are masculine, feminine, or neuter. In the first lesson only neuter nouns were introduced: **das Stück, das Papier.** In this lesson additional neuter nouns are used; a few feminines: **die Frau, die Jugend, die Mark, die Reise;** and one masculine noun: **der Bleistift.** The definite article in the nominative case for masculine nouns is **der;** for feminine nouns, **die;** and for neuter nouns, **das.** The article should be learned together with the noun. There is no general rule by which gender can be determined. Note that even inanimate objects are masculine, feminine, or neuter.

10. Verbs with Vowel Change. In the English verb *to do* there is a vowel change from the first person singular, *I do*, to the third person singular, *he does.* Many German verbs show a vowel change in the second and third persons of the singular:

ich sehe	**ich schlafe**	**ich fahre**
du siehst	**du schläfst**	**du fährst**
er sieht	**er schläft**	**er fährt**

Vowel changes will be indicated in the vocabulary as the verbs are introduced, e.g., **sehen (ie), schlafen (ä).**

11. Werden. The third most frequently used verb is **werden** (*to become*). It is irregular in the second and third persons of the singular:

ich werde	**wir werden**
du wirst	**ihr werdet**
er wird	**sie werden**

12. Irregular Ending of Second Person Singular. Verbs whose stems end in an *s*-sound have identical forms in the second and third persons singular:

du liest	**du sitzt**	**du reist**
er liest	**er sitzt**	**er reist**

13. Connecting e. It would be impossible to pronounce the second and third persons singular and second person plural of some verbs like **atmen** and **rechnen,** where the stems end in a consonant plus **m** or **n,** unless some vowel were inserted. In these forms an **e** is inserted between the stem and the ending:

ich atme	**ich rechne**
du atmest	**du rechnest**
er atmet	**er rechnet**
wir atmen	**wir rechnen**
ihr atmet	**ihr rechnet**
sie atmen	**sie rechnen**

EXERCISES

I

Answer in German: **1. Wer ist zufrieden? 2. Wie ist Meyers Haar? 3. Wie läuft sein Auto? 4. Wer raucht die Zigarre? 5. Was liest Herr Meyer? 6. Wer schläft schon? 7. Wie atmet Frau Meyer? 8. Wer fährt nach Berlin? 9. Wer wird wieder wach? 10. Was holt Herr Meyer? 11. Warum braucht Meyer kein Odontoschein?** (He has a set of false teeth.) **12. Was tut nun Herr Meyer? 13. Was bewahrt die Jugend? 14. Was bringt Odontoschein zurück? 15. Was tut Frau Meyer?**

II

Translate into German: 1. We read. 2. We are reading. 3. I am not old. 4. How does he write? 5. He gets pencil and paper. 6. Mr. Meyer brings Mrs. Meyer back. 7. His (**Sein**) hair is still thick. 8. Gustav travels to Berlin. 9. Who is getting (**wird**) old? 10. Mr. Meyer is reading the newspaper. 11. Who is running? 12. Is he sleeping now? 13. Meyer runs and breathes heavily. 14. Do you [*three forms*] see Mrs. Meyer? 15. She does not remain long. 16. Does he understand the woman? 17. He is watching the girl. 18 Are you [*three forms*] sleeping? 19. The pencil is red. 20. Who is contented?

III

Translate into English:

schön	**gehen**	**holen**
alles	**verstehen**	**man**
neben	**nach**	**gut**
schwer	**warum**	**zahlen**
wie	**noch**	**nur**

IV

Translate into German:

to hope	to be	to show	to report
to hear	again	to observe	already
nothing	to say	to fetch	to write

V

Conjugate in the present indicative:

werden	**haben**	**sehen**	**lesen**
sein	**schlafen**	**holen**	**atmen**

VI

Find the subject and predicate in each sentence of Texts A and B.

LESSON III

TEXT A

Ich habe kein Geld. Ich kann nicht zahlen. Du hast Geld. Du mußt zahlen.—Wir können alles verstehen.—Mußt du immer lachen?—Willst du schlafen?—Es ist schon spät, und er soll schlafen.—Darf ich heute abend gehen?—Du darfst nicht wieder lachen.—Warum können wir nicht bleiben?—Willst du schlafen? 5

Ich weiß nicht, ob er Geld hat.—Darf ich, darf ich fragen, wie alt Sie sind?—Ich will alles vergessen.—Ich kann es beweisen.—Ich mag das Kleid nicht.—Natürlich kostet das Papier viel zuviel.—Ich brauche ein Stück Papier.—Ich kann den Bleistift nicht finden.—Anna mag das Kleid nicht, aber ich finde es schön.—Ist das Kleid rot? 10

Wollt ihr die Zeitung lesen?—Meyer hat das Geld schon.—Heute muß ich hier bleiben.—Kann Hans gut rechnen?—Du mußt es versuchen.—Ich habe nichts zu berichten.

VOCABULARY

der Abend the *evening*
auswendig (know) by heart
bei at; with
bekommen to get, receive
bestimmt definitely
das Bett the *bed*
beweisen to prove
da there; then; since (*conj.*)
dünn *thin*
dürfen to be allowed to (cf. § 15)
erfahren (ä) to find out, learn
fast almost
die Gans the *goose*
gar (cf. Idioms)
gebrauchen to use
gewinnen to *win*
glauben to believe
heute today
immer always
interessant *interesting*
das Kleid the dress
kommen to *come*
können to be able to; know (cf. § 15)
kosten to *cost*
leider unfortunately
mögen to like, like to (cf. § 15)
müssen to have to (cf. § 15)
neidisch jealous, envious
nein *no*
ob whether; *if*
der Preis the *prize*; *price*
das Recht the *right*
reden to talk, speak

der Schnee the *snow*
sollen to be supposed to (cf. § 15)
spät late
still *still*, quiet
übrigens by the way
Uhr o'clock
  die Uhr the clock, watch
um at; around; about
vergessen (i) to *forget*
die Wand the wall
warten to wait
weiß *white*
wenn *when*, whenever; if
wissen to know (cf. § 19)
die Woche the *week*
wohnen to dwell, live
wollen to want to (cf. § 15)
zwischen between (*twixt*)

IDIOMS

gar (*strengthens or emphasizes*)
  gar nichts nothing at all
heute abend this evening
neidisch auf (*w. acc.*) envious of
noch nicht not yet
recht haben to be right; **er hat recht** he is right

TEXT B

Schmidts bei Fischers

Bei Schmidts. Herr Schmidt: „Ich weiß schon, du willst fragen: ‚Bekommt Meyer die fünfhundert (500) Mark?' Da[1] mußt du noch warten. Um acht (8) Uhr soll er es erfahren." Frau Schmidt: „Ich höre, er hat das Geld schon." Herr Schmidt: „Nein, nein, er hat es 5 noch nicht, das weiß ich bestimmt." Frau Schmidt: „Aber Frau Meyer hat schon ein Reisekleid. Sie sagt, es kostet hundert (100) Mark." Herr Schmidt: „Das beweist ja[1] gar nichts. Übrigens gehen wir um sieben (7) zu Fischers. Du weißt doch,[1] Fischers wohnen neben Meyers, und die Wand zwischen Meyers und Fischers ist so dünn, man 10 braucht nur still zu sein, dann kann man bei Fischers gut hören, was Meyers sagen." Frau Schmidt: „Das kann ja interessant werden, und ich brauche nicht so viel zu reden. Du weißt, ich mag Frau Fischer nicht."

* * *

Bei Meyers. Frau Meyer: „Gustav, wie spät ist es denn[1]?" Herr 15 Meyer: „Es ist nun sieben (7), sieben Uhr dreißig (7:30) Konzert, und um acht Uhr (8:00) Odontoschein-Programm."

Bei Fischers. Herr Fischer: „Meyer weiß schon, was Frau Meyer will. Er kann das Programm heute auswendig. Das kann man hören."

Bei Meyers. „Gustav, Frau Schmidt ist neidisch auf das Reisekleid.“ Herr Meyer: „Die Gans ist immer neidisch.“

Bei Fischers. „So, eine Gans bin ich. Und das muß man anhören“,[2] sagt Frau Schmidt.

Bei Meyers. „Was meinst du, Frau, bekommen wir das Geld? Ich glaube nicht.“—„Natürlich bekommen wir das Geld. Du weißt, Gustav, ich habe immer recht.“

Bei Fischers. „Frau Meyer muß jede[3] Woche eine Tube Zahnpasta[4] gebrauchen. Ihre[5] Zähne sollen[5] fast weiß sein.“—„Weiß oder nicht weiß, für Frau Meyer kommt die Jugend leider nicht zurück. Sie ist zu alt.“

Bei Meyers. „Also,[1] Frau, es ist acht Uhr (8:00). Still!“

Der Ansager[6]: „Guten[7] Abend, meine Damen und Herren.[7] Wenn Sie heute abend zu Bett gehen,[8] dürfen Sie nicht vergessen, Ihre[9] Zähne mit Odontoschein zu putzen.[9] Odontoschein ist gut für jung und alt. Das weiß auch Herr Meyer, Herr Gustav Meyer. Er gebraucht Odontoschein schon achtzehn (18) Jahre.[10] Seine Zähne[11] sind weiß wie Schnee.“

Bei Fischers. „Ha-ha-ha-ha! ‚Weiß wie Schnee!‘ “

Der Ansager[6]: „Herr Meyer, darf ich gratulieren[12]? Sie gewinnen den Preis. Sie haben recht. ‚Sind Sie jung? Odontoschein bewahrt die Jugend; sind Sie alt? Odontoschein bringt sie zurück.‘ “

NOTES. 1. The words **ja, da, doch, denn,** and **also** are flavoring particles (cf. § 22). 2. **anhören** listen to. 3. **jede** every. 4. **eine Tube Zahnpasta** a tube of toothpaste. 5. **Ihre Zähne sollen . . .** Her teeth are said to be . . . 6. **Der Ansager** the announcer. 7. **Guten . . . Herren** Good evening, ladies and gentlemen. 8. Observe verb-last position in dependent clause (cf. § 27). 9. **Ihre . . . putzen** to brush your teeth with Odontoschein. 10. **Jahre** years. 11. **Seine Zähne** his teeth. 12. **gratulieren** congratulate.

GRAMMAR

14. Modal Auxiliaries. As shown by the sentences *I can read* (**ich kann lesen**), *you may go* (**Sie dürfen gehen**), English and German have some verbal forms which indicate whether the action expressed by the following infinitive is possible, necessary, permissible, and so on. These verbs are called modal auxiliaries. However, the English modals are defective; they have no infinitives, no participles, and sometimes no past tense. The German modals are complete verbs, and the forms missing in English have to be paraphrased.

15. Meanings of Modals. The modals and their most common meanings are:

dürfen* to be allowed to, may (*idea of permission*)
können to be able to, can (*idea of ability, possibility*)
mögen† to want to, like to, like (*idea of inclination*)
müssen to be compelled to, must, have to (*idea of necessity*)
sollen to be to, be said to, be supposed to (*idea of obligation*)
wollen to want to, be about to, claim to (*idea of desire, immediate intention*)

Examples:

Darf ich gehen? May I go?
Ich kann gut sehen. I can see well.
Ich mag das Kleid nicht mehr sehen. I do not want to see the dress any more.
Ich muß heute gehen. I must go today.
Ich muß heute nicht gehen. I do not have to go today.
Er soll es heute erfahren. He is to find it out today.
Ich will das Kleid sehen. I want to see the dress.

Note that **können, mögen,** and **wollen** are also used as independent verbs. When so used, **können** means *to know.*

Können Sie Deutsch? Do you know German?
Meyer kann das Programm auswendig. Meyer knows the program by heart.
Er weiß, was er will. He knows what he wants.
Ich mag Frau Fischer nicht. I do not like Mrs. Fischer.

***Dürfen** in connection with negatives means *may not, cannot, must not*:

Du darfst nicht lachen. You must not laugh.
Wir dürfen nichts sagen. We cannot say anything.

†Mögen is used mainly in the subjunctive. See § 122.

16. Conjugation of Modals in the Present Tense

	dürfen	können	mögen	müssen	sollen	wollen
ich	darf	kann	mag	muß	soll	will
du	darfst	kannst	magst	mußt	sollst	willst
er	darf	kann	mag	muß	soll	will
wir	dürfen	können	mögen	müssen	sollen	wollen
ihr	dürft	könnt	mögt	müßt	sollt	wollt
sie	dürfen	können	mögen	müssen	sollen	wollen

17. Dependent Infinitive after Modals. The infinitive dependent upon a modal auxiliary stands at the end of the clause or sentence. Note that this infinitive does not take **zu.**

Das kann man hören. One can hear that.
Er will heute nicht gehen. He does not want to go today.

18. Omission of Dependent Infinitive. After modals the dependent infinitive is frequently omitted when it can be readily supplied from the context:

Ich will schlafen, aber ich kann nicht. I want to sleep but I can't.
Er will nach Amerika (**gehen** *understood*). He wants to go to America.

Cf. English: Do you want to (go, eat, sing)?

19. Wissen. The verb **wissen** is not a modal but is conjugated like one:

ich weiß	**wir wissen**
du weißt	**ihr wißt**
er weiß	**sie wissen**

20. Nominative and Accusative Cases. We would not think of saying "He gave I a pencil" or "She loves he." We recognize that certain pronouns (*I*, *he*, etc.) are reserved for the subject, whereas certain other pronouns (*me*, *him*, etc.) are reserved for the object. Because of this difference we may say, "She ignores him" and "Him she ignores" and not change the meaning.

In grammatical terminology the forms *I* and *he* are "nominatives" or are used in the "nominative case"; the forms *me* and *him* are used in the "objective case."

German pronouns show similar variations: **ich** and **er** (in the nominative case) and **mich** and **ihn** (in the accusative case, which is part of the objective case).

But, unlike English, German, by using distinct forms of the preceding article (or adjective), tends to differentiate also between cases of *nouns*. Thus, **Der Mann sieht den Schnee** means "The man sees the snow." And **Den Schnee sieht der Mann** has the identical meaning because the form **der** is the masculine definite article in the nominative, and the form **den** is the masculine definite article in the accusative.

Briefly stated, the subject of a sentence and the subjective complement or predicate noun (cf. John is my *friend*) are always in the nominative case. The direct object is always in the accusative (part of the English objective) case.

The nominative and accusative of the definite and indefinite articles are as follows:

	Definite Article (the)			**Indefinite Article (a)**		
	Masc.	**Fem.**	**Neut.**	**Masc.**	**Fem.**	**Neut.**
NOM.	**der**	**die**	**das**	**ein**	**eine**	**ein**
ACC.	**den**	**die**	**das**	**einen**	**eine**	**ein**

21. Use of Present Tense. The present tense is used more in German than in English. It is more frequently used to express future time:

Ich gehe heute abend bestimmt. I shall definitely go this evening.

It is always used where English uses the present perfect to denote what has been *and still is*:

Er gebraucht es schon achtzehn Jahre. He has been using it (for) eighteen years.

(In this usage **schon** is idiomatic and might be said to be the equivalent of English *for*.)

22. Flavoring Particles. Germans learning English discover that the "say" in "Say, she is beautiful" functions not as a verb but as a "flavoring" exclamation and expresses a note of admiration or surprise. Other flavoring words like *well* (Well, I don't know), *why* (Why, I didn't know that!) and *after all* (He is, after all, a child) lend almost imperceptible shades of meaning. In German a few short words like **also, da, denn, doch, ja, noch, schon,** and **wohl** serve a similar purpose. That is, they may be used as

a. normal words with a definite, translatable meaning (**Ja, ich weiß es.** Yes, I know it.)

b. flavoring words (**Das beweist ja gar nichts.** Why, that doesn't prove anything at all.)

Since the presence of such flavoring particles constitutes one of the main differences between idiomatic German and German that is merely grammatically correct, they will be used freely in this book. You will not be expected in first-year German to use them in writing or in speaking German, for their proper use is difficult. But when you find them in German passages and you are quite certain they may not be translated with their literal meanings, then you may be fairly sure they are used as flavoring particles, and you should probably not attempt to translate them.

EXERCISES

I

Answer in German: **1. Wer hat die fünfhundert (500) Mark noch nicht? 2. Was hat Frau Meyer schon? 3. Was kostet das Reisekleid? 4. Wann** (when) **gehen Schmidts zu Fischers? 5. Wo** (where) **wohnen Meyers? 6. Wie dünn ist die Wand zwischen Meyers und Fischers? 7. Was kann man bei Fischers hören? 8. Wer mag Frau Fischer nicht? 9. Wann** (when) **kommt das Odontoschein-Programm? 10. Wer kann heute das Programm auswendig? 11. Wer ist neidisch auf Frau Meyers Reisekleid? 12. Wer sagt: „Frau Schmidt ist eine Gans"? 13. Wer hat immer recht? 14. Sind Meyers Zähne weiß? Ja, . . . 15. Was bewahrt die Jugend? 16. Wer gewinnt den Preis?**

II

Translate into German: 1. I must go now. 2. I can see the paper. 3. I want to read the book. 4. We want to see the girl. 5. We must talk softly. 6. I don't* like the glass. 7. She is to come this evening. 8. We may not laugh. 9. Do you want to go now? 10. Do you want to come? 11. Must he come? 12. May I come? 13. Is he coming? 14. Do you see the snow? 15. I do not* want to forget Anna. 16. He already has the glass. 17. Today she is to find it out. 18. Why must we wait? 19. Does he want to come? 20. We must pay now.

III

Translate into English:

bekommen	**brauchen**	**leider**	**versuchen**
beweisen	**dicht**	**reden**	**werden**
tun	**fahren**	**übrigens**	**man**

IV

Translate into German:

alone	simple	to read	satisfied
to think	the dress	the piece	back

V

Underline each modal auxiliary in Text A and Text B.

VI

Conjugate in the present tense:

Ich muß gehen	**Ich will es heute abend erfahren**
Ich darf es nicht vergessen	**Ich kann den Preis gewinnen**

VII

Review all the words introduced through Lesson III. See pages 315–317.

---

*When **nicht** negates an entire clause, it stands as near the end of the clause as possible:

Er hat das Geld nicht. He hasn't the money.

Er kann heute nicht kommen. He cannot come today.

When **nicht** negates one particular element, it usually precedes that element:

Ich bin nicht neidisch auf Frau Meyers Kleid. I am not envious of Mrs. Meyer's dress.

Man kann nicht immer arbeiten. One cannot always work.

LESSON IV

TEXT A

Wenn es Frühling wird, arbeitet Kleinkopf auf dem Feld.—Es ist schon Frühling hier bei uns, aber ihr habt immer noch Schnee!—Hier bringe ich Ihnen eine Gans.—Nun, Herr Meyer, was haben Sie zu berichten? Leider nichts, gar nichts.—Warum antwortest du mir nicht? —Ich kann es dir nicht sagen.—Ich kann dich nicht verstehen.—Du 5 mußt den Apfel mit mir teilen.—Wohnst du nun in Berlin?—Ich bleibe bei dir.—Willst du mit mir oder mit ihm gehen?—Ich sehe dich gar nicht mehr.—Wir dürfen das Programm nicht vergessen.—Hier hast du ein Glas Wasser, das tut dir gut.—Die Frau gibt dem Fräulein ein Glas Wasser. Das Fräulein dankt ihr. Sie sagt: „Ich danke Ihnen." 10

Frank und Anna kommen aus der Klasse.—Du mußt nicht alles glauben. Einem Mädchen kann man immer glauben. Ich kann es dir beweisen.—Es steht in der Zeitung.—Sie ist nicht schön, aber sie ist intelligent.—Können Sie Deutsch?—Frau Meyers Kleid ist rot, das weiß ich bestimmt.—Herr Schmidt redet viel zuviel.—Sie ist mir zu 15 alt.—Atmet sie immer so schwer?—Ich weiß nicht, was sie tut.—Was tust du mit dem Geld?—Seit dem Krieg habe ich kein Geld.—Er nimmt mir alles.—Ich kann ihn nicht vergessen.—Ich mag ihn nicht.—Das ist mir recht.

VOCABULARY

also therefore
antworten (*w. dat.*) to *answer*; give an answer to
der Apfel the *apple*
die Arbeit the work
  arbeiten to work
aus *out* of, from; of
außerdem moreover, besides
beißen to *bite*
danken (*w. dat.*) to *thank*
daß *that* (*conj.*)
ehrlich honest
die Erbse (*pl.* **die Erbsen**) the pea (the peas)
die Erde the *earth*; ground
erzählen to relate, *tell*
das Feld the *field*
frisch *fresh*
der Frühling (the) spring
ganz whole, entire(ly), very
geben (i) to *give*
gerade straight; just; exact(ly)

gern gladly, willingly
das Geschäft the business, deal; store
die Geschichte the story; history
gleich *like*, same; immediately
halb *half*
  die Hälfte the *half*
der Herbst (the) autumn
der Hof the court; farm
in *in*, into
jemand somebody, someone
die Kartoffel (*pl.* **die Kartoffeln**) the potato
kaufen to buy
die Klasse the *class*
der Krieg the war
kurz short, shortly; *curt*
machen to *make*; do
mit with; along
nehmen (nimmst, nimmt) to take
oft *often*
ohne without
pflanzen to *plant*
recht *right* (cf. Idioms)
riechen to smell; (*reek*)
seit for; since
seitdem since that time
stehen to *stand*; to be
der Teil the share, the part
  teilen to divide, share
verlieren to lose
von of; from; by
vor before, in front of; ago
wachsen (ä) to grow; (*wax*)
werfen (i) to throw

IDIOMS

es ist mir ganz gleich it is all the same to me
es ist mir recht it is all right with me
glauben an to believe in (*w. acc.*)
immer noch or **noch immer** still
gern (*plus verb*) to like to . . .
  ich esse gern I like to eat
  ich schlafe gern I like to sleep
  ich kaufe gern I like to buy

TEXT B

Wer ist intelligent?

Heute erzählen wir Ihnen wieder eine Geschichte, die Geschichte von Kleinkopf und Windig. Wir hoffen, daß die Geschichte Ihnen nicht zu schwer ist.

Es ist Frühling. Die Erde riecht frisch und gut; und Kleinkopf steht auf dem Feld, beißt in einen Apfel und sieht in den Abend.

„Noch eine Woche, und ich muß Kartoffeln pflanzen", denkt er. „Ich verstehe nicht, warum Windig immer noch Erbsen pflanzt. Die Feldarbeit kostet ihm viel Geld; und für Erbsen bekommt man heute nicht mehr soviel wie vor dem Kriege." Kleinkopf wird wie immer neidisch,

wenn er an Windig denkt. Windigs Erbsenfeld liegt gleich neben Kleinkopfs Kartoffelfeld. Windig ist Advokat,[1] wohnt seit dem Kriege in Hamburg, braucht nicht mehr zu arbeiten und sagt: „Nur wenn jemand nicht intelligent ist, arbeitet er auf dem Felde.“

Kleinkopf geht zurück auf den Hof. Er denkt noch immer an Windig, denkt an das Erbsenfeld und meint: „Was ich habe, das macht mich nicht zufrieden; und gerade was man nicht hat, kann man oft so gut gebrauchen.“

Kurz nach dem Abendessen[2] kommt Windig zu Kleinkopf auf den Hof. „Kleinkopf“, sagt er, „ich will ein Geschäft mit dir machen. Ich weiß, du willst das Erbsenfeld kaufen. Nun, du kannst das Feld haben, wenn du mir im Herbst die Hälfte von allem gibst, was[3] auf dem Felde wächst.“ „Hm“, meint Kleinkopf, „und ich soll dir die Arbeit tun?“ „Natürlich“, antwortet der Advokat.[1] „Ich habe sozusagen das Kapital, und du tust die Arbeit. Das ist immer so. Außerdem bist du nicht intelligent. Feldarbeit kannst du tun. Aber wie man ohne Arbeit viel Geld machen kann, das weißt du nicht.“ „Nein, das weiß ich nicht“, sagt Kleinkopf.

„Ich will eine Wette[4] mit dir machen, Kleinkopf“, sagt Windig. „Du und ich, wir laufen um das Feld. Ich nehme einen Sack mit fünfundzwanzig (25) Pfund[5] auf die[6] Schulter[6], und du nimmst einen Sack mit hundert (100) Pfund. Wenn der Sack mir zu schwer wird, verliere ich; und wenn der Sack dir zu schwer wird, verlierst du. Wenn du verlierst, bekomme ich das Kartoffelfeld; und wenn ich verliere, bekommst du das Erbsenfeld.“ („Kleinkopf ist nicht intelligent“, denkt Windig. „Er weiß also nicht, daß er die Wette[4] verlieren muß, weiß nicht, daß ich das Kartoffelfeld, und nicht nur einen Teil von allem haben will, was[3] auf dem Erbsenfeld wächst.“) „Das ist mir recht“, antwortet Kleinkopf. „Ich laufe gern, und es ist mir ganz gleich, ob ich mit fünfundzwanzig (25) oder mit hundert (100) Pfund um das Feld laufe. Du kannst Freitag[7] auf den Hof kommen.“ (Er denkt: „Windig ist intelligent aber nicht ehrlich. Er glaubt, ich muß die Wette[4] verlieren. Aber er weiß nicht, daß es Freitag regnet[8] und daß er verlieren kann.“)

Der Freitag kommt. Kleinkopf gibt Windig einen Sack mit fünfundzwanzig Pfund Kartoffeln. Er nimmt einen Sack mit hundert Pfund Zucker.[9] Sie laufen um das Feld.

Um ein Uhr regnet[8] es, regnet auf den Sack mit dem Zucker.[9] Es regnet lange. Um drei[10] Uhr ist Kleinkopfs Sack gar nicht mehr so schwer. Windig aber hat eine Lungenentzündung,[11] wirft den Sack auf die Erde und verliert die Wette.[4] „Ich danke dir für das Erbsenfeld", sagt Kleinkopf. Dann bringt er Windig ins Hospital. Seitdem ist Kleinkopf zufrieden.

NOTES. 1. **Advokat** lawyer. (The indefinite article is omitted with nouns denoting professions.) 2. **Abendessen** supper. 3. **was** that, which. 4. **Wette** wager, bet. 5. **Pfund** pound(s). 6. **die Schulter** my shoulder. 7. **Freitag** Friday. 8. **regnet** will rain, rains. 9. **Zucker** sugar. 10. **drei** three. 11. **Lungenentzündung** pneumonia.

GRAMMAR

23. The Dative Case. In paragraph 20 you learned that German articles and pronouns have special forms for the nominative and accusative. They also have special forms for the dative. German divides, so to speak, the English objective case (used for the objects of prepositions and direct and indirect objects of verbs) into the dative and accusative. Certain rules govern the use of both cases.

I. USE

a. The dative is used to express the indirect object after German verbs of giving and taking where English frequently must use a preposition. German does not use the preposition. Examples:

Er gibt es mir. He gives it to me.
Er gibt mir ein Kleid. He gives me a dress (a dress to me).
Er nimmt es mir. He takes it from me.

b. The dative is used as the sole object of several verbs, such as **antworten** and **danken**:

Ich kann dir nicht antworten. I cannot answer you.
Ich danke Ihnen. (I) thank you.

Other such verbs will be so designated in the vocabulary as they are introduced. **Glauben** used without the preposition **an** takes the dative:

Ich glaube ihm nicht. I do not believe him.

c. The dative is governed by some adjectives, such as **interessant, recht,** and **schwer.** (To express the same idea English uses the prepositions *to*, *with*, or *for*.)

Das ist mir interessant. That is interesting to me.
Es ist ihm recht. It is all right with him.
Das ist mir zu schwer. That is too hard for me.

d. The dative is governed by the prepositions

aus	**außer**	**bei**	**mit**
nach	**seit**	**von**	**zu**

e. Compare § 28.

II. FORMS

Masc.	Fem.	Neut.
dem Hof(e)	**der Frau**	**dem Feld(e)**
einem Hof(e)	**einer Frau**	**einem Feld(e)**

Masculine and neuter nouns of one syllable may have an **-e** in the dative singular. Feminine nouns are not changed.

24. Contractions. The following prepositions and definite articles are generally contracted:

an dem to **am**	**von dem** to **vom**	**auf das** to **aufs**
in dem to **im**	**zu dem** to **zum**	**in das** to **ins**
bei dem to **beim**	**an das** to **ans**	**zu der** to **zur**

25. Personal Pronouns.

SINGULAR

	First Person	Second Person
NOM.	**ich** I	**du** (**Sie**) you
DAT.	**mir** (to) me	**dir** (**Ihnen**) (to) you
ACC.	**mich** me	**dich** (**Sie**) you

Third Person

NOM.	**er** he	**sie** she	**es** it
DAT.	**ihm** (to) him	**ihr** (to) her	**ihm** (to) it
ACC.	**ihn** him	**sie** her	**es** it

PLURAL

	First Person	Second Person	Third Person
NOM.	**wir** we	**ihr** (**Sie**) you	**sie** they
DAT.	**uns** (to) us	**euch** (**Ihnen**) (to) you	**ihnen** (to) them
ACC.	**uns** us	**euch** (**Sie**) you	**sie** them

26. **Agreement.** The personal pronoun of the third person must agree in gender and number with the noun to which it refers. English *it* may be **er, sie,** or **es** in the nominative, or it may be **ihn, sie,** or **es** in the accusative. Thus:

Wir sehen den Schnee; er ist weiß. We see the snow; it is white.
Siehst du die Zeitung? Sie ist weiß. Do you see the newspaper? It is white.

27. **Verb-Last Position.** In dependent or subordinate clauses the inflected verb is normally the *last* element of that clause:

Wir hoffen, daß die Geschichte nicht zu schwer *ist*. We hope that the story is not too hard.
Frau Meyer weiß, was sie *will*. Mrs. Meyer knows what she wants.
Wenn du heute abend zu Bett *gehst*, darfst du die Zeitung lesen. When you go to bed tonight, you may read the newspaper.

EXERCISES

I

Answer in German: **1. Ist die Geschichte Ihnen zu schwer? 2. Wie riecht die Erde? 3. Wo** (where) **steht Kleinkopf? 4. Was muß Kleinkopf nach einer Woche pflanzen? 5. Was kostet Windig viel Geld? 6. Was ist Windig? 7. Wo** (where) **wohnt Windig seit dem Kriege? 8. Was will Kleinkopf kaufen? 9. Wer soll die Arbeit tun? 10. Wer macht mit Kleinkopf eine Wette? 11. Was denkt Windig? 12. Wer läuft gern? 13. Wann** (when) **soll Windig auf den Hof kommen? 14. Ist Windig ehrlich? 15. Gibt Kleinkopf Windig einen Sack mit Kartoffeln oder einen Sack mit Erbsen? 16. Wann** (when) **ist Kleinkopfs Sack gar nicht mehr so schwer? 17. Was wirft Windig auf die Erde?**

II

Translate into German: 1. He sees me. 2. Karl, I thank you. 3. Mrs. Schmidt, we thank you. 4. He is just coming out of the class. 5. He is bringing us the newspaper. 6. They need him. 7. Who gets the prize? Franz gets it. 8. Do you want to go with her? 9. The wall is thin; we can hear you [*pl. familiar*]. Can you hear us? 10. We want to give them money. 11. What are they doing with the pencil? 12. Today I can give you* nothing. 13. You must not believe everything. 14. You may give him the money. 15. Mr. Meyer has a farm. 16. Fritz has a pencil; it is red. 17. I can see the snow; it is white. 18. Does he understand me (them, her, you)? 19. Can you see me (him, her, them)? 20. I don't† want to forget you (them, her, him).

III

Translate:

weiß	**jung**	**schon**	**die Zeitung**	**alt**
fast	**die Jugend**	**schön**	**gebrauchen**	**immer**
leise	**laufen**	**viel**	**der Bleistift**	**zwar**

IV

Translate:

to come	to show	the hair	to win	to breathe
always	the wall	more	to ask	but
no	to sit	jealous	to stay	to be sure

V

Learn the prepositions which take the dative; learn also the table of personal pronouns.

VI

Contract the following:

zu dem	**von dem**	**an das**
zu der	**an dem**	**in das**
in dem	**bei dem**	**auf das**

---

*Compare § 149*c*. In general the dative object precedes the accusative object unless the latter is a personal pronoun.

†See footnote, page 28.

VII

Conjugate in the present tense:

beißen pflanzen erzählen nehmen geben verlieren wachsen

VIII

Underscore in your text the inflected verbs in Text B and analyze the position of each.

IX

Draw one line under each dative form and two lines under each accusative form in Text A.

LESSON V

TEXT A

Unsere Zeitung liegt vor dem Hause.—Das Buch ist für meinen Mann, und die Zeitung ist für mich.—Ich lege das Buch in die Ecke.—Wo ist dein Pferd?—Ein gutes Pferd bekomme ich so leicht nicht wieder.—Er beißt in seinen Apfel.—Er wirft den Apfel auf das Feld.—Sie spielt oft auf unserem Felde.—Kartoffeln wachsen in der Erde, Erbsen wachsen 5 **über der Erde.—Kurz vor dem Krieg fährt Kleinkopf nach Berlin.—Hans läuft in den Wald.—Ohne ihn können wir nicht gehen.—Um die Ecke kommt mein Freund.—Euer Haus ist schön.—Er sitzt neben ihr.—In jenem Haus wohnt mein Freund.—Solche Arbeit mag ich nicht.—Dieses Buch gehört mir.** 10

VOCABULARY

arm poor
dauern to last; to take (of time)
denn for (*co-ord. conj.*) (cf. § 22)
dieser *this*
doch yet, however, but (cf. § 22)
die Ecke the corner
eng narrow
essen (i) to *eat*
etwas something; somewhat
der Freund the *friend*
gefallen (ä) to please (*w. dat.*)
  der Gefallen the favor
gehören (*w. dat.*) to belong to
genug *enough*
das Gesicht the face
glücklich happy
halten (**du hältst, er hält**) to *hold*; to keep
das Haus the *house*
der Held the hero
hinter *behind*
hungrig *hungry*
ja yes
das Jahr the *year*
jeder each, every
jener that
kaum scarcely
kennen to know (by acquaintance)
lassen (ä) to *let*; leave
leicht easy; *light*
lernen to *learn*
lieben to *love*
liegen to *lie*, be situated
mancher *many* a
der Mann the *man*; husband
nah close, near by
das Pferd the horse
solcher *such*
spielen to play
der Strumpf the stocking
der Student the *student*

studieren to *study*
unter *under*, below
verschwinden to disappear
vielleicht perhaps
der Wald the forest
wann *when* (*interrog. adv.*)
der Weg the *way*, road, path
weinen to weep, cry
welcher *which*, what
wo where
wohin whither, to what place
die Zeit the time

IDIOMS

es geht mir gut I am well
es geht ihm gut he is well
nach Hause gehen, kommen to go home, come home
um zu in order to; **um zu lernen** in order to learn; **um das Buch zu lesen** in order to read the book

TEXT B

Der Student aus dem Paradies[1]

Es ist gar nicht so einfach, eine Geschichte für unser Buch zu schreiben, wie Sie vielleicht glauben. Wenn die Geschichte zu schwer ist, dann werfen Sie das Buch in die Ecke und sagen: „Diese Geschichte kann man nicht verstehen; der Dativ ist einfach zu schwer.“ Wenn die Geschichte aber zu leicht ist, dann gehen Sie einfach zu Bett. Und im Bett lernt man den Dativ natürlich auch nicht.

Außerdem gehört zu jeder Geschichte ein Held; und eine Geschichte ohne Held ist einfach keine Geschichte. Aber leider gefällt nicht jeder Held jedem Leser,[2] und es ist schwer, es[3] jedem Leser recht zu machen.[3]

Joseph, unser neuer Held, gefällt uns ganz gut. Zwar lieben wir ihn nicht, aber wir sind mit ihm zufrieden. Er studiert in Paris. Geld hat er natürlich nicht. Doch weiß er den Weg zum Paradies[1]; denn er studiert Theologie. Aber Sie dürfen nicht glauben, daß er dem Paradies schon nahe ist. Denn der Weg zum Paradies ist, wie Sie wissen, eng und gerade; und ob das Haus, in dem Joseph gerade verschwindet, noch auf diesem Weg liegt, das wissen wir nicht.

„Grüß Gott!“[4] sagt unser Held und sieht gleich, daß die Frau allein ist und ihr Mann auf dem Felde sein muß. „Ich komme aus Paris und habe eine lange Reise hinter mir. Haben Sie vielleicht etwas zu essen für mich, gute Frau? Ich bin ein armer Student.“ Die Frau hört nicht gut. „Was“, meint sie, „Sie kommen aus dem Paradies? Da bin ich

aber glücklich. Da kennen Sie vielleicht auch Hans, meinen ersten[5] Mann. Er[6] ist schon drei Jahre tot,[6] aber ich kann ihn noch nicht vergessen. Er war[7] so gut und noch so jung!"—„Meinen Sie vielleicht den Hans Meyer?" fragt unser Student. „Das ist mein bester Freund im Paradies!"—„Ja, ja", weint die Frau, „das ist er! Ich hoffe, es geht ihm gut, meinem Mann."—„Leider nicht, gute Frau. Hans bekommt nicht genug zu essen, und oft ist er so hungrig, daß er kaum seine Harfe[8] spielen kann. Geld, um etwas kaufen zu können, hat er auch nicht."— „Guter Freund", meint da die Frau und weint noch mehr, „unter meinem Bett habe ich einen Strumpf mit hundert (100) Mark. Vielleicht tun Sie mir den Gefallen und bringen das Geld meinem Mann."— „Aber ja!" sagt Joseph, „ich habe zwar nicht gern so viel Geld bei mir. Aber was tut man nicht für seinen Freund?" Er nimmt Strumpf und Geld und verschwindet.

Es dauert nicht lang, da kommt der Mann nach Hause. Die Frau erzählt ihm alles. Es gefällt ihm gar nicht, daß der Strumpf mit dem Geld auf dem Wege zum Paradies ist. Er sagt nichts, holt sein Pferd, und nach kurzer Zeit sieht er einen Mann am Wege sitzen. Es ist Joseph, unser Freund, der[9] mit dem Strumpf ins Paradies will. Aber der Mann sieht nicht den Strumpf mit dem Geld, er sieht nur ein ehrliches Gesicht und fragt: „Haben[10] Sie vielleicht einen Mann mit einem Strumpf gesehen?"[10]—„Ja, natürlich!" antwortet Joseph. „Er ist da im Walde!"—„Hier, wollen Sie mein Pferd halten?" sagt der Mann und läuft in den Wald. Und Joseph, sein ehrliches Gesicht, der Strumpf und das Geld verschwinden mit dem Pferde.

Nach kurzer Zeit kommt der Mann zurück, ohne den Strumpf und ohne das Pferd. „Anna", sagt er, „du kannst den Mann doch nicht zu Fuß[11] ins Paradies gehen lassen! Ich[12] habe ihm mein Pferd gegeben[12]."

NOTES. 1. **Paradies** Paradise. 2. **Leser** reader. 3. **es jedem Leser recht zu machen** to please every reader. 4. South German greeting. 5. **ersten** first. 6. **Er . . . tot** He has been dead for three years. 7. **war** was. 8. **Harfe** harp. 9. **der** who. 10. **Haben . . . gesehen?** Have you perhaps seen a man with a stocking? 11. **zu Fuss** on foot. 12. **Ich . . . gegeben.** I gave him my horse.

GRAMMAR

28. Prepositions with Dative or Accusative. An, auf, hinter; in, neben, über; unter, vor, and **zwischen** govern the dative or accusative according to the following rule:

If the place expressed in the prepositional phrase is reached through the action of the verb, the preposition requires the accusative; conversely, if the entire action of the verb occurs at the place indicated by the preposition, the dative must be used.

Anna ist in dem Hause.	**Anna geht in das Haus.**
Das Buch liegt in der Ecke.	**Er wirft das Buch in die Ecke.**
Er schwimmt in dem Wasser.	**Er springt in das Wasser.**
(He swims in the water.)	(He jumps into the water.)

29. Prepositions with the Accusative. The following prepositions always govern the accusative: **durch** (*through*), **für, gegen** (*against*), **ohne,** and **um.**

30. Possessive Adjectives: ein-Words. The German possessive adjectives and their English equivalents are:

mein	my	**unser**	our
dein	your	**euer**	your
sein	his	**ihr**	their
ihr	her		
sein	its (one's)	**Ihr**	your

These words and **kein** take the same endings as the indefinite article **ein, eine, ein,** and therefore are frequently called the **ein**-words. (Note that the **er** of **unser** and **euer** belongs to the stem and is not an ending.) Examples:

Ein (mein, dein, unser) Buch ist interessant.
Eine (meine, deine) Gans kostet in diesem Jahre viel.
Meine (deine, unsere) Zeitung ist interessant.
Ich sehe ein (mein, dein, unser) Buch.
Du hast einen (meinen, deinen, unseren) Bleistift.

Review of **ein**-words and their endings:

	Masc.	Fem.	Neut.	Masc.	Fem.	Neut.
NOM.	**ein**	**eine**	**ein**	—	**e**	—
DAT.	**einem**	**einer**	**einem**	**em**	**er**	**em**
ACC.	**einen**	**eine**	**ein**	**en**	**e**	—

31. Pronominal Adjectives: der-Words. The pronominal adjectives **dieser, jeder, jener, mancher, solcher,** and **welcher** have endings very similar to those of the definite article and therefore are usually called **der**-words.

Review of **der**-words and their endings:

	Masc.	Fem.	Neut.	Masc.	Fem.	Neut.
NOM.	**dieser**	**diese**	**dieses**	**er**	**e**	**es**
DAT.	**diesem**	**dieser**	**diesem**	**em**	**er**	**em**
ACC.	**diesen**	**diese**	**dieses**	**en**	**e**	**es**

Table of Definite Article

	Masc.	Fem.	Neut.
NOM.	**der**	**die**	**das**
DAT.	**dem**	**der**	**dem**
ACC.	**den**	**die**	**das**

32. Pronominal Adjectives as Pronouns. When used without nouns **dieser (diese, dieses)** means *this one, the one*; **jener (jene, jenes)** means *that one, the other*; **jeder (jede, jedes)** means *each one, every one.*

Dieser also means *the latter*, and **jener** *the former*: **Hans liegt im Bett und Fritz studiert; dieser schreibt und jener schläft.** *Hans lies in bed and Fritz studies; the latter is writing and the former is sleeping.*

33. Predicate Adjectives. These never take an ending.

Sie ist alt. She is old. **Der Weg ist eng.** The way is narrow.

34. Strong Adjective Endings. When the endings of the **der**-words are added to adjectives, they are called strong adjective endings. They help the reader to see whether the first unit of a sentence is the subject, the direct, or the indirect object. Whenever an **ein**-word has *no* ending, the following adjective (if there is one) takes on the ending which the **ein**-word fails to show. It is the adjective in such cases which makes possible accurate reading. Examples:

d*er* Mann	(the man)	**dies*es* Haus**	(this house)
ein Mann	(a man)	**ein Haus**	(a house)
ein alt*er* Mann	(an old man)	**ein schön*es* Haus**	(a pretty house)

Da kommt ein arm*er* Student. There comes a poor student.
Er hat ein ehrlich*es* Gesicht. He has an honest face.

Sometimes a noun is used without any preceding **der-** or **ein**-word, leaving the noun's gender and case unindicated. Here German makes an adjective preceding that noun take over the function of the missing **ein**-word or **der**-word; the adjective takes a strong ending. Examples:

Arm*er* alt*er Mann!**	Poor old man!
Arm*e* Frau!	Poor woman!
Gut*es* Kind!	Good child!

In short, attributive adjectives (adjectives immediately preceding a noun) take strong endings when

a. A preceding **ein**-word shows no ending.
b. No **der-** or **ein**-word precedes.

EXERCISES

I

Answer in German: **1. Ist es einfach, eine Geschichte für dieses Buch zu schreiben? 2. Wann werfen Sie das Buch in die Ecke? 3. Wo liegt es nun? 4. Was tun Sie, wenn die Geschichte zu leicht ist? 5. Wo lernt man den Dativ nicht? 6. Was muß in jeder Geschichte sein? 7. Wo studiert Joseph? 8. Wie ist der Weg zum Paradies? 9. Was sieht Joseph gleich? 10. Was will Joseph von der Frau?** (He

*Adjectives in a series take the same ending.

wants something to eat.) **11. Wer kann Hans nicht vergessen? 12. Warum kann Hans nichts kaufen? 13. Wo hat die Frau den Strumpf mit ihrem Geld? 14. Wem** (to whom) **soll Joseph das Geld bringen?** (He is to take it to his friend.) **15. Wer kommt nach kurzer Zeit nach Hause? 16. Was holt der Mann? 17. Wer sitzt am Wege? 18. Wann kommt der Mann zurück?**

II

Translate into German: 1. I am a poor student. 2. Do you want to come into the house? 3. He knows (*use* **kennen**) every girl in this class. 4. Which book may I read? 5. Mr. Donnerwetter, may I throw my book into the corner? 6. This story is too hard for me. 7. Is he staying in (the) bed today? 8. The pencil is lying on your book. 9. I must go to bed. 10. He is already sitting on the horse. 11. The goose swims (**schwimmt**) in the water. 12. He comes home without his horse.

III

Translate into English:

also	**gerade**	**aber**	**stehen**
außerdem	**erzählen**	**wachsen**	**alles**
gleich	**der Frühling**	**jemand**	**auswendig**
weiß	**ohne**	**kurz**	**rechnen**

IV

Translate into German:

the evening	the war	to throw
honest	to take	thick
the business	to smell	almost
to buy	to lose	only

V

Conjugate:

essen	**lassen**	**spielen**
halten	**lernen**	**können**
kennen	**lieben**	**müssen**

VI

Supply the definite article in the following sentences:

1. Er kann _____ Geld nicht finden.
2. Er will _____ Frau nichts geben.
3. Sie wirft _____ Apfel in _____ Ecke.
4. Nach _____ Arbeit muß ich immer schlafen.
5. Es liegt auf _____ Buch.
6. Gehen Sie in _____ Haus?
7. Der Held in _____ Geschichte ist glücklich.
8. Die Gans spielt mit _____ Kartoffel.

VII

Supply the indefinite article in sentences 3, 5, 6, and 8 of Exercise VI.

VIII

Explain the difference between

Er läuft auf das Feld.	Er läuft auf dem Feld.
Er fällt auf den Weg.	Er fällt auf dem Wege.

IX

Learn the prepositions which govern the dative or accusative; learn those that take only the accusative. Learn the possessive adjectives.

X

Review all the words introduced through Lesson V. See pages 316–317.

LESSON VI

TEXT A

Ich höre, daß Frau Meyer einen Hut kaufen will. Sie hat ihn schon. Das ist nicht möglich! Die Farbe ihres Hutes gefällt mir nicht. Ihr alter Hut ist grün, aber ihr neuer Hut ist nicht grün, sondern blau. Der Hut, den Herr Meyer trägt, ist nicht blau und auch nicht grün, er hat sozusagen keine Farbe mehr. 5

Joseph ist ein Held, den jeder lieben muß. Das Haus, in dem Joseph gerade verschwindet, liegt nicht auf dem Weg ins Paradies. Siehst du die Frau, die da vor dem Hause steht? Es ist keine Frau, es ist Joseph, der mit dem Strumpf ins Paradies will.

Ich weiß nicht, ob ich Zeit habe.—Obgleich sie fast kein Geld hat, 10 **hat sie immer genug zu essen.—Während ich schlafe, darfst du nur ganz leise reden.—Weil die Erbsen schon etwas alt sind, will er sie** (them) **nicht essen.—Eine Geschichte, in der der Held das Mädchen bekommt, gefällt ihm.—Wer viel wissen will, muß auch viel studieren. —Ich weiß nicht, was er nun will.—Wer nichts verdient, kann auch** 15 **nichts kaufen.—Wer nicht für mich ist, ist gegen** (against) **mich.**

VOCABULARY

als than; when; as
die Art the manner; sort
außer besides; except (for)
behaupten to affirm, assert
bezahlen to pay for
blau *blue*
daher therefore
der Erfolg the success, result
erwarten to await; expect
das Fach the subject; drawer
der Fall the case
die Farbe the color
der Feind the enemy; (*fiend*)
die Gefahr the danger
grün *green*
heilig *holy*, sacred
helfen (i) (*w. dat.*) to *help*
der Hut the *hat*
je . . . desto the . . . the
das Kind the child
los loose
-los *-less*
  schlaflos sleepless
die Lösung the solution
der Markt the *market*
der Mensch the human being, person
möglich possible

die Mutter the *mother*
nämlich *namely*, you see
neu *new*
die Not the *need*; distress
obgleich although
scheinen to *shine*; seem
die Schuld the guilt, blame
  schuld(ig) guilty (to blame)
sondern but
sonst otherwise
sprechen (i) to speak
die Straße the *street*
suchen to *seek*
der Tag the *day*
tragen (ä) to bear, carry; wear
treffen (i) to hit; meet
trotz (*with genitive*) in spite of
  der Trotz the spite; haughtiness; obstinacy; defiance
verdienen to earn
verkaufen to sell
während (*with genitive*) while; during
wechseln to change; exchange
weil because, since
die Weise the manner, way
das Wort the *word*
die Zukunft the future

IDIOMS

auf diese Art und Weise in this manner and way
es gibt there is, there are
ganz gleich regardless
immer wieder again and again
mit gutem Recht rightly
ohne arbeiten zu müssen without having to work
ohne es zu wissen without knowing it
ohne zu sagen without saying
riechen nach to smell of

TEXT B

Vielleicht studieren Sie Deutsch, weil Sie Goethes *Faust* oder Schillers *Wilhelm Tell* lesen wollen. Vielleicht wollen Sie eine Reise nach Europa machen, und Sie lernen Deutsch, weil Sie in Deutschland ein Auto oder eine Kamera kaufen wollen. Vielleicht wollen Sie Philosophie
5 oder Geschichte studieren und lernen Deutsch, um Kants *Zum ewigen Frieden*[1] oder Spenglers *Der Untergang des Abendlandes*[2] im Original lesen zu können.

In diesem Falle dürfen Sie natürlich nicht erwarten, in unserem Buch eine Diskussion über Kants[3] oder Spenglers[3] Philosophie zu finden.
10 Wir sind zufrieden, wenn Sie nach einem Jahre ein deutsches Buch allein lesen können.

Wir geben Ihnen heute einen Text, der Ihnen zeigt, daß Sie schon auf dem Wege sind.

Arbeitslosigkeit und Maschine

Die Arbeitslosigkeit als soziales[4] Problem ist ein Kind unserer Zeit. Man darf mit gutem Recht behaupten, daß unsere Zivilisation nur dann eine Zukunft hat, wenn wir für dieses Problem eine Lösung finden.

„Arbeitslos sein" ist, wie Sie wissen, viel mehr als „keine Arbeit haben". Ein Mann, der so viel Geld hat, daß er gut leben[5] kann, ohne arbeiten zu müssen, ist nicht „arbeitslos"; und eine Mutter, die nicht „arbeitet", weil sie eine Familie hat, ist auch nicht „arbeitslos". Arbeitslos ist nur jemand, der Arbeit sucht, weil er arbeiten will oder arbeiten muß, und der doch keine Arbeit findet.

Oft aber sagt man heute einem Mann, der Arbeit sucht: „Wir brauchen leider keinen Arbeiter. Wir haben eine neue Maschine. Diese Maschine arbeitet bestimmt so gut wie ein guter Arbeiter, und doch kostet sie dem Arbeitgeber nicht so viel, wie ihm ein Arbeiter kostet." Oder man sagt dem Mann, der Arbeit sucht: „So, So! Sie sind ein Spezialist[6] für Turbinen.[6] Turbinen haben wir schon lange nicht mehr. Wir arbeiten mit Diesel-Motoren. Für einen Mann wie Sie haben wir leider keine Arbeit, und es ist gar nicht unmöglich, daß der Diesel-Motor Sie für immer arbeitslos macht."

Man kann es verstehen, wenn ein Spezialist, der auf diese Art und Weise immer wieder seine Arbeit verliert, nun bitter und unzufrieden wird. Man kann es verstehen, wenn er nicht mehr an die Zukunft glaubt und von nun an behauptet: „All meine Not kommt von der Maschine. Die Maschine allein ist schuld, daß ich nicht arbeiten darf, obgleich ich arbeiten will. Die Maschine ist eine Gefahr für unsere Zivilisation. Sie nimmt mir das Recht auf Arbeit; und dieses Recht ist mir heilig."

Aber die Maschine ist nicht nur ein Feind des Arbeitnehmers, den sie auf die Straße wirft und arbeitslos macht; sie ist auch ein Feind des Arbeitgebers.

Natürlich ist es jedem Arbeitgeber recht, wenn sein Arbeiter viel Geld verdient. Denn der Arbeitgeber weiß: je mehr der Arbeiter verdient, desto mehr kann er kaufen. Aber der Arbeitgeber will auch verdienen, und um Geld verdienen zu können, braucht er fast immer eine Maschine.

Eine Maschine aber kostet Geld. Und nicht jeder, der eine Idee[7] hat, wie man viel Geld verdienen kann, hat auch das Kapital, eine Maschine kaufen zu können. Er geht also zur Bank, und auf der Bank sagt man ihm: „Ihre Idee scheint gut zu sein. Wir geben Ihnen hunderttausend
5 (100 000) Mark (*marks*). Nach einem Jahre, so hoffen wir, können Sie dieses Kapital leicht zurückzahlen."

Der Mann kauft eine Maschine. Sie arbeitet gut. Sie läuft und macht an einem Tage hunderttausend (100 000) Tuben[8] Odontoschein.

„Odontoschein ist gut für jung und alt", spricht der Arbeitgeber, der
10 von nun an täglich 100 000 Tuben Odontoschein verkaufen muß, um kein Geld zu verlieren. „Odontoschein bringt die Jugend zurück!" behauptet Herr Meyer, weil er Geld braucht, um eine Reise nach Neuyork bezahlen zu können. „Wie kommt es, Fräulein Thusnelda, daß Sie trotz Ihrer Jugend jeden Freund verlieren, den Sie gewinnen? Odonto-
15 schein kann Ihnen helfen. Wenn Sie Odontoschein gebrauchen, verlieren Sie Ihren Freund nicht. Denn wer Odontoschein gebraucht, riecht wie eine Rose im Frühling. Warum versuchen Sie nicht auch Odontoschein, Fräulein Thusnelda? Noch ist es nicht zu spät!" schreibt die Zeitung. Und jedes Mädchen, ganz gleich ob sie Thusnelda heißt[9]
20 oder nicht, kauft eine Tube Odontoschein.

Der Arbeitgeber lacht. Er hat Erfolg. Er verdient Geld. Er ist zufrieden. Und die Maschine läuft und läuft und wirft täglich hunderttausend Tuben[8] Odontoschein auf den Markt.

Nach einem Jahre aber kann der Markt das Produkt der Odonto-
25 schein-Maschine nicht mehr aufnehmen. Das Odontoschein-Geschäft wird still, und daher muß die Maschine auch stillstehen.

Was kann der Arbeitgeber tun? Eine Maschine kostet Geld, kostet Geld, auch wenn sie nicht läuft!

Nun, eine Tube Odontoschein kostet im Geschäft an der Ecke eine
30 Mark. Man kann es verstehen, daß unser armer Joseph—und es gibt mehr als einen Joseph, obgleich sie nicht alle Theologie studieren—unmöglich eine Tube Odontoschein kaufen kann, wenn die Tube eine ganze Mark kostet. Der Arbeitgeber rechnet; er rechnet und findet einen Weg, wie man die Tube für fünfzig (50) Pfennig[10] verkaufen und
35 doch noch Geld verdienen kann.

„Von nun an können auch Sie Odontoschein gebrauchen", liest

Joseph während des Semesters in der Studentenzeitung. „Die Tube kostet von nun an nur fünfzig (50) Pfennig!"

Und nun liegt das Glück des Arbeitgebers in Josephs Hand. Der Arbeitgeber hofft, daß Joseph ihm hilft. Nun, wir kennen Joseph nicht so gut wie Sie, der Leser unseres Buches, ihn kennen. Alles, was wir von ihm wissen, ist, daß Theologie sein Fach ist. Ob er schon weiß, wann und wo man nach Odontoschein riechen muß, das wissen wir leider nicht. Wir können nur hoffen, daß er es lernt. Er muß es lernen, denn sonst steht die Odontoschein-Maschine wieder still.

Frau Meyer, das wissen wir, lernt viel leichter als Joseph. Sie weiß nicht nur, daß sie Odontoschein kaufen muß; sie weiß auch, daß sie einen Hut braucht. Frau Meyers Hut ist zwar noch ganz gut. Außer ihrer Freundin sieht kein Mensch, daß er schon ein Jahr alt ist. Aber Frau Meyers Hut ist grün, und der Hut ihrer Freundin ist blau, und Blau ist die Farbe des Jahres. „Diesen Hut", sagt Frau Meyer daher zu Gustav, ihrem Mann, „kann ich einfach nicht mehr tragen. Wenn du nicht willst, daß jede Frau, die ich treffe, mich fragt, ob mein Mann arbeitslos ist, dann muß ich Geld für einen Hut haben. Ich brauche einen Hut, der blau ist. Denn Blau ist, wie du weißt, die Farbe des Jahres." Ohne es zu wissen, tut Frau Meyer gerade das, was der Arbeitgeber will. Der Arbeitgeber muß nämlich verkaufen, wenn er verdienen will. Und weil er jeder Frau jedes Jahr „den Hut des Jahres" verkaufen will, so wechselt er, ohne ein Wort zu sagen, jedes Jahr die Farbe; denn sonst steht seine Maschine still.

Aber die Maschine darf nicht stillstehen, denn sonst werden wir alle arbeitslos. Und daher ist die Maschine eine Gefahr für unsere Zivilisation. Denn wir können nicht mehr tun, was wir wollen; wir müssen tun, was die Maschine will. Wir dürfen nicht mehr arbeiten, um kaufen zu können, sondern wir müssen kaufen, so scheint es, um arbeiten zu können.

NOTES. 1. **Zum ewigen Frieden** *On Perpetual Peace* 2. **Der Untergang des Abendlandes** *The Decline of the West.* 3. Observe absence of apostrophe. 4. **soziales** social. 5. **leben** to live. 6. **Spezialist für Turbinen** a specialist in turbine engines. 7. **Idee** idea. 8. **Tuben** tubes (of). 9. **heißt** is called, named. 10. **Pfennig** German coin; cognate is "penny."

BUILDING A PASSIVE VOCABULARY

An English-speaking student who knows the meaning of *to excite* is also expected to know the derivatives *excitable*, *excitability*, *excitement*, *excited*, *exciting*, *excitedly*, and so on. He is also expected to recognize compounds like *lovesick*, *love-worthy*, and *love story*, no matter whether they are spelled as one word, as two words, or with a hyphen. *Both in English and in German, derivatives and compounds constitute a large part of the vocabulary.* This is fortunate for the learner, since it is fairly easy to recognize words which are formed from familiar stems.

Derivative suffixes and prefixes will be introduced systematically later on. To assist the student to increase his vocabulary more rapidly, we offer following each Text B, from this lesson on, a section devoted to word families and difficult compounds used in Text B of the lesson. Here the words, in alphabetical arrangement, are shown with the elements which have already been introduced and with elements which are yet to be introduced or which may not be obvious to the learner. Translations then follow.

die Arbeit ***arbeiten*** to work, ***die Arbeit*** the work, ***der Arbeiter*** the worker, ***arbeitslos*** unemployed, ***die Arbeitslosigkeit*** the unemployment, ***der Arbeitgeber*** the work-giver *or* employer, ***der Arbeitnehmer*** the work-taker *or* employee

aufnehmen ***auf*** up, ***nehmen*** to take, ***aufnehmen*** to take up, absorb

Deutschland ***Deutsch*** German, ***Deutschland*** Germany

die Freundin ***der Freund*** the male friend, ***die Freundin*** the female friend

das Glück ***glücklich*** happy, ***das Glück*** happiness, luck, fate, fortune

leichter ***leicht*** easy, ***leichter*** easier, more easily

der Leser ***lesen*** to read, ***der Leser*** the reader

das Recht ***recht*** right, ***das Recht*** the right

täglich ***der Tag*** day, ***täglich*** daily

unmöglich ***möglich*** possible, ***unmöglich*** impossible

unzufrieden ***zufrieden*** contented, satisfied, ***unzufrieden*** discontented, dissatisfied

GRAMMAR

35. The Genitive Case. This case is generally used to denote possession. In English we may say either *the woman's hat* or *the hat of the woman.* German employs a separate case form: **der Hut *der* Frau.** In other words, the genitive article in German is equal to the apostrophe and *s* or the preposition *of* and the following article in English.

The endings of the **der**-words and **ein**-words in the genitive are:

Masculine	Feminine	Neuter
des, dieses	**der, dieser**	**des, dieses**
eines, meines	**einer, meiner**	**eines, meines**

Masculine and neuter nouns of one syllable add **-es** in the genitive: **des Buches, des Hutes**; masculine and neuter nouns of two or more syllables add **-s** in the genitive: **des Apfels, des Papiers.**

Feminine nouns remain unchanged throughout the singular.

Usually the genitive follows its governing noun:

Der Hut des Jahres ist grün. The hat of the year is green.
Die Farbe des Hutes ist grün. The color of the hat is green.

If a genitive precedes its governing noun, the latter drops its definite article. The normal order is, therefore, **der Herr des Hauses,** but the order can also be **des Hauses Herr.** (Both mean *the master of the house.*)

In front of their governing nouns, all personal names and words used as names add **-s** to form the genitive: **Karls Hut, Mutters Hut, Meyers Hut, Marias Hut, Hildegards Hut.**

Complete Tables of Endings in the Singular

	der-WORDS			ein-WORDS		
	Masc.	**Fem.**	**Neut.**	**Masc.**	**Fem.**	**Neut.**
NOM.	**er**	**e**	**es**	—	**e**	—
GEN.	**es**	**er**	**es**	**es**	**er**	**es**
DAT.	**em**	**er**	**em**	**em**	**er**	**em**
ACC.	**en**	**e**	**es**	**en**	**e**	—

Strong Adjective Endings

(Used only to compensate for the lack of a preceding **der-word** or the lack of an ending on a preceding **ein-word.**)

	Masc.	Fem.	Neut.
Nom.	**er**	**e**	**es**
Gen.	**(en)***	**er**	**(en)***
Dat.	**em**	**er**	**em**
Acc.	**en**	**e**	**es**

36. Relative Pronouns. English relative pronouns are as follows: *who* (nominative) *whose* (genitive), *whom* (dative and accusative), *that*, and *which* (both undeclined in English). The first three refer only to persons; *which* refers only to things; and *that* may refer to persons or things. There are two sets of relative pronouns in German: **der, die, das** and **welcher, welche, welches.** Both sets refer to persons or to things. The first one has a complete declension and is, with the exception of the genitive, identical with the definite article. The second has no genitive.

	Masculine		Feminine		Neuter	
Nom.	**der**	**welcher**	**die**	**welche**	**das**	**welches**
Gen.	**dessen**	—	**deren**	—	**dessen**	—
Dat.	**dem**	**welchem**	**der**	**welcher**	**dem**	**welchem**
Acc.	**den**	**welchen**	**die**	**welche**	**das**	**welches**

A relative pronoun agrees in gender and number with its antecedent; its case depends upon its use in its own clause:

Siehst du den Mann, der da vor dem Hause steht? Do you see the man who (that) is standing there in front of the house?
Joseph ist ein Held, den jeder lieben muß. Joseph is a hero whom (that) everyone must love.

Each form of **welcher, welche, welches** may be used interchangeably with the corresponding form of **der, die, das,** but the latter is used much more frequently.

---

*The genitive singular of strong adjective endings is of such low frequency that a discussion of its use is not within the scope of this book.

The relative pronoun is never omitted in German:

Der Hut, den ich kaufe, muß grün sein. The hat I buy must be green.

Clauses introduced by relative pronouns are set off by commas and require verb-last position. (See examples above and compare § 27.)

37. Indefinite Relative Pronouns: wer and was. The interrogative pronouns **wer** and **was** may be used as indefinite relative pronouns.

Wer when so used means *he who* or *whoever*. It is thus both antecedent and relative pronoun. For example:

Wer kein Geld hat, kann nichts kaufen. He who has no money can buy nothing.

Was (*whatever*) may also combine within itself both antecedent and relative pronoun:

Was er kauft, ist schön. Whatever he buys is beautiful.

But frequently **was** (*that, what*) has as its antecedent a neuter pronoun (**alles, nichts**) or an adjective used as a noun (to be explained later):

Er zeigt mir alles, was er kauft. He shows me everything (that) he buys.

38. Conjunctions. There are two main types of conjunctions, co-ordinating and subordinating conjunctions.

a. Co-ordinating conjunctions connect clauses, phrases, or single words. In this group are **aber, denn, oder, und,** and **sondern. Sondern** is used instead of **aber** in antitheses of the type *It is not A but B.*

Es ist nicht blau, sondern grün. It is not blue but green.*

---

*The statement *not A* excludes or contradicts a contrary assertion or assumption *A*, whereas the correction *but B* states the real situation. **Sondern,** therefore, is used only after a negation.

Verb-second position is used after co-ordinating conjunctions. (Cf. § 6.)

b. Subordinating conjunctions introduce dependent clauses. Those which have occurred so far are **als, daß, ob, obgleich, während, weil,** and **wenn.** (Five others will be introduced later.)

Verb-last position must be used in clauses introduced by subordinating conjunctions:

Ich höre, daß Frau Meyer einen Hut kaufen will. I hear that Mrs. Meyer wants to buy a hat.

A third type of conjunction is correlative (**entweder . . . oder,** *either . . . or*; **weder . . . noch,** *neither . . . nor*). The word order parallels that of English. Example:

Sie ist weder jung noch schön. She is neither young nor beautiful.

39. The Infinitive. The infinitive is preceded by its objects and other modifiers and thus usually stands at or near the end of a clause:

Ich will Goethes *Faust* lesen. I want to read Goethe's *Faust.*
Ich hoffe, dich heute abend zu sehen. I hope to see you this evening.

EXERCISES

I

Answer in German: **1. Ist Schillers *Wilhelm Tell* ein Drama? 2. Was kann man in Deutschland kaufen? 3. Wollen Sie eine Kamera kaufen? 4. Können Sie schon ein Buch in deutscher Sprache allein lesen? 5. Welches Problem ist ein Kind unserer Zeit? 6. Wer ist arbeitslos? 7. Kostet dem Arbeitgeber eine Maschine mehr als ein Arbeiter? 8. Für was ist die Maschine eine Gefahr? 9. Wohin** (where) **wirft die Maschine den Arbeiter? 10. Wer will auch Geld verdienen? 11. Warum braucht der Arbeitgeber eine Maschine? 12. Wann kann der Arbeitgeber das Geld zurückzahlen? 13. Was sagt der Arbeitgeber? 14. Warum behauptet Meyer: „Odontoschein bringt die Jugend zurück"? 15. Wer kauft dann Odontoschein? 16. Wer lacht? 17. Wer hat Erfolg? 18. Warum muß die Maschine stillstehen? 19. Wieviel kostet eine Tube Odontoschein? 20. Wo kann man eine Tube Odonto-**

schein kaufen? 21. Welche Zeitung liest Joseph? 22. Wo liegt das Glück des Arbeitgebers? 23. Wer lernt leichter als Joseph? 24. Wie alt ist Frau Meyers Hut? 25. Wer weiß, daß Frau Meyers Hut schon ein Jahr alt ist? 26. Was ist die Farbe des Jahres? 27. Warum wechselt der Arbeitgeber jedes Jahr die Hutfarbe? 28. Warum müssen wir heute kaufen?

II

Translate into German: 1. She is wearing the hat of the year. 2. I am reading the book of the week. 3. What is the price of this book? 4. What is the color of her dress? 5. Who is the hero of the story? 6. The mother of the girl is beautiful. 7. I have a hat that is green. 8. He is not going because he has no time. 9. The house in which we are living is good enough for me. 10. I do not believe that he can come. 11. Although you laugh when I play, I like to play. 12. Is that* the gentleman whom you want to see? 13. What is the color of her hat? 14. Is that* the house you want to buy? 15. He who wants to eat may eat. 16. Your mother's dress is beautiful. [*Use the pattern:* The dress of your mother . . .] 17. He is writing a history of the war. 18. The book of my mother is interesting. 19. The hero of this story pleases me.

III

Translate into English:

der Abend	**die Art**	**lassen**	**die Zeitung**
allein	**obgleich**	**die Geschichte**	**der Held**
atmen	**pflanzen**	**gebrauchen**	**zufrieden**

IV

Translate into German:

to give	enough	white
the war	to pay	blue
to hope	to prove	the child
to fetch	to sit	beautiful

---

*The neuter forms **das, dies,** and **es** are often used to introduce a sentence regardless of the gender or number of the predicate noun:

Das ist meine Mutter. That is my mother.
Dies ist eine schöne Farbe. This is a beautiful color.

V

Decline:

dieser Abend **mein Hut** **eine Klasse** **ein Buch**

VI

Change all nouns in the following sentences to the corresponding pronouns, thus: **Die Frau hilft dem Mann. Sie hilft ihm.** (Cf. § 26.) **1. Frank hat das Papier. 2. Frank sitzt neben Anna. 3. Hans beobachtet Marie. 4. Meyer liest die Zeitung. 5. Die Wand ist dünn. 6. Die Gans ist immer neidisch. 7. Ich kann den Weg nicht finden. 8. Ich kann die Geschichte nicht erzählen. 9. Er wirft den Apfel. 10. Man kann die Geschichte einfach nicht verstehen. 11. Frau Meyer will den Hut kaufen.**

VII

Supply the proper relative pronouns: **1. Das ist eine Farbe, _____ mir gefällt. 2. Er ist der Mann, _____ wir seit einer Woche suchen. 3. Ist das die Straße, in _____ Sie wohnen? 4. Heute ist der Tag, an _____ er kommt. 5. Ich liebe die Art nicht, in _____ er mit ihr spricht. 6. Hier ist das Kind, _____ Mutter leider kein Geld mehr hat. 7. Die Geschichte, _____ ich Ihnen erzählen will, gefällt Karl und Otto. 8. Der Bleistift, mit _____ ich schreibe, ist grün. 9. Das Bett, in _____ er schläft, ist viel zu kurz. 10. Glücklich (ist) der Mann, _____ Frau nicht zuviel redet. 11. Glücklich (ist) die Frau, _____ Mann nicht zuviel redet. 12. Ist das die Gans, _____ Sie uns verkaufen wollen? 13. Hier ist das Buch, _____ ich gerade lese.**

VIII

Find the inflected verb in each clause in Text B and explain its position.

IX

List the verbs that govern the dative.

X

Translate into English: **1. Was ist die Farbe (*a*) des Hutes? (*b*) jenes Buches? (*c*) des Apfels? (*d*) ihres Bleistiftes? (*e*) deines Papiers? 2. Was ist der Preis (*a*) dieses Stückes? (*b*) der Reise? (*c*) ihres Kleides? (*d*) der Zeitung? 3. Er ist ein Feind (*a*) des Mädchens (*b*) des Mannes (*c*) meiner Mutter (*d*) dieser Frau.**

LESSON VII

TEXT A

Ich weiß nicht, was ich unserer guten Mutter schenken soll. Sie hat alles, was sie braucht.—Im Frühling muß ich ihr einen Hut kaufen.—Außer ihrer Freundin sieht kein Mensch, daß Frau Meyer einen alten Hut trägt.—Ich suche schon lange, aber ich kann den grünen Rock nicht finden.—Ich kann nicht mehr warten. Es dauert mir zu lang.—Das Gesicht ihrer alten Mutter kann man einfach nicht vergessen.

Frank trifft Anna täglich in der Klasse. Sie wirft ihm einen Blick zu, der alles sagt.—Er kann es kaum glauben, daß sie ihn so haßt.—Kennst du mich nicht mehr?—Hast du einen roten oder einen grünen Bleistift für mich? Nein? Dann muß ich mir einen kaufen.—Siehst du den weißen Schnee vor unserem Haus? Ich spiele gern in frischem Schnee.

Der gute, alte Mann verdient nichts mehr.—Kleinkopf hat nun einen kleinen Hof.—Seit wann hast du das schöne Pferd?—Kleinkopf hat ein schönes Pferd.—Der Held dieser langen Geschichte gefällt mir nicht.—Obgleich die Wand dünn ist, kann ich nicht verstehen, was sie sagen. Sie sprechen viel zu leise.—Ich hoffe, deine Uhr geht richtig.

Wollen Sie nicht Platz nehmen?—Siehst du das kleine Schiffchen, das gerade abstoßen will?—Wann stoßen wir ab?—Ich darf noch nicht einsteigen.

„Ich steige in das kleine Schiffchen ein, nehme Platz, und wer sitzt da vor mir?"—„Wie soll ich das wissen, ein schönes Mädchen?"—„Nein, meine Mutter!"

VOCABULARY

ab *off*; down; away
ander different (*attr. adj*)
  anders different (*adv.*, *pr. adj.*)
der Augenblick the moment
die Bank the *bench*
begegnen (*w. dat.*) to meet, encounter
besser *better*
bis to, up to; until
blicken to look, glance
damit so that
das Dorf the town, village
ehe before
der Enkel the grandson
der Fisch the *fish*
fortsetzen to continue (*sep.*)

früh early
führen to lead, guide
die Gegenwart the presence; present time
grüßen to *greet*; wave (to)
der Hafen the harbor, port
hell bright, light
her (cf. § 41)
hin (cf. § 41)
hindern to *hinder*, prevent
jetzt now
klein small, little
das Land the *land*; country
das Meer the ocean, sea
morgen *tomorrow*
der Morgen the *morning*
der Name the *name*
nennen to *name*, call
der Platz the *place*; room
plötzlich suddenly
reizen to irritate; charm
richtig correct, accurate, *right*
der Rock the coat; skirt
schenken to give, present with
schieben to *shove*, push
das Schiff the *ship*, boat
schlank slender
schnell fast, quick(ly)
schwarz black
die Seite the *side*; page
die Sonne the *sun*
springen to *spring*, jump
steigen to climb
stoßen (ö) to push, thrust
treten (trittst, tritt) to step, walk
weder . . . noch neither . . . nor
weit far, distant; *wide*
der Wind the *wind*, breeze

IDIOMS

auf Wiedersehen good-by
bis zu until
Platz nehmen (Platz *is like a separable prefix*) to sit down
stehenbleiben (stehen *is a separable prefix*) to stop
warten auf to wait for (*with acc.*)

TEXT B

„L'Arrabbiata"[1] Eine Liebesgeschichte

„Heilige Maria, unser Padre[2] ist aber heute früh auf!" sagt eine alte Frau zu ihrer kleinen Enkelin, als der Pfarrer[2] eines italienischen[3] Fischerdorfes schon vor Sonnenaufgang zum Hafen herunterkommt und in ein kleines Boot[4] steigt, das auf ihn wartet. Dann grüßt sie zum Schiffchen
5 hinüber, das gerade abstoßen will. Antonio aber, der Fischer, springt wieder ans Land zurück und hilft einem schlanken, jungen Mädchen mit schwarzem Haar und lieblichem, frischem Gesicht ins Boot.

„Guten Tag, Laurella", grüßt sie der Pfarrer, „willst du mit nach Capri?"—„Wenn ich darf, Padre."—„Da mußt du den Antonio fragen",
10 meint der Pfarrer, „ihm gehört das Boot."—„Hier ist ein halber Carlin",[5]

sagt Laurella, ohne den jungen Schiffer anzusehen. „Nimmst du mich mit für einen halben Carlin?"—„Du kannst das Geld besser brauchen als ich", antwortet der junge Fischer und legt seinen Rock auf die Bank, damit das Mädchen besser sitzen kann. Aber Laurella schiebt den Rock wortlos auf die Seite und nimmt, ohne dem Schiffer noch einen Blick zuzuwerfen, neben dem Pfarrer Platz. 5

Die trotzige Art des Mädchens reizt den Fischer. „‚L'Arrabbiata', wie sie im Dorf jeder nennt, ist der richtige Name für sie", denkt er und sieht nicht gerade freundlich auf den Pfarrer, dem Laurella jetzt ihre ganze Aufmerksamkeit[6] schenkt. Immer wieder versucht er, an etwas anderes zu denken. Aber weder das stille Blau des Wassers, mit dem der leichte Morgenwind leise spielt, noch die unbeschreibliche Schönheit der Silhouette des Vesuvs[7] läßt ihn die Gegenwart des schönen Mädchens vergessen, dem seine ganze Liebe gehört. 10

Im Hafen von Capri trägt Antonio den Pfarrer ans Land, Laurella aber watet[8] schnell hinüber, ehe Antonio sie holen kann. Der Padre dankt dem jungen Fischer mit freundlichem Gruß, und auch Laurella sagt „Auf Wiedersehen!" „Du weißt, daß ich heute zurückfahre", meint Antonio, ohne Laurella anzusehen. „Ich warte auf dich bis zum Ave Maria.[9] Wenn du dann nicht kommst, ist es mir gleich." Laurella geht und steigt die enge Straße nach Anacapri hinauf. Nach kurzer Zeit bleibt sie stehen, wie[10] um Atem zu holen, und sieht zurück. Ihr Blick begegnet dem Blick Antonios, aber nur für einen Augenblick. Dann setzt sie ihren Weg fort. 15 20

Schon kurz nach zwölf (12) Uhr sitzt Antonio vor der Fischerschenke,[11] nicht weit von seinem Boot. Alle[12] fünf Minuten[12] springt er auf, tritt in die helle Sonne hinaus und blickt über den Weg, der von Anacapri zum Hafen herunterführt. Er sucht lange ohne Erfolg. Kurz vor dem Ave Maria aber, als Antonio, unglücklich über den Trotz des Mädchens, das Warten aufgeben will, steht Laurella plötzlich vor ihm. Und ehe sie es hindern kann, trägt Antonio sie wie ein Kind ins Boot. Einen[13] Augenblick[13] später fährt das kleine Schiff aufs stille Meer hinaus. 25 30

[Fortsetzung folgt. To be continued.]

NOTES. 1. Paul Heyse (1830–1914), winner of the Nobel Prize in literature in 1910, is the author of this charming story, which we have attempted to retell, in spite of obvious difficulties, in the hope that you will want to read the story later in the author's words. *L'Arrabbiata* is Italian; it means "Fury" or "Spitfire."

2. *Padre* (Italian) and Pfarrer (German), titles for clergymen. Here: priest, Father. 3. italienischen Italian. 4. Boot boat. 5. Carlin Italian coin. 6. Aufmerksamkeit attention. 7. Vesuv Vesuvius. 8. watet wades. 9. Ave Maria a prayer which is offered shortly after sunset. 10. wie as if. 11. Fischerschenke fishermen's tavern. 12. Alle fünf Minuten every five minutes. 13. einen Augenblick (*acc. of time.* Cf. § 72).

BUILDING A PASSIVE VOCABULARY

abstoßen ab off, stoßen to push, shove, abstoßen to shove off
der Atem atmen to breathe, der Atem the breath
der Blick blicken to look, glance, der Blick the look, glance
die Enkelin der Enkel the grandson, grandchild, die Enkelin the granddaughter
das Fischerdorf der Fisch the fish, der Fischer the fisherman, das Dorf the village, das Fischerdorf the fishing village
freundlich der Freund the friend, freundlich friendly, kind, pleasant(ly)
der Gruß grüßen to greet, der Gruß the greeting
lieblich lieben to love, die Liebe love, lieblich lovely
das Schiffchen das Schiff the ship, boat, das Schiffchen the little ship, boat, der Schiffer the boatman, sailor, skipper
die Schönheit schön beautiful, die Schönheit the beauty
der Sonnenaufgang die Sonne the sun, auf up, -gang *from* gehen to go, der Sonnenaufgang sunrise
später spät late, später later
trotzig der Trotz defiance, stubbornness; trotzig defiant, scornful, stubborn (Cf. § 93).
unbeschreiblich schreiben to write, beschreiben to describe, unbeschreiblich indescribable
wortlos das Wort the word, -los -less, without, wortlos silently, without saying a word

GRAMMAR

40. Separable Compounds

A. *Explanation and Importance:*

English often uses prepositions or adverbs as essential parts of verbs, e.g., *to cut off* (The operator *cut* us *off*), *to turn on* (He *turned on* the light *or* He *turned* the light *on*). Here the words *off* and *on* are not felt to be prepositions or adverbs but rather to be necessary parts of the verbs. German makes far greater use of such compounds, and this fact will enable you as a learner to increase your vocabulary much more rapidly than would otherwise be possible. Let us illustrate by using the verb fahren *to move, to ride, to drive* and several prepositions and adverbs. (Note that the latter elements are prefixed to the infinitive.) We will arrive at an astonishing number of new words, most of which you could guess, at least if you were to read them in context.

abfahren *to depart, set out*; auffahren *to ascend, to spring up*; ausfahren *to drive out, take a ride*; durchfahren *to pass through*; einfahren *to enter, drive into*; fortfahren *to continue*; mitfahren *to accompany*; überfahren *to cross over, ferry over, take over;* vorfahren *to drive up to a person's door*; zufahren *to drive to (a place)*; zurückfahren *to return.*

In German grammars such compounds are called separable compounds because the prepositions and adverbs, following well-defined rules, may either be prefixed to the verb: Ich kann nicht abstoßen *I cannot shove off*, or they may be placed at the end of the clause: Er stößt nun ab *He is shoving off now.* Your greatest difficulty will probably not be in understanding the meanings of the compounds, especially if you know the meanings of the elements, but in remembering to look to the end of the clause for the second—and very necessary—element. The following example will serve as an illustration: Er fährt heute mit seiner Mutter zurück. The word zurück is considered to be an integral part of the verb and changes its meaning so that the compound means "return." Thus the sentence in translation reads: *He is returning today with his mother.* The so-called "prefix" is so important that it receives the stress.

B. *Use:*

Separable prefixes are placed at the end of independent clauses when they are part of the *inflected* verb.

Er fährt heute mit seiner Mutter nicht **zurück.** He is not returning with his mother today.

Stoßen wir nun **ab**? Are we now shoving off?

Wann stoßen wir **ab**? When are we shoving off?

The separable prefix and verb are written as one word when

a. They occur at the end of a dependent clause (in verb-last position): e.g., Du weißt, daß ich heute zurückfahre. You know that I am returning today;

b. They are used as infinitives: Ich will heute zurückfahren. I want to return today;

c. The sign zu of the infinitive is placed between the prefix and the verb: Ich hoffe, morgen früh aufzustehen. I hope to get up early tomorrow.

Note also the following three important points:

1. A few nouns and verbs may also be used as prefixes. Examples: *a.* Noun: Sie nimmt neben dem Pfarrer Platz. She sits down next to the priest. *b.* Verb: Er bleibt vor dem Hause stehen. He stops in front of the house.

2. Three prefixes need special attention. When prefixed to a verb in takes the form ein (einsteigen, to climb in); auf assumes the meaning *up* (aufstehen, to stand up); unter assumes the meaning *down* (untergehen, to go down.)

3. The prefixes hin and her (cf. § 41) are often combined with prepositions.

41. Hin and her

Separable prefixes tend to develop figurative meanings and, therefore, must be treated carefully in both English and German. Such a statement as "He stepped out," for example, may merely indicate a change in location, but it can also mean in informal language that the person in question had a good time. Occasionally (there is no rule in this regard) English attempts to differentiate between the literal and the figurative meaning by changing the position of the adverb or preposition. Compare the position of the word *in* in the following sentences: "An efficient banker can bring in a lot of money" and "A man with a strong back can bring a lot of money in." Compare also "to throw in the towel" and "to throw the towel in."

German attempts to avoid ambiguity not by changing the position of the prefix but by attaching hin or her to the prefix (adverb or preposition) when the literal meaning is intended and nothing but a change of location is involved.

Hin is used to indicate motion away from the speaker or scene of action, and her to indicate motion toward the speaker or scene of action. Thus, Er tritt hinaus can mean only one thing: *He walks out (from wherever he is)*. But Er tritt aus may mean he is leaving the partnership.

Examples: Er kommt herunter. He is coming down (from above to the speaker or to the scene of action).

Er tritt in die helle Sonne hinaus. He steps out (from the shade or house) into the bright sun.

42. Weak Endings.* An adjective (or adjectives) preceded by a der-word (cf. § 31) or a declined form of an ein-word (cf. § 30) must take a so-called "weak" ending. The weak endings are:

	Masculine	Feminine	Neuter
NOM.	e	e	e
GEN.	en	en	en
DAT.	en	en	en
ACC.	en	e	e

Examples:

der alte Mann	die gute Frau	das schöne Kind
des guten Mannes	der guten Frau	des schönen Kindes
dem guten, alten Manne	der schönen, jungen Frau	dem guten Kinde
den guten, alten Mann	die schöne Frau	das kleine Kind

43. The Interrogative Pronoun wer. Wer is declined as follows:

NOM.	wer	who
Gen.	wessen	whose (of whom)
DAT.	wem	whom (to whom)
ACC.	wen	whom

*See § 35 for strong endings.

Examples:

Wer springt noch einmal ans Land zurück? Who jumps back to the land once more?

Wessen Gegenwart kann Antonio nicht vergessen? Whose presence can Antonio not forget?

Wem gehört seine ganze Liebe? To whom does his entire love belong?

Wen trägt Antonio ans Land? Whom does Antonio carry to the land?

EXERCISES

I

Answer in German: 1. Wer ist heute früh auf? 2. Mit wem spricht die alte Frau? 3. Wann kommt der Pfarrer zum Hafen herunter? 4. Was wartet auf ihn? 5. Wer springt wieder ans Land zurück? 6. Wie ist das Gesicht des jungen Mädchens? 7. Wer grüßt sie? 8. Wohin fährt der Padre? 9. Wem gehört das Schiffchen? 10. Wer kann das Geld besser brauchen als Antonio? 11. Warum legt Antonio seinen Rock auf die Bank? 12. Wohin schiebt Laurella den Rock? 13. Neben wem nimmt sie Platz? 14. Was reizt den Fischer? 15. Was nennt man Laurella im Dorf? 16. Wem schenkt Laurella ihre ganze Aufmerksamkeit? 17. Wessen Gegenwart kann Antonio nicht vergessen? 18. Wem gehört seine ganze Liebe? 19. Wen trägt Antonio im Hafen von Capri ans Land? 20. Wie lange will Antonio in Capri warten? 21. Wessen Blick begegnet dem Blick Laurellas? 22. Wann sitzt Antonio vor der Fischerschenke? 23. Wer will das Warten aufgeben? 24. Wer steht plötzlich vor ihm?

II

Translate into German: 1. Before he comes back, she jumps back into the house. 2. We must now shove off. 3. He steps out into the bright sun. 4. You know that I cannot* go up with you. 5. The old man goes down (hinunter) the street. 6. The young girl is slender and has a lovely face. 7. I cannot* understand the defiance of this beautiful girl. 8. He wants to stand up. 9. How long have you been studying German? (Cf. § 21.) 10. It is all the same to me. (Cf. idioms, p. 30.) 11. When are you sitting down?

*Cf. footnote, page 28.

12. Can you see the little old man? 13. What are we giving the good little child? 14. When are we shoving off? 15. Is he coming down now? 16. This poor man must sleep in a short bed. 17. Whose presence can Antonio not forget?

III

Translate the following words into English:

nur	berichten	unglücklich
nun	beobachten	die Schuld
jetzt	bekommen	der Schnee
jemand	lachen	schon
jener	mit	kennen

IV

Translate into German:

the earth	to eat	something
yes	scarcely	to lose
to understand	why	to last
honest	to grow	while
to change	again	to know
to know by acquaintance		

V

Conjugate in the present tense:

stehenbleiben	wollen	abstoßen	holen
aufgeben	fahren	heraufkommen	reden

VI

Underline all the separable prefixes in Text B. Find the subject and direct object (where there is a direct object) in each clause in Text B.

VII

Review § 35 and § 42 and decline:

ein kleiner Hof	unser schönes Haus
der alte Mann	diese arme Frau
ein gutes Buch	meine liebe Frau

LESSON VIII

TEXT A

„Komm schnell, wir haben nicht viel Zeit. Bis zum Hafen ist es ein langer Weg, und das Schiff wartet nicht auf uns. Steig ein, wir stoßen gleich ab.“—„Guten Tag, Frau Fischer, wollen Sie auch nach Köln?“—„Ja, ich will mir einen neuen Hut kaufen. Frau Meyer ist auch hier, sie will sich ein neues Kleid kaufen. Aber kommen Sie, wir gehen besser hinunter, es ist mir zu heiß hier in der Sonne.“

„Kann ich bei Ihnen arbeiten? Ich muß mir Geld für meine Reise nach Deutschland verdienen.“—„Ich suche zwar einen Arbeiter. Aber Sie nehme ich nicht. Ich kenne Sie. Sie denken bei der Arbeit immer an Nancy, und daher arbeiten Sie nicht schnell genug.“

„So, jetzt ist es Zeit für dich, zu Bett zu gehen, mein Kind. Hol mir noch die Zeitung und dann verschwinde und laß mich allein! Ich muß noch arbeiten.“—„Arbeite dich nur nicht tot!“

„Wer geht da gerade hinaus?“—„Herr Meyer! Er fragt, ob wir in diesem Herbst Kartoffeln von ihm kaufen wollen.“—„Ich kaufe nichts von Meyer. Bei ihm kostet alles mehr als im Geschäft.“

„Du mußt dich einfach zwingen, etwas zu essen, auch wenn du nicht hungrig bist. Wer dich sieht, muß glauben, du bekommst bei uns nicht genug zu essen. So! du magst keine Erbsen! Erbsen sind dir nicht gut genug? Laß mich das nicht wieder hören! In diesem Hause ißt jeder das, was Mutter und ich auch essen!“

Ich kann mich von dir nicht trennen.—Rettet euch!—Kannst du dich retten?—Ja, aber ich fürchte mich.—Fürchtest du dich nicht?—Folge mir!

Er ist die treibende Kraft hinter allem.—„Das Mädchen ist einfach reizend!“—„Gefällt sie dir?“—„Und wie! Sie hat so ein gewinnendes Lächeln (smile). Ich kenne sie zwar noch nicht lange, aber sie scheint mir intelligent zu sein.“—„Intelligent oder nicht, das ist mir gleich. Wenn sie nur schön ist!“

Ich weiß es selber (myself) nicht. Wir wissen es selber (ourselves) nicht.

LESSON VIII

VOCABULARY

das Auge the *eye*
das Bild the picture
binden to *bind*, tie
bitten (um) beg (for), ask (for)
das Blut the *blood*
der Boden the ground; *bottom*; floor
brechen (i) to *break*
derselbe the same
durch *through*
einander one *another*, each other
das Ende the *end*, close
ernst serious, *earnest*
das Fenster the window
fern *far*, distant
fließen to *flow*, run
folgen (*w.* dat.) to *follow*
fürchten (*refl.*) to *fear*, be afraid
die Hand the *hand*
hart *hard*
heben to lift, raise
heiß *hot*
das Herz the *heart*
innen within
der Kopf the head
die Kraft the force, power, strength
küssen to *kiss*
die Macht the power, *might*
der Mond the *moon*
die Nacht the *night*
öffnen to *open*
retten to save
der Rücken the back
schlagen (ä) to beat, strike
schreien to *cry*; shout
selber same; *self*
sinken to *sink*
stellen to place, put
strecken to *stretch*; extend
stürzen to rush; tumble; throw
tief *deep*; low
töten to kill
treiben to *drive*; put in motion; drift
trennen to separate
das Tuch the cloth; kerchief
die Tür the *door*
der Vater the *father*
verbergen (i) to hide, conceal
verwandeln to transform, change
wenden to turn
ziehen to pull, draw; move
zusammen together
zwingen to force, compel

IDIOMS

es geht Sie nichts an that is none of your business; was geht es dich an? what is that to you?
halten für to take to be, to consider to be
liebhaben to be fond of (lieb *is a separable prefix*)
sich fürchten vor to be afraid of

TEXT B

Fortsetzung von „L'Arrabbiata"

Laurella und Antonio wechseln lange Zeit kein Wort miteinander. Laurella sitzt vorn im Boot und wendet Antonio fast den Rücken zu, so daß er sie nur von der Seite sehen kann. Ihr Gesicht ist ernst, und ihr Blick verliert sich in weiter Ferne. Vor ihrem inneren Auge steht ein Bild aus ihrer Kindheit: der betrunkene[1] Vater, der mit harter Hand die Mutter schlägt, sich dann plötzlich verwandelt und die Mutter vom Boden aufhebt, um sie heiß und wild zu küssen. Und dieses Bild folgt Laurella Tag und Nacht, läßt sie auch jetzt nicht los, stellt sich trennend zwischen sie und Antonio, zwingt sie, ihre Liebe zu ihm zu verbergen.[2]

Antonio weiß nichts von der Not des Mädchens, hält ihre Furcht für Trotz, weiß nicht, daß sie ihn liebt. Seine ganze Kraft zusammennehmend, treibt er das Schiffchen mit schnellem Schlag ins offene Meer hinaus.

Dann läßt er die Ruder[3] fallen. Sie sind allein auf weitem Meere. Stille liegt über der blauen Tiefe.

„Es muß endlich heraus", bricht[4] Antonio los.[4] „Weißt du nicht, daß ich dich liebe? Hast du kein Herz, daß du nicht siehst, wie unglücklich du mich machst? Meinst du, daß ich es ansehen will, wenn du einen anderen nimmst?" —„Was geht es dich an?" sagt Laurella trotzig.—„Du Trotzkopf sollst mich nicht länger so unglücklich machen können. Weißt du, daß du hier in meiner Macht bist und tun mußt, was ich will?"—„Töte mich, wenn du willst!" trotzt Laurella. Antonio weiß nicht mehr, was er sagt und tut. „Du mußt mit mir ins Wasser, das Meer hat Platz für dich und mich!" schreit er und streckt seine Hand nach ihr aus. Aber im selben Augenblick zieht er die Hand zurück: aus einer tiefen Bißwunde[5] fließt Blut. „Muß ich tun, was du willst? Laß sehen, ob ich in deiner Macht bin!" Ehe Antonio es hindern kann, springt Laurella ins Wasser und verschwindet in der Tiefe. Doch sie kommt gleich wieder herauf und schwimmt[6] dem Lande zu. Antonio steht wie versteinert.[7] Dann stürzt er nach den Rudern und ist im Augenblick an ihrer Seite. „Vergib mir, Laurella!" bittet er. „Nein, du sollst mir nicht vergeben, nur dich retten und wieder einsteigen. Du kannst nicht bis ans Land schwimmen,[6] es ist zu weit. Und denk an deine Mutter!"

Ohne zu antworten, schwimmt Laurella ans Schiffchen. Antonio hilft ihr auf ihren alten Sitz. Dann sieht sie, daß er blutet, tritt zu ihm und bindet ihr weißes Kopftuch um die Wunde. Keiner[8] spricht mehr ein Wort.

Schlaflos liegt Antonio auf seinem Bett. Der Mond scheint durch das Fenster. Da hört er einen leichten Tritt vor seiner Tür. Er steht auf und öffnet. Laurella steht vor ihm.

„Wenn du mich noch liebhast, dann nimm mich und behalte mich. Ich liebe dich, liebe dich schon seit langem. Aber bis heute habe[9] ich dagegen gekämpft.[9] Nun will ich anders werden. Nun will ich dich auch küssen, und du weißt, Laurella küßt keinen[10] als den,[10] den sie zum Manne will."

Sie küßt ihn, dann macht sie sich los und sagt: „Gute Nacht, geh nun schlafen, und geh jetzt nicht mit mir, denn ich fürchte mich vor keinem Mann, nur vor dir." 5

NOTES. 1. betrunkene drunken. 2. verbergen hide. 3. die Ruder the oars. 4. bricht los bursts out. 5. Bißwunde wound caused by a bite. 6. schwimmt, schwimmen swims, swim. 7. wie versteinert as if turned to stone. 8. Keiner Neither. 9. habe . . . gekämpft I have fought against it. 10. keinen als den no one but him.

BUILDING A PASSIVE VOCABULARY

ansehen an on, at, sehen to see, look, ansehen to look on *or* at, watch
behalten halten to hold, behalten to keep
bluten das Blut the blood, bluten to bleed
endlich das Ende the end, endlich finally
die Ferne fern far, distant, die Ferne the distance
inner innen within, inside, inner inner
die Kindheit das Kind the child, die Kindheit (the) childhood
das Kopftuch der Kopf the head, das Tuch the cloth, das Kopftuch the scarf
länger lang long, länger longer
die Liebe lieben to love, die Liebe (the) love
offen öffnen to open, offen open
schlaflos schlafen to sleep, der Schlaf (the) sleep, -los -less *or* without, schlaflos sleepless(ly)
der Sitz sitzen to sit, der Sitz the seat
die Stille still still, quiet, die Stille (the) stillness
die Tiefe tief deep, die Tiefe the depth(s)
tot töten to kill, tot dead
der Tritt treten to step, der Tritt the step
trotzen, trotzig, der Trotzkopf der Trotz the defiance, stubbornness, trotzen to defy, trotzig defiant(ly), der Trotzkopf stubborn-head(ed person)
unglücklich das Glück the luck, good fortune, happiness, glücklich happy, unglücklich unhappy
vergib (*imperative of* vergeben) geben to give, vergeben to forgive
vorn vor in front of, vorn in front (*adverb*)

GRAMMAR

44. Reflexives

A. *Pronouns:* When the subject and the object of a verb are one and the same person or thing, English uses reflexive pronouns for the object: He pities *himself*; the heat made *itself* felt. German has no special reflexive pronoun for the first and second persons singular and plural, but uses the personal pronouns:

DAT.	mir	dir	uns	euch
ACC.	mich	dich	uns	euch

Examples:

Ich kaufe mir ein Auto. I am buying myself a car.
Du kaufst dir ein Auto.
Wir kaufen uns ein Auto.
Ihr kauft euch ein Auto.

Ich mache mich schön. I am making myself handsome (pretty).
Du machst dich schön.
Wir machen uns schön.
Ihr macht euch schön.

The reflexive pronoun for all genders and both numbers of the third person (including the polite Sie-form, which is really the third person verb form) is sich in both the dative and the accusative case. Examples:

Kauft er sich ein Auto? Is he buying himself a car?
Kauft sie sich ein Auto?
Kaufen sie sich ein Auto?
Kaufen Sie sich ein Auto?

Er macht sich schön. He is making himself handsome.
Sie macht sich schön.
Sie machen sich schön.
Sie machen sich schön.

NOTE. Almost all verbs are sometimes used with a reflexive dative or accusative pronoun object. Frequently this reflexive object need not be translated into English:

sich umdrehen: Er dreht sich um. He turns around.
sich wenden: Er wendet sich. He turns.

B. *Verbs.* An analysis of *I enjoyed the visit* and *I enjoyed myself* shows that the reflexive pronoun *oneself* is not a real object but simply belongs to the speech pattern. German has a few such verbs, too; and since the reflexive pronoun in such cases is no real object, it must not be translated.

sich fürchten Ich fürchte mich nicht. I am not afraid.
Ich fürchte mich vor dir. I am afraid of you.

45. Definite Article for Possessive Adjective. Where the possessor is clearly understood, German frequently uses the definite article instead of a possessive adjective:

Sie hält ein Buch in der Hand. She is holding a book in her hand.

Er hebt den Kopf und sieht das Mädchen. He raises his head and sees the girl.

Nimm den Hut ab! Take off your hat.

(Compare English "to get red in the face" and "to be weak in the knees.")

46. The Imperative in the Second Person. The most frequently used patterns to express a command in the second person are:

a. Singular familiar:

sag(e)! bring(e)! fall(e) nicht! gib!

As in English, the pronoun is not expressed. The ending -e is frequently dropped, especially in the case of irregular verbs. Only verbs like geben (ich gebe, du gibst) (cf. § 10), which change the stem vowel e to i or ie, show a vowel change in the imperative. These verbs never taken an ending, e.g., sieh! (from sehen):

brich!	hilf!	sprich!	verbirg!
iß!	lies!	triff!	vergiß!
gib!	nimm!	tritt!	wirf!

b. Plural familiar:

sagt! bringt! fallt nicht! gebt!

The pronoun is not expressed.

c. Polite form:

sagen Sie! bringen Sie! fallen Sie nicht! geben Sie!

Here the pronoun is always expressed, and it follows the verb. Observe the verb-first position.

Note the imperative forms of haben, sein, and werden.

habe!	habt!	haben Sie!
sei!	seid!	seien Sie!
werde!	werdet!	werden Sie!

Note also the imperative forms of verbs with a separable prefix.

geh nicht hinaus! geht heute nicht hinaus! gehen Sie nicht hinaus!

47. Word Formation. Agent Nouns in -er. The suffix -er is added to verb stems, as in English, to form masculine agent nouns denoting:

a. Persons:

der Arbeiter the worker — der Leser the reader
der Läufer the runner — der Käufer the buyer

b. Instruments:

der Hörer the receiver — der Fernsprecher the telephone

In some cases there is an umlaut, as can be seen in der Läufer and der Käufer.

48. Word Formation. Feminine Nouns in -in. Many masculine nouns add the suffix -in to form corresponding feminines:

der Held, die Heldin the hero, the heroine
der Enkel, die Enkelin the grandson, the granddaughter
der Freund, die Freundin the male friend, the female friend
der Arbeiter, die Arbeiterin the male worker, the female worker

49. Word Formation. Adjectives in -d. The suffix -d is added to infinitives to form adjectives. These correspond to English verbal adjectives ending in *-ing*. Such adjectives always describe the action of the noun they modify:

ein schreiendes Kind a crying child
das schlafende Mädchen the sleeping girl
die treibende Kraft the driving force
das untergehende Schiff the sinking ship
die wechselnde Farbe the changing color

Such adjectives are treated like other adjectives: they may take strong or weak endings; they may be used as predicate adjectives, as in Das Mädchen ist reizend, *The girl is charming*; they may be used as adverbs, as in Das Wasser ist beißend kalt, *The water is biting cold.* (Cf. § 71.)

LESSON VIII

EXERCISES

I

Answer in German: 1. Wo sitzt Laurella im Schiffchen? 2. Wen kann Antonio nur von der Seite sehen? 3. Wessen Gesicht ist ernst? 4. Welches Bild steht vor Laurellas innerem Auge? 5. Wer verwandelt sich plötzlich? 6. Was verbirgt Laurella vor Antonio? 7. Was weiß Antonio noch nicht? 8. Wer nimmt seine ganze Kraft zusammen, um das Schiffchen ins offene Meer hinauszutreiben? 9. Was liegt über der blauen Tiefe? 10. Wer macht Antonio unglücklich? 11. Nach wem streckt Antonio die Hand aus? 12. Was fließt aus der Bißwunde? 13. Was tut Laurella, ehe Antonio es hindern kann? 14. Wer soll sich retten? 15. Warum kann Laurella nicht bis ans Land schwimmen? 16. An wen soll Laurella denken? 17. Wem hilft Antonio ins Schiffchen? 18. Was bindet Laurella um die Wunde? 19. Wie liegt Antonio auf seinem Bett? 20. Wen will Laurella zum Manne haben? 21. Vor wem fürchtet sich Laurella?

II

Translate and be sure to write all three forms for the second person: 1. Do not* forget me. 2. Are you afraid? 3. He suddenly changes (*use* sich verwandeln). 4. Save yourself (yourselves). 5. Do not ask me why I am going. 6. You must ask her before she disappears. 7. Can you come? 8. Won't you sit down? 9. I am writing him a long letter (Brief, *masc.*). 10. Have you no money? 11. Don't work too hard. 12. Speak softly. 13. Follow me. 14. Don't eat too much. 15. Read this book.

III

Translate into English:

aber	zurück	wissen
zeigen	zufrieden	bestimmt
einfach	holen	ehrlich
auswendig	schlagen	der Krieg
schieben	leider	ohne
beobachten	die Wand	spielen

*Cf. footnote, page 28.

IV

Translate into German:

to hope
to laugh
difficult
to breathe
already

to pay
to do
to forget
white
almost

to prove
today
to bite
straight
to share

to take
happy
easy
to let
old

V

Translate the following compounds and derivatives*:

gefahrlos
zusammenbinden
farblos
die Windstille*
die Hausfrau
der Augenblickserfolg

die Haustür
die Haarfarbe
der Marktplatz
vaterlos
das Handtuch*
der Arbeitgeber
der Handarbeiter

der Kopfarbeiter
die Feindin
der Machthaber
der Langschläfer
der Verdiener
das Glasauge

ein weinendes, schreiendes, (schlafendes,) (spielendes) Kind
der Uhrzeiger (hand of clock *or* watch)

VI

Give the three imperative forms for each of the following verbs:

arbeiten
binden
sprechen
folgen

sich nicht fürchten
retten
sich retten
essen

tragen
werfen
lassen
lesen

vergessen
springen
sein
abstoßen

VII

Conjugate in the present tense:

sich retten
sich fürchten

sich verbergen
sich verwandeln

sich vor dem Winter fürchten

---

*Beginning with this lesson you will find in all lessons except Lesson IX an exercise section devoted to practice in recognizing and translating compounds and derivatives. The authors conceived this plan as a class exercise; but where the teaching method or lack of class time makes that plan undesirable or impossible, you may independently work out a large number of items. The most difficult entries and those which might be mistranslated may be found in the appendix on pages 291–293.

VIII

Translate into English: 1. Es geht ihr gut. 2. Wann fährst du nach Hause? 3. Denkt an euren alten Vater! 4. Herr Schmidt hat noch immer viel Geld, aber Herr Braun hat gar kein Geld.

IX

Explain the difference between

Er tötet sich and Er tötet ihn

X

Review all the words introduced through Lesson VIII. See pages 317–319.

LESSON IX

TEXT A

Das Mädchen grüßte zum Schiffchen hinüber, das gerade abstoßen wollte.—Die trotzige Art des Mädchens reizte den Fischer.—Immer wieder versuchte Antonio, an etwas anderes zu denken.—Antonio wußte nichts von der Not des Mädchens.—Laurella sah, daß Antonio blutete.—Sie küßte 5 ihn, dann machte sie sich los und sagte: „Gute Nacht."—Frau Meyer fiel ins Wasser und sank schnell.

„Guten Tag,[1] Frau Meyer. Nun, wie steht es mit Ihrer Reise nach Deutschland?"—„Ach, ich kann in diesem Jahre nicht fahren. Mein Onkel ist schon seit August arbeitslos und kann mir das Geld für die Reise nicht 10 geben."—„Ach, arbeitslos ist er? Nicht möglich! Ja, ja, so ein[2] Krieg bringt doch viel Not ins Land."—„Ja, und außerdem erwartet seine Frau im Frühling ein Kind und rechnet bestimmt auf meine Hilfe."[3] —„So, sie erwartet im Frühling ein Kind? Das ist ja interessant. Was macht denn Fritz?"—„Fritz studiert in Berlin Psychopathologie. Er will Psychiater 15 (psychiatrist) oder so etwas werden. Mir gefällt das gar nicht. Ich behaupte, er stürzt sich ins Unglück. Am Ende ist er selber (himself) nicht mehr normal."

Wolf ist auch arbeitslos, aber er hat nicht weit von seinem Hause ein kleines Feld. Gut ist der Boden zwar nicht, aber Kartoffeln oder Erbsen 20 kann er schon pflanzen. Er bekommt einen guten Preis, und auf diese Art und Weise kann er sich helfen. Auf jeden Fall braucht er nicht zu hungern.

Dein Rock ist schon wieder ganz weiß auf dem Rücken. Wie oft muß man dir denn sagen, daß du dich nicht mit dem Rücken gegen eine Wand stellen sollst?

25 Der Mond scheint so hell, man kann auf der Bank im Hof fast die Zeitung lesen.

NOTE. 1. Understood: Ich wünsche Ihnen einen . . . 2. so ein such a. 3. Hilfe help.

VOCABULARY

ach ah! oh! alas!
das Beispiel the example
der Charakter the *character*
fallen (ä) to *fall*
gegen against, toward; in comparison with

das Gegenteil the opposite
hassen to *hate*
leben to *live*
der Onkel the *uncle*
sogar even
die Tochter the *daughter*
die Vergangenheit the past
vorbei past, *by*; gone
wirklich real, really, genuine
wünschen to *wish*, desire

IDIOMS

am Ende in the long run; after all
auf jeden Fall at any rate; in any case
so etwas something of the kind
was die Zeit angeht as far as the time (tense) is concerned
wie steht es mit how about
zum Beispiel for example
zum Beweise as evidence

TEXT B

Der zerbrochene Krug[1]

Alle Zukunft wird Gegenwart, und alle Gegenwart muß Vergangenheit werden. Wir können daher auch in unserem Buche nicht immer nur die Gegenwart gebrauchen. Denn die Zeit fließt schnell an uns vorbei; und mancher junge Mann, der heute sagen kann: „Ich habe Geld", muß schon morgen sagen: „Ich hatte Geld." Übrigens ist die Vergangenheit gar nicht so schwer. Zum Beweise erzählen wir Ihnen wieder eine Liebesgeschichte. Für diese neue Liebesgeschichte brauchen wir nur ein kleines Vokabularium. Mit dem Vokabularium für eine (1) Liebesgeschichte aus der Gegenwart kann man nämlich hundert (100) aus der Vergangenheit erzählen. Statt[2] „Er liebt sie" sagt man einfach „Er liebte sie". Und von da an schreiben nicht wir die neue Geschichte. Die Liebe schreibt sie. Denn die Liebe ist auch heute noch, was sie schon immer war: Die treibende Kraft hinter allem.

Hildegard, die Heldin unserer neuen Liebesgeschichte, ist, ganz wie in „L'Arrabbiata", wieder jung, schön und schlank, kurz,[3] wieder ein Mädchen, welches das Herz jedes jungen Mannes schneller schlagen läßt.[4] Auch Paul, der Held, und Erich, sein Feind, sind für die Schwarz-Weiß-Technik[5] einer einfachen Liebesgeschichte gut zu gebrauchen. Paul ist ganz der junge Mann, wie ein Mädchen ihn sich wünscht: etwas älter als Hildegard natürlich, aber doch noch jung. Sein dichtes, schwarzes Haar, seine frische Gesichtsfarbe, seine jugendliche Kraft, sein männlicher Charakter, sein gutes Herz, seine ernste, ehrliche, gerade und einfache Art öffnen ihm die Tür jedes Hauses, in

dem eine Mutter auf einen Mann für ihre Tochter wartet. Von Erich, seinem Feinde, berichten wir nur, daß er Stück für Stück das Gegenteil Pauls war. Paul zum Beispiel war fünfundzwanzig (25), Erich zweiundfünfzig (52).—„War", denn auf dieser armen Erde ist leider nichts von
5 Dauer. Hildegard und Paul sind jetzt schon lange im Paradies, und für Erich wollen wir das Beste hoffen.

Auch für den Leser hoffen wir das Beste. Denn da Held und Heldin nicht mehr sind, müssen wir, wie wir schon sagten, die Geschichte ihrer Liebe leider in der Vergangenheit erzählen.

10 Als Hildegards Onkel aus dem Leben ging—er fiel aus seinem kleinen Schiff ins Wasser und kam nicht, wie Laurella, gleich wieder herauf—zog Hildegard mit ihrer Mutter von Hamburg nach Bacharach am Rhein und in das Haus des Onkels.

Es dauerte keine Woche, da wußte jeder junge Mann im Dorf, daß
15 Hildegard in diesem Hause wohnte und daß am ganzen Rhein kein Mädchen so schön wie sie zu finden[6] war. Wenn sie in ihrem reizenden grünen Kleidchen durch die enge Straße des kleinen Dorfes zum Markte ging, dann öffnete sich hier ein Fenster und da eine Tür. Und der junge Schmidt oder Schulz grüßte sie mit einem freundlichen „Guten Morgen" oder „Guten
20 Abend". Und Schmidt und Schulz brauchten Hildegard nur anzusehen, dann liebten sie sie schon und vergaßen die arme Maria. Maria Müller aber weinte, und es dauerte nicht lange, da sagte sie: „Hildegard ist an allem schuld." Dann sagte es auch Mutter Müller, dann sagte es auch Vater Müller, und endlich sagte es das ganze Dorf. Nur Paul sagte nichts. Und
25 das bewies dem Dorf, daß er keinen guten Charakter hatte.

Hildegard, in ihrer Unschuld, wußte natürlich von all dem[7] nichts und blieb freundlich gegen alle. Wer mit ihr sprach, mußte sie lieben, er konnte nicht anders. Der junge Müller vergab ihr zuerst[8] und sagte: „Ich weiß nicht, was ihr gegen Hildegard habt. Sie ist so schön—und bestimmt
30 unschuldig." Dann sagte es auch Vater Müller. Dann meinte es auch Mutter Müller. Und als die Tochter sah, daß ihr Freund keinen Erfolg bei Hildegard hatte, da meinte sie es auch, und endlich sagte es das ganze Dorf. Nur Paul sagte nichts. Und das bewies wieder, daß er keinen guten Charakter hatte.

35 Wenn er ihr auf der Straße begegnete, dann sah er zu Boden und ging ohne Gruß vorbei. Frau Müller behauptete sogar, daß er Hildegard haßte.

Und wirklich brauchte Paul Hildegard nur von fern zu sehen, dann stieg[9] ihm schon das Blut in den Kopf,[9] daß er ganz rot im Gesicht wurde—so haßte er sie. Denn warum soll ein junger Mann sonst rot werden, wenn er ein junges Mädchen sieht?

[Fortsetzung folgt. To be continued.]

NOTES. 1. Der zerbrochene Krug *The Broken Pitcher*; the story was written by Heinrich Zschokke (1771–1848). 2. statt instead of. 3. kurz in short. 4. läßt causes. 5. Schwarz-Weiß Technik light-and-shadow technique (black and white; that is, the hero with only good qualities, the villain with only bad ones). 6. zu finden to be found. 7. dem Dative of das, that. 8. zuerst first. 9. stieg . . . Kopf the blood rushed to his head.

BUILDING A PASSIVE VOCABULARY

älter alt old, älter older
von Dauer dauern to last, continue, von Dauer of duration, lasting, everlasting
freundlich der Freund the friend, freundlich friendly
jugendlich die Jugend the youth, jugendlich youthful
das Kleidchen das Kleid the dress, das Kleidchen the little dress
das Leben leben to live, das Leben (the) life
männlich der Mann the man, männlich manly
schneller schnell fast, schneller faster
die Sprache sprechen to speak, die Sprache the speech, language
die Unschuld die Schuld guilt, blame, die Unschuld innocence, unschuldig innocent
vergab (*past of* vergeben) geben to give, vergeben (*w. dat.*) to forgive

GRAMMAR: PAST TENSE

50. Weak and Strong Verbs. Both English and German verbs fall roughly into two large groups:

a. Those that have no vowel change in the past and past participle, like *play*, *played*, *played* (German spielen, spielte, gespielt). These are called "weak" verbs in German grammars.

b. Those that do show a vowel change in the past and past participle like *eat*, *ate*, *eaten*; *sing*, *sang*, *sung* (German essen, aß, gegessen and singen, sang, gesungen). These are called "strong" verbs in German grammars.

51. Weak Verbs. The principal parts—that is, the infinitive, past, and past participle—of this class of verbs are quite easy to learn; they follow the scheme:

spielen, spielte, gespielt to play, played, played
lachen, lachte, gelacht to laugh, laughed, laughed

In the past tense they add -te to the stem:

spielte	lachte	küßte	legte

The past participle is formed by prefixing ge- and adding -t to the stem:

gespielt	gelacht	geküßt	gelegt

Since the endings -te (in the past) and -t (in the past participle) are characteristic features of weak verbs, they must in all cases be clearly audible. Hence in the past there is a connecting e between stems ending in -d or -t and all personal endings (ich antwortete, du antwortetest, and so on), and in the past participle (geantwortet). For similar reasons an extra e is found in verbs like atmen and rechnen (ich atmete, ich rechnete, geatmet, gerechnet). (Cf. §§ 5 and 13.)

52. Conjugation of Past Tense of Weak Verbs

ich	lachte	spielte	antwortete
du	lachtest	spieltest	antwortetest
er	lachte	spielte	antwortete
wir	lachten	spielten	antworteten
ihr	lachtet	spieltet	antwortetet
sie	lachten	spielten	antworteten

53. Strong Verbs. Even those students who want only a reading knowledge of German must learn the principal parts of strong verbs. To the principal parts as given in English grammars it is necessary to add and to learn in German:

a. The third person singular of the present of verbs which have a vowel change in the present (cf. § 10). (Since one learns faster and more easily when following a rhythmical pattern, the third person singular is given even when it shows no vowel change.)

b. The auxiliary verb used to form compound tenses. This auxiliary in English is always *to have* (*I have eaten, he has spoken*); in German the auxiliary verb is either haben or sein. (The rule stating which verbs require haben and which take sein may be found in § 76.)

Thus the principal parts of schreiben (which has as its auxiliary haben) and fallen (whose auxiliary is sein) are:

schreiben	schrieb	hat geschrieben	schreibt	to write
fallen	fiel	ist gefallen	fällt	to fall

54. Conjugation of Past Tense of Strong Verbs. The endings of strong verbs in the *past* are the same as those of the modal auxiliaries in the *present* tense:

ich sprach	ging	schrieb
du sprachst	gingst	schriebst
er sprach	ging	schrieb
wir sprachen	gingen	schrieben
ihr spracht	gingt	schriebt
sie sprachen	gingen	schrieben

In order to pronounce second person familiar forms which end in -d or -t and add -st or -t, an e is inserted (cf. § 5): du fandest, ihr fandet; du bandest, ihr bandet.

55. Weak Verbs with Vowel Change. About a dozen weak verbs have a vowel in the past and past participle which is different from that of the infinitive. Their past forms are regular in other respects.

müssen, mußte (*no umlaut*), gemußt, muß to be obliged to
können, konnte, gekonnt, kann to be able to
wissen, wußte, gewußt, weiß to know
kennen, kannte, gekannt, kennt to know by acquaintance

56. Conjugation of Past Tense of Weak Verbs with Vowel Change können, kennen, and wissen

ich	konnte	kannte	wußte
du	konntest	kanntest	wußtest
er	konnte	kannte	wußte
wir	konnten	kannten	wußten
ihr	konntet	kanntet	wußtet
sie	konnten	kannten	wußten

57. Conjugation of haben, sein, and werden in the Past

ich	hatte	war	wurde
du	hattest	warst	wurdest
er	hatte	war	wurde
wir	hatten	waren	wurden
ihr	hattet	wart	wurdet
sie	hatten	waren	wurden

58. Word Order. The same rules of word order which apply to the present tense hold for the past tense. In questions the inflected verb takes the same position as in English; in declarative sentences it is the second element; and in dependent clauses it is last. Separable prefixes stand at the end of main clauses:

Er kam nicht gleich wieder herauf. He did not immediately come up again.
Er ging ohne Gruß vorbei. He walked past without (a) greeting.

Again the infinitive stands at the end of a clause:

Er wollte es ihm nicht sagen. He did not want to tell it to him.

59. Progressive Form. Remember that German has no progressive or emphatic forms. This is true of all tenses. Thus ich lachte expresses *I laughed*, *I was laughing*, or *I did laugh*; ich ging may be translated, depending on the context, as *I went*, *I was going*, and *I did go*.

Learn the principal parts of the following verbs as a part of this lesson. (It should be considerably easier to memorize principal parts in future lessons if these are learned well, since most of the types are found below.)

LESSON IX

Infinitive	Past	Pres. Perfect	3d Sing. Pres.	Meaning
ſchreiben	ſchrieb	hat geſchrieben	ſchreibt	to write
bleiben	blieb	iſt geblieben	bleibt	to stay, remain
beweiſen	bewies	hat bewieſen*	beweiſt	to prove
ſchreien	ſchrie	hat geſchrieen	ſchreit	to cry
ſteigen	ſtieg	iſt geſtiegen	ſteigt	to climb
fließen	floß	iſt gefloſſen	fließt	to flow
riechen	roch	hat gerochen	riecht	to smell
ſchieben	ſchōb†	hat geſchōben	ſchiebt	to shove
verlieren	verlōr	hat verlōren*	verliert	to lose
ziehen	zōg	hat gezōgen	zieht	to pull
ziehen	zōg	iſt gezōgen	zieht	to move, go
ſinken	ſank	iſt geſunken	ſinkt	to sink
finden	fand	hat gefunden	findet	to find
binden	band	hat gebunden	bindet	to bind, tie
ſprechen	ſprāch	hat geſprochen	ſpricht	to speak
ſēhen	ſāh	hat geſēhen	ſieht	to see
vergeſſen	vergāß	hat vergeſſen*	vergißt	to forget
fallen	fiel	iſt gefallen	fällt	to fall
kommen	kām	iſt gekommen	kommt	to come
gēhen	ging	iſt gegangen	geht	to go
ſein	wār	iſt gewēſen	iſt	to be
werden	wurde	iſt geworden	wird	to become
hāben	hatte	hat gehābt	hat	to have
dürfen	durfte	hat gedurft	darf	to be permitted to
können	konnte	hat gekonnt	kann	to be able to
mȫgen	mochte	hat gemocht	māg	to like to
müſſen	mußte	hat gemußt	muß	to have to
ſollen	ſollte	hat geſollt	ſoll	to be to, be said to, *etc.*
wollen	wollte	hat gewollt	will	to want to
wiſſen	wußte	hat gewußt	weiß	to know

---

*The absence of the ge- prefix is explained in § 79.

†As an aid to memorization and to correctness of pronunciation, vowel length is indicated.

EXERCISES

I

Answer in German: 1. Was muß alle Gegenwart werden? 2. Was fließt schnell an uns vorbei? 3. Was muß mancher junge Mann schon morgen sagen? 4. Was ist die Liebe? 5. Wer ist Hildegard? 6. Ist Hildegard alt? 7. Ist sie jung? 8. Wer ist der Held unserer Geschichte? 9. Wie ist Pauls Herz? 10. Wer hat ein gutes Herz? 11. Wer war Stück für Stück das Gegenteil Pauls? 12. Was ist auf dieser Erde von Dauer? 13. Wo sind Hildegard und Paul schon lange? 14. Was wollen wir für Erich hoffen? 15. Wer ging aus dem Leben? 16. Wohin zog Hildegard mit ihrer Mutter? 17. Wie lange dauerte es, ehe jeder junge Mann im Dorf wußte, daß Hildegard in dem Hause wohnte? 18. Was war die Farbe ihres Kleidchens? 19. Wie grüßte sie der junge Schmidt oder Schulz? 20. Wen vergaß der junge Schmidt, als er Hildegard sah? 21. Wer weinte dann? 22. Wer sagte nichts? 23. Was bewies das? 24. Gegen wen blieb Hildegard freundlich? 25. Wer mußte Hildegard lieben? 26. Wer vergab Hildegard zuerst? 27. Wer hatte bei Hildegard keinen Erfolg? 28. Was behauptete Frau Müller? 29. Was stieg dem Paul in den Kopf? 30. Wie wurde er dann im Gesicht?

II

Translate into German: 1. He does not[1] know me. 2. I did not find him. 3. What did you have against her? 4. He fell into the water. 5. He stayed with (bei) me. 6. She was not there. 7. Karl threw (warf) an apple into the sea. 8. I could not[1] help the man. 9. I had to stay with (bei) them. 10. When I came, he was there. 11. We were speaking with an old woman. 12. It was not on the little bench. 13. I had the newspaper in my hand.

NOTE. 1. Cf. footnote, page 28.

III

Translate into English:

ehrlich	teilen	plötzlich
erwarten	übrigens	ohne
laufen	das Wort	neidisch
das Papier	vielleicht	die Straße
sollen	schon	auch

IV

Translate into German:

to take	to thank	deep
red	then	the place
possible	naturally	to hate
to lead	next to	hot
to use	hard	always
the danger	to see	to belong to

V

Translate into English:

er will nach Hause gehen
du hast recht
er blieb stehen
das war ja gar nichts
wollen Sie nicht Platz nehmen?

VI

Conjugate in the past tense:

ziehen	lachen	sagen	sein	haben
gehen	schreiben	wissen	können	binden

VII

Give the infinitive of each of the verbs used in the last four paragraphs of Text B in this lesson.

VIII

Read the last three paragraphs of Text B in the present tense, changing the inflected verb wherever necessary.

IX

Underline all past tense forms in the first paragraph of Text A.

LESSON X

TEXT A

Der Pfarrer[1] von Bacharach war ein alter, feiner Mann, den im Dorfe jeder liebte und auf dessen Urteil man sehr viel gab (prized highly). Er war nämlich nicht nur ein guter Pfarrer, der seine Bibel fast auswendig konnte, er war vor allem (above all) ein guter Mensch. Man konnte mit jedem Problem zu ihm gehen und sich sagen: Wenn es für mein Problem eine Lösung gibt, weiß unser Pfarrer sie bestimmt. Wenn jemand in Not war und Hilfe brauchte, teilte der Pfarrer mit ihm sein letztes Geld und trennte[2] sich,[2] wenn nötig, von seinem besten Rock. Ja, er war dem Dorf wirklich ein Vater, das Dorf ihm eine große Familie. Wer unrecht tat, brauchte nicht zu versuchen, es vor dem Pfarrer zu verbergen. Der Pfarrer erfuhr es doch und zwang jeden, sein Unrecht wiedergutzumachen.[3]

NOTES. 1. Pfarrer priest, Father. 2. trennte sich von parted with. 3. wiedergutzumachen make amends for.

VOCABULARY

besuchen to visit
böse angry, bad
dienen (*w. dat.*) to serve
einzig only, sole; unique; single
erst first, at first, not until; only
ewig eternal
fein *fine*; excellent
fressen to eat (*of animals*)
(der) Gott *God*
der Himmel the sky; heaven
irgend- any; some (cf. Vocab.)
  irgendwo anywhere
  irgendein Mann any man
kalt *cold*
die Kirche the *church*
die Krone the *crown*
letzt *last*
der Löwe the lion
das Mal the time (instance)
meist *most*; usually
der Mund the *mouth*
der Mut the courage
niemand nobody, no one
nötig necessary
das Schaf the *sheep*
schließen to close; lock; conclude
schweigen to be silent
sehr very
der Stein the *stone*, rock
der Tisch the table
die Vernunft the reason; senses
versprechen to promise

warm *warm*
das Weib the woman; *wife*
wirken to *work*; effect; be

IDIOMS

bitten um to ask for (cf. § 67)
fragen nach to ask for (cf. § 67)
im Gegenteil on the contrary
kennenlernen to make the acquaintance of (*sep. prefix*)
nach und nach little by little
zum ersten Mal for the first time

TEXT B

Der zerbrochene Krug, Teil II

Der Pfarrer[1] des Dorfes, der schon so alt war, daß er kaum noch hören konnte und nur verstand, was er verstehen wollte, tat sein Bestes, den hartherzigen Paul zur Vernunft zu bringen. Er sprach in der Kirche ernst und lang über den Text: „Es ist nicht gut, daß der Mensch allein ist; ein gutes Weib ist ihres Mannes Krone, und ein Weib, das schweigen kann, ist eine Gabe des ewigen Gottes." Aber obgleich er mit dem Wort schloß: „Liebet euch untereinander!"[2] blieb Pauls Herz hart wie Stein. Er sah zwar nach der Bank hinüber, auf der Hildegard saß, und Hildegard sah auch zu ihm hinüber. Aber was der gute Pfarrer sagte, half trotzdem nicht. Im Gegenteil.

Auf dem Jahrmarkt[3] in Oberwesel, den Hildegard mit ihrer Mutter im Spätherbst jenes Jahres besuchte, folgte Paul der armen Hildegard von Stand zu Stand, grüßte dieses Mädchen, redete mit jenem, wechselte aber mit Hildegard nicht ein einziges Wort—aus Trotz. „Um sie neidisch zu machen", meinte Frau Müller, die auch auf dem Markt war.

Auf diesem Jahrmarkte[3] nun sah Hildegard *den* Krug.[4] Nicht irgendeinen Krug, sondern *den* Krug. Denn von ihm haben wir noch viel zu berichten. Dieser Krug war aus feinem, durchscheinendem Porzellan, fast so dünn wie Papier, mit einem Bild auf jeder Seite. Das Bild auf der einen (1) Seite zeigte Adam und Eva im Paradies. Und der Apfel, zu dem Eva hinaufblickte, wirkte in seinem hellen Rot so natürlich, daß[5] der guten Hildegard das Wasser im Mund zusammenlief[5] und sie zum ersten Mal verstand, warum Eva da hineinbeißen mußte. Außerdem stand da ein Löwe ganz zufrieden neben einem Schaf, das sich gar nicht fürchtete. Man konnte sehen, der gute Löwe wußte noch nicht, daß er das Schaf einen Augenblick später fressen sollte. Das Bild auf der anderen Seite zeigte die Mutter Gottes mit dem Christuskind und dem Heiligen Joseph.

Als Hildegard diesen Krug[4] sah, konnte sie ihr Auge lange Zeit nicht abwenden. Sie vergaß sogar, daß Paul dicht hinter ihr stand und sie beobachtete. Endlich nahm sie all ihren Mut zusammen und fragte den Verkäufer nach dem Preise. „Hundert (100) Mark", antwortete dieser kaltblütig. Da schwieg Hildegard und ging, denn soviel Geld hatte sie nicht. Paul aber blieb.

Als niemand mehr von Bacharach auf dem Markte war, warf er dem Verkäufer hundert (100) Mark auf den Tisch, ließ[6] den Krug in eine Schachtel[7] legen und ging dann durch den tiefen Schnee allein nach Bacharach zurück.

Nicht weit vom Dorfe begegnete er dem alten August, dem Diener Erichs. August war ein ganz guter Mensch, aber nicht sehr intelligent. „August", sagte Paul zu ihm, „ich gebe dir eine Mark, wenn du diese Schachtel in das Haus Hildegards trägst und sie da liegen läßt. Wenn dich jemand sieht und fragt, von wem diese Schachtel kommt, so erzähle ihm irgendeine Geschichte, aber sage auf keinen Fall, daß sie von mir kommt!" August nahm erst die Mark und dann die Schachtel und versprach, alles richtig zu machen.

Er wollte gerade im Hause Hildegards verschwinden, da fiel er fast über Erich. Erich nämlich, sein Herr—es wird Zeit, daß der Leser ihn kennenlernt—war ein Junggeselle[8] in jenem gefährlichen Alter, in dem ein Mann glücklich sein muß, wenn er noch ein Mädchen findet, das seine Frau werden will. Und da Erich Geld und eine gute Stellung hatte, wurde es der Mutter ganz warm ums Herz, wenn Erich sie, die Mutter, manchmal besuchte, ihr oft etwas schenkte und sie dann nach und nach vergaß, um mit der Tochter über das himmlische Wort „Liebet[2] euch untereinander[2]" zu sprechen.

Erich also, um auf den Krug zurückzukommen, kam gerade aus dem Hause, als August, sein Diener, hineinwollte. „August", fragte Erich, „was trägst du da?"—„Eine Schachtel für Hildegard, Herr", antwortete August. „Aber ich darf nicht sagen, von wem sie kommt, sonst ist mir Paul böse."—„Es ist gut, daß du schweigen kannst, August. Aber es ist schon spät. Gib mir die Schachtel! Ich kann sie Hildegard morgen geben, denn ich muß wieder zu ihrer Mutter."

So kam die Schachtel mit dem Krug an Erich. Erich nahm sie mit nach Hause, öffnete sie, sah den Krug und sagte „Aha!" Er brachte Krug und Schachtel am folgenden Morgen zu Hildegard und sprach: „Diesen Krug und mein liebendes Herz lege ich zu Ihren Füßen."[9] Hildegard aber wandte sich um und sagte: „Ich darf weder Ihr Herz noch Ihren Krug nehmen." Dann lief sie weinend hinaus. Da nahm die Mutter den Krug und versprach, ihre Tochter zu überreden, Erichs Herz zu nehmen.

[Fortsetzung folgt]

NOTES. 1. Pfarrer priest, Father. 2. Liebet . . . untereinander love one another. 3. Jahrmarkt annual fair. 4. Krug pitcher. 5. daß . . . zusammenlief that Hildegard's mouth watered. 6. ließ. Cf. § 64. 7. Schachtel (paper) box. 8. Junggeselle bachelor. 9. Füßen feet.

BUILDING A PASSIVE VOCABULARY

das Alter alt old, das Alter age
durchscheinend durch through, scheinen to shine, durchscheinend translucent
endlich das Ende the end, endlich final(ly)
der Fall auf keinen Fall in no case (*cf.* Idioms, Lesson IX)
die Gabe geben to give, die Gabe the gift
gefährlich die Gefahr the danger, gefährlich dangerous
hartherzig hart hard, das Herz the heart, hartherzig hardhearted
himmlisch der Himmel heaven, himmlisch heavenly
jawohl ja yes, jawohl yes, sir!
kaltblütig kalt cold, das Blut the blood, kaltblütig cold-blooded(ly)
manchmal mancher many a, das Mal the time, manchmal sometimes
trotzdem der Trotz the spite, defiance, trotz (*preposition*) in spite of, trotzdem in spite of it, nevertheless
überreden* über over, above, reden to talk, speak, überreden to persuade.

GRAMMAR

60. Word Formation: The Prefix un=. The prefix un= is added to adjectives and nouns to reverse the meaning:

interessant interesting	ehrlich honest
uninteressant uninteresting	unehrlich dishonest
glücklich happy	die Schuld the guilt
unglücklich unhappy	die Unschuld the innocence

*This is a verb with über as an inseparable prefix. The accent is on reden.

61. Word Formation: The Suffixes -chen and -lein. The suffixes -chen and -lein are added to nouns to form neuter diminutives. Usually these diminutives have an umlaut if the vowel is capable of change. Frequently they express affection rather than smallness. Examples are:

das Bett	das Bettchen	das Glas	das Gläschen
der Kopf	das Köpfchen	die Mutter	das Mütterlein
das Buch	das Büchlein	das Herz	das Herzchen

62. Word Formation: Infinitives. Infinitives are used as neuter nouns which correspond roughly to English verbal nouns—gerunds (*Running is good exercise*) or infinitives (*To read is profitable*):

Er hat ein gewinnendes Lachen. He has a winning laugh.
Beim Aussteigen verlor er das Geld. In getting out he lost the money.
Geben ist besser als Nehmen. To give is better than to receive.

63. Word Formation: The Suffix -ung. The suffix -ung added to verb stems forms feminine nouns corresponding in most cases to English derivatives ending in *-ing*, *-tion*, and *-ment*:

Die Atmung the breathing	die Behauptung the assertion
die Bezahlung the payment	die Stellung the position

64. Lassen. This verb is usually used like the modal auxiliaries. As with the modals, the infinitive dependent upon lassen does not take zu. In this use it has two meanings:

a. To let, allow.

Laß sie kommen! Let them come.

b. To cause, have (*someone do*).

Er ließ den Doktor kommen. He had the doctor come, ***or*** He sent for the doctor.

The dependent infinitive frequently has a passive meaning:

a. Sie ließ sich nicht überreden. She did not allow herself to be persuaded, was not to be persuaded.

b. Er ließ den Krug in eine Schachtel legen. He had the pitcher put into a box.

65. Wann, als, and wenn. All three words mean *when.*
Wann is used only in direct and indirect questions:

Wann darf ich gehen? When may I go?
Ich weiß nicht, wann er nach Hause kommt. I don't know (the answer to the question) when he is coming home.

Als is a subordinating conjunction and indicates one single occurrence or state in the past:

Erich kam aus dem Haus, als August hineinwollte. Erich was coming out of the house when August wanted to go in.
Als ich ein Kind war, spielte ich gern auf dem Felde. When I was a child, I liked to play in the field.

Wenn is used for all other meanings of *when.* It also means *whenever* and *if*:

Wenn er ihr auf der Straße (begegnet) begegnete, (sieht) sah er zu Boden. When he (meets) met her on the street, he (looks) looked at the ground (down).
Wenn das Kleid nicht zuviel kostet, kaufe ich es. If the dress doesn't cost too much, I'll buy it.

66. Kennen and wissen. Both words mean *to know.*
Kennen means *to be acquainted with a person or a thing*:

Ich kenne deinen Onkel. I know your uncle.
Kennen Sie dieses Buch? Do you know this book?

Wissen means *to know something as a fact*:

Ich weiß, daß er Geld hat. I know that he has money.
Antonio wußte nicht, daß sie ihn liebte. Antonio didn't know that she loved him.

67. Fragen and bitten. Both words mean *to ask.*
Fragen means *to ask for information*:

Er fragte sie: „Wie alt sind Sie?" He asked her, "How old are you?"
Er fragte mich nach meiner Mutter. He asked me about my mother.

Bitten means *to ask for a gift or favor*:

„Geh nicht mit mir!" bat Laurella. "Don't go with me!" Laurella pleaded.

Er bat seinen Vater um Geld. He asked his father for money.

Learn the principal parts of the following verbs as a part of this lesson. (The verbs in small type were listed in the previous lesson; they are repeated as an aid to learning the new verbs.)

schreiben	schrieb	hat geschrieben	schreibt	to write
schweigen	schwieg	hat geschwiegen	schweigt	to be silent
fließen	floß	ist geflossen	fließt	to flow
schließen	schloß	hat geschlossen	schließt	to close
sinken	sank	ist gesunken	sinkt	to sink
springen	sprang	ist gesprungen	springt	to jump
zwingen	zwang	hat gezwungen	zwingt	to force
sprechen	sprāch	hat gesprochen	spricht	to speak
versprechen	versprāch	hat versprochen*	verspricht	to promise
brechen	brāch	hat gebrochen	bricht	to break
treffen	trāf	hat getroffen	trifft	to meet
helfen	half	hat geholfen	hilft	to help
werfen	warf	hat geworfen	wirft	to throw
nēhmen	nāhm	hat genommen	nimmt	to take
sēhen	sāh	hat gesēhen	sieht	to see
gēben	gāb	hat gegēben	gībt	to give
lēsen	lās	hat gelēsen	liest	to read
trēten	trāt	ist getrēten	tritt	to step
sitzen	sāß	hat gesessen	sitzt	to sit
bitten	bāt	hat gebēten	bittet	to ask
fāhren	fūhr	ist gefāhren	fährt	to ride
erfāhren	erfūhr	hat erfāhren*	erfährt	to find out
trāgen	trūg	hat getrāgen	trägt	to carry
fallen	fiel	ist gefallen	fällt	to fall
lassen	ließ	hat gelassen	läßt	to let
schlāfen	schlief	hat geschlāfen	schläft	to sleep
laufen	lief	ist gelaufen	läuft	to run

*The absence of the ge- is explained in § 79.

LESSON X

stēhen	stand	hat gestanden	stēht	to stand
verstēhen	verstand	hat verstanden*	verstēht	to understand
tūn	tāt	hat getān	tūt	to do
bringen	brachte	hat gebracht	bringt	to bring
denken	dachte	hat gedacht	denkt	to think
wenden	wendete wandte	hat gewendet hat gewandt	wendet	to turn

EXERCISES

I

Answer in German: 1. Wen versuchte der Pfarrer, zur Vernunft zu bringen? 2. Wo sprach er ernst und lange? 3. Wer soll nicht allein sein? 4. Was ist die Krone eines Mannes? 5. Wie blieb Pauls Herz? 6. Wohin sah er? 7. Zu wem sah Hildegard hinüber? 8. Wo war der Jahrmarkt? 9. Wann besuchte Hildegard den Jahrmarkt? 10. Wem folgte Paul von Stand zu Stand? 11. Mit wem wechselte Paul kein Wort? 12. Wer war auch auf dem Markt? 13. Was sah Hildegard auf dem Jahrmarkt? 14. Was war auf jeder Seite des Kruges? 15. Wie wirkte der Apfel? 16. Was verstand Hildegard zum ersten Mal? 17. Wie war der Löwe? 18. Wen vergaß Hildegard, als sie den Krug sah? 19. Wem gab Paul hundert Mark? 20. Wo begegnete Paul dem Diener Erichs? 21. Was sollte August mit der Schachtel tun? 22. Wem schenkte Erich oft etwas? 23. Mit wem sprach er über den Text „Liebet euch untereinander"? 24. Woher kam Erich, als August ins Haus gehen wollte? 25. Was nahm Erich mit nach Hause? 26. Was sagte Erich, als er Hildegard die Schachtel brachte? 27. Was tat Hildegard? 28. Wie lief sie hinaus? 29. Was versprach Hildegards Mutter?

II

Translate into German: 1. He needed them, but they did not want to come. 2. She brought us a beautiful book. 3. He did not know that you are my uncle. 4. Where were they sitting in the church? 5. She ran around the corner. 6. She asked him (*use*

*The absence of the ge= is explained in § 79.

accusative) for a glass [of]* water. 7. He asked, "How old are you?" 8. When I came home, my mother was sleeping. 9. When may I see them? 10. Whenever I see the moon, I think of you. 11. She took it away (ab) from him (cf. §23). 12. When he said that, you were silent. 13. I know what you were thinking. 14. I was reading a book. 15. Why did you go into the forest? 16. I do not know your mother.

III

Translate into English:

die Arbeit	stoßen	das Urteil
behaupten	eng	zwischen
die Jugend	nennen	die Vergangenheit
der Enkel	das Gegenteil	die Zukunft
nein	erfahren	ziehen
der Platz	plötzlich	grüßen

IV

Translate into German:

the wall	the head	the hand
slender	happy	hot
fast	to cost	the bed
nothing	against	the hat
new	the corner	early
or	short	to find

V

Translate into English the following compounds and derivatives:

das Äpfelchen, das Vaterland, unmöglich, die Stellung, die Wasserkraft, die Pferdekraft, die Pflanzung, der Wochentag; wir hatten einen Wortwechsel mitein= ander; ungerade, die Erwartung, taghell, das Kindlein, der Uhrmacher, ungleich; ich bin sprachlos; das Fräulein, die Sonnenuhr, die Trennung, schneeweiß, die 5 Wendung, der Reiseführer, das Papiergeld, undeutsch, der Notfall, die Mutter=

*English words in brackets are not to be translated.

sprache, das Mutterherz, das Muttergottesbild; die Menschwerdung Gottes war ein Wunder; das Hänschen, das Häuschen, der Markttag, ein herzloser Mensch, die Erzählung, der Marktpreis, der Herbstmorgen, das Gänslein, der Geschäftsmann, die Meinung, die Glastür, die Arbeitsteilung, die Verwandlung, unbestimmt, ungern, die Führung, unheilig, unrichtig, das Händchen, unnatürlich, das Wäldchen, das Schifflein, unschön, unweit, die Begegnung, unwissend, das Herzchen; rede nicht beim[1] Essen! das Hütchen, die Beobachtung, das Stückchen; er fiel beim[1] Einsteigen ins Wasser; die Fortsetzung, die Wanduhr

NOTE. 1. beim in the act of, while.

VI

Conjugate in the past tense:

sein	bringen	leben	fahren	binden
haben	denken	nehmen	bitten	führen

VII

Give the infinitive of each of the verbs used in the first three paragraphs of Text B.

VIII

Read the last six paragraphs of Text B in the present tense, changing the inflected verb wherever necessary.

IX

Review the principal parts of the verbs learned in Lesson IX.

LESSON XI

TEXT A

Du bist nicht sehr höflich, Kind. Du sollst „Danke schön" sagen, wenn dir Onkel Kurt einen Apfel gibt.—Ein modernes Hotel muß in jedem Zimmer (room) fließendes warmes und kaltes Wasser haben.—„Das Schiff sinkt! Frau Meyer, wollen Sie sich nicht retten?"—„Nein, ich bleibe bei Gustav und gehe mit ihm unter."—Ich kaufe meine Butter jetzt bei Schmidts. Meyers Butter riecht oft nicht gut.—Du findest Frau Meyer schön? Ich nicht. Sie hat doch solch einen großen Mund.—Schon streckte der Einbrecher[1] die Hand nach dem Strumpf aus, in dem Frau Meyer ihr Geld verborgen hielt, schon lächelte er siegesfroh,[2] als Herr Pinkerton, der Meisterdetektiv aus Neuyork, mit einem Revolverschuß seinem Leben ein Ende machte.—Jeden Morgen trieb August das einzige Schaf der Familie erst auf das Feld und dann in den Wald.—Wir wurden zwischen drei (3) und vier (4) Uhr wach.—Er wandte seinen Blick zum Himmel.—Der Tod (death) ist nur eine Verwandlung, kein Schlaf, aus dem man nicht wiederaufwacht.—Während ich am Bette der Mutter blieb, holte mein Vater den Arzt.

NOTES. 1. der Einbrecher the burglar. 2. siegesfroh happily, triumphantly

VOCABULARY

der Arm the *arm*
der Arzt the physician
der Brunnen the well, fountain
die Brust the *breast*; chest
die Butter the *butter*
deutlich clear, plain
(der) Dienstag *Tuesday*
(der) Donnerstag Thursday
drücken to press, squeeze
eigen *own*
das Eis the *ice*
erinnern an to remind of
sich erinnern an to remember
die Familie the *family*
das Faß the barrel, cask
fertig ready; finished
fest firm, solid, *fast*
froh glad, happy, joyful
gegenüber (*w. dat.*) opposite
gewöhnlich usual, customary
groß *great*, large; tall
heiraten to marry
klar *clear*, plain
der Kuchen the *cake*
lächeln to smile
langsam slow(ly)

laut *loud*, noisy
der Meister the *master*; champion
(der) Mittwoch Wednesday
nicken to nod
nie, niemals *never*
die Pflicht the duty
rufen to call, shout
die Sache the thing, affair
schicken to send
schießen to *shoot*
der Schmerz the pain, grief
der Sieg the victory
sogleich immediately, at once
(der) Sonntag *Sunday*
statt (anstatt) *instead* of
die Stunde the hour, lesson
trauen to marry (unite in marriage); trust
trösten to console
der Wein the *wine*
wenig little; wenige few
ein wenig a little
wild *wild*
der Winter the *winter*
zittern to tremble

IDIOMS

danke schön thank you; much obliged
halten von to think of
morgen früh tomorrow morning
nach meiner Meinung in my opinion
so geht es im Leben such is life
solange as long as
statt zu geben instead of giving

TEXT B

Der zerbrochene Krug, Teil III

[Schluß]

Um sich an den Geber zu gewöhnen, mußte die arme Hildegard nun jeden Morgen mit dem Krug zum Brunnen gehen und Wasser holen. Aber es half nichts. Es wurde Winter, es wurde Frühling, und Erichs Herz lag noch immer zu Hildegards Füßen.[1] Doch das Mädchen ließ sich nicht überreden,[2] es aufzuheben. 5

Der gute Pfarrer wechselte am Sonntag seinen Text und sprach ernst und lange über das Wort: „Die Fügungen[3] des Himmels sind wunderbar."[3]

Und wirklich verlor Hildegard am folgenden Tage am Brunnen ein Hutband, ein schönes blaues Band, das man im ganzen Dorfe kannte. Paul, der es fand, kannte es auch. Aber statt es Hildegard zurückzugeben, band er 10 es um seinen eigenen Hut. Und das bewies wieder, daß er keinen guten Charakter hatte. Denn wenn man ein Mädchen nicht liebt, trägt man auch nicht ihr Hutband. Und daß Paul Hildegard haßte, das wußte man im Dorfe ja. (Frau Müller behauptete es immer noch.)

Erich wußte es auch. Nur nicht mehr so bestimmt wie früher. „Die Sache kann nicht so weitergehen!" dachte er und ging noch am selben Abend zur Mutter Hildegards.

Die Mutter wußte natürlich schon alles. (Kein Wunder! Frau Müller wohnte ihr[4] gerade gegenüber,[4] in dem kleinen Häuschen auf der anderen Seite der Straße.) Trotzdem ließ sie Erich die ganze Geschichte von Paul und dem Hutband noch einmal erzählen. „Sie haben recht", meinte sie, als Erich fertig war, „die Sache kann nicht so weitergehen. Hildegard muß heiraten, und zwar sogleich. Natürlich kann man sie nicht zwingen, aber was halten Sie von folgendem Plan? Ich schicke Hildegard am kommenden Donnerstag mit irgendeinem Geschenk zum Pfarrer. Der Pfarrer muß dann das Mädchen an ihre Pflicht erinnern und ihr klarmachen, daß sie als meine Tochter zu tun hat, was nach meiner Meinung gut für sie ist. Sie gehen eine halbe Stunde später als Hildegard zum Pfarrer. Und der alte Mann muß euch zwei[5] dann trauen, ehe sie wieder an ihr Hutband denken kann."

Die arme Hildegard wußte von all dem nichts und ging am Dienstag wie sonst zum Brunnen, um Wasser zu holen. „Guten Morgen", sagte da jemand zu ihr. Hildegard wandte sich um und wurde blutrot im Gesicht. Es war Paul, und noch immer trug er ihr Band um den Hut. „Warum tragen Sie mein Band?" fragte Hildegard trotzig und stellte den Krug auf den Boden. „Ich gab es Ihnen nicht. Geben Sie es mir zurück!"

Paul nahm den Hut ab, sah auf das Band, sah auf Hildegard, sah wieder auf das Band und sagte leise: „Liebe Hildegard, gib mir das Band!" Hildegard sah erst auf Paul, dann auf das Band und dann wieder auf Paul. Ihr Blick verlor sich ganz in seinem Blick. Und so kam es, daß sie sich versprach[6] und „Nein!" sagte, obgleich sie „Ja!" sagen wollte. Da ärgerte[7] sich[7] Paul, und er wurde plötzlich ganz weiß im Gesicht und schrie in wildem Schmerz: „Da hast du das Band!" Und er warf Hut und Band so unglücklich auf den Krug, daß der schöne Krug zerbrach und Hildegard weinend nach Hause lief.

Doch die Mutter weinte nicht, als Hildegard mit dem zerbrochenen Krug nach Hause kam, sondern tröstete ihre Tochter und meinte: „So geht es im Leben. Versprich mir, mein Kind, das nächste Mal, wenn dich ein Mann um Band oder Herz bittet, dann sagst du ‚Ja!'" Das versprach Hildegard gern. Nur dachte sie an Paul, während ihre Mutter an Erich dachte.

Und die Mutter ging am nächsten Morgen, Mittwoch, wieder zum Pfarrer. Der gute alte Mann war wie immer sehr freundlich, nickte zu allem, was die Mutter sagte, und versprach, sein Bestes zu tun.

Der Donnerstag kam, und Hildegard ging, ein Bild der Unschuld, mit einem großen Kuchen zum Pfarrer. Erich, der hinter seinem Fenster stand 5 und wartete, sah sie vorbeigehen, zog schnell seinen besten Rock an und ging eine halbe Stunde später auch zum Pfarrer—siegesfroh[8] lächelnd.[8]

Aber die Fügungen[3] Gottes sind wirklich wunderbar.[3] Gerade an diesem Donnerstag kam Paul der Gedanke, dem Pfarrer ein kleines Fäßchen Wein zu bringen. Und Wein und Kuchen trafen sich am Brunnen, erfuhren, daß 10 sie denselben Weg hatten, und gingen zusammen weiter. Und da Paul seinen Wein auf der einen Seite, Hildegard aber ihren Kuchen auf der anderen Seite trug, so war es ganz natürlich, daß Paul Hildegards Hand in seine Hand nahm. Hildegard zitterte ein wenig. Aber nur ein wenig, denn sie dachte an ihr Versprechen, nie wieder nein zu sagen. Und dieser Gedanke gab ihr 15 Kraft.

Der Pfarrer war wie immer sehr freundlich, nickte wieder zu allem und sprach noch einmal ernst und väterlich über das schöne Wort: „Liebet euch untereinander!" Da schmolz[9] das Eis um Pauls Herz wie Butter vor der Sonne, und auch Hildegards kleines Herz öffnete sich weit. „Ach!" 20 rief sie, „ich liebe ihn ja schon lange, aber er haßt mich."—„Ich hasse dich nicht!" rief Paul. „Ich liebe dich! Aber ich hatte nicht den Mut, es dir zu sagen. Du warst so kalt und unfreundlich gegen mich. Wie konnte ich wissen, daß du mich liebst?"

Da sank Hildegard an Pauls Brust, und Paul drückte sie leise, doch fest 25 an sich. Sie vergaßen alles um sich her.[10] Fast ohne es zu wissen, folgten sie dem Pfarrer in die Kirche und sagten laut und deutlich „Ja!"

Vor der Kirche aber stand Erich in seinem besten Rock und wartete. Als er Hildegard am Arme Pauls aus der Kirche kommen sah, da wußte er alles. Sein Herz, das noch immer zu Hildegards Füßen[1] lag, hob er nun selber 30 auf. Es schlug nur sehr, sehr langsam.

NOTES. 1. Füßen feet. 2. überreden be persuaded (cf. § 64). 3. Die . . . wunderbar. The ways (methods) of heaven (of God) are wonderful. 4. ihr gegenüber opposite her (object precedes preposition). 5. zwei two. 6. sich versprach made a mistake. 7. ärgerte sich became angry. 8. siegesfroh lächelnd smiling happily in anticipation of victory. 9. schmolz melted. 10. her. Do not translate.

BUILDING A PASSIVE VOCABULARY

anziehen an on, ziehen to draw, pull, anziehen to put on, dress
früher früh early, früher earlier, formerly, before
der Gedanke denken to think, der Gedanke the thought
das Geschenk schenken to give, das Geschenk the gift
sich gewöhnen an gewöhnlich usual, customary, sich gewöhnen an to become accustomed to
lieb lieben to love, die Liebe love, lieb dear
nächst nah near, nächst (*superlative form*) nearest, next
siegesfroh der Sieg the victory, froh glad, happy, siegesfroh happy (in anticipation of victory)
trotzig der Trotz defiance, trotzig defiantly
weiter weit far, distant, weiter farther, *here* on, weitergehen to continue
zerbrach (*from* zerbrechen) brechen to break, zerbrechen to break to pieces, smash

GRAMMAR

68. Word Formation: Noun-Verb Pairs. Just as in English there are such noun-verb pairs as *the work* and *to work*, so in German there are a great many nouns corresponding to verbs (or vice versa):

die Arbeit (work), arbeiten (to work) das Blut (blood), bluten (to bleed)
der Teil (share), teilen (to share, divide)

The German feminines frequently end in -e:

die Liebe (love), lieben (to love) die Reise (trip), reisen (to travel)

English has a few, German a great many, nouns whose stem vowels differ from those of the infinitive:

the shot, to shoot the song, to sing

der Biß (bite), beißen (to bite) das Band (bond, ribbon), binden (to tie)
der Tritt (step, footstep), treten (to step)

69. Word Formation: Adjectives in -lich. The suffix -lich is added to *nouns* and forms adjectives which either correspond to English adjectives ending in *-ly* or *-like* or mean *typical of*. (They usually have the umlaut.)

der Tag, täglich daily	der Vater, väterlich fatherly
die Nacht, nächtlich nightly	der Feind, feindlich hostile
der Mann, männlich manly	die Mutter, mütterlich motherly

der Hof, höflich courteous, polite

70. Word Formation: Adjectives in -lich and -bar. The suffixes -lich or -bar are added to *verb* stems to form adjectives which correspond to English adjectives ending in *-able* (*-ible*):

fraglich questionable	brauchbar usable	eßbar edible
unglaublich unbelievable	lesbar readable	tragbar portable

71. Word Formation: Adverbs from Adjectives. Adjectives in their uninflected forms, that is, the forms given in the vocabulary, are used as adverbs:

Er war ernst (*predicate adjective*). He was earnest.
Er redete ernst (*adverb*). He talked earnestly.
Das Essen war gut. The food was good.
Wir aßen gut. We ate well.
Er war sehr freundlich. He was very friendly (pleasant).
Er sprach sehr freundlich. He spoke very pleasantly.

Adjectives which in their uninflected forms end in -e retain the e on becoming adverbs:

Er sprach leise. He spoke softly.
Er lachte böse. He laughed maliciously.

Some writers regularly write the following adverbs with an -e:

gern (gerne), lang (lange), nah (nahe)

72. Accusative of Time. Sometimes a noun like der Tag is used to answer the question "*When?*" (*When* is he going to work?) If the answer includes a declinable word as in "every (jed- plus ending) day," German must perforce use one of the four cases, for there is no undeclined form reserved for such needs. It is an established practice in German when expressing definite time and duration of time with nouns to use the accusative case when there is no preceding preposition. Examples:

Hildegard ging jeden Tag zum Brunnen. Hildegard went every day to the well.

Das nächste Mal sage ich ja. The next time I'll say yes.

Er liest schon den ganzen Morgen. He has been reading the entire morning.

NOTE. The greetings Guten Morgen, Guten Abend, Guten Tag are direct objects; *I wish you* is understood.

73. The Article in Expressing Time. The article is used with names of the seasons, months, days, and divisions of the day:

im Winter im Januar am Montag am Abend

74. The Days of the Week. In German the days of the week are:

Montag, Dienstag, Mittwoch, Donnerstag, Freitag, Sonnabend (or Samstag), and Sonntag

They are all masculine.

75. The Months of the Year. In German the months are:

Januar, Februar, März, April, Mai, Juni, Juli, August, September, Oktober, November, Dezember

The months are likewise masculine.

Learn the principal parts of the following verbs as a part of this lesson. (The verbs in small type were listed in previous lessons.)

schreiben	schrieb	hat geschrieben	schreibt	to write
scheinen	schien	hat geschienen	scheint	to shine
treiben	trieb	hat getrieben	treibt	to drive
treiben	trieb	ist getrieben	treibt	to drift
beißen	biß	hat gebissen	beißt	to bite
schließen	schloß	hat geschlossen	schließt	to close
schießen	schoß	hat geschossen	schießt	to shoot
hēben	hōb	hat gehōben	hēbt	to lift
sinken	sank	ist gesunken	sinkt	to sink
verschwinden	verschwand	ist verschwunden	verschwindet	to disappear
gewinnen	gewann	hat gewonnen	gewinnt	to win

helfen	half	hat geholfen	hilft	to help
verbergen	verbarg	hat verborgen	verbirgt	to hide
vergessen	vergāß	hat vergessen	vergißt	to forget
essen	āß	hat gegessen	ißt	to eat
fressen	frāß	hat gefressen	frißt	to eat (*of animals*)
liegen	lāg	hat gelēgen	liegt	to lie
fāhren	fūhr	ist gefāhren	fāhrt	to ride
schlāgen	schlūg	hat geschlāgen	schlāgt	to beat
wachsen	wuchs	ist gewachsen	wächst	to grow
fallen	fiel	ist gefallen	fällt	to fall
gefallen	gefiel	hat gefallen	gefällt	to please
halten	hielt	hat gehalten	hält	to hold
stōßen	stieß	hat gestōßen	stōßt	to push
rūfen	rief	hat gerūfen	rūft	to call
kommen	kām	ist gekommen	kommt	to come
bekommen	bekām	hat bekommen	bekommt	to receive
kennen	kannte	hat gekannt	kennt	to know
nennen	nannte	hat genannt	nennt	to name

EXERCISES

I

Answer in German: 1. An wen sollte sich Hildegard gewöhnen? 2. Wohin ging sie jeden Morgen? 3. Was holte sie da? 4. Zu wessen Füßen lag Erichs Herz? 5. Wer wechselte seinen Text? 6. Wann verlor Hildegard ihr Hutband? 7. Wer fand es? 8. Was machte Paul mit dem Band? 9. Wer behauptete immer noch, daß Paul Hildegard haßte? 10. An welchem Tage wollte Hildegards Mutter ihre Tochter zum Pfarrer schicken? 11. Wohin ging Hildegard am Dienstag? 12. Sprach Paul laut oder leise? 13. Was wollte Hildegard sagen? 14. Wurde Paul wieder rot im Gesicht? 15. Wohin warf er seinen Hut? 16. Wie lief Hildegard nach Hause? 17. Wen tröstete die Mutter? 18. An wen dachte Hildegard? 19. Was zog Erich an, als er Hildegard sah? 20. Wer nahm schweigend wessen Hand? 21. Wie war der Pfarrer? 22. Wie schmolz das Eis um Pauls Herz? 23. Was vergaßen Hildegard und Paul? 24. Wem folgten sie in die Kirche? 25. Wie sagten sie „Ja"? 26. Wo wartete Erich? 27. Wen sah er aus der Kirche kommen? 28. Was wußte er nun? 29. Was hob er auf? 30. Wie schlug sein Herz?

II

Translate into German: 1. Every evening he brought me home. 2. While you were talking with him, I ate an apple. 3. I did not like the apple. 4. I gave the horse an apple. 5. The student held her horse. 6. The man disappeared in (*dat. or acc.*) the forest. 7. On that evening she did not remain long. 8. Hans was reading the newspaper. 9. Who was writing? 10. I could not forget you. 11. He was just coming out of the class. 12. He knew every girl in the class. 13. I knew that you were in front of the door. 14. The pencil was lying on your book.

III

Translate into English:

die Weise	wohnen	die Lösung	richtig	ehe	die Not
weil	kaufen	hell	zahlen	der Feind	glauben
welcher	leicht	der Rücken	spielen	stürzen	jetzt

IV

Translate into German:

the wind	to learn	the solution
the week	the power	simple
the country (land)	to push	the window
to kiss	the ship	the uncle
young	to wish	suddenly

V

Translate the following compounds and derivatives:

die Wohnung, der Eckstein; er fiel kopfüber ins Wasser; sie spielte Beethovens
„Mondschein-Sonate"; augenblicklich schläft er; die Zeit ist unendlich; ein
herbstlicher Morgen; der Besucher; Hildegard war unbeschreiblich schön; unweit
von der Kirche stand Erich; das ist undenkbar; das Kirchlein; sie atmete hörbar;
5 ein zusammenlegbares Bett, brauchbar, eine sehr fragliche Lösung; dieses Kleid
ist nicht käuflich: ein unabwendbares Unglück, das Butterfaß, das Weinfaß, ein
schriftlicher (written) Bericht. ein mündlicher Bericht, die Löwin; der Lauf,
laufen; die Pflanze, pflanzen; der Schuß, schießen; der Schein, scheinen; der
Schlaf, schlafen; das Haus, hausen; das Kleid, kleiden; das Urteil, urteilen;

der Schluß, schließen; geben, die Gabe; fragen, die Frage; springen, der Sprung; die Furcht, fürchten; das Mündchen, das Dörflein, eine böse Erfahrung (experience); Hildegard traf Paul beim Wasserholen

VI

Conjugate in the present and past tenses:

ich will gehen
ich kann schnell arbeiten
ich spreche mit ihm
ich denke an ihn
ich tröste das Kind
ich verliere den Weg
ich lese die Zeitung
ich tue es nicht

VII

Read the first four paragraphs of Text B in Lesson VII and all of Text B in Lesson VIII in the past, changing all inflected verbs that are not in quotation marks.

VIII

Make the necessary verb changes and read the first six paragraphs of Text B of this lesson in the present tense.

IX

Review the principal parts of the strong verbs listed in Lessons IX and X.

LESSON XII

TEXT A

John schläft. Nach einer Stunde steht er auf und sagt: „Ich habe gut geschlafen."—Kurzhals und seine Frau sitzen am Tisch und essen. Nach einer Stunde kommt ihre Tochter nach Hause und Frau Kurzhals sagt: „Du mußt allein essen; Vater und ich haben schon gegessen."--„Gib mir
5 das Buch. Ich will es lesen. Ich weiß, du hast es schon gelesen. (Ich weiß, daß du es schon gelesen hast.)"—„Ja, ich habe es schnell durchgelesen."

„Darf ich meinen Freund Paul Windig besuchen?"—„Herr Windig ist leider letzte Nacht gestorben."—„Das tut mir leid. Ich kannte ihn seit langer Zeit. Er und seine Frau lebten in einer sehr glücklichen Ehe."

10 „Hast du den Brief (letter) an Vater schon geschrieben?"—„Nein, ich habe ihn noch nicht angefangen."

„Ich habe heute einen Brief von meinem Vater bekommen. Er behauptet, meinen letzten Brief nicht bekommen zu haben."

„Ich habe Paula lange nicht gesehen. Ich hoffe, sie ist nicht gestorben."—
15 „Sie kann nicht gestorben sein, denn ich habe sie erst vor einer Stunde gesehen."

Nachdem Antonio lange gewartet hatte, stand Laurella plötzlich vor ihm.

Kaum hatte Meyer sein Geld bekommen, da verlor er es.

Als Hildegard und Paul in die Kirche gegangen waren, kam Erich und
20 wartete, bis sie wieder herauskamen.

„Darf ich dich um eine Tasse Kaffee bitten? Ich bin eine ganze Stunde durch diesen Regen gelaufen und durch und durch kalt geworden."

„Wenn du mir einen Gefallen tun willst, so kaufe mir auf dem Nachhauseweg ein Buch, damit ich Sonntag etwas zu lesen habe."

VOCABULARY

anfangen to begin, start
ankommen to arrive
der Bart the *beard*
eben, soeben just now
die Ehe the marriage
einzeln single, individual
empfangen to receive
entschließen (*refl.*) to decide
erklären to explain; declare
etwa about; perhaps

frei *free*; vacant
sich freuen to be glad
genau exact, precise
die Gesellschaft the company; party
greifen to seize; reach; grasp
der Grund the *ground*; cause; reason
heißen to be called; call; command
hoch (hoh-) *high*, tall
der Kaffee the *coffee*
die Linie the *line*
die Luft the air
der Mantel the cloak, *mantle*
merken to *mark*, note
der Monat the *month*
nachdem after (*conj.*)
die Nase the *nose*
die Person the *person*
der Pfennig the *penny*
der Regen the *rain*
ruhen to rest
der Schreck(en) the fright
der See the lake
die See the *sea*, ocean
spitz pointed, acute
die Stadt the city, town
stark strong; stout; heavy
sterben to die
die Stimme the voice
der Sturm the *storm*, tempest
die Tasche the pocket
die Tasse the cup
trinken to *drink*
überhaupt at all, on the whole
verlangen to demand, require; desire
vollkommen complete, perfect
vorher before, previously
wagen to dare, risk
wiederholen to repeat (*insep. prefix*)
zählen to count
zuhören (*sep. prefix*) to listen

IDIOMS

beim Aufstehen in standing up
beim Aussteigen in getting out, off
das heißt that is to say
es tut mir leid I am sorry
greifen nach to reach for
jawohl yes, indeed
sonst noch etwas anything (something) else
vor einer Stunde an hour ago
vor einer Woche a week ago
eine Woche lang for a week
eine Zeitlang for a time

TEXT B

Der Herr mit der großen roten Nase

Es ist nicht unsere Schuld, daß wir soviel Zeit gebraucht haben, um Paul und Hildegard vor den Altar zu bringen. Denn was kann man machen? Wer eine Geschichte schreibt, muß Held und Heldin nehmen, wie Gott sie gemacht hat. Und Paul und Hildegard hatte er leider etwas zurückhaltend gemacht. Auf jeden Fall waren sie nicht so stürmisch wie Laurella 5 und Antonio geworden. Wirklich, wir hatten eine Zeitlang selber alle Hoffnung aufgegeben und sind nun mehr als froh, sie endlich zusammengebracht zu haben.

Wir können nun in Ruhe auf Meyer zurückkommen. Jawohl, auf Gustav mit dem schneeweißen Odontoscheingebiß.[1]—Weder er noch seine Frau ist inzwischen gestorben oder ins Wasser gefallen. Auch in Neuyork sind sie nie angekommen. Hören Sie zu!

Meyer fuhr gleich am nächsten Morgen, nachdem er für sein Urteil den Preis gewonnen hatte, in die Stadt, um sein Geld zu holen. Und zwar mit dem Omnibus und nicht mit seinem kleinen Auto. Und das war so gekommen:

Gustav hatte mit Paula, seiner Frau, (Hatten wir Ihnen schon erzählt, daß seine Frau Paula heißt?) einen kleinen Wortwechsel gehabt. Seine Frau nämlich hatte am Abend vorher in der Garage eine Glasvase zerbrochen, und Gustav war mit seinem Auto in das Glas gefahren. Das heißt, nach Paulas Behauptung war der Boden der Garage vollkommen frei von Glas gewesen. Sie erinnerte sich genau, jedes einzelne Stückchen aufgehoben zu haben und konnte sich nicht erklären, wie trotzdem ein Glasstück in Gustavs Vorderreifen[2] gekommen war. Gustav konnte es sich auch nicht erklären und wagte—wagte ist das richtige Wort—die Behauptung: „Dann hast du nicht jedes einzelne Stückchen aufgehoben." Aber er hatte diese vollkommen grundlose (?) Behauptung kaum ausgesprochen, da tat es ihm schon leid, überhaupt etwas gesagt zu haben. Er sagte also gar nichts mehr, hörte still zu und wartete, bis seiner Paula, genau wie seinem Vorderreifen, die Luft ausging. Dann nahm er den Omnibus.

Und das war der Anfang vom Ende.

Das heißt, zuerst ging alles gut. Der Direktor der Odontoschein-Gesellschaft, ein alter Herr, dem sein Odontoschein die Jugend nicht zurückgebracht hatte, empfing Gustav persönlich, gab ihm die fünfhundert (500) Mark, und um zehn (10) Uhr saß Gustav schon wieder im Omnibus.

Nun sind fünfhundert Mark nicht einfach fünfhundert Mark. Man kann sie zum Beispiel gern oder ungern ausgeben. Schon mancher verliebte junge Mann hat gern seinen letzten Pfennig für das Lächeln eines schönen Mädchens ausgegeben; schon mancher Reisende in schwerem Sturm auf hoher See (hat) der Kirche all sein Geld wenigstens versprochen. Aber was ist das Lächeln eines Mädchens, was (ist) die Ruhe nach dem Sturm gegen den

Sonnenschein, der in jeder Ehe auf kurzen, starken Regen folgt! Und da in jeder Ehe die Sonne scheint, wenn der Mann mit fünfhundert Mark nach Hause kommt, dachte Gustav nicht mehr an das Glas, in das er mit seinem Auto gefahren (war), nicht mehr an den kalten Regen, der auf ihn herabgekommen war. Er dachte nur an den warmen Sonnenschein, den er für fünfhundert Mark von seiner Paula erwartete.

Kein Wunder, daß er in Erwartung dieses Glücks oft nach seiner Brieftasche[3] griff, um das Geld noch einmal zu zählen. Kein Wunder, daß er die Brieftasche, gerade als der Omnibus hielt, mit einem zufriedenen Lächeln auf dem Gesicht nicht in seine *Tasche*, sondern zwischen Rock und Regenmantel steckte[4] und dann ausstieg. Kein Wunder auch, daß Gustav, gerade als der Omnibus um die nächste Ecke gefahren war, plötzlich schneeweiß wurde und schnell in ein Café ging und einen Whisky verlangte.

Aber erst nachdem er auch eine Tasse Kaffee getrunken hatte, merkte er, daß ihm gegenüber ein Herr am Tisch saß, ein Herr mit einem spitzen Bart und einer großen roten Nase. „Denken Sie nur", meinte Gustav, der sich freute, jemand gefunden zu haben, mit dem er reden konnte, „ich habe eben im Omnibus eine Brieftasche mit fünfhundert Mark verloren."—„Eine Brieftasche mit fünfhundert Mark?" wiederholte der spitze Bart. „Aber läuft ein vernünftiger Mensch mit fünfhundert Mark in der Brieftasche herum*?"—„Nein", sagte Gustav, „ein vernünftiger Mensch nicht. Aber ich bin mit dem Geld auch nicht herumgelaufen. Ich hatte es gerade geholt und wollte nach Hause fahren. Schrecklich, noch vor zehn (10) Minuten habe ich die Brieftasche im Omnibus in der Hand gehabt. Dann bin ich hier an der Ecke ausgestiegen und habe sogleich gemerkt, daß ich sie verloren hatte. Jemand muß sie mir beim Aussteigen gestohlen[5] haben. Vielleicht habe ich sie auch nicht richtig in die Rocktasche gesteckt,[4] und sie ist beim Aufstehen auf den Boden gefallen."—„War sonst noch etwas in der Brieftasche?" fragte der Herr mit der roten Nase. „Nein, gar nichts", antwortete Gustav, „es war eine neue, schwarze Brieftasche, die mir meine Frau erst letzten Monat geschenkt hat und die ich sonst nie gebrauche."

„Nun", meinte die große Nase, „trösten Sie sich! Vielleicht hat sie jemand gefunden, der ehrlich ist. Warten Sie bis heute abend! Dann gehen Sie zum Fundbüro[6] der Omnibuslinie! Vielleicht gibt der Finder sie da ab."

---

*See § 144.

Noch lange, fast eine ganze Stunde, saß Gustav allein an seinem Tisch. Dann kam er plötzlich zu einem Entschluß. „Vielleicht", sagte er sich, „hat irgendein ehrlicher Mensch das Geld schon abgegeben."

Er stand auf und ging zum Telephon. „Hier[7] Gustav Meyer!" sagte er. 5 „Ich habe vor etwa einer Stunde hier an der Ecke beim Aussteigen eine schwarze Brieftasche mit fünfhundert Mark verloren. Hat sie vielleicht jemand schon abgegeben?"—„Jawohl!" kam eine Stimme durchs Telephon zurück. „Aber ein Herr mit einem spitzen Bart und einer großen roten Nase hat vor einer halben Stunde dieselbe Geschichte erzählt, und ihm haben wir 10 sie gegeben." Da hing Gustav den Hörer ab[8]; sein Glaube an Ehrlichkeit und Menschenliebe war für immer zerbrochen.

NOTES. 1. See Lessons II and III. 2. Vorderreifen front tire. 3. Brieftasche wallet, billfold. 4. steckte, gesteckt put. 5. gestohlen stolen. 6. Fundbüro lost-and-found office. 7. Hier This is. 8. hing . . . ab hung up.

BUILDING A PASSIVE VOCABULARY

abgeben ab off, away, geben to give, abgeben to turn in
ausgeben aus out, geben to give, ausgeben to spend
ausgesprochen aus out, sprechen to speak, aussprechen to utter
aussteigen aus out, off, steigen to climb (*here* get), aussteigen to get off
Ehrlichkeit ehrlich honest, die Ehrlichkeit (the) honesty
inzwischen in in, zwischen between, inzwischen meanwhile
persönlich die Person the person, persönlich personally
die Ruhe, in Ruhe ruhen to rest, in Ruhe in peace
schrecklich der Schreck the fright, schrecklich frightful, awful
stürmisch der Sturm the storm, stürmisch stormy, emotional
verliebt lieben to love, verliebt in love
wenigstens wenig few, wenigstens at least
Wortwechsel Wort word, wechseln to exchange, Wortwechsel exchange of words, argument
zerbrochen brechen to break, zerbrechen to shatter, zerbrochen shattered
zurückhaltend zurück back, haltend holding, zurückhaltend reserved, bashful

GRAMMAR

76. The Compound Tenses. Both English and German have six tenses: the present, *I sing* ich singe; the past, *I sang* ich sang; the present perfect, *I have sung* ich habe gesungen; the past perfect,

I had sung ich hatte geſungen; the future; and the future perfect. This lesson deals with the present perfect and past perfect tenses.

To form the present perfect, English always employs as the auxiliary the present tense of the verb *to have* together with the past participle of the main verb:

I have eaten, you have eaten, he has eaten.

In the past perfect the same auxiliary, *to have*, is used in the past tense:

I had eaten, you had eaten, he had eaten.

German uses two auxiliaries in a similar way to form these two tenses:

a. Haben is used with all transitive and most intransitive verbs.

b. Sein is used with those intransitive verbs, both weak and strong, which show a change of position or condition of the subject* (gehen, laufen, ſtürzen, werden, ſterben). Sein and bleiben are exceptions to this rule and take ſein.

NOTE. In German only verbs which can take an *accusative* object are considered to be transitive. Thus folgen and begegnen, which take a dative object, are intransitive and take ſein.

The student is already familiar with the auxiliaries of the strong verbs which have been introduced. Those which have hat as the third element of the principal parts take haben (er hat gegeſſen); those which have iſt take ſein (er iſt nach Hauſe gegangen). Examples:

PRESENT PERFECT

Auxiliary haben			*Auxiliary* ſein		
ich	habe	gegeſſen, gelacht	ich	bin	gelaufen, gefallen
du	haſt	gegeſſen, gelacht	du	biſt	gelaufen, gefallen
er	hat	gegeſſen, gelacht	er	iſt	gelaufen, gefallen

*Cf. Matthew 8:1, "When he *was* come down from the mountain . . ."; John 20:17, ". . . for I *am* not yet ascended to my Father . . ."

wir haben	gegeſſen, gelacht	wir ſind	gelaufen, gefallen
ihr habt	gegeſſen, gelacht	ihr ſeid	gelaufen, gefallen
ſie haben	gegeſſen, gelacht	ſie ſind	gelaufen, gefallen

I have eaten, laughed
you have eaten, laughed,
etc.

I have run, fallen
you have run, fallen,
etc.

PAST PERFECT

ich hatte	gegeſſen, gelacht	ich war	gelaufen, gefallen
du hatteſt	gegeſſen, gelacht	du warſt	gelaufen, gefallen
er hatte	gegeſſen, gelacht	er war	gelaufen, gefallen
wir hatten	gegeſſen, gelacht	wir waren	gelaufen, gefallen
ihr hattet	gegeſſen, gelacht	ihr wart	gelaufen, gefallen
ſie hatten	gegeſſen, gelacht	ſie waren	gelaufen, gefallen

I had eaten, laughed
you had eaten, laughed,
etc.

I had run, fallen
you had run, fallen,
etc.

77. Position of Auxiliary, Past Participle, and Past Infinitive

I. *The Auxiliary.* In compound tenses the auxiliary is the inflected verb and is the first, second, or last element in the clause as stated in paragraphs 6, 7, and 27.

a. Verb-first position:

Haſt du heute ſchon gegeſſen? Have you already eaten today?

b. Verb-second position:

Ich habe heute ſchon gegeſſen. I have already eaten today.
Was haſt du heute gegeſſen? What did you eat today?

c. Verb-last position:

Ich wußte nicht, daß du heute ſchon gegeſſen hatteſt. I didn't know that you had already eaten today.

II. *The Past Participle.* The past participle stands at the end of the clause except in dependent clauses, when it precedes the inflected verb. See examples above.

III. *The Past Infinitive.* A form like "to have lost" (he is said to have lost) or "have eaten" (I believe he must have eaten) is called a past infinitive. In German when this form is used, the past participle comes first and the auxiliary comes last. Examples:

Er freute sich, jemand gefunden zu haben. He was happy to have found somebody.
Es tat ihm leid, etwas gesagt zu haben. He was sorry to have said anything.
Er kann nicht gestorben sein. He can't have died. (Note the omission of zu after modals (cf. § 17).)

Note that the past infinitive, like the present infinitive, stands at the end of its phrase or clause.

78. Past Participles of Separable Compounds. The prefix of separable compounds precedes the participle and is written with it as one word:

abgelaufen, untergegangen, heraufgekommen, zusammengestellt

Sie haben schon abgestoßen. They have already shoved off.
Das Schiff ist untergegangen. The ship has sunk.

79. Verbs with Inseparable Prefixes. Verbs with the unaccented prefixes be= (bekommen), emp= (empfangen), ent= (entkommen), er= (erfahren), ge= (gefallen), ver= (versprechen), zer= (zerbrechen) are conjugated like other verbs except that the past participle does not add the ge= prefix. (Verbs in =ieren also form the past participle without the ge= prefix.) Examples:

Er hat mir nichts versprochen. He has promised me nothing.
Er hat leider nichts bekommen. Unfortunately he got nothing.
Er ist nicht entkommen. He hasn't escaped.

80. Omission or Suppression of the Auxiliary. When two past participles take the same auxiliary form, only one of the auxiliaries need be expressed; the other is felt to be superfluous and is sometimes omitted:

Schon mancher junge Mann hat seinen letzten Pfennig ausgegeben, schon mancher Reisende (hat) der Kirche sein ganzes Geld versprochen. Many a young man has spent his last penny; many a traveler has promised the church all his money.

Aber was ist das Lächeln eines Mädchens, was (ist) die Ruhe nach dem Sturm gegen . . . But what is the smile of a girl, what is the calm after the storm in comparison with . . .

Er dachte an die Frau, die er geliebt, und an den Mann, den er gehaßt hatte. He thought of the woman whom he had loved and of the man whom he had hated.

A single auxiliary in dependent clauses is sometimes omitted when the auxiliary is clearly understood:

Ich warf noch einmal einen Blick auf die Bank, wo Minna und ich Hand in Hand so oft gesessen. (Hatten is clearly understood.) I cast once more a look at the bench where Minna and I, hand in hand, had sat so often.

81. Use of the Past and Present Perfect Tenses. The past tense is used:

a. When the speaker is narrating a series of connected events in the past:

Paul nahm den Hut ab, sah auf das Band, sah auf Hildegard, sah wieder auf das Band und sagte leise . . . Paul took off his hat, looked at the ribbon, looked at Hildegard, looked at the ribbon again, and said softly . . . .

Schlaflos lag Antonio auf seinem Bett. Der Mond schien durch das Fenster. Da hörte er einen leichten Tritt vor seiner Tür. Er stand auf und öffnete. Laurella stand vor ihm. Antonio lay sleepless on his bed. The moon shone through the window. Then he heard a light step before his door. He stood up and opened it. Laurella stood before him.

b. When English uses the past perfect to denote what had been and still was (at a given moment in the past):

Ich kannte ihn seit langer Zeit. I had known him for a long time.

The present perfect, which occurs more often in German than in English, is used:

a. When English uses the present perfect:

Ich habe ihn noch nicht gesehen. I have not yet seen him. Was hast du getan? What have you done?

But see § 21.

b. When the speaker does not narrate a series of past events in their succession but reports an event just as a fact, detaching it from its context:

Herr Müller ist letzten Monat gestorben. Mr. Müller died last month.
Goethe hat ein langes Leben gehabt. Goethe had a long life.

▭

Learn or review the principal parts of the following verbs:

beißen	biß	hat gebissen	beißt	to bite
greifen	griff	hat gegriffen	greift	to seize
schließen	schloß	hat geschlossen	schließt	to close
entschließen	entschloß	hat entschlossen	entschließt	to decide
sinken	sank	ist gesunken	sinkt	to sink
trinken	trank	hat getrunken	trinkt	to drink
helfen	half	hat geholfen	hilft	to help
sterben	starb	ist gestorben	stirbt	to die
heißen	hieß	hat geheißen	heißt	to be called
anfangen	fing an	hat angefangen	fängt an	to begin
empfangen	empfing	hat empfangen	empfängt	to receive
ankommen	kām an	ist angekommen	kommt an	to arrive

EXERCISES

I

Answer in German: 1. Wie muß man Held und Heldin nehmen? 2. War Paul zurückhaltend? 3. War auch Hildegard leider etwas zurückhaltend? 4. Wer war nicht so stürmisch wie Laurella und Antonio geworden? 5. Sind Gustav und seine Frau in Neuyork angekommen? 6. Wann fuhr Meyer in die Stadt, um sein Geld zu holen? 7. Wie heißt Gustavs Frau? 8. Mit wem hatte Gustav einen Wortwechsel gehabt? 9. Was hatte Paula in der Garage zerbrochen? 10. Wie war der Garagenboden nach Paulas Behauptung gewesen? 11. Wer wagte eine Behauptung? 12. War die Behauptung vollkommen grundlos? 13. Wem ging die Luft aus? 14. Wie ging alles zuerst? 15. Wer empfing Gustav persönlich? 16. Für was hat mancher verliebte junge Mann seinen letzten Pfennig ausgegeben? 17. Was hat mancher Reisende der Kirche wenigstens versprochen? 18. Was erwartete Gustav von Paula? 19. Warum griff Gustav oft nach seiner Brieftasche? 20. Wohin steckte Herr Meyer die Brieftasche? 21. Wie wurde Gustav, als der Omnibus um die nächste Ecke gefahren war? 22. Wohin ging Gustav schnell? 23. Was verlangte er? 24. Warum freute sich Gustav? 25. Wohin war die Brieftasche gefallen? 26. Wer hatte Gustav die Brieftasche geschenkt? 27. Wohin sollte Gustav gehen? 28. Wie lange saß Gustav am Tisch? 29. Wer hatte dieselbe Geschichte erzählt? 30. Wessen Glaube an Menschenliebe und Ehrlichkeit war für immer zerbrochen?

II

Translate into German the following sentences, using in the first eleven sentences the present perfect: 1. What did you do with the pencil? 2. Has he already eaten? 3. Why did you ask? 4. He has not come yet. 5. Have you seen her? 6. Did they jump into the water? 7. She has forgotten her hat. 8. My father has written an interesting book. 9. I went to the city. 10. Unfortunately I did not hear him. 11. The old man died last week. 12. He has been working the entire morning (cf. § 21). 13. He has been sleeping since Sunday.

III

Translate into English:

das Stück	leise	hindern	verdienen	verkaufen	das Meer
retten	der Hafen	heben	der Hof	die Wand	leider
rechnen	heute	töten	kaufen	seit	schon

IV

Translate into German:

the apple	the door	black	everything
often	the blood	the forest	nothing
where	the moon	to show	good
who	the night	to try	bad
how			the book

V

Translate into English:

das Mäntelchen, unmerklich, monatlich, der Winterregen; die Ruhe, ruhen; das Taschentuch, trinkbar, das Verlangen, die Wiederholung, unzählbar; der Zuhörer, die Zuhörerin; der Empfang, empfangen; bartlos; der Ehemann, die Ehefrau, das Eheglück; entschließen, der Entschluß; anfangen, der Anfang, der Anfänger; der Empfänger; die Erklärung, unerklärlich; das Gesellschafts- 5 spiel; der Grund, grundlos; hochheben, hochhalten; der Kaffeetrinker, das Kaffeehaus, die Kaffeetasse; das Luftschiff, die Luftlinie

VI

Translate into English:

auf jeden Fall	bitten um	zum letzten Mal	danke schön
einen Monat lang	zum Beispiel	das heißt	warten auf

VII

In each blank supply the proper form of the auxiliary to form the present perfect tense (as, ich habe geantwortet):

ich ----- gearbeitet	ihr ----- genommen
er ----- behauptet	sie (they) ----- getragen
Sie ----- gebeten	ich ----- geblieben
sie (she) ----- gefallen	er ----- gestorben
ihr ----- gegangen	die Sonne ----- untergegangen
er ----- vergessen	sie (she) ----- geweint

VIII

In each blank, as in VII, supply the proper form of the auxiliary to form the past perfect (as, ich hatte gewonnen):

er _____ gebunden
er _____ gehalten
wir _____ verloren
ich _____ geweſen
ihr _____ geſchoben
ſie (they) _____ gefallen
wir _____ gefahren
ſie (they) _____ ſchon angefangen
er _____ noch nicht abgeſtoßen

IX

Conjugate in the present perfect and past perfect tenses:

tun ſprechen werden wachſen warten ſein haben

X

Give the third person singular of the present, past, present perfect, and past perfect tenses (as, er geht, er ging, er iſt geganaen, er war gegangen):

fragen	bringen	helfen	haben
treten	wiſſen	leſen	ſein

XI

Translate the following sentences and explain the use of the auxiliary verb in each:

a. Ich bin nach der Schule ſogleich nach Hauſe gelaufen.
b. Er hat heute ein (1) Kilometer in drei (3) Minuten gelaufen.
c. Das Pferd hat den Wagen von Hamburg nach Berlin gezogen.
d. Ich bin von Berlin nach Hamburg gezogen.

XII

Review all the words introduced through Lesson XII. See pages 319–323.

LESSON XIII

TEXT A

Heute muß ich früh zu Bett gehen. Heute ist Freitag, und ich muß früh zu Bett. Am Dienstag mußte ich früh zu Bett gehen. Auch am Mittwoch habe ich früh zu Bett gemußt. Am Donnerstag habe ich früh zu Bett gehen müssen. Jawohl, ich muß immer früh zu Bett.

Er wollte nicht. Er hat nicht gewollt. Er wollte nicht arbeiten. Er hat nicht arbeiten wollen. Ich habe die ganze Nacht nicht geschlafen. Ich habe die ganze Nacht nicht schlafen können.

Ich habe ihn nie gehört. Ich habe ihn nie reden hören. Ich habe sie nie gesehen. Ich habe sie nie tanzen (dance) sehen.

Ich ließ ihn kommen. Ich habe ihn kommen lassen. Er ließ ihn ohne Geld nach Hause fahren. Er hat ihn ohne Geld nach Hause fahren lassen. Ich konnte ihn nicht ohne Geld nach Hause fahren lassen. Ich habe ihn nicht ohne Geld nach Hause fahren lassen können.

Er muß es getan haben. Er muß sie Freitag gesehen haben. Er soll nach Deutschland gefahren sein. Frau Schmidt soll am Sonnabend gestorben sein. Meyer soll sein Geld verloren haben. Er hat es nicht verlieren müssen. Schulz ist reich und hat nie arbeiten müssen.

Diesen Kaffee kann ich dir empfehlen. Er *riecht* nicht nur frisch, er *ist* auch frisch.—Ich kann nicht soviel reisen wie du. Ich habe immer für meine Familie sorgen müssen.

Ich habe heute im Traum mein Mädchen geküßt.—Ich träume leider nie. Aber warum küßt du sie nur im Traum?—Sie ist stolz und trotzig und hat sich noch von niemand küssen lassen.

Bist du gefallen? Du blutest ja am Knie.

Wir haben Paul und Hildegard nicht sehr schnell vor den Altar bringen können. Mit Laurella und Antonio haben wir es leichter gehabt.

Antonio hat das Mädchen leider nicht ans Land tragen können.

Kleinkopf hat den schweren Sack nicht lange tragen müssen. Denn der Sack wurde sehr schnell leicht.

Meyer wollte seiner Frau das Geld bringen. Er hat Paula das Geld bringen wollen.

VOCABULARY

angenehm agreeable, pleasant
außerordentlich extraordinary
der Brief the letter
der Bruder the *brother*
das Dach the roof
dunkel dark, obscure
edel noble; lofty
eilen to hasten, hurry
empfehlen to recommend
erlauben to *allow*, permit
der Garten the *garden*
geboren *born*
gemein *mean*, common; general
gering slight; inferior
gesund healthy, *sound*
das Gold the *gold*
das Gras the *grass*
grau *gray*
herbei here, hither
herrlich excellent, splendid
hervor forth, out
jedoch however
klingeln to ring
klopfen to knock, beat, pound
das Knie the *knee*
leiden to suffer; tolerate
messen to *measure*
die Milch the *milk*
der Nachbar the *neighbor*
nachher afterwards
nieder low; mean; down
der Punkt the *point*, period, dot
reich *rich*
reichen to *reach*; hand to; suffice
der Schatten the *shade*; *shadow*
der Schatz the treasure; beloved
schätzen to value, estimate
schmecken to taste
sicher safe; certain, steady
sorgen to care
stecken to *stick*; put (in pocket); pin
stolz proud (Stolz pride)
der Teufel *devil*
träumen to *dream*
-wärts (aufwärts) *-ward, -wards* (*upwards*)
die Weile the *while*, space (of time)
die Welt the *world*
wohl *well*; no doubt
ziemlich rather; considerable
das Zimmer the room
zurückkehren (*sep. prefix*), return
der Zweck the purpose (use)

IDIOMS

auch wenn (wenn auch) even if
auf der Stelle at once, on the spot
sich auf den Weg machen to set out, start
vorwärtskommen to get ahead
zuerst at first

TEXT B

Einem neugeborenen Kind kann man leider nicht gleich am ersten Tage Sauerkraut geben. Das heißt, man kann schon, aber es hat nicht viel Zweck. Man gibt ihm zuerst besser Milch. Nach etwa einem Monat kann man dann mit dem Spinat[1] anfangen, und noch viel später bringt man das erste Sauerkraut auf den Tisch.

Mit Ihnen haben wir, wenn wir uns so ausdrücken dürfen, genau dasselbe getan und tun müssen; wir haben auch Ihnen zuerst Milch gegeben und Sie „ich gehe, du gehst, er geht" lernen lassen. Mit blutendem Herzen (!) haben wir Sie beim Dativ schreien hören—und einfach schreien lassen. Mit väterlichem Stolz (!) haben wir Sie wachsen sehen und Ihnen—Sie haben recht, es war gemein—schon beim Genitiv den ersten Spinat[1] gegeben. Der Erfolg war besser, als wir erwartet hatten. Natürlich haben Sie den Spinat zuerst kaum essen können, vielleicht auch, seien Sie ehrlich, nicht essen wollen. Aber jetzt schmeckt er schon ganz gut, und es wird Zeit, das Sauerkraut auf den Tisch zu bringen.

Peter Schlemihl*

In Afrika, den 1. Juli 17—.

Mein lieber Freund!

Ich weiß, Du hast Deinen Peter Schlemihl nicht vergessen, auch wenn ich Dich seit langer Zeit nicht mehr habe sehen dürfen. „Und warum", fragst Du, „hast du mich nicht sehen dürfen?" Ich überreiche Dir hiermit die Geschichte meines Lebens. Lies sie und urteile nicht zu hart über einen Freund, dessen Leben durch seine eigene Schuld ein einziges Leiden gewesen ist. „Gewesen ist", denn ich bin am Ende meiner Kraft und dem Tode nahe.

Dein

Peter Schlemihl.

. . . .

Nach einer stürmischen und für mich sehr unangenehmen Seefahrt erreichten wir endlich den Hafen, und froh, wieder festen Boden unter mir zu haben, ging ich sogleich in den „Goldenen Löwen",[2] wo mich der Hausdiener nach einem schnellen Blick auf meine Kleidung in ein kleines Zimmer unter dem Dach führte. Da es noch früh am Tage war, holte ich sogleich meinen

*We found it quite impossible to avoid taking liberties in the retelling of this *Novelle* by Adelbert von Chamisso (1781–1838). The story is fantastic in nature. Just what the Schatten symbolizes, no one seems to know. Perhaps it would be wisest to follow Chamisso's advice and simply not hunt for a solution.

neu gewendeten schwarzen Rock hervor, steckte den Empfehlungsbrief an Herrn John in die Tasche und machte mich auf den Weg zu diesem Manne, der mir, wie ich hoffte, helfen sollte, in der Welt vorwärtszukommen.

Es dauerte nicht lang, und ich konnte das helle Rot und Weiß des großen Steinhauses durch das Grüne sehen. Mit klopfendem Herzen zog ich die Klingel. Die Tür sprang auf. Ein Diener maß mich und meinen gewendeten Rock mit einem nicht sehr freundlichen Blick, verschwand jedoch, als er meinen Empfehlungsbrief sah, und führte mich, nachdem ich eine Zeitlang hatte warten müssen, in den Park, wo Herr John einer kleinen Gesellschaft soeben den Plan eines neuen Gartenhauses erklärte. Er empfing mich, wie ein Reicher einen armen Teufel empfängt, und ich überreichte ihm meinen Empfehlungsbrief. „So, so", sagte er, nachdem er den Brief gelesen hatte, „von meinem Bruder. Er hat mir lange nicht geschrieben. Nun, bleiben Sie hier, junger Freund, vielleicht finde ich nachher Zeit, mit Ihnen zu sprechen. Dann wollen wir sehen, was ich für Ihre Zukunft tun kann. Mein Bruder ist doch noch gesund?" Er schien jedoch keine Antwort auf diese Frage zu erwarten, denn er wandte sich wieder zu der Gesellschaft, und man ging, ohne von mir weiter Notiz[3] zu nehmen[3], einer Stelle des Parkes zu, von der man einen weiten Blick auf das Meer hatte.

Der Anblick war wirklich schön und herrlich. Am Horizont erschien zwischen dem dunkelen Grün der See und dem tiefen Blau des Himmels ein weißer Punkt. „Bring mir ein Teleskop!" rief Herr John. Aber ehe der Diener ins Haus laufen konnte, zog ein stiller, dünner, grau gekleideter Mann, der dicht vor mir stand und auch zur Gesellschaft zu gehören schien, ein langes Teleskop aus seiner Rocktasche und überreichte es Herrn John. „Ein Schiff!" rief dieser und reichte dann das Instrument seiner Nachbarin.

Während das ziemlich lange und schwere Teleskop von Hand zu Hand ging, sah ich erstaunt[4] auf den grauen Mann und konnte mir nicht erklären, wie er das große Instrument in seiner Tasche hatte haben können. Aber außer mir schien niemand etwas Außerordentliches dabei[5] zu finden.

Niemand verlor ein Wort, und niemand dankte dem Geber, als der graue Mann nach einer Weile aus derselben kleinen Rocktasche ein Fäßchen Wein, einen Tisch und schließlich sogar ein Pferd hervorzog.

Mir aber wurde die Situation so schrecklich, daß ich mich entschloß, nicht länger zu bleiben. Aber gerade als ich den Garten verlassen wollte, sah ich den grauen Mann zu meinem Schreck herbeieilen und auf mich zu-kommen. Er nahm höflich den Hut vor mir ab und sagte mit leiser, etwas unsicherer Stimme: „Ich habe soeben mit unaussprechlicher Bewunderung Ihren schönen Schatten beobachten können. Darf ich Sie bitten, mir diesen Schatten zu verkaufen?"

„Er muß nicht ganz richtig im Kopf sein", dachte ich und antwortete: 5 „Guter Freund, haben Sie denn nicht an Ihrem eigenen Schatten genug?"— Er ließ mich nicht weiterreden und sagte: „Ich habe in meiner Tasche etwas, was dem Herrn vielleicht gefällt, denn für diesen schönen, unschätzbaren Schatten ist auch der höchste Preis zu gering."

Diese Tasche! Es[6] lief mir heiß und kalt über den Rücken,[6] und ich 10 wunderte mich, wie ich ihn hatte „guter Freund" nennen können. „Aber, mein Herr[7]", nahm ich schließlich wieder das Wort, „ich verstehe Sie wohl nicht recht. Wie kann ich Ihnen denn meinen Schatten verkaufen?"— „Erlauben Sie mir nur, diesen edelen Schatten hier auf der Stelle aufzuheben und mit mir zu nehmen. Wie ich das mache, das lassen Sie meine 15 Sorge sein!" Er steckte die Hand in seinen grauen Rock und holte einen kleinen Geldsäckel[8] hervor. „Hier ist ein Glückssäckel",[9] sagte er, „vielleicht versucht der Herr ihn einmal!" Ich griff schnell in den Glückssäckel und zog ein Goldstück hervor, und wieder eins, und wieder eins, und wieder eins. „Für diesen Säckel[8] können Sie gern meinen Schatten haben!" rief ich 20 lachend. Der graue Mann aber kniete nieder, und ich sah ihn meinen Schatten leise vom Grase aufheben, zusammenrollen und zuletzt in die Rocktasche stecken. Einen Augenblick später war er im Park verschwunden. Ich glaube, ich habe ihn lachen hören.

Wie im Traum verließ ich Park und Haus und ging zur Stadt zurück, 25 die ich als armer, hilfesuchender junger Mann verlassen hatte und in die ich jetzt reich, doch ohne Schatten, zurückkehrte.

[Fortsetzung folgt]

NOTES. 1. Spinat spinach. 2. Goldenen Löwen the Golden Lion (name of inn). 3. Notiz zu nehmen pay attention to. 4. erstaunt astonished. 5. dabei in it (the act). 6. Es . . . Rücken A chill went up and down my spine. 7. mein Herr sir. 8. Geldsäckel, Säckel purse. 9. Glückssäckel magic purse.

BUILDING A PASSIVE VOCABULARY

der Anblick an at, der Blick the look, glance, der Anblick view
ausdrücken aus out (*Latin* ex), drücken to press, ausdrücken to express
die Bewunderung das Wunder the wonder, wundern to wonder, die Bewunderung the admiration
erreichen reichen to reach, hand to, erreichen to attain, gain, reach
erscheinen scheinen to shine, seem, appear, erscheinen to appear
höchst *superlative form of* hoch, highest, greatest
höflich der Hof the court, höflich courteous, polite
schließlich schließen to close, shut, conclude, schließlich finally
schrecklich der Schreck the fright, schrecklich frightful, terrible
stürmisch der Sturm the storm, stürmisch stormy
der Tod töten to kill, der Tod (the) death
überreichen über over, reichen to reach, hand over, überreichen to hand to, offer
unaussprechlich un in, aus out [*Latin* ex], sprechen to speak, utter, say, unaussprechlich inexpressible
unschätzbar schätzen to value, esteem, schätzbar estimable, unschätzbar inestimable, invaluable, priceless
verlassen lassen to let, to leave, verlassen to leave, abandon
weiter weit far, distant, weiter (*comparative form*) further. Weiter *frequently means* on; *as*, weiterreden to talk on, go on talking

GRAMMAR

82. Past Participles of Modal Auxiliaries. Each of the six modals has *two* past participles:

a. The participle which was learned in Lesson IX:

gedurft gekonnt gemocht gemußt gesollt gewollt

This form is used only when the dependent infinitive is not expressed:

Ich wollte es tun, aber ich habe es nicht gekonnt. I wanted to do it but I haven't been able to.

Warum hat er nicht gegessen? Er hat nicht gewollt. Why hasn't he eaten? He didn't want to.

b. A form without the ge- prefix which is *identical with the infinitive*:

dürfen können mögen müssen sollen wollen

This participle *always* stands last. The dependent infinitive always immediately precedes it. These two verb forms are commonly referred to as the "double infinitive." Examples:

Antonio hat das Mädchen leider nicht ans Land tragen können. Antonio was unfortunately not able to carry the girl to the land.

Ich habe dich seit langer Zeit nicht sehen dürfen. I have not been permitted to see you for a long time.

The inflected verb in dependent clauses usually comes just before the double infinitive. This is an exception to the verb-last position. Example:

Es tut mir leid, daß du es nicht hast essen können. I am sorry that you haven't been able to eat it.

Note the difference between

Er hat nicht essen können. He has not been able to eat.
Er kann nicht gegessen haben. He cannot have eaten.

83. Double Infinitive with hören, lassen, sehen. The double infinitive construction is used with a few verbs besides the modals, notably hören, lassen, and sehen. Examples:

Wir haben Sie beim Dativ schreien hören. We heard (have heard) you cry at the dative.

Wir haben Sie wachsen sehen. We have seen (watched) you grow.

Wir haben Sie einfach schreien lassen. We (have) simply let you cry.

84. Declension of das Herz and der Herr in the Singular. Both das Herz and der Herr are irregular in the singular:

das Herz	der Herr
des Herzens	des Herrn (*no* s)
dem Herzen	dem Herrn
das Herz	den Herrn

85. Word Formation: Past Participles as Adjectives and Adverbs. The past participle may be used as a predicate adjective and then, of course, requires no ending: Die Tür ist geschlossen. It may also be used and declined as an attributive adjective:

das geschriebene Wort, ein geschriebenes Wort the written word, a written word.
Er hat mir das versprochene Buch gegeben. He has given me the promised book.
Das muß einen verborgenen Zweck haben. That must have a hidden purpose.

The past participle may also be used adverbially:

Er kam unerwartet. He came unexpectedly.
Er hat es wiederholt gesagt. He has said it repeatedly.

86. Word Formation: Adjectives as Nouns. German adjectives may be used as nouns; when so used, they are capitalized, and their inflectional endings are retained:

ein Deutscher a German ein Armer a poor man
der Deutsche the German der Arme the poor man
die Schöne the beautiful girl *or* woman

Neuters are generally abstract:

das Schöne the beautiful

87. Neuter Nouns Formed from Adjectives. Adjectives modifying and forming one part of speech with etwas *something*, nichts *nothing*, viel *much*, mehr *more*, wenig *little*, and alles *everything* are (for the English-speaking student illogically) capitalized. They take strong neuter adjective endings except after alles, which governs weak endings. Examples:

Das ist etwas Außerordentliches. That is something (which is) unusual.
Verlange nichts Unmögliches. Do not expect anything (which is) impossible.
Er hatte viel Neues zu berichten. He had much (that was) new to report.
Ich wünsche dir alles Gute. I wish you everything (that is) good.

However:

Und Hildegard und Paul hatte er leider **etwas zurückhaltend** gemacht. Unfortunately he had made Hildegard and Paul somewhat bashful. (Etwas *modifies the adjective.*)

Learn or review the principal parts of the following verbs:

beißen	biß	hat gebissen	beißt	to bite
leiden	litt	hat gelitten	leidet	to suffer
nehmen	nāhm	hat genommen	nimmt	to take
empfēhlen	empfāhl	hat empfōhlen	empfiehlt	to recommend
essen	āß	hat gegessen	ißt	to eat
messen	māß	hat gemessen	mißt	to measure

EXERCISES

I

Answer in German: 1. Was kann man einem neugeborenen Kind nicht gleich am ersten Tage geben? 2. Was gibt man ihm zuerst? 3. Wann kann man mit dem Spinat anfangen? 4. Wann bringt man das erste Sauerkraut auf den Tisch? 5. Was hat man Ihnen zuerst gegeben? 6. Wann haben Sie geschrieen? 7. War es gemein, Ihnen so früh den ersten Spinat zu geben? 8. Was haben Sie zuerst nicht essen wollen? 9. Fürchten Sie sich vor dem Sauerkraut? 10. Wo hat Peter die Geschichte geschrieben? 11. Wie soll der Freund urteilen? 12. Wer ist am Ende seiner Kraft? 13. Wie war die Seefahrt? 14. Wer war froh, wieder festen Boden unter sich zu haben? 15. Wohin führte der Diener Peter? 16. Warum machte Peter sich sogleich auf den Weg zu Herrn John? 17. War sein Rock neu? 18. Was steckte Peter in die Tasche? 19. Wohin führte der Diener unseren Freund? 20. Empfing Herr John Peter freundlich? 21. Von wem war der Empfehlungsbrief? 22. Was erschien am Horizont? 23. Wer zog ein Teleskop aus der Tasche? 24. Wem überreichte Herr John das Instrument? 25. Zog der Graue nur ein Teleskop aus seiner Tasche? 26. Warum entschloß sich Peter, die Gesellschaft zu verlassen? 27. Was hatte der Mann beobachten können? 28. Wer wollte Peters Schatten kaufen? 29. Wo hatte der Mann den Glückssäckel? 30. Was tat er mit Peters Schatten? 31. Wie verließ Peter Haus und Park?

II

Translate into German: 1. He has not been able to eat since Sunday. 2. He has fallen into the snow. 3. She has had to work every day. 4. When are you coming? 5. Naturally I have wanted to do it. 6. Has he been permitted to see her? 7. He was a beaten man. 8. Give him everything* you have. 9. I have sent him my last penny. 10. Stuttgart is a fast-growing city. 11. I have forgotten my watch. 12. I know Mr. Miller, your old friend. 13. Although I have wanted to go since Tuesday, I have had no time.

III

Translate into English:

steigen	der Boden	daher	richtig	verwandeln	hell
reizen	bezahlen	damit	schlank	der Markt	zwar
beißen	bis	riechen	heilig	die Lösung	nahe

IV

Translate into German:

the rain	to marry	the spring	complete
the city	March	ready	to listen
the line	July	the voice	together
last	to console	the cup	definitely

V

Translate the following compounds and derivatives:

der Regenmantel; du bist mein Augapfel; grasgrün; die Bruderliebe; das Hausdach; der Traum, träumen, der Träumer; der Briefträger; er ist der Letzte in der Klasse; ein viel gelesenes Buch; unerklärlich; beißen, der Biß; unentschlossen; greifen, der Griff; nachbarlich; meßbar; ein vielsagender Blick; 5 ein Täßchen Kaffee; das Veilchen; zwecklos; brüderlich; der Kuß, küssen; er war ausgesprochen unfreundlich; himmelblau, dunkelrot; ein Armer, der Reiche, eine Deutsche; das Nasenbluten

---

*Cf. §37, page 53.

VI

Translate into English:

morgen früh	das heißt	zum letzten Mal	noch nicht	noch immer
auf Wiedersehen	noch einmal	es tut mir leid	heute morgen	gar nichts

VII

Conjugate in the present perfect and past perfect tenses:

ich habe arbeiten müssen
ich habe teilen wollen
ich habe nicht sprechen dürfen
ich habe nicht schlafen können
ich habe jeden Tag gehen wollen
ich habe ihn kommen sehen
ich habe ihn reden hören

VIII

Underline the double infinitives in Text A and Text B.

IX [Review]

In each blank supply the correct relative pronoun: 1. Dies ist das Kind, _____ Bett zu kurz ist. 2. Eine Frau, _____ Hut grün ist, muß einen neuen Hut kaufen. 3. Ist das die Gans, _____ du verkaufen willst? 4. Ist das der Herr, _____ Frau so schön ist? 5. Das Buch, _____ sie jetzt liest, ist interessant. 6. Ich komme gerade aus einer Klasse, in _____ man nicht lachen darf. 7. Er ist der Herr, _____ ich mein ganzes Geld gegeben habe. 8. Er hat den Apfel, _____ ich essen wollte.

X

Change all nouns to corresponding (personal) pronouns: 1. Die Frau hilft dem Mann. 2. Frau Meyer macht eine Reise. 3. Herr Meyer liest die Zeitung. 4. Anna sitzt neben Frank. 5. Paul glaubt nicht an den Teufel. 6. Hans kann die Geschichte nicht verstehen.

LESSON XIV

TEXT A

„Mutter, darf ich ein Stückchen Apfelkuchen haben?"—„Nein, mein Kind, jetzt nicht. Wir essen gleich, und wenn du jetzt Apfelkuchen ißt, magst du nachher nichts mehr essen."—„Was gibt es denn heute abend?"—„Du weißt doch, Vater hat eine Gans geschossen."—„Ach ja! Nun, dann kannst du mir noch ein Stück Apfelkuchen geben. Gans mag ich immer, auch wenn ich schon Apfelkuchen gegessen habe. Hm! Der Kuchen schmeckt heute nicht so gut wie sonst."—„Die Äpfel für den Kuchen habe ich in dem kleinen Geschäft an der Ecke gekauft. Sie sind hart und noch ganz grün. Frau Müller, wo kaufen Sie Ihre Äpfel?"—„Wir brauchen keine Äpfel zu kaufen. Wir haben im Garten einen großen Apfelbaum (apple tree). Ihre Kleine hat übrigens einen guten Appetit, Frau Schmidt. Essen Ihre anderen Töchter auch so gut?"—„Nein, junge Mädchen über vierzehn (14) wollen schlank bleiben."—„Seit wann wohnen Sie in diesem Hause, Frau Schmidt?"—„Seit etwa einem Jahre, Frau Müller. Unser altes Haus hatte nur drei (3) Schlafzimmer und wurde uns langsam zu klein. Jetzt haben wir ein Schlafzimmer mehr. Leider sind die Böden in allen Zimmern so alt, daß wir im ganzen Haus Linoleum legen lassen müssen."—„Die Gärten in dieser Straße sind so schön, Frau Schmidt."—„Ich hoffe, der Winter kommt dieses Jahr nicht wieder so früh. Die letzten drei (3) Winter waren wirklich kalt."

„Aber Maria, du hast schon wieder das Licht im Spielzimmer brennen lassen. Deck jetzt den Tisch!"

Die Statistik zeigt, daß nach einem großen Kriege immer mehr Jungens[1] als Mädchen auf die Welt kommen. Die Natur verbessert die Fehler, die wir in unserer Unvernunft machen.

Trauere nicht um etwas, was du nicht ändern kannst! Laß die Vergangenheit Vergangenheit sein und denke an die Zukunft!

NOTE. 1. Jungens boys. (This is one of the very *few* nouns in German that form their plural in -s.)

LESSON XIV

VOCABULARY

bald soon
befehlen to command
bewegen to move, budge
brennen to *burn*
der Bürger the citizen, *burgher*
decken to cover; set (table)
dort there
der Durst the *thirst*
einschlafen to go to sleep
fehlen to miss; be lacking to
der Fehler the mistake, error
das Feuer the *fire*
der Finger the *finger*
der Friede(n) the peace
das Gebäude the building
gelingen (*impers. w. dat.*) to succeed
geschehen to happen, take place
gießen to pour; cast
glänzen to glitter, gleam
der Haufe(n) the *heap*, pile; crowd
das Heil the happiness; salvation; welfare
hundert *hundred*
jagen to hunt; chase
lehren to teach
die Leute the people
das Licht the *light*
die Mauer the (outside) wall
die Menge the crowd; quantity
das (or der) Meter the *meter*
müde tired
der Narr the fool
der Ort the place; town
das Paar the *pair*; couple
ein paar a few
das Rathaus the city hall
schreiten to step, pace; walk
die Schule the *school*
singen to *sing*
der Sinn the sense; mind
das Tier the animal, beast
trauern to grieve, mourn
treu *true*, faithful
der Vogel the bird, *fowl*
voll *full* (of), filled (with)
vorschlagen to propose, move
der Wagen the *wagon*, carriage, car
wahr true, real
der Wirt the innkeeper, landlord
zunächst first of all; at first
der Zweifel the doubt

IDIOMS

es gelingt mir I succeed
noch einmal again
noch nie never before
sobald (*conj.*) as soon as
über und über all over, thoroughly

TEXT B

Peter Schlemihl

[Fortsetzung]

Noch heute, nach so langer Zeit, habe ich die Schrecken jenes Tages nicht vergessen. Wie heiß habe ich gewünscht, wie oft in unsagbarer Not zu Gott geschrieen, nur diesen e i n e n Tag meines Lebens noch einmal leben zu

dürfen! Aber obgleich der Allmächtige uns unsere Fehler vergibt, kann er sie nicht ungeschehen machen. Noch immer ziehe ich schattenlos durch die Welt und habe lange an keinem Orte Ruhe oder Frieden finden können. Wie jung, wie unerfahren muß ich gewesen sein, als ich an jenem Tage mit
5 leichtem Herzen und frohem Sinn zur Stadt zog! Noch nie, so glaubte ich, hatte die Sonne so hell vom Himmel geschienen; noch nie, so schien es mir, hatte ich die Vögel in den Gärten so herrlich singen hören. „Mir ist es gleich", so sagte ich mir mit jugendlich leichtem Sinn, „ob ich einen Schatten habe oder nicht. Ohne Schatten kann man leben, ohne Geld nicht. Und
10 wenn die Leute neidisch werden und mit Fingern auf mich zeigen, so laß sie doch! Geld ist Macht, Geld tut Wunder, Geld macht frei." So unterdrückte ich alle Zweifel. Ich Narr!

Kaum war ich ein paar hundert Meter gegangen, da hörte ich hinter mir jemand laut schreien: „He, he, junger Herr, Sie haben ja Ihren Schatten
15 verloren!"—„Danke, Mütterchen!" sagte ich, warf der alten Frau ein Goldstück zu und setzte meinen Weg fort. „Aber wo hat denn der feine Herr seinen Schatten gelassen?" fragte beißend ein Mann im Vorbeigehen; und „Heilige Maria, der arme Mensch hat keinen Schatten!" riefen ein paar Mädchen, die am Brunnen vor der Stadtmauer spielten, wie aus e i n e m
20 Mund. Das fing an, mir unangenehm zu werden, und ich versuchte, so wenig wie möglich in die Sonne zu treten. Zu meinem Unheil kam ich gerade in dem Augenblick auf den Markt, als die Schule zu Ende war und die Schüler aus der Klasse auf die Straße stürzten. Ein frischer kleiner Bengel,[1] ich sehe ihn noch heute, merkte gleich, daß mir der Schatten fehlte,
25 und sogleich folgte mir die ganze Gesellschaft mit großem Geschrei. Bald lief die ganze Stadt, Schüler, Väter, Mütter, Töchter, Hafenarbeiter, Meister, Lehrer und junge Hunde[2] hinter mir her, und wie ein gejagtes wildes Tier lief ich, um mein Leben zu retten. In meiner Not warf ich endlich, um Zeit zu gewinnen, Gold unter die Menge. Das half. Es gelang
30 mir, einen Wagen zu finden, ein paar gute Bürger halfen mir hinein und retteten so mein Leben.

Allein im Wagen, fing ich an, bitterlich zu weinen. Schon in jenem Augenblick muß es mir klar geworden sein, daß alles Gold der Welt ein Nichts ist gegen den Schatten, gegen „diesen unschätzbaren Schatten", wie ihn
35 der graue Mann so wahr und richtig genannt hatte. Es tat mir leid, daß ich ihn verkauft hatte. „Was", so fragte ich mich, „was soll aus dir noch werden?"

Im „Goldenen Löwen" angekommen, warf ich dem Diener, demselben, der mich am Morgen in ein kleines Zimmer unter dem Dach geführt hatte trotzig ein Goldstück hin, bezahlte meine Rechnung und gab den Befehl, vor das beste Hotel zu fahren. Dort ließ ich mir die besten Zimmer geben und schloß mich ein, sobald ich konnte. 5

Und was glaubst Du, lieber Freund, was ich machte, als ich allein auf meinem Zimmer war? O, urteile nicht zu hart! Ich zog den unglücklichen Glückssäckel[3] hervor, griff hinein, holte Gold heraus, und Gold, und Gold, und immer wieder Gold, ließ es langsam durch meine Finger laufen, freute mich an seinem Glanze, legte es auf den Tisch, warf es auf den Boden, zog 10 neues Gold hervor und warf es wieder von mir, bis der Boden meiner Zimmer über und über mit Gold bedeckt war und ganze Haufen Gold auf Tisch und Bett lagen. So kam der Abend. Ich schloß die Tür nicht auf. Die Nacht fand mich, schon todmüde, noch immer mit dem Golde spielend. Auf dem Golde liegend schlief ich schließlich ein. 15

Am folgenden Morgen erwachte ich wie jemand, der einen bösen Traum gehabt hat und noch nicht ganz sicher ist, ob es wirklich nur ein Traum war. Ich fürchtete mich, und eine Zeitlang wagte ich nicht, die Augen[2] zu öffnen. „Es muß nur ein Traum gewesen sein", sagte ich mir. Aber mein Rücken schmerzte von dem harten Gold, auf dem ich eingeschlafen war, und diese 20 Schmerzen waren wirklich.

Hungrig, durstig und niedergeschlagen stand ich endlich auf. Die helle Morgensonne schien schon durch die Fenster, schien auf die roten Goldstücke[2] am Boden, und ihr Licht brannte wie Feuer in meine Augen.[2] Ich versuchte, das Gold wieder in den Säckel[3] zu stecken. Gold herausnehmen konnte 25 man, soviel man wollte, Gold hineinstecken nur soviel wie in jeden anderen Säckel auch. Ich hob also das ganze Gold Stück für Stück vom Boden auf und verbarg es in meinem Schlafzimmer. Dann ließ ich mir eine Tasse Kaffee und etwas zu essen bringen.

Den ganzen Tag wagte ich keinen Schritt aus meiner Tür und hielt mich 30 in meinen Zimmern eingeschlossen, ausgeschlossen für immer aus aller menschlichen Gesellschaft. Ein armer Reicher stand ich hinter meinen Fenstern und sah voll Neid auf die Straße und auf den Marktplatz gegenüber. Aber ich sah nicht auf die Leute, sondern auf ihre Schatten.

Diese Schatten! Sie wurden langsam, langsam kürzer und langsam, 35 langsam wieder länger. Die Zeiger[4] der großen Rathausuhr, die ich von meinen Fenstern aus[5] beobachten konnte, schienen sich nicht von der Stelle bewegen zu wollen. Noch nie war mir ein Tag in meinem Leben so lang gewesen wie dieser, der eine Ewigkeit zu dauern schien.

Erst spät am Abend, als der Mond schon voll am Himmel stand und sein weißes Licht über die Stadt goß, machte ich mich zum Ausgehen fertig, warf mir meinen Abendmantel um, drückte den Hut tief ins Gesicht und verließ, mich zunächst vorsichtig im Schatten der Gebäude haltend, mit klopfendem Herzen das Haus, um noch einmal mein Urteil aus dem Munde der Leute zu hören.

O, lieber Freund, verlange nichts Unmögliches! Ich kann, ich kann Dir nicht wiederholen, was ich an jenem Abend erfahren mußte. Ich hörte mein Urteil aus jedem Wort, las es aus jedem Blick: Ausgestoßen aus aller menschlichen Gesellschaft, erst im Tode wieder Frieden zu finden.

Noch blieb mir *eine* Hoffnung. Ich mußte den grauen Mann finden. Ich schickte also Bendel, meinen neuen Diener, den mir der Wirt als treu und ehrlich empfohlen hatte und der mir bald zum Freund wurde, am nächsten Morgen zum Hause des Herrn John. Traurig kam er am Abend zurück. Niemand aus der Gesellschaft—er hatte mit allen persönlich gesprochen—hatte sich an den Mann im grauen Rock erinnern können. Das neue Teleskop war noch da, aber niemand wußte, wo es überhaupt hergekommen war.

Ich war am Ende meiner Kraft und bat den guten Bendel, mich allein zu lassen. Er blieb: „Erlauben Sie mir noch zu berichten, daß ich heute morgen[6] vor der Tür einem Mann begegnet bin, der mir im Vorbeigehen zurief: ‚Sagen Sie Ihrem Herrn, daß ich leider eine Reise machen muß und ihn daher heute nicht besuchen kann. Aber ich komme nach genau einem Jahre wieder und kann ihm dann vielleicht ein besseres Geschäft vorschlagen. Herr Schlemihl weiß schon, was ich meine.'"

Mein Diener ging. Ich war allein. Ein Jahr hatte er gesagt, ein ganzes Jahr! Und jeder Tag eine Ewigkeit!

[Fortsetzung folgt]

NOTES. 1. Bengel fellow, rascal. 2. Hunde, Augen, Goldstücke (plural forms) dogs, eyes, gold pieces. 3. Glückssäckel magic purse; Säckel purse. 4. Zeiger hands. 5. aus. Omit in translating. 6. heute morgen this morning

LESSON XIV

BUILDING A PASSIVE VOCABULARY

ändern ander other, different, anders different(ly), otherwise, ändern to make different, to change, alter

aufschließen auf open, schließen to close, shut, lock, aufschließen to unlock. (Zuschließen to lock up. Zu to, closed)

aufstehen auf upon, up (cf. § 40), stehen to stand, aufstehen to stand up, get up, arise

ausgeschlossen aus out, schließen to close, lock, ausgeschlossen locked out, excluded

ausgestoßen aus out, stoßen to thrust, push, ausgestoßen pushed out, cast out, rejected, exiled

bedeckt decken to cover, bedeckt covered, covered up

beißend beißen to bite, beißend bitingly, sharply, sarcastically

eingeschlossen ein in (*cf.* § 40), schließen to close, lock, eingeschlossen locked in

erwachte wach awake, erwachte awakened

die Ewigkeit ewig eternal, die Ewigkeit eternity

das Geschrei schreien to cry, shout, das Geschrei the cry, shout(ing)

kürzer kurz short, kürzer shorter

länger lang long, länger longer

der Neid neidisch envious, der Neid envy, jealousy

niedergeschlagen nieder down, schlagen to beat, strike, niedergeschlagen beaten down, dejected

der Schüler die Schule the school, der Schüler the schoolboy

unerfahren un in, erfahren (past part.) experienced, unerfahren inexperienced, naïve, unsophisticated

ungeschehen geschehen to happen, take place, ungeschehen (unhappened) undone

unterdrücken unter under, down (cf. § 40), drücken to press, unterdrücken to hold down, suppress

urteilen das Urteil the judgment, urteilen to judge

vergeben geben to give, vergeben to forgive

verließ *past tense of* verlassen to leave, forsake

vorsichtig vor before, Sicht (*from* sehen to see) sight, vorsichtig seeing beforehand, cautious, careful(ly)

GRAMMAR

88. Plural of Nouns. There are in German only a very few nouns that form their plural by adding -s. Most of them are foreign nouns with un-German sound combinations, as: Leutnant, Auto, Orang-Utan, Café. With few exceptions German nouns form their plural in one of four ways:

a. By adding nothing (but sometimes taking an umlaut).
b. By adding an -e (and sometimes an umlaut).
c. By adding -er (and the umlaut whenever possible).
d. By adding -n or -en (and never an umlaut).

The verb form, a preceding der- or ein-word, or the adjective ending usually indicates whether a noun is singular or plural. Sometimes, however, these aids fail. It is therefore suggested that even students who wish merely reading ability make themselves acquainted with the four types of plural formation and also learn the plural of those nouns which are introduced in the vocabularies of each lesson. (The student will not be expected to learn the genders and plurals of nouns of verb-noun pairs (cf. § 68) where the verb is introduced.)

In order to simplify the learning of the plurals they will be taken up in the order given above, one group or class being given in each lesson.

89. Nouns of the First Class. Nouns of this class do not add an ending to form the plural. Some of them (there is no rule in this respect) add the umlaut. To this class belong:

a. Most masculine and neuter nouns ending in -el, -en, -er. Examples:

der Apfel	der Kuchen	der Vater
die Äpfel	die Kuchen	die Väter

b. All diminutives, that is, nouns ending in -chen and -lein. Examples:

das Mädchen, die Mädchen   das Fräulein, die Fräulein

(Cf. § 61.)

c. Two feminines:

die Mutter, die Mütter	die Tochter, die Töchter

d. A few neuters which have the prefix Ge- and the suffix -e, of which only das Gebäude (plural, die Gebäude) *the building*, and das Gemüse (plural, die Gemüse) *the vegetable*, will be used in this book.

The nouns in this class which have been introduced are:

a. Those which require the umlaut in the plural:

der Apfel	der Bruder	der Hafen	der Vater
der Boden	der Garten	der Mantel	der Vogel

b. Those which do not add an umlaut in the plural:

der Brunnen	das Feuer	der Meister	der Rücken	der Winter
der Bürger	der Finger	das Meter	der Schatten	das Wunder
der Enkel	der Himmel	der Morgen	der Wagen	das Zimmer
der Fehler	der Kuchen	der Onkel	das Wasser	der Zweifel

In this class belong a few masculines which are regular except in the nominative singular. They include:

SINGULAR

NOM.	der Friede(n)	der Haufe(n)	der Name
GEN.	des Friedens	des Haufens	des Namens
DAT.	dem Frieden	dem Haufen	dem Namen
ACC.	den Frieden	den Haufen	den Namen

PLURAL

NOM.		die Haufen	die Namen
GEN.	*No*	der Haufen	der Namen
DAT.	*plural*	den Haufen	den Namen
ACC.		die Haufen	die Namen

Henceforth plural forms of words belonging in the classes which have been studied will be given together with the words in the vocabularies as they are introduced.

90. Dative Plural. In the dative plural all nouns end in =n. Thus, if the plural form does not end in =n, this ending must be added. If, however, the plural form already ends in =n, no change is made.

91. Der=Words, Relative Pronouns, ein=Words, and Adjective Endings in the Plural. The plural forms for these words are the same for all genders.

	der=Words		Relative Pronouns		ein=Words	Strong Adjective Endings
Nom.	die	diese	die	welche	meine	gute
Gen.	der	dieser	deren	—	meiner	guter
Dat.	den	diesen	denen	welchen	meinen	guten
Acc.	die	diese	die	welche	meine	gute

92. Review of Strong and Weak Adjective Endings

STRONG

[Used only to compensate for the lack of a preceding der=word or the lack of an ending on a preceding ein=word.]

WEAK

[After *der*-words or inflected *ein*-words.]

	Strong Masc.	Strong Fem.	Strong Neut.	Strong Pl.	Weak Masc.	Weak Fem.	Weak Neut.	Weak Pl.
Nom.	er	e	es	e	e	e	e	en
Gen.	es*	er	es*	er	en	en	en	en
Dat.	em	er	em	en	en	en	en	en
Acc.	en	e	es	e	en	e	e	en

93. Word Formation: Adjectives in =ig. The suffix =ig may be added to nouns and adverbs to form adjectives denoting possession of the quality indicated in the stem (cf. English *-y*):

der Hunger, hungrig (hungry)
der Durst, durstig (thirsty)
die Vorsicht (care, precaution), vorsichtig (careful)
der Trotz, trotzig (defiant)

---

*Cf. footnote page 52.

die Ruhe (ruhen), ruhig (restful, peaceful, calm)
die Vernunft, vernünftig (sensible)
am heutigen Tage on this day

Learn or review the principal parts of the following verbs as a part of this lesson:

beißen	biß	hat gebissen	beißt	to bite
schreiten	schritt	ist geschritten	schreitet	to step
schließen	schloß	hat geschlossen	schließt	to close
gießen	goß	hat gegossen	gießt	to pour
sinken	sank	ist gesunken	sinkt	to sink
singen	sang	hat gesungen	singt	to sing
gelingen	gelang	ist gelungen	gelingt	to succeed
empfēhlen	empfāhl	hat empfōhlen	empfiehlt	to recommend
befēhlen	befāhl	hat befōhlen	befiehlt	to command
sēhen	sāh	hat gesēhen	sieht	to see
geschēhen	geschāh	ist geschēhen	geschieht	to happen
schlāgen	schlūg	hat geschlāgen	schlāgt	to beat
vorschlāgen	schlūg vor	hat vorgeschlāgen	schlāgt vor	to suggest
schlāfen	schlief	hat geschlāfen	schlāft	to sleep
einschlāfen	schlief ein	ist eingeschlāfen	schlāft ein	to go to sleep
kennen	kannte	hat gekannt	kennt	to know
brennen	brannte	hat gebrannt	brennt	to burn

EXERCISES

I

Answer in German: 1. Was konnte Peter noch nicht vergessen? 2. Zu wem hat er in unsagbarer Not geschrieen? 3. Was vergibt uns der Allmächtige? 4. Was konnte Peter nicht finden? 5. Wohin zog er? 6. Wo sangen die Vögel? 7. Was schrie jemand hinter ihm? 8. Was warf er der alten Frau zu? 9. Was riefen die Mädchen? 10. Was war gerade zu Ende, als Peter auf den Markt kam? 11. Wer stürzte auf die Straße? 12. Wer lief hinter ihm her? 13. Wie lief er? 14. Warum warf er Gold unter die Menge? 15. Wer half ihm in den Wagen? 16. Was tat er, als er im Wagen war? 17. Wer hatte den Schatten „unschätzbar" genannt?

18. Wie warf Schlemihl dem Diener ein Goldstück zu? 19. Welche Zimmer im Hotel nahm er? 20. Was holte er aus seinem Säckel? 21. Wohin warf er das Gold? 22. Wo schlief er ein? 23. Was wagte er eine Zeitlang nicht? 24. Was sagte er sich? 25. Wo verbarg er den Schatz? 26. Wie lange blieb er in seinen Zimmern? 27. Beobachtete er die Leute? 28. Was schien sich nicht von der Stelle bewegen zu wollen? 29. Wurde ihm der Tag lang? 30. Wann verließ er das Haus? 31. Wann konnte er hoffen, wieder Frieden zu finden? 32. Wen mußte er finden? 33. Wer hatte Bendel empfohlen? 34. Wohin schickte Peter seinen Diener? 35. Wer war am Ende seiner Kraft? 36. Wem war der Diener begegnet? 37. Wann will der graue Mann wiederkommen?

II

Translate into German: 1. The citizens of the city were otherwise satisfied. 2. They have no grandsons. 3. We have wanted to eat the cakes. 4. Where are the apples we saw Saturday? 5. In our class we make few mistakes. 6. His fingers are rather short. 7. He has bought a large house with many rooms. 8. We were working on the roof of the building when someone suddenly cried, "You have forgotten the windows!" 9. My brothers died when I was young. 10. The birds return every spring. 11. She has more[1] uncles than brothers. 12. The windows were closed. 13. We have not been able to work. 14. I know that she has wanted to go.

NOTE. 1. mehr is never inflected.

III

Translate into English:

leise	die Zukunft	gewöhnlich	Dienstag	gemein
Freitag	die Vergangenheit	nahe	das Faß	der Pfennig
daher	ehrlich	sogleich	böse	der Sieg
damit	der Hafen	sogar	fest	die Spitze
		erwarten		

IV

Translate into German:

the church	to pull	to begin
to cost	the newspaper	the beard

the war	to be sure	to explain
to smile	Wednesday	the peace
to hide	March	proud

V

Translate the following compounds and derivatives:

das Blut, bluten, blutig; der Träumer; der Ruf, rufen; die Heilsarmee; kräftig, mächtig, allmächtig, der Allmächtige; der Schatten, schattig; die Schuld, schuldig, die Unschuld, unschuldig, schuldlos; windig, trotzig, unerklärlich, unerklärbar, teilbar, brechbar, meßbar; rückwärts; der Empfang; die Wiederholung; zuhören, der Zuhörer; der Arbeiter, die Arbeiter; der Besucher, die Besucher; der Erzähler, die Erzähler; dienen, der Diener, die Diener; lehren, der Lehrer, die Lehrerin, die Lehrer; führen, der Führer, die Führer; der Sprecher, die Sprecher; der Schmerz, schmerzen; hassen, der Haß; die Luftlinie; schattenlos; der Schatz, schätzen; die Antwort, antworten; je mehr . . . desto besser; das Näslein

VI

Translate into English:

auf der Stelle	sie soll glücklich sein
über und über rot	Sie waren nicht zu Hause
auf Wiedersehen	er wiederholt es gern
nach und nach	ihr habt recht

VII

Decline in the singular and plural:

der Meister	kein blauer Vogel	dein schöner Name
unser guter Kuchen	jener kalte Brunnen	mein Fenster
dieses kleine Zimmer	der große Haufe	der rote Apfel

VIII

In each blank supply the proper ending: 1. Mein_____ klein_____ Enkel ist letzte Woche gestorben. 2. D_____ Zimmer in dies_____ Haus sind viel zu klein. 3. Dies_____ Kuchen sind für Sie. 4. Wir müssen unser_____ Wagen (*sing.*) waschen (wash). 5. Wir müssen unser_____ Wagen (*pl.*) waschen. 6. D_____ gut_____ Bürger d_____ alt_____ Stadt riefen hurra. 7. Er gab mein_____ Brüdern viel Geld. 8. D_____ Schrecken des Krieges waren groß. 9. England hat gut_____ Häfen.

IX

Conjugate in the past:

befehlen	vorschlagen	einschlafen	singen dürfen	verdienen können
ankommen	singen	schreiten	helfen müssen	wollen

X

Conjugate the above verbs in the present perfect.

LESSON XV

TEXT A

Der Mensch, so hört man oft von Leuten, die durch den Krieg nichts gelernt haben, ist das höchste, das edelste und das schönste Wesen, das die Natur hervorgebracht hat. Vielleicht haben sie trotz allem recht, vielleicht sind wir etwas zu pessimistisch. Aber wir wollen vorsichtig sein und sagen daher nur: Der Mensch ist das höchste Wesen, das die Natur hervorbringen 5 will. Trotzdem ist der Mensch oft unvernünftiger als das vernunftlose Tier. Wir haben zum Beispiel die Möglichkeit, die ganze Erde in einen Garten zu verwandeln. Aber uns fehlt oft der gute Wille. Statt unsere Städte wohnlicher und unser Land schöner zu machen, stecken wir unsere Arbeit und unser Geld in Kriegsschiffe und Tanks und führen[1] Kriege, die unsre Enkel bezahlen 10 müssen. Auch im eigenen Lande kämpft eine Klasse gegen die andere, und jeder will sich das Leben auf[2] Kosten anderer[2] leichter machen.

„Ich habe leider einen sehr starken Bart, einen außerordentlich starken Bart sogar. Können Sie mir eine besonders gute Rasier-Creme[3] empfehlen?"—„Gewiß, mein Herr, mein Bart ist ebenso stark wie Ihr Bart, 15 vielleicht noch etwas stärker. Aber wie die meisten Herren mit einem starken Bart gebrauche ich schon seit Jahren ‚Ososchnell'. Versuchen Sie es einmal. Wenn Sie mit der Wirkung nicht zufrieden sind, gebe ich Ihnen Ihr Geld gern zurück."

Durch Schweigen erreicht man oft mehr als durch viele Worte. Was du 20 tun mußt, tue heute! Schiebe nichts von einem Tag auf den anderen!

Das Schaf auf dem Bild im „Zerbrochenen Krug" fraß Gras. Der Löwe fraß zuerst auch Gras, aber dann wurde er leider blutdürstig und fraß das arme Schaf.

„Ich höre, dein Mann spricht Englisch fließender[4] als Deutsch."—„So, 25 das ist mir neu. Aber vielleicht hast du recht. Er macht zwar viele Fehler, aber wenn er einmal anfängt, hört er so bald nicht wieder auf."[5]

„Unsere Eva geht so gern in die Sonntagsschule, Frau Müller. Sie fängt schon Montags an, ihren Bibelvers zu lernen, damit sie ihn Sonntags auch ja auswendig kann. Sie ist wirklich ein gutes Kind, nicht wahr?"— 30 „Ich weiß, warum Ihre Eva so gerne in die Sonntagsschule geht. Wir

halten die Sonntagsschule nämlich in demselben Raum, in dem Mittwoch abends der Missionsverein zusammenkommt, um für die armen Eskimos in Alaska Strümpfe zu stricken.[6] Und für die kleinen Mädchen haben wir da einen Eskimo aus Gips.[7] Wenn man ihm einen Pfennig in den Mund
5 wirft, dann nickt er mit dem Kopf und sagt ‚Danke schön!'"

NOTES. 1. führen wage. 2. auf Kosten anderer at the expense of others. 3. Rasier=Creme shaving cream. 4. fließender more fluently. 5. hört... auf does not stop. 6. stricken knit. 7. Gips plaster.

VOCABULARY

der Baum, ⸗e the tree (*beam*)
besonder special
die Blume the flower (*bloom*)
damals then, at that time
dringen to enter by force; penetrate
die Ehre the honor
die Eltern the parents
die Feder the pen; *feather*; spring
feiern to celebrate
das Fest, –e the *feast*; festival
fliegen to *fly*
die Freude the joy, pleasure
die Frucht, ⸗e the *fruit*
der Gast, ⸗e the *guest*
die Gewalt the power; force
gewiß certain, sure
der Graf the count
der Kampf, ⸗e the combat, battle; struggle
der König, –e the *king*
die Lust, ⸗e the desire; pleasure
die Mitte the *middle*, center
der Raum, ⸗e the *room*; space
das Reich, –e the realm; empire
reiten to *ride* (horseback)
scheiden to separate; part
schneiden to cut
schwach *weak*, feeble
setzen to *set*, place, put
sonder= special . . .
  besonders especially
  sonderbar peculiar, strange
der Stern, –e the *star*
stumpf dull, blunt
der Ton, ⸗e the sound, *tone*
der Verein, –e the club, organization
voraus ahead; in advance
weg *away*; off; gone
das Wesen, – the being; creature; essence
das Wetter, – the *weather*
das Ziel, –e the aim, goal
der Zustand, ⸗e the condition

IDIOMS

auf dem Lande sein to be in the country
auf das Land gehen to go to the country
immer öfter more and more frequently
nicht wahr? isn't that so?
vor allem above all

LESSON XV

TEXT B

Peter Schlemihl [Fortsetzung]

Hast Du gewußt, mein Freund, daß ein Mensch noch viele Jahre leben kann, auch wenn sein Herz schon lange gestorben ist? Ich hoffe, Du brauchst es nie zu erfahren. Ich—ich habe es erfahren.

Wenn leben mehr ist als essen, trinken und schlafen, wenn Lust und Leid, Freude und Schmerz, wenn Lachen, Weinen und Lieben auch zum Leben 5 gehören, dann war jenes Jahr, in dem ich auf den grauen Mann wartete, das letzte meines Lebens. Noch esse, schlafe und arbeite ich, noch halten meine schwachen Finger die Feder. Doch mein Herz ist kalt und tot. Meine Sinne sind stumpf. Das Feuer ist ausgebrannt.

Es ist mir unmöglich, Dir, mein Freund, mit farblosen, nichtssagenden 10 Worten ein treues Bild jener Tage zu geben. Nicht der Peter, der heute diese Worte schreibt, hat damals Dienern Befehle gegeben, Feste gefeiert, Gäste empfangen, Goldstücke wie Pfennige weggeworfen und an langen Tischen in großen Räumen seinen Freunden die besten Weine und die feinsten Früchte vorgesetzt. Nein, nicht ich habe damals in dunklen Nächten, wenn 15 der Mond nicht schien, das lieblichste aller Wesen in meinen Armen gehalten und ihren Mund mit Küssen bedeckt. Nicht ich. Jener Schlemihl starb, als . . .

Doch ich will nicht mit dem Ende anfangen.

Als alle Versuche, den grauen Mann zu finden, erfolglos geblieben waren, 20 als an jeder Ecke schon die Bürger die Köpfe zusammensteckten und mit vielsagenden, bösen Blicken immer öfter über den Mann ohne Schatten redeten, machte ich mich endlich reisefertig und ritt eines Morgens mit Bendel und fünf anderen Dienern unbeobachtet aus der Stadt—im Regen, als man weder von den Pferden noch von den Reitern einen Schatten ver- 25 langen konnte.

Ich war fest entschlossen, in einem kleinen Städtchen auf dem Lande ein Jahr lang so verborgen und zurückgezogen wie möglich zu leben—und auf den grauen Mann zu warten.

Doch es kam ganz, ganz anders. 30

Ich hatte einen meiner Diener vorausgeschickt, mir eine Wohnung zu suchen. Er mußte sich aber wohl etwas zu unbestimmt über meine Person ausgedrückt haben. Auf jeden Fall schienen die guten Leute des Städtchens

die sonderbarsten Gedanken über mich zu haben. Denn als ich nach drei oder vier Tagen mit meinem Wagen, den ich Schattenloser des[1] schönen Wetters wegen[1] hatte nehmen müssen, ankam, sahen wir etwa eine halbe Stunde vor der Stadt eine festlich gekleidete Menge auf dem Wege stehen und
5 warten. Kanonenschüsse durchschnitten die Luft, als man den Wagen näher kommen sah, und laute Hurrarufe drangen zu mir herüber. Die guten Leute hielten mich, wie ich zu meinem größten Schreck herausfand, für den König des Landes. Der Bürgermeister begrüßte mich im Namen der Bürger und der verschiedenen Vereine, und ein liebliches, schlankes Mädchen kniete
10 vor meinem Wagen nieder. Frühlingsblumen[2] hielt sie in den Händen.

Und diese Szene,[3] lieber Freund, in der hellsten Sonne! Zwei Schritte vor mir kniete das schönste, reizendste aller Mädchen. Und ich, ohne Schatten, konnte nicht zu ihr hinüberspringen, nicht vor diesem Bild der Jugend auf die Knie fallen. Ach, alle Schätze und Königreiche der Welt waren in jenem
15 Augenblick ein Nichts gegen den Schatten.

Mein treuer Bendel rettete mich schließlich aus dieser für mich sehr unangenehmen Situation. Er sprang auf der anderen Seite aus dem Wagen und sagte, sich an den Bürgermeister wendend: „Es tut mir leid, Herr Bürgermeister, aber mein Herr ist wirklich nicht der König, wie Sie zu
20 glauben scheinen. Er kann daher unmöglich die unverdiente Ehre dieses Empfanges annehmen. Er dankt den Bürgern jedoch für ihre guten Wünsche." Nicht ganz sicher, ob Bendel die Wahrheit sprach oder nicht, gab die Menge den Pferden Raum, und bald hielten wir vor meinem Hause. Mit dem Befehl, niemand zu mir zu lassen, verschwand ich in meine Zimmer.
25 Noch lange schrie der Haufe, der dem Wagen gefolgt war, unter meinen Fenstern hurra. Und ich Narr ließ noch Goldstücke auf die Straße regnen.

Jenes Mädchen, welches ich mit Blumen[2] in der Hand vor meinem Wagen hatte knien sehen, kam[4] mir nicht wieder aus dem Sinn.[4] Ich wußte, es war sinnlos, in meinem Zustand, ohne Schatten, an Liebe und Ehe zu
30 denken. Denn war es nicht genug, daß ich allein unglücklich war? Hatte ich das Recht, auch noch ein Mädchen ins Unglück zu stürzen? Nein, ich durfte mich an niemand binden, durfte vor allem niemand an mich binden. Doch ich tröstete mich schließlich: „Nicht lange", so sagte ich mir, „und du siehst den grauen Mann wieder. Wenn nötig, zwingst du ihn mit Gewalt, dir deinen
35 Schatten zurückzugeben." Ach, im Grunde meines Herzens wußte ich wohl, das war nicht wahr. Ihn zwingen, mit Gewalt?! Aber ich hörte nicht auf

diese Stimme, wollte nicht auf sie hören, ich fürchtete mich vor ihr. Und wie so oft, ging auch diesmal aus dem Kampf zwischen Herz und Vernunft das Herz als Sieger hervor. Ich unterdrückte alle Zweifel und bat fast die ganze Stadt zu einem Fest, das ich am folgenden Abend unter den Bäumen vor meinem Hause geben wollte. 5

Und sie kam!

Wie aller Glanz der Sterne vor der Sonne verschwindet, so überstrahlte[5] sie in ihrer Schönheit den Glanz des Festes. Und mit jener Gewißheit, die einem kalten Herzen unerklärlich ist, wußten wir, daß wir einander liebten, und trugen die Gewißheit dieser Liebe in unsrem[6] Herzen, als wir uns 10 trennten.

Für eine kurze Weile schien mir das Leben wieder Zweck, Sinn und Ziel zu haben. Solange die Sonne schien, blieb ich eingeschlossen in meinen Zimmern: Graf Peter—so nannte man mich—„arbeitete". Abends aber gab ich Empfänge und Feste, von denen die Leute des Städtchens nicht 15 müde wurden zu reden. Und abends, wenn es dunkel war und auch die alten Bäume im Garten ihrer Eltern keine Schatten warfen, ging ich zu ihr, zu meiner Minna.

O mein guter Freund, ich hoffe, Du hast nicht vergessen, was Liebe ist. Verlange nicht, daß ich jene ach so ferne Zeit noch einmal ins Leben rufe. Ich 20 kann es nicht. Genug, daß sie Liebe um Liebe gab, mich liebte mit der vollen jugendlichen Kraft eines unschuldigen Herzens.

So ging die Zeit vorbei wie im Fluge. Und der Tag, an dem ich den grauen Mann wiedersehen, der Tag, an dem ich frei werden sollte, kam näher, kam heran.[7] Schon am Abend vorher schloß ich mich ein und nahm soviel 25 Gold aus meinem Säckel, wie ich in meinen Zimmern verbergen konnte. Dann wartete ich. Die Uhr schlug zwölf. Niemand erschien. Langsam sah ich die Zeiger[8] sich weiter und weiter bewegen. Es wurde Morgen. Niemand kam. Es wurde Mittag, es wurde Abend, und nichts erschien. Ich saß und wartete. Dann standen die Zeiger[8] der großen Wanduhr wieder auf zwölf. 30 Sie schlug. Und mit dem Ton des letzten Schlages sank ich hoffnungslos zu Boden.

[Fortsetzung folgt]

NOTES. 1. des . . . wegen on account of the beautiful weather. 2. Frühlingsblumen, Blumen spring flowers, flowers. 3. Szene scene. 4. kam . . . Sinn In translating read: kam nicht wieder aus meinem Sinn. 5. überstrahlte outshone, did she outshine. 6. in unsrem Herzen in our hearts (singular in German). 7. heran up. 8. Zeiger hands.

BUILDING A PASSIVE VOCABULARY

annehmen an on, nehmen to take, annehmen to accept
ausdrücken (ausgedrückt) aus out (*Latin* ex), drücken to press, ausdrücken to express
bedeckt decken to cover, bedecken to cover, bedeckt covered
begrüßen grüßen to greet, begrüßen to greet
erscheinen (erschien) scheinen to seem, erscheinen to appear, seem
Gedanken (*pl. of* der Gedanke) denken to think, der Gedanke the thought
Königreiche der König the king, das Reich the realm, das Königreich the kingdom, die Königreiche the kingdoms
Mittag die Mitte the middle, der Tag the day, Mittag midday, noon
nichtssagend nichts nothing, sagen to say, nichtssagend empty, meaningless
Sieger der Sieg the victory, als Sieger as victor
tot töten to kill, tot dead. (Der Tod death)
unterdrücken unter under, down, drücken to press, unterdrücken to press down, suppress
verschieden *belongs to the word family* scheiden to separate, part, verschieden various, different
vielsagend viel much, sagen to say, vielsagend expressive, significant
zurückgezogen zurück back, gezogen (*from* ziehen) pulled, drawn, zurückgezogen drawn back, withdrawn, secluded

GRAMMAR

94. Nouns of the Second Class. Nouns of this class add ⸗e to form the plural. In this group there are many monosyllabic and a few polysyllabic masculines and relatively few feminines and neuters. Examples are:

der Arm	der Baum	der Feind	die Hand	das Jahr
die Arme	die Bäume	die Feinde	die Hände	die Jahre

The nouns of this class which have already been introduced are:
a. Masculines which take umlaut:

der Arzt	der Grund	der Markt	der Strumpf
der Bart	der Hof	der Platz	der Sturm
der Baum	der Hut	der Raum	der Ton
der Fall	der Kampf	der Rock	der Zuſtand
der Gaſt	der Kopf	der Schatz	

b. Masculines which do not add umlaut:

der Abend	der Fiſch	der Mund	der Tag
der Arm	der Freund	der Ort	der Teil
der Augenblick	der Frühling	der Preis	der Tiſch
der Bleiſtift	der Herbſt	der Punkt	der Verein
der Brief	der König	der Sieg	der Weg
der Charakter	der Krieg	der Sinn	der Wein
der Erfolg	der Monat	der Stein	der Wind
der Feind	der Mond	der Stern	der Wirt

der Zweck

c. Feminines, all of which add umlaut:

die Bank	die Frucht	die Hand	die Luft	die Macht	die Not
die Bruſt	die Gans	die Kraft	die Luſt	die Nacht	die Stadt

die Wand

d. Neuters, none of which adds umlaut:

das Beiſpiel	das Haar	das Meer	das Recht	das Stück
das Feſt	das Jahr	das Paar	das Reich	das Tier
das Gegenteil	das Knie*	das Papier	das Schaf	das Urteil
das Geſchäft	das Mal	das Pferd	das Schiff	das Wort

das Ziel

95. Comparison of Adjectives: Formation. The comparative is formed by adding -er and the superlative by adding -ſt to the stem of the positive:

klein, kleiner, (der) kleinſt(e); angenehm, angenehmer, (der) angenehmſt(e) small, smaller, the smallest; pleasant, more pleasant, the most pleasant

---

*Das Knie has two plurals: die Knie and die Kniee. Both forms are pronounced with two syllables.

The following seventeen adjectives (of about eighty used in this book) always umlaut the stem vowel in the comparative and superlative degrees:

alt, arm, groß, hart, hoch, jung, kalt, krank (sick, ill), kurz, lang, nah, oft, scharf (sharp), schwach, schwarz, stark, warm.

Examples:

alt, älter, (der) ältest(e) arm, ärmer, (der) ärmst(e)

In the superlative the ending -st must be clearly audible. Hence the ending est is added when the adjective ends in -d, -t, or an *s*-sound:

kalt, kälter, (der) kältest(e) cold, colder, coldest
weiß, weißer, (der) weißest(e) white, whiter, whitest

The English way of expressing the comparative and superlative with *more* and *most* is rarely found in German,* the -er and -(e)st endings being added no matter how many syllables the adjective has.

96. Comparison of Adjectives: Use. *The Comparative.* The usual strong or weak endings are added to the comparative suffix -er when adjectives are used *attributively*:

das bessere Buch, ein besseres Buch the better book, a better book
die kleinere Kirche, eine kleinere Kirche the smaller church, a smaller church
der kürzere Weg, ein kürzerer Weg the shorter way, a shorter way

When used predicatively or adverbially, no inflectional endings are added:

Ich bin jünger als du. I am younger than you.
Du mußt deutlicher sprechen. You must speak more distinctly.

The Superlative. When the superlative is used *attributively*, the usual case endings are added to the superlative suffix -st:

das interessanteste Buch, des interessantesten Buches the most interesting book, of the most interesting book
die älteste Kirche, der ältesten Kirche the oldest church, of the oldest church

*A discussion of this usage is not within the scope of this book.

(This rule covers all cases where the noun is suppressed and can easily be supplied: Sie ist die schönste (Frau) von allen; she is the most beautiful (woman) of all.)

When the superlative is used *adverbially* or *predicatively*, a phrase with the contraction am (an dem) plus the dative weak ending is used:

Maria sang am schönsten von allen. Maria sang most beautifully of all.
Im Frühling sind die Kartoffeln am teuersten. Potatoes are most expensive in the spring.

English has expressions such as:

She is a most beautiful girl.
He spoke most clearly.
That is most unusual.

In these sentences no direct comparison is made, but only a high degree of the quality involved is expressed. In such cases German likewise uses a positive adjective, strengthened, however, NOT by the German meist but by the uninflected superlatives höchst or äußerst or simply by sehr or außerordentlich. Thus, English *That is a most interesting book* is Das ist ein höchst interessantes Buch (or äußerst, sehr, or außerordentlich). Similarly, *That is most disagreeable to me* is Das ist mir äußerst unangenehm; *That is extremely important*, Das ist äußerst wichtig.

97. Irregular Forms. The following adjectives and adverbs show irregularities in their comparison:

gern (*adverb only*)	lieber	am liebsten
groß	größer	der größte
gut	besser	der beste
hoch	höher	der höchste
lieb (dear, *adj. only*)	lieber	der liebste
nah	näher	der nächste
viel	mehr	der meiste

98. Als and wie. In making comparisons, wie is used after a positive where English uses *as* (*as big as*, so groß wie); als expresses, in the comparative, English *than*:

Du bist so ernst wie ich. You are as serious as I.
Er ist ernster als du. He is more serious than you.

99. Omission of the e. When the comparative suffix -er or a case ending (strong or weak) is added to adjectives which end in -el, -en, -er, like dunkel, offen, and teuer (including the possessive adjectives unser and euer), the e of the stem is usually dropped:*

Mein Haar ist dunkler geworden. Ein edlerer Mensch als er hat nie gelebt. Ein dunkler Tag, ein offnes Fenster, eine andre Frau, unsre besten Freunde, eure schönsten Äpfel

100. Adverbial Genitive. In a number of set phrases the genitive case of nouns is used adverbially. When used with a preceding article they are capitalized; but when used without the article, they are felt to be adverbs and are not capitalized. In the latter case and with the definite article, recurrence of time is implied:

des Morgens, morgens in the morning, of a morning
des Abends, abends in the evening, of an evening
des Nachts, nachts at night
vormittags in the forenoon (morning)
nachmittags in the afternoon
Donnerstags, Freitags, etc. (*days of the week retain capitals*) Thursday, on Thursday, Friday
eines Tages, eines Abends, eines Morgens, eines Nachts, eines Samstags one (a certain) day, evening, morning, night, Saturday

101. Word Formation: Nouns in -heit, -keit, -igkeit. The suffixes -heit, -keit, and -igkeit are added to adjectives to form feminine abstracts; they frequently correspond to the English suffixes *-ty* or *-ness*:

gewiß, die Gewißheit certain, certainty
deutlich, die Deutlichkeit distinct, distinctness
hoffnungslos, die Hoffnungslosigkeit hopeless, hopelessness

*Adjectives like böse, gerade, leise, weise, whose undeclined forms end in -e, are treated as if they had no such -e when inflectional endings are added:

ein weiser Mann, eine geradere Linie a wise man, a straighter line

schön, die Schönheit beautiful, beauty
wahr, die Wahrheit true, truth

102. Cardinal Numbers. The cardinal numbers from one to twelve are as follows: eins, zwei, drei, vier, fünf, sechs, sieben, acht, neun, zehn, elf, zwölf.

They are indeclinable. Note that eins is used in counting only when no noun follows. When a noun follows, eins is replaced by the indefinite article ein, which then functions as the adjective "one."

Learn the principal parts of the following verbs as a part of this lesson:

schreiben	schrieb	hat geschrieben	schreibt	to write
scheiden	schied	hat geschieden	scheidet	to separate
beißen	biß	hat gebissen	beißt	to bite
reiten	ritt	ist geritten	reitet	to ride
schneiden	schnitt	hat geschnitten	schneidet	to cut
ziehen	zōg	hat gezōgen	zieht	to pull
fliegen	flōg	ist geflōgen	fliegt	to fly
sinken	sank	ist gesunken	sinkt	to sink
dringen	drang	ist gedrungen	dringt	to penetrate

EXERCISES

I

Answer the following questions in German: 1. Was gehört auch zum Leben? 2. Was tut Peter immer noch? 3. Wie sind seine Finger? 4. Wie ist sein Herz? 5. Wie sind seine Sinne? 6. Was kann Peter nicht tun? 7. Was hatte Peter früher getan? 8. Wann hielt Peter Minna in seinen Armen? 9. Wo will er mit seiner Geschichte nicht anfangen? 10. Mit wem ritt Peter aus der Stadt? 11. Was konnte man weder von den Pferden noch von den Reitern verlangen? 12. Wo wollte er ein Jahr lang leben? 13. Wie wollte er leben? 14. Auf wen wollte er warten? 15. Warum hatte Peter einen Diener vorausgeschickt? 16. Warum hatte Peter einen Wagen nehmen müssen? 17. Was durchschnitt die Luft?

18. Was riefen die Leute? 19. Für wen hielten die Leute unsren Peter? 20. Wer begrüßte ihn? 21. Was hielt das liebliche Mädchen in den Händen? 22. Warum konnte Peter nicht aussteigen? 23. Wer rettete Peter endlich aus seiner Not? 24. Was befahl Peter seinen Dienern? 25. Was ließ Peter aus den Fenstern regnen? 26. Hatte Peter das Recht, ein Mädchen ins Unglück zu stürzen? 27. Warum hörte Peter nicht auf die Stimme? 28. Ging das Herz oder die Vernunft aus dem Kampf als Sieger hervor? 29. Wann wollte Peter ein Fest geben? 30. Wo wollte er es geben? 31. Wo blieb Peter, solange die Sonne schien? 32. Wann gab er Empfänge und Feste? 33. Wie ging die Zeit vorbei? 34. Was tat Peter am Abend vor dem großen Tag? 35. Wieviel Geld nahm er aus seinem Säckel? 36. Was tat er mit dem Geld? 37. Wie bewegten sich die Zeiger? 38. Was tat Schlemihl den ganzen Tag? 39. Was tat er, als die Uhr zwölf schlug?

II

Translate into German: 1. Two physicians have died in this little city in the last three months. 2. Is the water clearer than it was last week? 3. My four friends and I wanted to go to the country. 4. We had many guests. 5. It[1] was a dark night and we counted the stars. 6. We threw rocks into the water. 7. The nights were colder than we had expected. 8. She is getting more and more beautiful. 9. He is getting older but not better. 10. We have ten fingers, two hands, and one head. 11. The most beautiful flowers (Blumen) do not always smell best. 12. He can run the fastest of all. 13. The horse had run away. 14. His wife is ten years younger than he [is]. 15. Of an evening he never works. 16. One evening my father came home rather late.

NOTE. 1. Cf. footnote, page 55.

III

Translate into English:

atmen	der Brunnen	einschlafen	erinnern	März
behaupten	das Dach	eng	erlauben	der Ort
besuchen	ehe	das Fach	jagen	Sonnabend
der Bleistift	eilen	das Faß	die Krone	zunächst

IV

Translate into German:

the apple	thin	the goose
May	the parents	the building
to bite	the enemy	the danger
the brother	the fish	mean
the village	early	the mouth

V

Translate the following compounds and derivatives:

das Bäumchen, die Baumart; befehlen, der Befehl, der Befehlshaber; bewegen, die Bewegung, beweglich, die Beweglichkeit; brennen, die Brennbarkeit; der Briefwechsel; der Bruder, brüderlich; Freiheit, Gleichheit, Brüderlichkeit; dunkelblau, die Dunkelheit; die Ehe, die Ehescheidung, ehelos; die Ehre, ehren, ehrbar, die Ehrbarkeit, das Ehrenwort, die Ehrenlegion; eilen, die Eile, eilig, 5 der Eilbrief (the special delivery letter); ein einseitiges Buch; der Empfänger; entschließen, der Entschluß, die Entschlußkraft; schießen, der Schuß, der Fehlschuß; feurig, die Feuergefahr; der Ringfinger; fliegen, der Flug, der Flieger, der Flugplatz; frei, die Freiheit, der Freiheitskrieg; die Frucht, fruchtlos, die Fruchtlosigkeit; das Gastzimmer; greifen, der Griff; je deutlicher desto besser; meter- 10 lang; schmecken, der Schmecker; die Buttermilch; die Gesundheit, die Ewigkeit

VI

Translate into English: 1. Die gerade Linie ist der kürzeste Weg zwischen zwei Punkten. 2. Es wurde immer heller. 3. Er läuft immer schneller. 4. Die Kartoffeln werden immer teurer. 5. Köln ist nicht so weit von hier wie Berlin. 6. Diese Kirche ist die schönste im ganzen Lande. 7. Es gelang mir, zwei neue Hüte zu kaufen. 8. Tut es auf der Stelle! 9. Eines Morgens gingen wir auf das Land.

VII

Form feminine abstracts, (*a*) with -heit: gesund, klar, schlank, wild; (*b*) with -keit: heilig, herrlich, langsam, richtig; (*c*) with -igkeit: genau, schnell.

VIII

Compare the following adjectives:

angenehm	schnell	süß	stark
dünn	schön	alt	schwach
früh	spät	kurz	lang

IX

Decline in the singular and plural:

das Fräulein	das blaue Meer	der größte Baum
der Fehler	die kalte Nacht	mein älterer Hut
	der schönere Weg	

X

Conjugate in the present, past, present perfect, and past perfect the following verbs:

fliegen schneiden zeigen laufen zahlen bezahlen

XI

Learn the cardinal numerals from one to twelve.

LESSON XVI

TEXT A

Auf der Bank saß eine Frau, die ein Buch in der Hand hielt. Auf der Bank saß eine Frau; die hielt ein Buch in der Hand. Da geht der reiche Schmidt, dem die halbe Stadt gehört. Da geht der reiche Schmidt. Dem gehört die halbe Stadt. Ich denke noch oft an meinen Freund. Ich denke noch oft an ihn. An den denke ich noch oft. An wen denkst du, an ihn (an den)? Ich denke noch oft an unsre Reise, die wir zusammen gemacht haben. Ja, ich denke noch oft an sie zurück. Ja, an die denke ich noch oft zurück. Ich denke noch oft daran zurück. An was denkst du, an unsere Reise? Woran denkst du, an unsere Reise? Diese Reise, an die (an welche, woran) ich noch oft zurückdenken muß, war wirklich die schönste meines Lebens.

Gib mir einen andren Bleistift! Mit dem kann ich nicht schreiben. Damit kann ich nicht schreiben. In dem Zimmer stand ein großer Tisch. Und auf diesem Tisch (auf ihm, auf dem, darauf) lag ein dickes Buch. In dem Zimmer stand ein Tisch, auf dem (auf welchem, worauf) ein dickes Buch lag.

Ich fürchte mich vor dem Sterben. Rede nicht vom Sterben! Ich fürchte mich davor. Vor dem fürchte ich mich. Wovor fürchtest du dich, vor dem Sterben?

Fritz hat an deinen Vater geschrieben. So, davon habe ich nichts gewußt.

Ich treffe meine Freundin jeden Abend um sechs Uhr am Postamt. Ihre Eltern wissen nichts davon, denn wir halten unsere Liebe noch geheim.—Was raten Sie mir, soll ich mir ein teureres Kleid kaufen?—Viele Kinder haben Angst vor Pferden.—Ich trinke süßen Wein nicht gern.

Große Hitze ist für uns gefährlicher als große Kälte, denn Wärme können wir ja immer produzieren,[1] wenn es draußen kälter wird. Doch wenn die Kälte draußen zu groß wird, genügt[2] das Feuer in uns nicht mehr. Wenn sich z. B. (zum Beispiel) ein Tier unter eine bestimmte Temperatur abkühlt, so wird es zunächst unruhig. Es bewegt sich schneller, atmet tiefer, zeigt größere Freßlust, einen schnelleren Puls und einen höheren Blutdruck. Es versucht sozusagen, mit Gewalt mehr Hitze zu produzieren, um dem Tode zu entgehen.[3] Denn sein tieferes Atmen, sein höherer Blutdruck und seine ungewöhnlich große Freßlust haben natürlich nur den Zweck, mehr Wärme zu produzieren. Wenn jedoch die Bluttemperatur noch weiter sinkt, etwa unter vierunddreißig (34) Grad[4] Celsius, so beginnt das Tier, langsamer zu atmen. Der Puls sinkt auf eine sehr niedrige Zahl, und schließlich schläft das Tier ein. Von da ab geht es äußerst[5] schnell abwärts, bis bei etwa neunzehn (19) Grad der Tod eintritt. Für uns folgt daraus, daß eine Rettung bei dreißig (30) Grad noch möglich ist. Ja, es ist den Ärzten sogar gelungen, Leuten das Leben wiederzugeben, deren Temperatur auf sechsundzwanzig (26) Grad gesunken war.

NOTES. 1. produzieren produce, generate. 2. genügt suffices (cf. genug). 3. entgehen escape. 4. Grad degrees. 5. äußerst extremely.

VOCABULARY

die Absicht the intention
allerdings to be sure
das Amt, ⸚er the office; duty
die Angst, ⸚e the anxiety; fear
die Aufgabe the lesson, assignment; duty
außen outside
draußen outside, out of doors
die Backe the cheek
beginnen to *begin*
bereit *ready*, prepared
das Blatt, ⸚er the leaf; sheet
der Blitz, –e the lightning
dennoch nevertheless
dick *thick*
doppelt *double*
durchaus thoroughly; absolutely
empfinden to feel, perceive
entweder . . . oder either . . . or
fühlen to *feel*; touch
geheim secret
genießen to enjoy
die Gestalt the form, figure
gestatten to allow, permit
gestern *yesterday*
das Glied, –er the limb; member
das Gut, ⸚er the estate; *goods*
indes (indessen) meanwhile; nevertheless
irren to *err*; stray, wander
kühl *cool*
der Leib, –er the body; waist
das Lied, –er the song
das Maul, ⸚er the mouth (of animal)
mischen to *mix*
das Nest, –er the *nest*
prüfen to test, examine
raten to advise; guess
die Reihe the *row*, rank; series
reißen to tear
der Ring, –e the *ring*
die Rose the *rose*
rühren to stir; move
die Schlacht the battle (*slaughter*)
die Seele the *soul*
der Soldat the *soldier*

streiten to dispute, quarrel
streng severe, strict, stern
süß *sweet*
der Tau the *dew*
der Verlust, -e the *loss*
vorkommen to occur, happen; come forward; seem
der Wert, -e the value, *worth*
das Zeichen, - the sign; signal
der Zufall, ⸗e the chance; accident

IDIOMS

auf und ab up and down; back and forth
hin *frequently* gone
mit einem Male suddenly

TEXT B

Peter Schlemihl

[Fortsetzung]

Es war noch früh, als ich am folgenden Morgen wach wurde. Meine Augen[1] brannten, und meine Glieder schmerzten, als ich mich müde streckte. Mein treuer Bendel schien vor der Tür einen Streit mit Raskal, einem anderen meiner Diener, zu haben. Sie redeten laut und schnell. Das meiste konnte ich nicht verstehen, aber ein paarmal hörte ich deutlich das Wort 5 Schatten. Mein Herz klopfte. Ich klingelte. Niemand hörte mich. Da warf ich mich schnell in meine Kleider und riß die Tür auf. „Was willst du!" fragte ich Raskal streng mit dem Tone eines Mannes, der ans Befehlen gewöhnt ist. Er trat zwei Schritte zurück und antwortete beißend: „Darf ich Sie bitten, Herr Graf, mich einmal Ihren Schatten sehen zu lassen? 10 Die Sonne scheint eben so schön auf dem Hofe." Ich stand wie vom Blitz getroffen. Außer Bendel, so hatte ich geglaubt, wußte niemand um mein Geheimnis. Wie hatte Raskal dieses Geheimnis erfahren können? Und gerade an diesem Morgen! Noch gestern war ich sicher gewesen, heute wieder im Besitze[2] meines Schattens zu sein. Wußte Raskal mehr, als er sagte? 15 Auf jeden Fall konnte er ein gefährlicher Feind werden. Es dauerte lange, bis ich meine Sprache wiederfand. „Wie kann ein Diener sich erlauben, gegen seinen Herrn solche Worte zu gebrauchen?" fragte ich schließlich mit ziemlich unsicherer Stimme. Er sah mich stolz an und antwortete: „Ein Diener kann ein sehr ehrlicher Mensch sein und einem Schattenlosen nicht 20 dienen wollen. Herr Graf, entweder zeigen Sie mir Ihren Schatten, oder ich gehe." Ich suchte hilflos nach Worten. Er ging.

Mechanisch[3] nahm ich einen Brief, den, wie Bendel berichtete, ein Diener soeben mit der Bitte abgegeben hatte, ihn mir sogleich zu überreichen.

Mechanisch wollte ich das Schreiben eben öffnen, als ich sah: Der Brief war von Minnas Vater. Ich zitterte an allen Gliedern. Ich brauchte den Brief nun nicht mehr zu lesen. Ich legte ihn ungeöffnet auf den Schreibtisch. Ich wußte: Das war das Ende.

5 Ich ließ mir meinen Mantel bringen, warf ihn um und verließ das Haus, obgleich draußen die Morgensonne schon hoch am klarblauen Himmel stand.

Eine große Ruhe kam über mich. Wie ein Soldat vor der Schlacht im Angesicht des Todes Süße und Schönheit des Lebens noch einmal mit 10 doppelter Stärke empfindet, so genoß ich, den Tod im Herzen, noch einmal die Schönheit dieses Frühlingsmorgens.

Ein leichter Wind spielte leise mit den Blättern der Bäume vor meinem Hause. Ein paar rotbäckige Kinder spielten „Ringlein, Ringlein, Rose" in der Sonne, und die einfache Melodie ihrer kleinen Lieder rief längstvergessene 15 Jugendbilder in mir wach und rührte mich so, daß ich dem Weinen nahe war. Kaum merkte ich, daß ein paar Weiber,[4] die am Brunnen vor dem Rathaus standen, ihr interessantes Gespräch plötzlich abbrachen und mir mit offenen Mäulern[4] und erschrockenen Gesichtern nachsahen, als ich ohne Schatten an ihnen vorbeiging. Ich beobachtete die Schwalben,[5] die, vor ein paar Tagen 20 aus fernen Ländern zurückgekehrt, jetzt eilig hin und her flogen und unter den Dächern der langen Häuserreihe an ihren Nestern arbeiteten. Und draußen vor dem Städtchen lag das Land im Glanze der Frühlingssonne. Der frische Tau in den Gräsern spielte[6] in allen Farben.[6] Die Luft war frisch und kühl und roch nach Erde. In tiefem Frieden lagen die Dörfer 25 zwischen den Feldern. Die Welt, so kam es mir vor, war nie schöner gewesen.

Wie träumend und dennoch ganz wach ging ich den Weg zu Minnas Haus, deren Eltern etwa eine halbe Stunde vor der Stadt ein großes Gut besaßen.[2] Minna und ich reichten[7] uns still und ernst die Hand,[7] wie Menschen,[8] die wissen, sie sehen einander zum letzten Male. Und wie sie so vor 30 mir stand, in der lieblichen Schönheit ihrer Jugend, keinen Vorwurf,[9] nur Traurigkeit in ihrem Blick, da war meine Ruhe hin, und mit schmerzender Klarheit erkannte ich, wieviel ich verloren hatte.

Der Vater stürmte mit schnellen Schritten den engen Gartenweg auf und ab. In der Hand hielt er ein Papier, einen Brief von Raskal, wie ich später 35 erfuhr. Mit einem Male blieb er vor mir stehen, sah, daß ich keinen Schatten warf, blickte mich prüfend an und sagte: „Erinnern Sie sich, mein schatten=

loser Graf, vielleicht an einen gewissen Peter Schlemihl?"—„Allerdings, der bin ich." Meine Offenheit nahm ihm die Sprache. „Gut, mein Herr", begann er nach einer Weile wieder, „durch welchen—nun nennen wir es Zufall, Sie Ihren Schatten verloren haben, ist mir persönlich gleich. Ich habe durchaus nicht die Absicht, mich in eine Sache zu mischen, die mich nichts angeht. Indes, Sie behaupten, meine Tochter zu lieben. Sie gestatten, daß ich an diese Liebe nicht glaube. Man stürzt nicht jemand ins Unglück, den man liebt. Auf jeden Fall habe ich als Vater das Amt und die Aufgabe, für meine Tochter zu sorgen. Es ist meine Pflicht, zu verhindern, daß sie sich an einen Mann bindet, der keinen Schatten hat. Ich gebe Ihnen bis Mittwoch Zeit. Wenn Sie Mittwoch mit einem Schatten wiederkommen, können Sie Minna noch am selben Tage heiraten. Wenn nicht, so ist meine Tochter, das verspreche ich Ihnen, am Donnerstag die Frau eines andern."

Ich wollte noch versuchen, ein Wort mit Minna zu reden. Aber sie blickte traurig und hilfesuchend auf ihre Mutter, und diese machte mir ein Zeichen zu gehen. Ich ging. Und alles, was eines Mannes Leben lebenswert macht, blieb hinter mir zurück.

Gewiß, tief im Herzen hatte ich gewußt: Eure Liebe ist ohne Hoffnung, euer Glück muß ein böses Ende nehmen. Aber nun war der Schlag doch zu plötzlich gekommen und hatte mich vollkommen unvorbereitet getroffen. Ich sah keinen Ausweg, keine Hoffnung. Minnas Bild vor meiner Seele, irrte ich verloren durch Wälder und Felder. Und vor diesem Bild ihrer geliebten Gestalt mußte ich mich schämen.[10] Wie hatte ich Schattenloser dieses junge, unschuldige Wesen an mich binden können? Ich haßte mich.

Ich weiß nicht, wie lange ich gegangen war, als ich plötzlich eine Hand auf meinem Arm fühlte. Ich stand still und sah mich um: Es war der Mann im grauen Rock!

Er nahm sogleich das Wort: „Lassen Sie den Mut nicht sinken, mein Freund! Noch ist der Kampf nicht verloren. Sie haben in Ihrer Rechnung einen Fehler gemacht und mich einen Tag zu früh erwartet. Folgen Sie meinem Rat und kehren Sie gleich wieder zurück! Ihren Schatten gebe ich Ihnen gerne wieder."

Ich stand wie im Schlafe da. „Einen Tag zu früh erwartet?" Wie hatte ich einen solchen Fehler machen können? Aber er hatte recht, ich hatte ihn wirklich einen Tag zu früh erwartet. Ein[11] Stein fiel mir vom Herzen.[11]

Ich riß sogleich den Säckel aus meiner Brusttasche. Er riet meine Absicht und sagte: „Nein, nein, nicht nötig, Herr Graf, der Säckel ist in guten Händen, und ich brauche ihn nicht. Nur um eine Kleinigkeit muß ich Sie bitten. Seien Sie so gut und unterschreiben Sie dies hier mit Ihrem
5 richtigen Namen."

Er überreichte mir ein Stück Papier. Ich las:

„Dem Besitzer[2] dieses Dokuments gehört meine Seele nach ihrer natürlichen Trennung von meinem Leibe."

[Fortsetzung folgt]

NOTES. 1. Augen, Händen *plural forms* eyes, hands. 2. Besitz possession; besaßen possessed, owned, had; Besitzer possessor. 3. Mechanisch mechanically. 4. Weiber, Mäulern. These two words, Weiber and Mäuler, show Peter's contempt for the women standing with open mouths. The words are used in a derogatory sense. 5. Schwalben swallows. 6. spielte in allen Farben glistened in all colors. 7. reichten uns . . . die Hand clasped, pressed hands. 8. Menschen people. 9. Vorwurf reproach. 10. mußte . . . schämen I had to be ashamed of myself. 11. Ein . . . Herzen A weight fell from my heart.

BUILDING A PASSIVE VOCABULARY

das Angesicht *same as* Gesicht
erkannte (erkennen) kennen to know, erkennen to recognize
erschrocken der Schreck the fright, erschrocken frightened
das Geheimnis geheim secret, das Geheimnis the secret
das Gespräch sprechen to speak, talk, das Gespräch the conversation
gewöhnt (an etwas gewöhnt sein) gewöhnlich usual, customary, an etwas gewöhnt sein to be accustomed to something
Herr Graf *The title* Herr *precedes such titles as* Graf, Doktor, Professor, *and the like. It is best left out in translating*
niedrige *The adjective* nieder *has a second form* niedrig
ein paarmal das Paar pair, couple, ein paar some, few, das Mal time, ein paarmal a few times
die Sprache sprechen to speak, die Sprache speech (words)
unterschreiben unter under, below, schreiben to write, unterschreiben to sign
unvorbereitet bereit prepared, unvorbereitet unprepared
verhindern *same as* hindern
verließ (verlassen) lassen to let, allow, leave, verlassen to leave
die Zahl zählen to count, die Zahl the number

GRAMMAR

103. Nouns of the Third Class. Nouns of this class add ⸗er to form the plural and umlaut the vowel whenever possible. In this group there are many monosyllabic neuters, a few monosyllabic masculines (of which only five will be found in this book), but no feminines.

The neuter nouns which have already been introduced are:

das Amt	das Dach	das Feld	das Gut	das Licht	das Rathaus
das Bild	das Dorf	das Gesicht	das Haus	das Lied	das Tuch
das Blatt	das Fach	das Glas	das Kind	das Maul	das Weib
das Buch	das Faß	das Glied	das Kleid	das Nest	das Wort*
		das Gras	das Land		

The following masculines have been introduced:

der Gott der Leib der Mann der Wald

104. The Demonstrative Pronoun der, die, das. When the third person of the personal pronoun (er, sie, es, sie) is emphasized, it is frequently replaced by the demonstrative pronoun (der, die, das, die), which is identical in form with the relative. The reader can distinguish between the relative der and the demonstrative der only by the position of the inflected verb: with verb-second position it is a demonstrative; with verb-last position it is a relative:

Auf dem Jahrmarkt sah Hildegard einen Krug, { der hatte ein Bild auf jeder Seite. / der ein Bild auf jeder Seite hatte. }

At the annual fair Hildegard saw a pitcher { . It had a picture on each side. / which had a picture on each side. }

An der Ecke traf er Eva, { deren Gesicht wurde ganz rot. / deren Gesicht ganz rot wurde. }

On the corner he met Eva { . Her face became very red. / , whose face became very red. }

*Das Wort has two plurals, die Worte (connected discourse) and die Wörter (isolated or disconnected words, as in a dictionary).

105. The Pronoun Substitute da=. When governed by prepositions, personal pronouns in the third person referring to things (or ideas) are usually replaced by the word da= (dar= before vowels) compounded with and preceding the preposition in question.* Thus, mit ihm, mit ihr, mit ihnen, are all expressed by damit; an ihn, an sie, an es, are expressed by daran. Examples:

Hast du Vaters Bleistift gesehen? Ich schreibe gerade damit. Have you seen father's pencil? I am writing with it.

Vor zwei Tagen war das Eis noch gefährlich dünn. Heute aber kann man schon darauf spielen. Two days ago the ice was still dangerously thin. Today, however, one can play on it all right (or one can already play on it).

Examples of substitute referring to an entire clause or idea:

Ich höre, ihr habt euer Haus verloren. Ja, aber sprecht nicht davon. Karl hat es nicht gern. I hear you have lost your house. Yes, but don't talk about it (*in formal English* our having lost it). Karl doesn't like it (i.e., anyone's talking about the loss).

Wolltest du nicht heute deinen Onkel besuchen? Ach, ich habe gar nicht mehr daran gedacht. Didn't you want to visit your uncle today? Oh, I hadn't thought about that at all.

106. The Pronoun Substitute wo=. The interrogative pronoun was when governed by prepositions is usually replaced by the word wo= (wor= before vowels) and is compounded with and precedes the preposition in question.† Thus, mit was becomes womit; an was, woran. Examples:

Woran arbeitest du? What are you working on?

Womit schreibst du denn da, mit Vaters Feder? Say, what are you writing with, with father's pen?

Worauf schläfst du? What are you sleeping on? *or* On what do you sleep?

---

*Cf. thereby, thereat, therefrom.

†Cf: whereto, whereon, wherewith

Relatives, when referring to things, are frequently replaced in a like manner. Examples:

Der Bleistift, mit dem (mit welchem, **womit**) ich schreibe, . . . *All three forms mean* with which: The pencil with which I am writing . . .
Das Buch, in dem (in welchem, **worin**) ich las, . . . The book in which I was reading . . .

107. Absolute Accusative. The accusative is often used absolutely, that is, without depending upon a verb or preposition. Sometimes *having* and sometimes *with* is understood:

Den Tod im Herzen, genoß ich noch einmal die Schönheit des Frühlingsmorgens. Minnas Bild vor meiner Seele, irrte ich verloren durch Wälder und Felder. With death in my heart I enjoyed once more the beauty of the spring morning. With Minna's picture before my soul I strayed lost through forests and fields.

108. Word Formation: Feminine Abstracts in -e. The suffix -e is added to adjectives to form abstract feminine nouns. The umlaut is added whenever possible:

süß sweet, die Süße the sweetness
treu faithful, die Treue the faithfulness
fern distant, die Ferne the distance
stark strong, die Stärke the strength

Hence:

die Größe the greatness *or* size
die Hitze (*from* heiß) the heat
die Frühe the morning
die Nähe the nearness, proximity
die Schwere the heaviness, weight

Learn the principal parts of the following verbs as a part of this lesson:

beißen	biß	hat gebissen	beißt	to bite
reißen	riß	hat gerissen	reißt	to tear
streiten	stritt	hat gestritten	streitet	to quarrel

schließen	schloß	hat geschlossen	schließt	to close
genießen	genoß	hat genossen	genießt	to enjoy
sinken	sank	ist gesunken	sinkt	to sink
empfinden	empfand	hat empfunden	empfindet	to feel
gewinnen	gewann	hat gewonnen	gewinnt	to win
beginnen	begann	hat begonnen	beginnt	to begin
schlāfen	schlief	hat geschlāfen	schlāft	to sleep
rāten	riet	hat gerāten	rāt	to advise
kommen	kām	ist gekommen	kommt	to come
vorkommen	kām vor	ist vorgekommen	kommt vor	to occur

EXERCISES

I

Answer the following questions in German: 1. Wann wurde Peter wach? 2. Mit wem hatte Bendel einen Streit? 3. Woran war Peter gewöhnt? 4. Wie antwortete Raskal? 5. Was wollte Raskal sehen? 6. Wonach suchte Peter hilflos? 7. Warum ging Raskal? 8. Von wem war der Brief, den der Diener soeben abgegeben hatte? 9. Was wußte Peter? 10. Was ließ Peter sich bringen? 11. Wie war das Wetter draußen? 12. Was genoß Peter mit doppelter Stärke? 13. Womit spielte der Wind? 14. Was spielten die Kinder? 15. Was rief die Melodie ihrer Lieder in ihm wach? 16. Wovor standen die Frauen? 17. Warum hatten sie erschrockene Gesichter? 18. Woher kamen die Schwalben? 19. Woran arbeiteten sie? 20. Wo waren die Schwalbennester? 21. Wonach roch die Luft? 22. Wo lagen die Dörfer? 23. Wohin ging Peter? 24. Was besaßen Minnas Eltern vor der Stadt? 25. Was erkannte Peter, als Minna vor ihm stand? 26. Was hielt Minnas Vater in der Hand? 27. Was nahm ihm die Sprache? 28. Wen stürzt man nicht ins Unglück? 29. Bis wann hatte Peter Zeit, seinen Schatten wiederzubekommen? 30. Wer machte Peter ein Zeichen zu gehen? 31. Was ließ er zurück? 32. Was war zu plötzlich gekommen? 33. Was konnte Peter nicht sehen? 34. Wovor mußte Peter sich schämen? 35. Was fühlte er plötzlich an seinem Arm? 36. Worin hatte Peter einen Fehler gemacht? 37. Warum riß Peter den Glückssäckel aus seiner Brusttasche? 38. Was überreichte der Graue unsrem Peter? 39. Was war der Preis, den der Graue für Peters Schatten verlangte?

II

Translate into German: 1. It is a charming house; we have three pictures of it. 2. They now have five children. 3. She has bought four dresses in the last six months. 4. What does she do with them? 5. What are you doing with so many books? 6. Three men were riding on one horse. 7. They have a large house in the country, but they do not live in it. 8. In the new book we found many words that we never use. 9. What are they doing on the ice? 10. How long have you been eating? 11. I am much older than my brother. 12. The roofs of the houses in Rothenburg are red. 13. May I see your new pen? May I write with it? 14. We could hear you best because you were singing loudest.

III

Translate into English:

genau	lehren	die Lust	die Mauer	fehlen
gering	der Gott	die Luft	der Nachbar	zehn
innen	die Linie	die Wand	nachdem	der Zustand

IV

Translate into German:

to happen	to ring	the power	the pen
the company	to knock	the sea	Monday
to pour	the cake	the crowd	the victory
June	to smile	the milk	Saturday
the church	loud	the middle	to listen

V

Translate the following compounds and derivatives:

die Ferne; die Hälfte; tun, tat, getan, die Tat, die Gewalttat; glänzen; der Steinhaufen; hervorholen, herbeiholen, hervorkommen; genießen, der Genuß; das Hochland, hochstehend; das Jahrhundert (century), die Jahrhundertfeier; der Jäger; der Kampf, kämpfen, der Kämpfer, kampfbereit, der Einzelkampf; der König, die Königin, königlich, die Königskrone, das Königreich; die Schwäche; 5 die Blindheit, die Schnelligkeit; der Graf, die Gräfin; die Strenge, die Süße;

die Lehrmethode; das Sonnenlicht; ein Heißluft-Apparat; messen, das Maß, die Meßbarkeit; die Helle, die Helligkeit; der Durst, dürsten; der Edelmann; die Gemeinheit; der Wein schmeckt nach dem Faß; das Verlangen; vorausgehen; weglaufen; wirken, die Wirkung; lang, die Länge, Armeslänge

VI

Translate the following sentences into English: 1. Du wirst immer schöner. 2. Vater wird immer dicker. 3. Sag es noch einmal. 4. Morgen früh wollen wir wieder zu Hause sein. 5. Es tut mir leid, daß du nicht mitgehen kannst. 6. Die Verkäuferin fragte uns, ob wir sonst noch etwas kaufen wollten. 7. Mit einem Male war er nicht mehr da. 8. Hin ist hin! Verloren ist verloren!

VII

Form feminine abstracts in -e and translate into English:

dick　gut　kurz　schwach　treu
eng　hart　rot　still　tief

VIII

Decline in the singular and plural:

das Faß　mein Gast　der freundliche Lehrer
das Glas　dieses Lied　der lange Bleistift
das Mädchen　das grüne Blatt　jener Wald
der Baum

IX

Give the third person singular form of the following verbs in the present, past, present perfect, and past perfect:

sterben　teilen　wollen
stoßen　treiben　arbeiten können
vorschlagen

X

Give the correct pronoun substitute for the following underlined words. Example: Er schreibt mit einem Bleistift. Er schreibt damit.

1. Er arbeitet an einem Buch. 2. Er hilft bei der Arbeit. 3. Sie spielen vor der Kirche. 4. Er lag auf dem Schnee. 5. Er sitzt hinter dem Tisch. 6. Wir saßen lange in der Kirche. 7. Er saß am (an dem) Fenster. 8. Sie spielten auf dem Dache.

XI

Give pronoun substitutes for the following relatives: 1. Der Bleistift, mit dem du schreibst, ist stumpf. 2. Das Glas, aus dem du sonst trinkst, ist letzte Woche auf den Boden gefallen. 3. Das Zimmer, in dem die armen Kinder schlafen müssen, hat gar keine Fenster. 4. Mein Enkel hat mir das Buch gegeben, über das wir vor drei oder vier Tagen gesprochen haben. 5. Wir wollen einen Wagen kaufen, in dem sechs Leute gut sitzen können.

LESSON XVII

TEXT A

Münchhausen erzählt eine Geschichte

„Meine letzte Reise nach Moskau machte ich absichtlich mitten im Winter. Denn man kommt auf dieser Reise durch eine Provinz,[1] wo es im Herbst so außerordentlich stark und lange regnet, daß Felder und Wälder unter dem Wasser verschwinden und sich das Land in einen großen See verwandelt— was übrigens für die Menschen, die dort wohnen, gar nicht so unangenehm ist, wie Sie vielleicht glauben. Die Kirchen, die Rathäuser, die Schulen, überhaupt alle größeren Gebäude stehen auf hohen Steinmauern und kommen selbst dann nicht in Gefahr, wenn das Wasser zehn oder zwölf Meter höher steigt als gewöhnlich. Die anderen Häuser sind aus[2] Holz und treiben[3] zur Regenzeit[3] wie Schiffe auf dem Wasser. Wenn sich die Leute eines Dorfes besuchen wollen, so warten sie einfach, bis der Wind ihre Häuser nahe aneinander treibt. Und sobald die Dächer zusammenstoßen, springt man von seinem Dach auf das des Bruders, Onkels oder Nachbarn. Schafe, Pferde und andere Haustiere[4] in dieser Provinz bekommen im Herbst ein dichtes Federkleid, leben dann während der Regenzeit wie Gänse auf dem Wasser und fressen die Fische, die jedes Jahr in großen Mengen aus dem Meere kommen, um einmal Süßwasser[5] zu genießen.

Sie können sich denken, daß kaum jemand Lust hat, während der Monate, in denen es Tag und Nacht gießt, durch diese Provinz zu reisen, wenn es nicht absolut notwendig ist, besonders dann nicht, wenn man, wie ich, gerne reitet. Die meisten warten, bis die Regenzeit vorbei ist, und reisen erst, wenn die strenge Winterkälte das Wasser in Eis verwandelt hat, was oft in einer einzigen Nacht geschieht. Dann kann man allerdings in dieser Provinz schneller vorwärts kommen als in jedem anderen Lande, das ich kenne. Man ist dann nicht mehr an die Wege gebunden und kann sozusagen auf der Luftlinie reisen, besonders wenn man, wie ich, ein Pferd hat, das Ski laufen[6] kann.

Doch ich sehe, daß Sie ungläubig lächeln. Ich erlaube mir, den Damen und Herren vorzuschlagen, daß Sie einmal selber im Herbst in diese Provinz fahren, die dortigen Zustände zur Regenzeit studieren und mir dann berichten, ob ich mich in irgendeinem Punkte von der Wahrheit entfernt habe, oder ob man mir trauen und meinen Behauptungen Glauben[7] schenken[7] darf."

[Fortsetzung folgt. Siehe Aufgabe XIX]

NOTES. 1. Provinz province. 2. aus Holz of wood. 3. treiben zur Regenzeit float, drift in the rainy season. 4. Haustiere domestic animals. 5. Süßwasser fresh water. 6. Ski laufen to ski. 7. Glauben schenken lend *or* give credence to.

VOCABULARY

ähnlich similar
anzünden (*sep. prefix*) to light, ignite
begleiten to accompany
beide *both*; two
das Bein, –e the leg
bilden to form, shape; educate
brav good; well-behaved
die Dame, –n the lady
der Dieb, –e the *thief*
das Ding, –e the *thing*
dumm stupid, "*dumb*"
einsam lonesome; solitary
einst *once*; formerly
falsch *false*; forged
fangen to catch
fassen to seize; contain
fordern to demand; challenge
die Form, –en the *form*, shape, figure
freilich certainly; to be sure
frieren to *freeze*
füllen to *fill*
der Fürst, –en the prince; sovereign
der Fuß, ⁻̈e the *foot*
der Geist, –er the spirit, *ghost*; mind
die Grenze, –n the limit; boundary
der Hals, ⁻̈e the throat, neck
die Heide, –n the *heath*
der Hund, –e the dog, *hound*
je ever
der Knabe, –n the boy, lad
kochen to *cook*; boil
leer empty, vacant
die Linde, –n the *linden* (tree)
link left
  links to the left
die Lippe, –n the *lip*
die Musik the *music*
notwendig necessary
das Ohr, –en the *ear*
recht *right* (hand)
  rechts to the right
reif *ripe*; mature
scharf *sharp*
stechen to prick, pierce, sting
die Sünde, –n the *sin*
überall everywhere
unterrichten to instruct; inform
der Ursprung, ⁻̈e the origin
vorziehen to prefer; pull out
wählen to choose, select; elect
weise *wise*, prudent
die Wolke, –n the cloud

IDIOMS

Glück haben to be fortunate
um . . . willen for the sake of
was für ein what sort of; what a

TEXT B

Peter Schlemihl [Fortsetzung]

Sprachlos sah ich abwechselnd auf das Stück Papier in meinen Händen und auf den grauen Mann neben mir. Träumte ich? Der Graue, das Papier, überhaupt die ganze Szene[1] kam mir so unwirklich vor. War das Ganze ein Produkt meiner Phantasie[2]? Ja, in meiner Jugend, da hatte ich
5 die Historia von Doktor Johannes Faust und andere Geschichten gelesen, in denen ein Mann seine Seele verkauft und ähnliche Dokumente unterschrieben hatte. Aber nie, auch nicht als Knabe, hatte ich geglaubt, daß es so[3] etwas[3] wirklich gibt, wollte es auch jetzt nicht glauben. Aber derselbe Wind, der mit meinem Haar spielte und mein Gesicht kühlte, bewegte auch leise das Papier
10 in meiner Hand.

Soviel war klar: ich war in Gefahr. Der Graue war mein Feind. Ich mußte all meinen Mut zusammennehmen, um aus dem Kampf, der jetzt kommen mußte, als Sieger hervorzugehen. „Mein Herr", sagte ich nach einer Weile, „das unterschreibe ich nicht."—„Nicht?" wiederholte der
15 Graue, „und warum nicht?"—„Es scheint mir doch sehr unweise zu sein, meine Seele für einen Schatten wegzugeben."—„Unweise! Haha!" lachte der Graue. „Wissen Sie denn wirklich, was für ein Ding Ihre Seele ist? Haben Sie sie je gesehen? Sind Sie überhaupt sicher, daß Sie eine Seele haben? Und was wollen Sie denn machen mit dieser Seele, wenn Sie
20 einst tot sind? Seien Sie doch froh, einen Dummen gefunden zu haben, der Ihnen für dieses Ding noch vor Ihrem Tode etwas Wirkliches, nämlich Ihren Schatten geben will! Ihren Schatten, durch den Sie Ihre geliebte Minna zurückgewinnen und zur Erfüllung all Ihrer Wünsche kommen können. Wollen Sie etwa, daß Minna, das arme Ding, Raskal heiratet?
25 Sie wissen doch, es war Raskal, der so gemein war, den Brief an den Vater zu schreiben, und der Minna am Donnerstag heiraten will. Hier, seien Sie kein Narr und unterschreiben Sie!"

Daß der Graue mich mit meiner Liebe zu Minna zwingen wollte, etwas Böses zu tun, brachte mein Blut zum Kochen. Ich haßte ihn aus dem
30 Grunde meiner Seele, und ich glaube, dieser Haß allein hat mich damals zurückgehalten, ihm sogleich die geforderte Unterschrift zu geben.

„Mein Herr", sagte ich laut und versuchte, ruhig zu bleiben, „ich habe Ihnen vor einem Jahre meinen Schatten verkauft. Ein zweites Geschäft dieser Art kommt nicht in Frage. Meine Seele verkaufe ich Ihnen nicht. Entweder Sie geben mir meinen Schatten gegen den Säckel zurück, oder jeder von uns behält, was er hat, und wir scheiden voneinander. Und zwar je eher, desto besser!“—„Es tut mir leid, Herr Graf, daß Sie vorziehen, bis an das Ende Ihres Lebens ohne Schatten zu bleiben. Indessen, vielleicht habe ich ein andermal mehr Glück. Auf Wiedersehen!—Übrigens gestatten Sie mir, Ihnen zu zeigen, daß ich die Sachen, die ich kaufe, nicht verkaufe. Ihr Schatten ist mir mehr wert als alles Gold der Welt.“ Mit diesen Worten zog der graue Mann meinen Schatten aus der Rocktasche, faßte ihn bei den Beinen, warf ihn auf die Heide und legte ihn so an seine Füße, daß er auf zwei Seiten statt auf einer einen Schatten zu haben schien, seinen eigenen Schatten auf der rechten und meinen auf der linken Seite. „Sie brauchen durchaus nicht so traurig auf Ihren Schatten zu sehen“, meinte er. „Ein Federzug ist alles, was nötig ist, damit der Schatten wieder Ihnen gehört. Nur ein Federzug, und Ihre Minna hat in den Armen des geliebten Grafen bald alles Leid vergessen.“

Er schwieg einen Augenblick und schien irgendwohin in die Ferne zu sehen. „Kommen Sie“, sagte er, „unterrichten Sie sich mit Ihren eigenen Augen und Ohren über die Absichten Ihres ‚treuen‘ Dieners Raskal! Ziehen Sie diese Tarnkappe[4] über den Kopf, und wir können Herrn Raskal ungesehen beobachten.“ Er zog etwas aus der Tasche, das wie ein Mantel aussah, warf es mir um und ging voraus, ohne zu warten,[5] ob ich ihm folgte. Ich eilte ihm nach, und schweigend machten wir uns auf den Weg zu Minnas Garten.

Fast wie einen Hund hatte mich der Vater vor wenigen Stunden aus dem Garten gejagt. Wie ein Dieb kehrte ich zurück. Aber war das wirklich noch derselbe Garten? Mir kam alles so verändert vor. Und war das meine Minna, die da wie leblos auf der Bank zwischen den beiden Linden saß, meine Minna, die hier so oft ihre Arme um meinen Hals gelegt, so oft ihre Lippen auf meine gedrückt hatte? Wie tot, keinen Tropfen[6] Blut im Gesicht, sah sie mit leerem Blick in die Ferne. Der Anblick schnitt mir ins Herz. „Sehen Sie sich das arme Ding an!“ sagte mein Begleiter leise. „Ihre Schuld! Nur weil Sie nicht unterschreiben wollen.“

Ich zitterte.

Der Vater ging wieder, die Hände auf dem Rücken, mit schnellen Schritten den Gartenweg auf und ab. „Freilich“, sagte er nach einer Weile und blieb vor ihr stehen, „ich verstehe es ja, daß du ihn geliebt hast. Ich selbst habe ihn geliebt. Aber du mußt dir diese Liebe aus dem Herzen reißen, mußt diesen Ehr- und Schattenlosen vergessen, mußt zu stolz sein, noch an ihn zu denken. Was! Jeder Hund hat seinen Schatten, und mein einziges Kind soll einen Menschen heiraten, der keinen Schatten hat? Nein, das können, das dürfen deine Eltern nicht erlauben. Ich weiß, du bist vernünftig, du denkst nicht mehr an ihn. Raskal ist zwar kein Fürst, kein Graf, aber er ist gesund, er ist reich, er ist nicht zu alt und kann dich vielleicht glücklich machen. Auf jeden Fall kannst du dich mit ihm in der Sonne sehen lassen. Nein, antworte nichts! Sei eine brave Tochter und laß deinen Vater für dich sorgen! Versprich mir, dem Herrn Raskal deine Hand zu geben!" Minna nickte müde und antwortete mit leiser Stimme: „Ich habe keine Wünsche mehr auf dieser Erde. Tu mit mir, was du willst!"

Mein Begleiter sah mir prüfend ins Gesicht: „Und dabei bleiben Sie ruhig?" fragte er mit beißender Schärfe. „Fließt denn Wasser statt Blut in Ihren Adern[9]?" Er zog eine Feder aus der Tasche und stach mir damit in die Hand. „Wahrhaftig, Herr Graf", meinte er, „rotes Blut!" Er fing einen Tropfen auf und reichte mir Feder und Papier. „Hier, unterschreiben Sie, rechts, da unten: Peter Schlemihl!"

Ich nahm Feder und Papier. . . .

Ich weiß nicht, wie es kam, daß ich gerade in dem Augenblick in eine tiefe Ohnmacht fiel, als ich meine Unterschrift unter das Dokument setzen wollte. Ich war entschlossen, den geforderten Preis zu zahlen. Nicht für mein Glück, sondern um dieses unschuldige Wesen vor einem Manne zu retten, den sie nicht liebte.

Aber ich bin zufrieden, daß alles so kam, wie es gekommen ist. Ich habe gelernt, daß es überall in der Welt und auch im Leben der Menschen eine allweise Vorsehung gibt, die dem Einzelnen zwar eine gewisse Freiheit läßt für seine persönlichen Wünsche, aber diesen Wünschen auch eine Grenze setzt, an der unsere Macht endet. Ich habe gelernt, daß diese Vorsehung, höher als unsere enge Menschenvernunft, zwar oft erlaubt, daß wir Fehler machen und schuldig werden, aber nur, um uns zu bilden und zu formen, bis wir reif werden und sie als Anfang und Ende, als Ursprung und Ziel aller Dinge verehren. Ich weiß heute, daß diese übernatürliche Macht, als ich um Minnas willen eine Sünde tun wollte, für mich und für Minna das Bessere gewählt hat.

Der Graue stand noch immer neben mir, als ich wieder zu mir kam. „Sie altes Weib!" begrüßte er mich freundlich. Aber ich war noch schwach, und es dauerte eine Weile, bis mir klar wurde, was überhaupt geschehen war. Wir waren noch immer in Minnas Garten. Der volle Mond zog durch die Wolken. Im Hause hatte man die Lichter angezündet, und aus den Räumen 5 drangen helle Frauenstimmen und festliche Musik zu uns herüber.

Ein paar Gäste gingen auf den Gartenwegen auf und ab. Ein junges Paar nahm nicht weit von mir auf derselben Bank Platz, auf der ich so oft mit Minna gesessen hatte. Sie sprachen von Raskal und seiner jungen Frau. „Nach meiner Meinung hat sie wirklich Glück gehabt", hörte ich die Dame 10 sagen, „so schnell einen Mann zu finden, der sie heiraten wollte nach dieser bösen Geschichte mit dem falschen Grafen."

Es war also geschehen. Minna, meine Minna, war die Frau eines anderen.

[Fortsetzung folgt]

NOTES. 1. Szene scene. 2. Phantasie imagination. 3. so etwas such a thing (a thing like that). 4. Tarnkappe magic cloak (which makes the wearer invisible). 5. ohne zu warten without waiting (to see). 6. Tropfen drop. 7. Adern veins.

BUILDING A PASSIVE VOCABULARY

abwechselnd ab off, wechseln to change, abwechselnd changing "off" (that is, looking first at one and then at the other), alternately
der Anblick an on, at, blicken to look, der Anblick sight
aussah aussehen to look, appear
behält (behalten) halten to hold, behalten to keep
entfernt fern far, distant, entfernt (*past part.*) departed
Erfüllung füllen to fill, erfüllen fulfill, Erfüllung fulfillment
Federzug die Feder the pen, der Zug (*from* ziehen to move) the movement, der Federzug stroke of the pen
geliebt lieben to love, geliebt (*past part. as adj.*) beloved
machen tun
nach meiner Meinung in my opinion
Ohnmacht ohne without, die Macht power, might, die Ohnmacht, faint
der Tod, tot töten to kill, der Tod death, tot dead
übernatürlich über over, super-, natürlich natural. übernatürlich supernatural
unten unter under, below, unten (*adv.*) below, at the bottom

unterschreiben, die Unterschrift unter under, below, schreiben to write, unterschreiben to sign, die Unterschrift the signature
verändert anders different, ändern to change, verändert changed
verehren die Ehre the honor, verehren to honor, respect
vor ago (vor wenigen Stunden a few hours ago); note that English "ago" follows the noun.
die Vorsehung Providence
wahrhaftig wahr true, wahrhaftig truly, really
zweites zwei two, zweites (*ordinal number*) second

GRAMMAR

109. Nouns of the Fourth Class. Nouns of this class add -n or -en to form the plural. They do not take the umlaut. This is the group to which almost all feminines belong; there are relatively few masculines and neuters in it.

a. The feminine nouns that have already been introduced and which add -n are:

die Aufgabe	die Familie	die Klasse	die Reihe	die Straße
die Backe	die Farbe	die Krone	die Rose	die Stunde
die Blume	die Feder	die Linde	die Sache	die Sünde
die Dame	die Freude	die Linie	die Schule	die Tasche
die Ecke	die Geschichte	die Lippe	die Seele	die Tasse
die Ehe	die Grenze	die Mauer	die Seite	die Weise
die Ehre	die Kartoffel	die Menge	die Spitze	die Woche
die Erbse	die Kirche	die Nase	die Stimme	die Wolke

b. The feminines which add -en are:

die Absicht	die Gesellschaft	die Pflicht	die Uhr
die Art	die Gestalt	die Schlacht	die Welt
die Form	die Gewalt	die Schuld	die Zeit
die Frau	die Person	die Tür	die Zeitung
die Gefahr			

c. The following neuters* and masculines* add -en (-n if they end in -e):

* These nouns are regular in the singular; as, das Auge, des Auges, dem Auge, das Auge; der Doktor, des Doktors, dem Doktor, den Doktor.

das Auge
das Bett
der Doktor
das Ende
das Ohr
der Schmerz
der See

d. The following masculines add -n or -en (as indicated) to the nominative singular form in all of the other cases, singular and plural. (They are all irregular in the genitive singular in that they do not add -s.)

der Fürst (–en)
der Graf (–en)
der Held (–en)
der Knabe (–n)
der Löwe (–n)
der Mensch (–en)
der Nachbar* (–n)
der Narr (–en)
der Soldat (–en)

e. The plural of der Herr is die Herren; of das Herz, die Herzen. (Cf. § 84 for singular forms.)

110. Reciprocal Pronouns. Reflexive pronouns when used in the plural may have a reciprocal sense and mean *each other*:

Wir sehen uns oft. We see each other often.
Sie küßten sich. They kissed each other (one another).

111. The Dative of Interest. The dative of interest is a variety of the indirect object. It denotes the person to whom something is done or to whom something happens. It is especially frequent when, as stated in § 45, the definite article replaces the possessive adjective (Cf. *Look me in the eye*):

Mein Begleiter sah mir ins Gesicht. My companion looked into my face
Der Anblick schnitt mir ins Herz. The sight cut me to the heart.
Du mußt dir diese Liebe aus dem Herzen reißen. You must tear (cast) this love from your heart.
Er hat sich in den Finger geschnitten. He cut his finger.

112. Intensifiers. To give particular emphasis to a personal pronoun, English uses the corresponding reflexive pronoun: *I myself say it. He says it himself.* Compare:

Reflexive Pronouns	**Intensifiers**
She loves herself.	She loves him herself.

*Nachbar may also be declined regularly (like Vater) in the singular.

German does not use reflexives (Cf. § 44) as intensifiers. Instead it places one of two indeclinable and interchangeable words, selbst and selber, after the emphasized noun or pronoun:

Ich selbst (selber) habe ihn geliebt. I myself loved him.
Das haben wir selber (selbst) gesehen. We saw that ourselves.

Selbst may precede a noun or pronoun; and when it does, it means *even*:

Selbst ein Hund hat einen Schatten. Even a dog has a shadow.

Learn the principal parts of the following verbs:

empfangen	empfing	hat empfangen	empfängt	to receive
fangen	fing	hat gefangen	fängt	to catch
ziehen	zōg	hat gezōgen	zieht	to pull
vorziehen	zōg vor	hat vorgezōgen	zieht vor	to prefer
frieren	frōr	ist gefrōren	friert	to freeze
sprechen	sprāch	hat gesprochen	spricht	to speak
stechen	stāch	hat gestochen	sticht	to sting

EXERCISES

I

Answer in German: 1. Wer war sprachlos? 2. Wer stand neben Peter? 3. Was kam ihm unwirklich vor? 4. Was hatte er in seiner Jugend gelesen? 5. Was hatte Doktor Faust verkauft? 6. Was bewegte der Wind? 7. Warum wollte Peter das Papier nicht unterschreiben? 8. Wodurch konnte Peter Minna zurückgewinnen? 9. Was wollte der Graue dem armen Peter für seine Seele geben? 10. Wer hatte den Brief an Minnas Vater geschrieben? 11. Wann sollte Raskal Minna heiraten? 12. Wen haßte Peter aus dem Grunde der Seele? 13. Was hielt Peter zurück, dem Grauen seine Unterschrift zu geben? 14. Woraus zog dieser den Schatten? 15. Wohin warf er den Schatten? 16. Worauf sah Peter so traurig? 17. Was sollte Peter über den Kopf ziehen? 18. Woraus zog der Graue die Tarnkappe? 19. Wie sah die Tarnkappe aus? 20. Wohin gingen die beiden? 21. Wann hatte der Vater den hilflosen Peter aus dem Garten gejagt? 22. Worauf saß Minna? 23. Wo stand die Bank? 24. Wer redete mit Minna? 25. Was hat jeder Hund? 26. Wer wollte für Minna sorgen? 27. Wie sah Peters Begleiter ihm ins Gesicht? 28. Womit stach der Graue dem unglücklichen Peter in die Hand? 29. Warum unterschrieb Peter nicht? 30. Was waren die ersten (first) Worte des grauen Mannes, als Peter wieder zu sich kam? 31. Was hatte man im Hause angezündet? 32. Woraus drangen helle Frauenstimmen? 33. Worauf nahm das junge Paar Platz? 34. Von wem sprachen die beiden? 35. Was sagte die Dame? 36. Wessen Frau war Minna nun?

II

Translate into German: 1. My three friends and I want to go to Germany. 2. What are your intentions? 3. In the garden we saw many beautiful roses and other flowers. 4. (My) Ladies and gentlemen, you may count on (auf *with acc.*) me. 5. To be sure, I haven't much money. 6. Even the children want to buy themselves a couple of things. 7. A coat often has four or five pockets. 8. I myself have three pens. Yes, I write with them. 9. These narrow streets remind me of Dinkelsbühl. 10. Potatoes and peas are not enough for a child that is still growing. 11. He has broken his left arm. (*Use dative of interest.*) 12. She has a book in [her] (the) hand.* 13. On Sunday she wears a ring on [her] (the) finger.* 14. What are you writing with?

III

Translate into English:

geheim	das Reich	die Schlacht	übrigens
herbeieilen	die Reihe	der Stern	der Vogel
nicken	reiten	stolz	vollkommen
der Ort	schenken	strecken	das Zeichen
die Pflanze	schicken	trauern	der Zufall

IV

Translate into German:

the uncle	the rain	to taste	blunt
the penny	the sheep	to cut	the dew
the duty	to separate	the school	the animal
the point	to shove	to study	the past

*Cf. § 45.

V

Translate the following compounds and derivatives:

der Letzte des Monats, der Letztgenannte; lichtblau, ein Lichtchen; das Liederbuch, ein Liedchen; die Lust, die Unlust, lustig; der Wintermantel; merkbar, merklich, unmerklich; milchweiß, die Milchstraße, eine Milchfrau; die Mischung; der Mittag, der Nachmittag; der Schlaf, das Schläfchen, das Nachmittagsschläfchen; die Mittagshitze, die Mitternacht; monatlich, der Monatsbericht; töten, tot; todmüde, die Müdigkeit; er ist sehr musikliebend; die Nachbarin, das Nachbardorf, nachbarlich; der Narr, die Närrin, das Narrenhaus; das Näslein; das Vogelnest; niederlegen, niederwerfen; der Ohrenschmerz; prüfen, die Prüfung; raten, der Rat, er hilft mit Rat und Tat; reif, reifen; er lief wie der Blitz; ein amtlicher Brief; doppelt so gut; rühr dich nicht von der Stelle; eintönig (monotonous); Hans fehlte zwei Tage in der Schule; feiern, die Schulfeier; die Rose, das Röslein; der Streit, streiten; wertlos

VI

Translate the following sentences into English: 1. Die Sonne scheint mir ins Gesicht. 2. Er warf ihnen das Geld vor die Füße. 3. Mein Vater kaufte mir einen Hut. 4. Er nahm mir mein ganzes Geld. 5. Das Herz blutet mir. 6. Meinem Onkel fallen die Zähne (teeth) aus. 7. Sie weint sich die Augen aus. 8. Das kommt mir nicht aus dem Sinn. 9. Nimm dir ein Stück Kuchen. 10. Mariechen, nimm den Finger aus dem Mund! 11. Selbst mein bester Freund konnte mir nicht helfen.

VII

Give the definite articles and plurals of:

Person   Wagen   Arzt   Brief
Bild   Wolke   Apfel   Recht
Tasse   Licht   Gesicht   Form

VIII

Decline in the singular and plural:

das Zimmer   der letzte Fehler   die Seite
die grüne Wand   mein Gast   der Bleistift
unsere gute Mutter

IX

Compare:

früh	groß	laut	warm	kurz	schnell

X

Give the principal parts of:

zeigen	empfehlen	bringen	wissen
leiden	erlauben	können	kennen

XI

Give the third person singular form of the following verbs in the present, past, present perfect, and past perfect:

lachen	wenden	bekommen	wollen
anfangen	verschwinden	arbeiten	dürfen

XII

Review § 82 in preparation for the next lesson and translate again sentences 1, 3, 5, 6, 13 of exercise II in Lesson XIII.

LESSON XVIII

TEXT A

Mein Mann ist jetzt tot. Als er noch lebte, ging es mir gut, und ich brauchte nicht zu arbeiten. Wenn er heute noch lebte, brauchte ich nicht zu arbeiten.

Als du mir letztes Jahr sagtest: „Ich liebe dich!" glaubte ich dir. Heute
5 weiß ich, daß man dir nicht glauben kann. Wenn du mir heute sagtest: „Ich liebe dich!" glaubte ich es nicht.—Ich weiß, du liebst mich nicht, und daher kann ich dir nicht in ein fernes Land folgen. Wenn du mich liebtest, folgte ich dir bis an das Ende der Welt.

Als ich für Meyer arbeitete, verdiente ich viel Geld. Leider arbeite ich
10 heute für Schmidt. Wenn ich für Meyer arbeitete, verdiente ich heute noch viel Geld.—Warum hat Meyer sich ein neues Haus gekauft, das soviel Geld kostet? Wenn er noch in seinem alten Hause wohnte, brauchte er nicht so schwer zu arbeiten.—Wenn ich ihm im Dunkeln begegnete, fürchtete ich mich.

15 Es wäre schön, wenn mein Vater mir ein Auto schenkte. Aber ich weiß, er hat kein Geld. Wenn er mehr Geld hätte, kaufte er mir alles, was ich brauche.—Meine Mutter ist leider tot. Wenn sie noch lebte, schenkte sie mir jeden Monat zweihundert Mark.—Wenn du mir den Tee selber machtest, schmeckte er mir besser.

20 „Weißt du nicht, daß Meyer krank ist und keinen Wein trinken darf? Ich hoffe, du hast ihm keinen Wein gegeben; denn wenn du ihm Wein gegeben hast, ist er vielleicht schon tot."—„Nein, ich habe ihm keinen Wein gegeben. Wenn ich ihm Wein gegeben hätte, lebte er jetzt nicht mehr."—„Weißt du, ob Johann noch krank ist? Wenn er noch krank ist, müssen wir
25 ihn besuchen."—„Nein, er ist wieder gesund. Aber du hast recht. Wenn er noch krank wäre, müßten wir ihn besuchen."—„Wissen Sie, ob der Mörder (murderer) noch lebt? Wenn er noch lebt, kann kein Mensch in dieser Stadt ruhig schlafen."—„Man hat ihn gestern tot in seiner Wohnung gefunden. Wenn er noch lebte, könnte kein Mensch ruhig schlafen. Wenn er sich nicht
30 getötet hätte, könnte kein Mensch ruhig schlafen."

Ich rettete dich nicht, wenn du dich ins Wasser stürztest.—Wie wäre es, wenn du ein paar Freunde holtest?—Es wäre unrecht, wenn ich das täte.—

Ich bliebe sehr gerne hier und kochte euch Kaffee.—Für deine Hilfe wäre ich sehr dankbar.—Sie sind alt genug, daß Sie mein Vater sein könnten.—Ich bleibe hier, denn in der Dunkelheit fände ich den Weg nicht durch den Wald.—Wenn er gleich ins Wasser gesprungen wäre, lebte das Kind vielleicht noch.—Es ist gut, daß er nie viel Geld gehabt hat. Wer weiß, was er damit getan hätte.—Wenn der Krieg nicht gekommen wäre, wäre heute alles anders.—Wenn er nur bald käme!—Käme er nur bald!—Ich möchte wissen, ob Herr Lehmann hier wohnt.—Wenn ich die Stelle bekäme, könnten wir heiraten.

Ich hätte ins Wasser springen mögen.—Ich glaube, es wäre gut für euch, wenn ihr eine Reise machtet.—Alles hätte anders sein können.—Unser Vater hätte sich gefreut, wenn er euer neues Haus gesehen hätte.—Unser Vater hätte sich gefreut, wenn er euer neues Haus hätte sehen können.—Du könntest die zwei Apfelsinen deiner Mutter bringen.—Er hätte für dich und deine Mutter besser sorgen können, als du es nun kannst.—Ich ginge nicht in das Haus, wenn ich du wäre.—Ich hätte dich nicht zurückgehalten, wenn es dein fester Wunsch gewesen wäre.

VOCABULARY

die Apfelsine, –n the orange
der Bach, ⸚e the brook
bellen to bark
der Berg, –e the mountain
biegen to bend, turn
das Brot, –e (the loaf of) *bread*
der Busch, ⸚e the *bush*
das Ei, –er the *egg*
die Eiche, –n the *oak*
einige a few, some
entlang *along*
⸗erlei . . . kind(s) of
  allerlei all kinds of
der Felsen, – the rock
fördern to *further*, advance, bring out
fort away, gone; on
das Frühstück the breakfast
der Fuchs, ⸚e the *fox*
die Gabel, –n the fork
der Gegenstand, ⸚e the object
gelb *yellow*
hängen to *hang*
das Haupt, ⸚er the head; chief
das Hemd, –en the shirt
die Herde, –n the *herd*
das Holz, ⸚er the wood
die Hose, –n the trousers
der Käse, – the *cheese*
der Knochen, – the bone
der Laden, ⸚ the store, shop
lieber rather
der Löffel, – the spoon
das Messer, – the knife

der Nebel, – the fog, mist
ost=, öst= *east-*
der Osten the *east*
schlecht bad, wicked
der Schuh, –e the *shoe*
die Schulter, –n the *shoulder*
die Stirn, –en the forehead
süd= *south-*
der Süden the *south*
die Tanne, –n the fir (tree)
der Tee the *tea*
der Teller, – the plate
teuer *dear*, expensive
trocken *dry*
das Ufer, – the shore, bank
der Vorteil, –e the advantage
wahrscheinlich probable, likely
weh tun to hurt, pain
west= *west-*
der Westen the *west*
zugleich at the same time

IDIOMS

es tut mir weh it hurts me
es war mir it seemed to me
jedenfalls at any rate
loswerden (*w. acc.*) to get rid of
(es ist) schade (it is) too bad
tun, als ob act as if
zum Glück luckily, by good fortune

TEXT B

Peter Schlemihl [Fortsetzung]

Jeden Augenblick konnte Minna am Arme Raskals in den Garten kommen, und dieser Anblick wäre für mein armes Herz zuviel gewesen. Ich mußte fort. Ich stand auf, warf noch einmal einen letzten Blick auf den Gartenweg, auf dem ich mit Minna so oft gegangen war, auf die Rosen=
5 büsche am Wege, die Minna so liebte, auf die Bank zwischen den beiden Linden, wo wir Hand in Hand so oft gesessen. Und dann ging ich. Ein Mensch ohne Zukunft, ohne Hoffnung, ohne Ziel. Der graue Mann folgte mir.

Es gelang uns, mit Hilfe der Tarnkappe[1] unbemerkt den Marktplatz zu
10 erreichen. Ich eilte schnell ins Haus, nahm weinend von meinem treuen Bendel Abschied, steckte schnell ein Bild Minnas in meinen Mantel und eilte wieder auf den Marktplatz, wo der Graue mit zwei Pferden, die er indessen aus seiner Rocktasche gezogen hatte, am Rathausbrunnen auf mich wartete. In derselben Nacht noch ritten wir über die nahe Grenze des
15 kleinen Königreiches, bogen gegen Morgen von der Hauptstraße ab, ritten ein paar Stunden zwischen hohen Bergen an einem Bach entlang und stiegen schließlich in einem hohen Tannenwalde ab. Todmüde warf ich mir

eine Decke um die Schultern, suchte mir in dem dichten Unterholz ein trockenes Plätzchen und schlief bald fest ein.

Die Sonne stand schon wieder im Osten, als ich endlich wach wurde. Der Graue führte gerade die Pferde an den Bach und ließ sie trinken.

Ich stand auf. Mein Rücken schmerzte von dem harten Boden, alle Knochen im Leibe taten mir weh.

„Ja", meinte der Graue trocken, als er zurückkehrte, „wenn Sie mir Ihre schöne Seele zur rechten Zeit verkauft hätten, wären Sie jetzt noch immer der Herr Graf und könnten bis ans Ende Ihres Lebens in einem Federbette schlafen. Wahrscheinlich säßen Sie jetzt gerade am Frühstückstisch und tränken den heißen Tee, den die Gräfin Ihnen selber gemacht hätte. Jungverheiratete Frauen machen den Tee nämlich meistens selber. Später, wenn die Liebe abgekühlt ist, tut es der Mann. Nun, Herr Raskal weiß[2] Tee und Gräfin sicher auch zu schätzen[2]."

Ich wäre dem Grauen am liebsten an den Hals gesprungen. Aber er tat, als ob er nichts merkte, steckte die Hand in die Rocktasche, holte für jeden einen Teller, eine Gabel und ein Messer heraus, ließ Brot und Käse folgen, förderte außerdem noch für jeden zwei Eier und einen kleinen Löffel ans Tageslicht und sagte, nachdem wir uns beide gesetzt hatten: „Sehen Sie, ich denke natürlich vor allem an meinen eigenen Vorteil. Andere Leute, die lieber ein Mädchen ins Unglück stürzen als ihre Seele verkaufen, tun das zwar auch. Aber solche Leute sind nicht so ehrlich wie ich. Und glauben Sie mir, ich denke zugleich an Ihren Vorteil, wenn ich Ihnen noch einmal dringend rate, doch endlich vernünftig zu werden und zu unterschreiben. Wenn Sie nicht unterschreiben, müssen Sie die Hoffnung, je wieder unter Menschen wohnen zu können, für immer aufgeben. Einen Schattenlosen, das haben Sie ja erfahren, will niemand unter seinem Dache haben. Ich verstehe ja, daß man sich nicht gern von etwas trennt, was man noch nie gesehen hat. Sie sind nicht der erste Fall dieser Art. Aber glauben Sie mir, bis jetzt hat noch jeder, der mir einmal seinen Schatten verkauft hatte, diesen Schatten auch wieder zurückgekauft. Warum sollten gerade Sie anders sein als die anderen? Vielleicht insofern, als Sie schlechter sind und lieber ein Mädchen als Ihre Seele aufgeben."

Oh, der Graue war ein guter Menschenkenner. Mit jedem Wort, das er sprach, schnitt er mir tief ins Herz. Ich kann Dir gar nicht sagen, mein teurer Freund, was für einen brennenden Haß gegen diesen Teufel ich in mir fühlte. Jedem anderen als ihm hätte ich damals gerne meine Seele gegeben, nur um ihn endlich loszuwerden.

Ich war also nicht der erste Fall. Wahrscheinlich hatte der Fuchs schon unzählige Menschen auf diese Art und Weise ins Unglück gestürzt. Gestalten
5 der Vergangenheit traten vor meine Seele. „Haben Sie auch von Herrn John eine Unterschrift?" fragte ich ihn. Er lächelte: „So, so! Sie erinnern sich noch an ihn. Freilich hatte ich eine Unterschrift von Herrn John, obgleich das bei einem so guten Freunde kaum nötig gewesen wäre. Übrigens ist er vor einigen Wochen gestorben."—„Wo ist er?" rief ich, meinen Haß
10 nicht länger verbergend. „Bei Gott, ich will es wissen!"

Merkte der Graue plötzlich, daß er sein Spiel verloren hatte, daß ich mich eher in Stücke hätte reißen lassen, als ihm meine Seele zu verkaufen? Ich weiß es nicht. Jedenfalls ließ er nun seine höfliche Maske fallen, wilder Haß leuchtete ihm aus den Augen, und mit einem Lachen, das ich nicht vergessen
15 kann, zog er die Gestalt des unglücklichen John bei den Haaren aus seiner Rocktasche. Ich fiel fast in Ohnmacht, als sich die kalten Lippen zu den schweren Worten bewegten:

"Justo judicio Dei judicatus sum.
Justo judicio Dei condemnatus sum[3]."

20 Dann aber war es mir, als käme mir von irgendwoher neue Kraft. Ich riß den Säckel aus der Brusttasche, warf ihn dem Grauen vor die Füße und rief: „Ich befehle dir im Namen Gottes, mich allein zu lassen und mir nie wieder vor die Augen zu kommen!" Und an dem Namen des Allmächtigen brach die Gewalt des Grauen. Er verschwand zwischen den Felsen. Den
25 Säckel nahm er mit.

Da saß ich, ohne Schatten und ohne Geld. Aber ich war nicht traurig. Hätte ich meine Minna nicht verloren, oder hätte ich mich frei von jeder Schuld an diesem Verlust fühlen dürfen, ich glaube, ich hätte glücklich sein können. Ich durchsuchte meine Taschen und fand noch einige Goldstücke.
30 Ich zählte sie und lachte. Und da die Sonne noch hoch am Himmel stand, legte ich mich in den Schatten der nächsten Bäume und schlief ruhig ein.

Die Sonne stand tief im Westen, als ich die Augen wieder öffnete. Die Pferde waren nicht zu finden. Wahrscheinlich waren sie dem Grauen nachgelaufen. Ich machte mich also zu Fuß auf den Weg, stieg über Steine
35 und Felsen, kam gegen Morgen wieder auf die Hauptstraße und sah bald ein

kleines Städtchen vor mir zwischen den Bergen liegen. Zu meinem Glück hingen schwere, graue Regenwolken am Himmel, so daß kein Mensch von mir einen Schatten verlangen konnte.

Ich brauchte dringend ein Paar Schuhe, denn die Schuhe, welche ich trug, hatte ich für den reichen Grafen Peter, nicht für den armen Teufel Schlemihl gekauft. Die scharfen Steine hatten sie vollkommen unbrauchbar gemacht. Nach einigem Suchen fand ich denn auch in einer engen Seitenstraße einen kleinen Laden, in dem eine lange Reihe alter Schuhe neben allerlei anderen gebrauchten Gegenständen im Fenster stand. Der Laden war noch geschlossen, denn es war noch früh, gerade sieben Uhr. Ich klingelte also. Ein altes, dünnes Männchen öffnete mir und zeigte mir stolz seine Schätze. Ich wählte ein Paar Schuhe aus, die mir noch ziemlich gut und stark zu sein schienen, kaufte mir noch ein neues Hemd und eine neue Hose, zog Schuhe, Hemd und Hose gleich im Laden an und trat wieder auf die Straße. Mir war ein herrlicher Gedanke gekommen: „Wie wäre es“, sagte ich mir, „wenn du in einem der Silberbergwerke[4] in diesen Bergen eine Stelle bekommen könntest! Dann wärest du bei Tage unter der Erde und brauchtest nichts zu fürchten. Schade, daß dir dieser Gedanke nicht früher gekommen ist! Du hättest Minna dann wahrscheinlich nie getroffen, und das gute Mädchen wäre heute nicht so unglücklich.“

Ich blickte auf, um mich nach jemand umzusehen, den ich nach dem Weg zum nächsten Bergwerk[4] fragen könnte. Aber irgendwie war ich von der Straße abgekommen. Zu meinem Schrecken stand ich mitten in einem hohen Eichenwalde. Von dem Städtchen war nichts zu sehen. Ich drang ein paar Schritte weiter vor, und auch der Wald war hinter mir verschwunden. Ich stand auf einem großen Eisberg. Die Luft war schneidend kalt, um mich war Totenstille, und soweit das Auge reichte, sah ich nichts als Eis und schweren, dicken Nebel. Die Sonne stand blutigrot dicht am Horizonte. Noch ein paar Schritte, und ich stand am Ufer eines Meeres. Auf grünlich weißen Eisbergen saßen Vögel, wie ich sie nie vorher gesehen hatte. Eine ganze Herde von Seelöwen stürzte sich ins Wasser, als ich plötzlich mitten unter ihnen stand. Ich folgte diesem Ufer nach Süden, und nach wenigen Minuten wurde es so heiß, daß mir das Wasser von der Stirn lief und ich kaum noch atmen konnte. Ich mußte mich in den Schatten eines Baumes setzen, um auszuruhen. Der Baum hing voll schöner, reifer Apfelsinen. Zwei Männer, die wie bei uns die Mädchen einen langen Zopf[5] auf dem Rücken trugen, liefen lautschreiend herbei und riefen mir in einer Sprache, die ich nicht verstand, etwas zu; und ihr gelber Hund, der wie ein kleiner Löwe aussah, bellte mich an. Ich machte zwei Schritte, um sie zu begrüßen—die Männer waren verschwunden, und wieder war alles um mich 5 her[6] verändert. Kein Zweifel, ich hatte Siebenmeilenstiefel[7] an den Füßen.

[Fortsetzung folgt]

NOTES. 1. Tarnkappe magic cloak (which makes the wearer invisible). 2. weiß ... zu schätzen knows how to appreciate. 3. Justo ... condemnatus sum. By the just judgment of God I am judged. By the just judgment of God I am condemned. 4. Silberbergwerke, Bergwerk silver mines, mine. 5. Zopf braid(s) 6. her Do not translate. 7. Siebenmeilenstiefel seven-league boots.

BUILDING A PASSIVE VOCABULARY

Abschied nehmen Abschied (*from* scheiden to separate, part) leave, Abschied nehmen to take leave

dringend dringen to penetrate, crowd, urge, dringend urgently

der Gedanke denken to think, der Gedanke the thought

das Gefühl fühlen to feel, das Gefühl the feeling

irgendwie somehow

jungverheiratet jung young, recent, verheiratet (heiraten) married, jungverheiratet recently married

das Königreich der König the king, das Reich the realm, das Königreich the kingdom

leuchtete das Licht the light, leuchten to emit light, leuchtete gleamed

meistens meist most, meistens mostly, usually

der Menschenkenner der Mensch the man, human, der Kenner the knower, der Menschenkenner the psychologist

die Sprache sprechen to speak, die Sprache the language

das Unterholz unter under, below, beneath, das Holz the wood, das Unterholz the underbrush

unzählig zählen to count, unzählig countless, innumerable

verändert anders different, ändern, verändern to make different, change, verändert changed

GRAMMAR

113. The Subjunctive. The indicative forms of the verb state facts. Even "if-clauses" require the indicative as long as they express what might possibly be a fact. Present: If Meyer is still living, he is a very old man. Wenn Meyer noch lebt, ist er ein sehr alter Mann. Past: If he was still living last year, he could probably no longer work. Wenn er letztes Jahr noch lebte, konnte er wahrscheinlich nicht mehr arbeiten.

Only indicative forms have been used so far in this book. We now propose to introduce the subjunctive, of which there are two kinds in German:

a. The Imaginative Subjunctive, used to refer to imagined situations.

b. The Indirect-Discourse Subjunctive, used to report another person's words or opinions. (See Lesson XXI.)

114. The Present Imaginative Subjunctive. A situation imagined to be true in the present (but actually known or expected not to be true) is called a contrary-to-fact condition. To express such imaginary conditions English uses a past tense in the "if-clause" and a conditional form in the main clause:

If I were you, I'd go to Europe.
If I had more money, I'd buy a new car.
If Fred really loved me, he would write regularly.

German uses a simple past (or past-like) form in both clauses:

Wenn sie mich liebte, heiratete ich sie. If she loved me, I'd marry her. (Literally, If she loved me, I married her.)

This pattern corresponds exactly to the pattern of archaic English:

It were different if I had some independence.*
Caesar were no lion, if Romans were not hinds.†

In order to avoid confusion, the term *present imaginative* is used whenever a past or past-like form refers to the *present time.*

---

*Lytton, *My Novel,* I, III, Ch. XIX.

†Shakespeare's words are as follows: "He were no lion, were not Romans hinds," *Julius Cæsar,* I, iii.

115. Formation of the Present Imaginative. The present imaginative subjunctive is formed as follows:

Weak verbs use the indicative forms of the past tense without change, requiring even the same personal endings (⸗te, ⸗teſt, ⸗te; ⸗ten, ⸗tet, ⸗ten):

Wenn ich in Berlin wohnte, brauchte ich mehr Geld. If I lived in Berlin, I'd need more money.

Wenn du in Berlin wohnteſt, brauchteſt du mehr Geld. If you lived in Berlin, you'd need more money.

Strong verbs umlaut, whenever possible, the stem vowel of the past indicative forms and add the endings of the weak verbs minus the t:

Wenn ich jünger wäre, ginge ich mit dir. If I were younger, I'd go with you.

Wenn wir jünger wären, gingen wir mit dir. If we were younger, we'd go with you.

Exceptions:

ich hülfe (helfen) ich ſtürbe (ſterben) ich würfe (werfen)

Weak verbs with vowel change (*and all modals*) are treated like regular weak verbs and retain the stem vowel of the infinitive:

Ich könnte, wenn ich wollte. I could if I wished.

ich dürfte, ich möchte, ich müßte, ich ſollte, ich ſendete, ich rennte.

Exceptions:

ich brächte (bringen) ich dächte (denken) ich wüßte (wiſſen)

Examples:

Weak	Strong		Modal
ich lebte	gäbe	ginge	möchte
du lebteſt	gäbeſt	gingeſt	möchteſt
er lebte	gäbe	ginge	möchte
wir lebten	gäben	gingen	möchten
ihr lebtet	gäbet	ginget	möchtet
ſie lebten	gäben	gingen	möchten

sein		haben	
ich wäre	wir wären	ich hätte	wir hätten
du wärest	ihr wäret	du hättest	ihr hättet
er wäre	sie wären	er hätte	sie hätten

werden

ich würde	wir würden
du würdest	ihr würdet
er würde	sie würden

116. Use of the Present Imaginative to Refer to Future Time. From sentences like Ich fahre morgen nach Berlin the student is already familiar with the fact that the present of the indicative is frequently used to refer to future time (Cf. § 21). The forms of the present imaginative subjunctive are used in the same way:

Es wäre gut für dich, wenn du eine Reise machtest. It would be good for you if you took (would take) a trip.

117. Past Imaginative. In imagination we sometimes ask ourselves what would have happened if the past had been different from what it actually was. To express such bygone possibilities, English uses a past perfect in the "if-clause" and a conditional in the conclusion: If you had been here, my brother would not have died. (Revised Version, John 11:21.) German uses a past perfect form in both clauses:

Wenn du hier gewesen wärest, wäre mein Bruder nicht gestorben.

Compare the King James Version:

If thou hadst been here, my brother had not died.

The term *past imaginative* is used whenever a past perfect (or past perfect-like) form refers to imagined situations in the *past*. The three past tenses of the indicative (past, present perfect, and past perfect) merge into this one *past imaginative*.

As can be seen in the foregoing example, the past imaginative is formed by adding the past participle to ich hätte, du hättest, etc., or to ich wäre, du wärest, etc.

Examples in both German and English:

German	English "if-clause"	English conclusion
ich hätte gesehen	(if) I had seen	I'd have seen
du hättest gesehen	(if) you had seen	you'd have seen
ich wäre gewesen	(if) I had been	I'd have been
du wärest gewesen	(if) you had been	you'd have been

The "double infinitive" construction, with which the student is familiar from indicative phrases like Ich hatte sehen können *I had been able to see*, is found in the subjunctive: Ich hätte sehen können. *I'd have been able to see.* (Here again the dependent infinitive may be omitted. Cf. § 18. Das hätte ich nicht gekonnt for Das hätte ich nicht tun können *I couldn't have done that.*)

118. So, dann. In conclusions either of the adverbs so and dann is frequently used to repeat, as it were, the idea of the preceding *if*-clause: Wenn ich den Preis gewänne, dann wäre ich glücklich. If I won the prize, I'd be happy.

119. Omission of wenn. The wenn in *if*-clauses is frequently omitted, in which case the *if*-clause shows verb-first position instead of verb-last position and precedes the conclusion:

Wenn ich das Geld bekäme, (so) (dann) könnten wir heiraten. Bekäme ich das Geld, so könnten wir heiraten. If I were to get (*or* were I to get) the money, then we could marry.

120. Als ob, als wenn. After als ob and als wenn German has the same tense patterns as English after "as if":

Er tat, als ob er Geld hätte.	He acted as if he had money.
Er tat, als ob er schliefe.	He acted as if he were sleeping.
Er tat, als ob er geschlafen hätte.	He acted as if he had slept.

The wenn or ob may be omitted. In that case the verb follows als.

Er tat, als schliefe er. He acted as if he were sleeping.

121. Wishes. The imaginative subjunctive is used to express wishes like *If he were only here* or *If he had only been here*:

Wenn er nur hier wäre (*or without the* wenn: Wäre er nur hier).
Wenn er nur hier gewesen wäre. Wäre er nur hier gewesen.

Such wishes are *if*-clauses without conclusions.

122. Mögen and sollen. The imaginative subjunctive forms of these verbs are:

Ich möchte singen. Ich hätte singen mögen.
Ich sollte singen. Ich hätte singen sollen.

Ich möchte singen means *I should like to sing*; Ich hätte singen mögen, *I should have liked to sing*. The subjunctive of sollen in the *main* clause means *ought to*. Thus:

Ich sollte singen. I ought to sing.
Ich hätte singen sollen. I ought to have sung.

In the *dependent* clause the subjunctive of sollen means *should* or *were to* and implies improbability:

Wenn er wirklich kommen sollte, haben wir immer noch Zeit, Tee für ihn zu kochen. If he really should come, we shall still have (enough) time to make him some tea.

123. Sein plus the Infinitive with zu. In expressions like Von der Stadt war nichts zu sehen the infinitive has a passive meaning and is translated into English with the passive infinitive. (*To be seen* is the passive infinitive of *to see*.) Thus, Von der Stadt war nichts zu sehen is translated, *There was nothing to be seen of the city.*

Learn the principal parts of the following verbs:

schieben	schōb	hat geschōben	schiebt	to shove
biegen	bōg	hat gebōgen	biegt	to bend
fangen	fing	hat gefangen	fängt	to catch
hängen	hing	hat gehangen	hängt	to hang

EXERCISES

I

Answer in German: 1. Wohin blickte Peter noch einmal? 2. Wer war ein Mensch ohne Hoffnung? 3. Von wem nahm Peter Abschied? 4. Was steckte er in seinen Mantel? 5. Woraus hatte der Graue die Pferde gezogen? 6. Was warf sich Peter um die Schultern? 7. Wo stand die Sonne, als er wieder wach wurde? 8. Was tat unserm Peter weh, als er aufwachte? 9. Was wäre Peter immer noch, wenn er unterschrieben hätte? 10. Worin hätte er schlafen können? 11. Wo säße er wahrscheinlich jetzt? 12. Wem wäre Peter nun am liebsten an den Hals gesprungen? 13. Was holte der Graue hervor? 14. An wessen Vorteil dachte der Graue vor allem? 15. Wer war ein guter Menschenkenner? 16. Gegen wen fühlte Peter einen brennenden Haß? 17. Wann war Herr John gestorben? 18. Wer sprach die lateinischen (Latin) Worte? 19. In welcher Tasche hatte Peter den Säckel getragen? 20. Sollte der Graue zurückkommen? 21. Ließ der Graue den Säckel liegen? 22. Wen hatte Peter verloren? 23. Fühlte er sich frei von jeder Schuld? 24. Was fand er noch in seinen Taschen? 25. Wo stand die Sonne, als er die Augen öffnete? 26. Wem waren die Pferde wahrscheinlich nachgelaufen? 27. Was sah Peter zwischen den Bergen vor sich liegen? 28. Was konnte niemand von Peter verlangen? 29. Was hatte seine Schuhe unbrauchbar gemacht? 30. Was fand er nach einigem Suchen? 31. Warum war der Laden noch geschlossen? 32. Wie waren die Schuhe, die er sich auswählte? 33. Was kaufte er sich auch noch? 34. Wo zog er Hemd, Hose und Schuhe an? 35. Wen hätte er wahrscheinlich nie getroffen, wenn er früher auf diesen Gedanken gekommen wäre? 36. Wovon war nichts zu sehen? 37. Worauf stand er auf einmal? 38. Wie war die Luft auf dem Eisberg? 39. Was konnte er um sich sehen? 40. Was taten die Seelöwen, als er plötzlich mitten unter ihnen stand? 41. Warum setzte er sich unter einen Baum? 42. Was hing an dem Baum? 43. Wie sah der Hund aus? 44. Was hatte er ohne Zweifel an den Füßen?

II

Translate into German: 1. If I worked longer, I'd earn more money. 2. I'd be very unhappy if I didn't have you. 3. If it were not so cold, he'd stay longer. 4. They would have brought it back if they had known that. 5. If I needed him, I'd say it. 6. They could marry if they were older. 7. If I had a pencil, I could write faster. 8. If he would come, we'd help him. 9. If he had talked (reden) less, he would have been happier. 10. I could go next week if he would allow it. 11. I'd have gone yesterday if he had been here. 12. If my father had given me money, I could have gone too. 13. If he is still sleeping, he must stay home. 14. My poor husband. If he hadn't eaten so much, he wouldn't have died. 15. If I had not met (treffen) you (fam. sing.), I'd not be so happy today. 16. We'd have won if it hadn't been so cold. 17. I'd buy more books if they didn't cost so much. 18. I could work better if I had my own room. 19. If you had come earlier, you would have been permitted to see him. 20. Hildegard would not have moved to Bacharach if her uncle had not fallen into the water. 21. I should like to see him.

III

Translate into English:

acht	sieben	das Fach	bilden	voraus
das Amt	einsam	feiern	der Blitz	vorziehen
begleiten	der Enkel	gering	durchaus	freilich
deutlich	auswendig	das Heil	einst	bestimmt
ewig	das Blatt	allerdings	die Sünde	zwar

IV

Translate into German:

to ignite	noble	the fish
the beard	to recommend	Friday
to meet	the fruit	to share
the example	the crown	to mix
to visit	to catch	everywhere
the brother	the barrel	twelve

V

Translate the following compounds and derivatives:

der Waldbach, das Bächlein; der Bergsteiger, die Bergspitze; zurückbiegen, biegbar; arbeitslos werden, das heißt brotlos werden; die Vogeleier; die

Ohrringe; weggehen; der Eichbaum; dreierlei Weine gab es zu trinken; das Nachthemd; die Füchsin; der Weg gabelt sich, die Weggabelung; ein Bild aufhängen; der Holzhaufe; eine Herde wilder Pferde; Hosenträger (suspenders); käseweiß im Gesicht werden; die Ladentür; westlich, westwärts, südwärts; die
5 Schlechtigkeit; die Hausschuhe, Tennisschuhe; das Schulterstück; breitstirnig; der Tannenbaum; die Ähnlichkeit; doppelte Freude; der Dummkopf; durstig; die Fürstin; geheim halten; die Knabenschule; er ist sehr musikliebend; das ist keinen Pfennig wert; der Prüfer; weder rechts noch links; der Unterricht; der Vorschlag; zufällig

VI

Make up six original sentences using the imaginative subjunctive in each one. Some of the sentences should refer to present and the others to past time.

VII

Give the third person singular of the present imaginative subjunctive (example: kommen, er käme) of:

schreiben	finden	fahren	mögen
fangen	helfen	schlafen	können
ziehen	gehen	tun	sollen
fliegen	sitzen	wissen	spielen

VIII

Give the third person singular of the past imaginative subjunctive of the verbs above (example: er wäre gekommen).

LESSON XIX

TEXT A

[Fortsetzung der Münchhausen-Geschichte]

„Aber Herr Graf", riefen die Damen und Herren der Gesellschaft wie aus einem Munde, „Sie tun uns unrecht! Wir kennen Ihre Wahrheitsliebe und wissen, daß wir Ihnen trauen dürfen. Wir glauben Ihnen daher jedes Wort." Da lächelte der Graf zufrieden. „Jawohl, Wahrheitsliebe", wiederholte er und nickte mit dem Kopf, „das haben Sie sehr fein 5
gesagt. Wir alle sollten für die Wahrheit kämpfen, und ich wünschte, man könnte allen Menschen so trauen wie mir." Dann griff er nach dem Glas, das ihm ein Diener mit feurigem Wein gefüllt hatte, und begann wieder:

„Ich machte also aus dem eben genannten Grunde meine Reise nach Moskau mitten im Winter, eine Reise, die ich, das muß ich sagen, nicht 10
vergessen werde, auch wenn ich hundert Jahre alt würde. Es gelang mir, viel schneller über das Eis zu fahren, als ich erwartet hatte, und zwar indem ich meinen Mantel aufmachte, beide Arme ausstreckte und mich von dem diesmal ganz besonders starken Rückenwind treiben ließ. Zwar kam der Wind oft von der Seite, aber mein braves Pferd hielt sich, indem[1] es 15
den Schwanz als Steuer gebrauchte,[1] trotzdem auf einer vollkommen geraden Linie. Die Dörfer, die Rathäuser und die Schulen flogen an uns vorbei, und nachdem wir festen Boden unter den Füßen hatten, wäre ich sicher in einem Tage nach Moskau gekommen, wenn ich nicht noch zuletzt auf eine mir zuerst ganz unerklärliche Art und Weise den Weg verloren hätte. 20
Das war unangenehm und hätte bei der strengen Kälte noch viel unangenehmer werden können. Jedoch tröstete ich mich und traute meinem Glück. Ich ritt, bis Nacht und Dunkelheit mich überfielen, und stieg endlich unter freiem Himmel ab.

Kein Dorf war zu sehen. Mir war, als ob der Pfosten,[2] der vor mir so 25
fest im Schnee stand und an den ich mein Pferd gebunden hatte, genau in der Mitte eines großen, einsamen Schneefeldes stände. Indes, ich verlor den Mut nicht. Im Gegenteil. Mit dem festen Entschluß, am nächsten Morgen die Suche nach dem verlorenen Wege wieder aufzunehmen, legte ich mich ruhig auf den Schnee, deckte mich mit meinem schweren Mantel zu 30
und war bald fest eingeschlafen. Um ganz sicher zu sein, hatte ich meine Pistole noch unter den Arm gesteckt.

Ohne jede Störung schlief ich so tief und herrlich, daß ich nicht eher aufwachte, als bis es heller Tag war und die Sonne schon hoch am Himmel stand. Wie groß war aber mein Erstaunen,[3] als ich herausfand, daß ich mitten in einem Dorfe auf dem Kirchhof lag. Sie werden mir das vielleicht nicht glauben, und ich selber glaubte es auch nicht. Aber da standen vor mir ein paar alte Weiber, der Schulmeister und der dicke Pastor. Die wußten sich meine Gegenwart nicht zu erklären und glaubten, jemand vor sich zu sehen, der aus dem Reiche der Toten auf Besuch gekommen war. Mir selbst kam es fast auch so vor. Ich stand auf, setzte mich auf einen Stein und sah um mich. Die Luft, die am Tage vorher noch schneidend kalt gewesen war, war jetzt warm, und die Wassertropfen[4] im Grase glänzten im Lichte der Morgensonne, als ob der Frühling gekommen wäre. Mein Pferd war nicht zu sehen. Doch hörte ich es bald irgendwo über mir wiehern.[5] Als ich hinaufblickte, sah ich es zu meinem Erstaunen[3] von der Spitze des Kirchturms[6] herunterhängen. Es wieherte[5] und klopfte mit den Beinen auf das Dach, weil es sah, daß ich wach war. Da wurde mir langsam klar, was geschehen war: Das ganze Dorf hatte unter einer hohen Schneedecke gelegen und war mir daher verborgen geblieben. Wie mir der Pastor erzählte, war von Sonntag morgen bis Montag abend so viel Schnee gefallen, daß das Dorf am Dienstag verschwunden war. In der Nacht von Mittwoch auf Donnerstag war es dann plötzlich warm geworden, der Schnee war geschmolzen,[7] und ich war langsam in den Kirchhof hinabgesunken. Und was ich Narr für einen Pfosten[2] gehalten hatte, war in Wirklichkeit die Spitze des Kirchturms[6] gewesen. Ich nahm also meine Pistole, schoß nach dem Zügel,[8] der Zügel zerriß, mein Pferd kam glücklich wieder auf die Erde, und ich konnte meine Reise fortsetzen.

Am nächsten Tage schon überreichte ich dem Kaiser den Brief, den ihm der König durch mich hatte schicken lassen. Der Kaiser hatte schon Angst um mich gehabt und empfing mich außerordentlich herzlich."

Der Graf sah nach seiner Uhr. „Ich sehe, es ist schon spät geworden", sagte er. „Erlauben Sie mir, daß ich mich zurückziehe. Ich wünsche den Damen und Herren gute Nacht. Auf Wiedersehen!"

NOTES. 1. indem . . . gebrauchte by using its tail as rudder. 2. Pfosten post. 3. Erstaunen amazement. 4. Wassertropfen dewdrops. 5. wiehern, wieherte whinny, whinnied. 6. Kirchturm church steeple. 7. geschmolzen melted. 8. Zügel reins.

LESSON XIX

VOCABULARY

aufmachen (*sep. prefix*) to open
die Beere, –n the *berry*
blühen to *bloom*
breit *broad*
die Brücke, –n the *bridge*
darstellen (*sep. prefix*) to present; represent
drucken to print
der Eifer the zeal, ardor, eagerness
England *England*
sich erkälten to catch *cold*
fliehen to *flee*
das Futter the *fodder*, *feed*
die Gunst the favor
das Heft, –e the notebook
das Heim, –e the *home*
hinzu besides, in addition; there
hohl *hollow*
indem while (cf. § 127)
die Karte, –n the *card*; map; ticket
die Katze, –n the *cat*
krank ill, sick
die Kuh, ⸚e the *cow*
die Kunst, ⸚e the art; skill
die Lampe, –n the *lamp*
das Mahl, –e the *meal*
  die Mahlzeit, –en the *meal*
der Marsch, ⸚e the *march*
der Norden the *north*
die Nuß, ⸚e the *nut*
oben *above*, upstairs
der Ofen, ⸚ the stove, *oven*
das Salz the *salt*
sammeln to collect, gather
schwierig difficult
selten *seldom*, rare
der Sommer, – the *summer*
der Stamm, ⸚e *stem*; trunk; tribe, race
stets always
der Stoff, –e the material; cloth
stören to disturb, interrupt
das Stroh the *straw*
der Strom, ⸚e the large river; *stream*, current
der Stuhl, ⸚e the chair
verfassen to write, compose
das Volk, ⸚er the people, nation, *folk*
vollständig complete
das Werk, –e the *work*
wiegen to *weigh*
die Wurzel, –n the root
der Zahn, ⸚e the tooth
die Ziege, –n the goat

IDIOMS

auf einmal suddenly
her ago (lange her long ago)
nicht einmal not even
zuerst at first
zuletzt at last

TEXT B

Peter Schlemihl [Schluß]

Mein lieber Freund, man redet nicht gerne von Dingen, die einem heilig sind. Und mit Recht. Das Beste und Tiefste läßt sich nicht mit Worten sagen. Gerade für das, was unser Herz ausfüllt zum Zerspringen, ist die

Sprache viel zu arm. Aber das muß und darf ich sagen: Was ich in jener Stunde, als es mir klar wurde, daß ich Siebenmeilenstiefel[1] an den Füßen hatte, in mir aufsteigen fühlte, das zwang mich nieder auf die Kniee und füllte mein Herz mit Dank gegen den Allmächtigen. Worte, um zu sagen, was ich fühlte, fand ich nicht. Aber ich bin sicher, der Allmächtige hat meinen Dank auch ohne Worte verstanden.

Noch am Tage vorher hatte die Zukunft schwarz und dunkel und trostlos vor mir gelegen. Eine Zeitlang hatte ich sogar mit dem Gedanken gespielt, ob es nicht besser wäre, mir das Leben zu nehmen. Und nun stand auf einmal eine Möglichkeit vor mir, die auch das Herz in Deiner Brust, mein Freund, hätte schneller schlagen lassen. Mir, der sich durch eigene Schuld für immer von menschlicher Gesellschaft ausgeschlossen hatte, mir, für den es keine Hoffnung gab, je wieder als Bürger unter Bürgern leben zu können, mir Armem hatte Gott in seiner Güte ein Arbeitsfeld gegeben. Mein Leben hatte auf einmal wieder einen Sinn, ein Ziel: das Studium der Natur. Die ganze Erde stand mir offen. Pflanzen, Tiere, Menschen, Völker, über die sich andere Leute nur durch Bücher unterrichten können, konnte ich in Zukunft mit eigenen Augen sehen. Und Länder, die, weil Menschen nicht darin leben können, allen andern stets unerreichbar bleiben werden, konnte ich von nun an in schnellem Marsch durcheilen. Ich habe damals nicht gewählt, nicht nach langem Suchen einen Ausweg gefunden, ich habe einfach aus der Hand des Allmächtigen ein Geschenk genommen. Und seitdem habe ich mit heiligem Eifer in stiller Arbeit Material für ein Werk gesammelt, das den Titel „Unsere Erde, ihre Geographie, ihre Fauna und Flora" tragen soll. Ich werde darin die Pflanzen- und Tierwelt mit einer Vollständigkeit darstellen, wie sie bis jetzt noch niemand erreicht hat. Ich weiß, dieses Werk wird, wie alles, was aus Menschenhänden kommt, unvollkommen bleiben; und das Ideal, das mir in jener Stunde auf den Bergen Tibets vor mein inneres Auge trat, werde ich nicht erreichen. Aber was ich tun konnte, habe ich getan, und ich bin nur dann mit mir selbst zufrieden gewesen, wenn es mir gelungen war, das gesammelte Material klar und verständlich darzustellen.

Ich stand also, wie gesagt, auf einer Hochebene[2] im Inneren Asiens,[2] und die Sonne, die in Deutschland erst vor wenigen Stunden aufgegangen war, stand hier schon ziemlich tief am Abendhimmel. Ich durcheilte Asien von Osten nach Westen, sah die Sonne bald wieder über mir stehen, ging durch Palästina nach Afrika hinüber und durcheilte auch diesen Kontinent noch am selben Tage mehrere Male von Osten nach Westen und von Süden nach Norden.

Nur wenige Schritte von den Pyramiden Ägyptens fand ich eine Oase,[3] deren Namen Du auf keiner Karte finden wirst, aus dem einfachen Grunde, weil sie außer mir noch niemand gesehen hat. Und in dieser Oase fand ich in 5 einem Felsen eine große Höhle. M e i n e Höhle darf ich sie wohl nennen, denn sie ist mir in den letzten Jahren Haus, Heim und Studierzimmer gewesen. (Auch jetzt, mein Freund, sitze ich im Schatten einer hohen Kokosnußpalme vor dieser meiner Höhle, halte das Heft, das Du bald in Deinen Händen halten wirst, auf den Knieen und schreibe.) 10

Ich war müde. Und da es kühl wurde und ich nicht wußte, ob etwa wilde Tiere in der Nähe waren, zündete ich vor dem engen Eingang der Höhle ein Feuer an, legte den Kopf auf meinen Mantel und war bald fest eingeschlafen.

In der folgenden Woche ließ ich es dann meine erste Sorge sein, die Höhle etwas wohnlicher zu machen und alles herbeizuholen, was ich zum Leben und 15 zum Studium dringend brauchte.

Zunächst kaufte ich mir von den wenigen Goldstücken, die mir geblieben waren, ein Paar Überschuhe, denn ich hatte erfahren, wie unangenehm es war, meine Schritte nicht anders kürzer machen zu können, als indem ich meine Siebenmeilenstiefel auszog. Ein Paar Schuhe aus Stoff, über die 20 Stiefel[1] gezogen, hatte ganz die Wirkung, die ich mir davon versprach. Später habe ich sogar immer zwei Paar bei mir getragen, weil ich oft ein Paar in aller Eile von den Füßen werfen mußte, wenn mich Löwen, Tiger, Wildkatzen oder Menschen beim Sammeln störten.

Alle Instrumente, die ich für meine Arbeit brauchte, holte ich nach und 25 nach in Deutschland, England oder Amerika, und zwar immer dort, wo es gerade regnete oder wo Nebel und Wolken den Leuten meine Schattenlosigkeit verbargen. Natürlich mußte ich alles auf meinen Schultern selber in die Oase tragen. Es hatte also keinen Zweck, etwas zu kaufen, was ich nicht in meine Taschen stecken oder auf die Schultern nehmen konnte. Sachen, 30 die viel wiegen, sind daher in meiner Höhle nicht zu finden. Ich habe einen Strohsack, auf dem ich schlafe, nur einen einzigen Stuhl, einen Tisch, an dem ich esse und schreibe, eine Lampe, einen sehr kleinen Ofen, auf dem ich mir meine Mahlzeiten koche, und das ist alles.

Ich lebe außerordentlich einfach. Eßbare Wurzeln, Beeren und Früchte 35 finde ich auf meinen Expeditionen mehr als genug. Und in Alaska und anderen nördlichen Ländern gibt es wilde Vögel in solchen Mengen, daß es mir auch an frischen Eiern nicht fehlt. Ich nehme sie einfach aus den Nestern. Meine braven Ziegen, die ich als ganz junge Tiere hierher gebracht habe—ich hätte ja lieber eine Kuh gehabt, und es dauerte lange, bis mir die Ziegenmilch wirklich gut schmeckte. Aber wie hätte ich eine Kuh in meine Oase bringen sollen?—meine Ziegen geben so viel Milch, daß auch mein Hund noch etwas davon bekommt. Zu füttern brauche ich sie nicht, denn Gras und frisches Wasser hat meine Oase genug. Oft bringe ich ihnen eine Handvoll Salz mit. Wenn ich Geld brauche, suche ich mir in den afrikanischen Wäldern einen Elefantenzahn und verkaufe ihn in London.

Doch genug von diesen Dingen.

Nachdem ich so aus der Höhle ein Schlaf-, Studier- und Wohnzimmer gemacht hatte, begann ich sogleich mit meiner Arbeit. Das ist jetzt etwa fünfundzwanzig (25) Jahre her. Und in diesen fünfundzwanzig Jahren habe ich alle Länder und Kontinente durchsucht, die ich mit meinen Wunderschuhen erreichen konnte. Ich habe seltene Steine, Pflanzen und Tiere gesammelt, habe die Stärke der Winde und die Temperaturen von Luft und Wasser gemessen. Ich habe—und das war das Interessanteste—die Lebensweise und die Kunst von Völkerstämmen studiert, von deren Existenz ich vorher noch nicht einmal etwas gehört hatte. Wurde es auf der nördlichen Hälfte unserer Erde Winter, dann habe ich auf der südlichen weitergearbeitet, solange es da Sommer war und die Pflanzen blühten, die ich sammeln wollte. Hohe Berge, Flüsse, ja Ströme haben mich bei meinen Märschen nicht gehindert. Selbst über den Amazonenstrom, der mehrere Kilometer breit ist, komme ich ohne Brücke hinüber. Meine botanische, zoologische und anthropologische Sammlung ist so von Jahr zu Jahr gewachsen.

Vor etwa zwei Jahren habe ich meine Materialsammlung dann abgeschlossen, und seitdem ist fast nichts Neues mehr hinzugekommen. Ich fühlte damals, daß ich schwächer wurde und alle Kraft, die mir geblieben war, für die Ausarbeitung der Darstellung gebrauchen mußte, wenn meine Arbeit nicht verlorengehen sollte. In wenigen Wochen werde ich mein Werk im Manuskript fertig haben. Ich werde mir dann erlauben, es Dir, mein Freund, in Berlin zu überreichen. Wahrscheinlich werde ich es, ehe die Sonne aufgegangen ist, Deinem Diener geben.

Niemand hat den Frieden meines kleinen Königreiches je gestört. Weder gesellschaftliche Pflichten noch Familiensorgen oder Geldschwierigkeiten haben mir jemals Zeit und Energie genommen. Und auch den Frieden der Seele, den ich in Minnas Garten verlor, habe ich hier wiedergefunden.

Als ich einst nicht weit vom Nordpol seltene Vogeleier sammelte, trat mir plötzlich um die Ecke eines Felsens ein Eisbär[4] entgegen.[5] Ich warf die Überschuhe weg und wollte auf eine Insel[6] fliehen. Ich trat mit dem linken Fuß auf einen Eisberg, der zwischen mir und der nahen Insel im Wasser trieb. Dann aber stürzte ich auf der anderen Seite des Eisbergs ins Meer, weil mir der eine Überschuh am rechten Fuß hängen geblieben war. Ich fühlte sehr bald einen stechenden Schmerz in der Brust, glaubte zuerst aber, ich hätte mich nur erkältet, und blieb noch einige Tage in der Nähe des Pols. Dann aber wurde ich doch plötzlich so krank, daß ich meine Oase nicht mehr erreichen konnte und irgendwo in Deutschland in Ohnmacht fiel.

Als ich aufwachte, lag ich in einem Krankenhaus, das zu meinem Erstaunen[7] „Schlemihlium" hieß. Mein alter Diener Bendel, so erfuhr ich, hatte es von dem Golde, das ich in meiner Wohnung hinter mir hatte zurücklassen müssen, zusammen mit Minna gegründet. Ich erfuhr ferner, daß Raskal nach ganz kurzer Ehe gestorben war. Minna selbst kam täglich mit Bendel ins Krankenhaus und ging durch alle Zimmer. Für jeden hatte sie ein Wort des Trostes, auch für mich, den sie nicht erkannte. Aber vielleicht erinnerte sie mein Gesicht doch an alte Zeiten, denn eines Tages fing sie an, vor meinem Bett mit Bendel von mir zu reden. „Ich bin sicher", sagte sie, „daß es unserm Freunde Peter nun besser geht. Ich selbst bin ja mit meinem Leben zufrieden und freue mich auf ein Wiedersehen mit ihm in einer andern Welt." Ich aber wollte den Frieden ihrer Seele nicht stören. Nur diese Worte ließ ich für sie zurück: „Deinem Freunde geht es wirklich besser. Auch er freut sich auf ein Wiedersehen in einer andern Welt."

Die Gewißheit, daß Minna nicht an der Seite eines Mannes leben muß, den sie nicht liebt, hat mir seitdem meine Arbeit leichter gemacht.

Ich werde versuchen, Dich, wenn möglich, nicht zu sehen. Du wirst verstehen, daß ich mich auch Dir nicht ohne Schatten zeigen möchte. Du könntest Fragen stellen, die Dir mein Brief viel besser beantworten wird, als meine Worte es könnten. Und ich hoffe, Du wirst mir, wenn Du diesen Brief gelesen hast, meine Unhöflichkeit vergeben.

Nun möchte ich Dich, mein Freund, um eine Gunst bitten. Laß mein Werk, wenn Deine Zeit es erlaubt, möglichst bald[8] drucken! Ich bin nicht mehr jung und möchte noch die Freude haben, ein Buch in den Händen zu halten, das einen gewissen Peter Schlemihl zum Verfasser hat. Dafür werde ich Dir immer dankbar sein.

Dein alter Freund
Peter Schlemihl.

NOTES. 1. Siebenmeilenstiefel, Stiefel seven-league boots, boots. 2. Hochebene ... Asiens plateau in inner Asia. 3. Oase oasis. 4. Eisbär (ice bear) polar bear. 5. entgegen toward. 6. Insel island. 7. Erstaunen astonishment. 8. möglichst bald as soon as possible.

BUILDING A PASSIVE VOCABULARY

auszog aus out (*here*, off), ziehen to pull, auszog pulled off, drew off, took off

Eingang ein in, Gang *from* gehen to go, Eingang entrance

erkannte kennen to know, erkennen to recognize

erreichen reichen to reach, hand to, be sufficient, erreichen to attain, unerreichbar unobtainable, inaccessible

der Fluß fließen to flow, der Fluß the river

gegründet der Grund the ground, gründen to ground, establish

das Geschenk schenken to give, das Geschenk the gift

das Glück *here*, luck

die Höhle hohl hollow, die Höhle the cave

der Kirchhof die Kirche the church, der Hof the yard, der Kirchhof the churchyard, cemetery

das Krankenhaus krank sick, das Haus the house, das Krankenhaus the hospital

mehrere mehr more, mehrere several

nördlich der Norden the north, nördlich northern. *Similarly* südlich, westlich, östlich

die Ohnmacht ohne without, die Macht the might, power, (die) Ohnmacht (the) faint

das Studium studieren to study, das Studium the study

unerreichbar *see* erreichen *above*

GRAMMAR

124. The Future Tense.* This tense consists of the present of werden, used as an auxiliary, and the infinitive of the main verb (which stands at the end of a main clause):

ich werde arbeiten	ich werde schneiden	ich werde bringen
du wirst arbeiten	du wirst schneiden	du wirst bringen
er wird arbeiten	er wird schneiden	er wird bringen
wir werden arbeiten	wir werden schneiden	wir werden bringen
ihr werdet arbeiten	ihr werdet schneiden	ihr werdet bringen
sie werden arbeiten	sie werden schneiden	sie werden bringen
I shall work	I shall cut	I shall bring
you will work	you will cut	you will bring
etc.	etc.	etc.

125. Inseparable Prefixes. The six prefixes which were listed in § 79 have meanings which they give the verbs to which they are prefixed. Two of the prefixes, ent= and zer=, have meanings which the student can readily learn:

Ent= denotes *separation* (*away from*):

entgehen to escape
entdecken to discover (take away the cover)
entehren to dishonor
entkleiden to undress

Zer= means *to pieces, in pieces*:

zerbrechen to break to pieces, to smash
zerreißen to tear to pieces
zergliedern to dissect, analyze
zerspringen to burst

---

*The future perfect tense (*I shall have eaten*) is seldom used in English or in German. It is formed like the simple future, except that the past infinitive is used instead of the present infinitive. Thus:

I shall have eaten, ich werde gegessen haben; you will have seen him, du wirst ihn gesehen haben; he will have gone, er wird gegangen sein.

The prefix **be=** is frequently used to form transitive verbs from nouns and verbs:

antworten, beantworten (Er antwortete mir auf meine Frage. Er beantwortete meine Frage. He answered my question); treten, betreten (Er trat ins Haus. Er betrat das Haus. He entered the house); begrenzen (*from* Grenze), to limit (Amerika ist das Land der unbegrenzten Möglichkeiten. America is the land of unlimited possibilities.)

126. Man. The pronoun man is declined as follows:

NOM.	man
GEN.	—
DAT.	einem
ACC.	einen

127. Indem-Clauses. Indem-clauses denote (*a*) simultaneousness or, frequently, (*b*) the method used to accomplish something:

a. Simultaneousness:

„Guten Tag", sagte er, indem er den Hut abnahm. "Good day," he said, as he took off his hat.

b. Method:

Ich kam schnell vorwärts, indem ich meinen Mantel aufmachte und mich vom Wind vorwärts treiben ließ. I made rapid progress by opening my coat and letting the wind push me ahead.

Er rettete Frau Meyer, indem er sie aus dem Wasser zog. He saved Mrs. Meyer by pulling her out of the water.

Learn the principal parts of the following verbs:

ziehen	zōg	hat gezōgen	zieht	to pull
fliehen	flōh	ist geflōhen	flieht	to flee
wiegen	wōg	hat gewōgen	wiegt	to weigh

LESSON XIX

EXERCISES

I

Answer in German (Beantworten Sie auf Deutsch!): 1. Wovon redet man nicht gern? 2. Was läßt sich nicht mit Worten sagen? 3. Wer hat Peters Dank sicher verstanden? 4. Wie hatte die Zukunft vor Peter gelegen? 5. Was stand plötzlich als Ziel vor ihm? 6. Was stand ihm nun offen? 7. Wofür hat Peter Material gesammelt? 8. Was bleibt immer unvollkommen? 9. Wann war Peter mit sich selbst zufrieden? 10. Wo stand in Asien schon die Sonne? 11. Wo fand Peter eine Oase? 12. Warum steht der Name der Oase auf keiner Karte? 13. Was fand er in einem Felsen? 14. Warum zündete Peter vor dem Eingang der Höhle ein Feuer an? 15. Was machte Peter in der folgenden Woche? 16. Wovon kaufte er sich ein Paar Überschuhe? 17. Welche Wirkung hatten die Überschuhe? 18. Warum trug Peter immer zwei Paar bei sich? 19. Wo holte er die notwendigen Instrumente? 20. Wie brachte er die Sachen in seine Oase? 21. Warum kaufte er nichts, was viel wiegt? 22. Worauf schlief er? 23. Wie viele Stühle waren in seiner Höhle? 24. Worauf kochte er seine Mahlzeiten? 25. Wie lebte er? 26. Hatte er anfangs Ziegenmilch gern? 27. Wie viele lebende Wesen gab es in der Oase? 28. Wo gibt es Elefantenzähne? 29. Womit begann Peter, nachdem er seine Höhle wohnlich gemacht hatte? 30. Was sammelte er? 31. Was maß er? 32. Warum schloß er seine Materialsammlung ab? 33. Wann will er sein Manuskript fertig haben? 34. Wo sammelte er einst seltene Eier? 35. Warum stürzte er ins Wasser? 36. Warum konnte er seine Oase nicht erreichen? 37. Wo lag er, als er aufwachte? 38. Wer hatte das Krankenhaus gegründet? 39. Wer war nach kurzer Ehe gestorben? 40. Wer hatte für jeden ein Wort des Trostes? 41. Mit wem redete Minna über Peter? 42. Worauf freute sich Minna? 43. Warum wollte Peter seinen Freund nicht sehen? 44. Was soll der Freund mit Peters Werk tun?

II

Translate into German: 1. I shall see you Friday. 2. Next week he will be here. 3. That will cost you your head. 4. In the summer we shall go to the country. 5. He will help you if you wish (*use* wollen). 6. He would help you if you did not sleep so long. 7. I know that you will be very happy. 8. We shall have to drink goat's milk. 9. We should (would) have to drink wine. 10. I shall show you how I do that. 11. He will report [to] us what he has seen. 12. We shall not be permitted to see him. 13. Shall you be able to come? 14. With your book you will have a big success. 15. You will soon be as slender as I. 16. We shall soon be ready.

III

Translate into English:

weh tun	die Dame	der Knochen	das Brot
rühren	freilich	März	der Fürst
gelingen	jagen	das Maul	leer
der Fuß	streiten	das Hemd	prüfen
dringen	stumpf	der Bach	überall
die Blume	der Punkt	bellen	vier

IV

Translate into German:

thick	the wood	the office	to be sure
the thief	the trousers	to meet	thoroughly
seven	the fool	to cover	the neck
six	the ring	the thing	ripe
eight	the knife	double	the sin
holy	the middle	the fire	to report

V

Translate the following compounds and derivatives:

blühende Apfelbäume; breitstirnig; die Rheinbrücke, eine Hängebrücke; die Darstellung, der Darsteller, die Darstellerin; der Druck, drucken, der Drucker, druckfertig, der Druckfehler; der Eifer, eifrig, eifrig bei (at) der Arbeit sein; England, der Engländer, die Engländerin; eine Erkältung haben; das Pferdefutter, das Hundefutter, Fütterung der Löwen um sechs Uhr; die Gunst, die Mißgunst, ein günstiger Wind; ich bin auf der Heimfahrt, die Heimreise; der Hohlkopf; die Spielkarten, der Kartenspieler; die Katzenmusik, das Kätzlein, die Hauskatze; krank, der Kranke, ein Kranker, die Kranken, das Krankenhaus (hospital), das Krankenbett; die Kunst, der Künstler (the artist), die Kunstgeschichte, die Kunstschule; das Festmahl (banquet); die Marschmusik; eine hohle

Nuß, der Nußbaum, das Nüßchen; die Ofentür, der Gasofen; salzig, das Salzwasser; sammeln, die Sammlung, der Sammler; der Sommerregen, sommerlich, Sommernachtstraum; der Baumstamm; entlaufen, zerfallen, zerkleinern, entführen, entziehen; der Apfelsinenbaum, der Lindenbaum; die Mischung; gelblich; der Feiertag; das Ladenfenster; das Löffelchen, das Tellerchen; vorauseilen; „die lustigen Weiber von Windsor" 5

VI

Change to the future tense: 1. Wir besuchen sie jedes Jahr. 2. Ich sehe ihn nie wieder. 3. Ich habe nichts zu verlieren. 4. Ich schreibe Dir bald einen längeren Brief. 5. Jeden Morgen arbeite ich drei Stunden. 6. Ich verkaufe heute gar nichts. 7. Ich trinke eine Tasse Tee. 8. Im Sommer essen wir neue Kartoffeln und frische Erbsen. 9. Schicken dir deine Eltern Geld? 10. Wann beginnen wir?

VII

Conjugate in the future tense:

rufen laufen kommen eilen finden schreiben

VIII

Give the plural of the following nouns:

der Lehrer	die Rose	das Blatt	die Hand	die Karte
das Buch	der Mantel	der Brief	der Tag	das Lied
der Mann	der Bleistift	der Finger	die Mutter	die Lippe

IX

Give the third person plural indicative of the present, past, present perfect, past perfect, and future of the following verbs:

danken	essen	helfen	arbeiten	einschlafen
aufmachen	fahren	machen	schneiden	frieren

X

Make up four original sentences using the future tense; make up four sentences using the imaginative subjunctive; make up two sentences using indem. Be sure to use at least three verbs with inseparable prefixes in the ten sentences.

LESSON XX

TEXT A

Active	Passive
Die Mutter ruft ihre Tochter.	Die Tochter wird von der Mutter gerufen.
Marie deckt den Tisch.	Der Tisch wird von Marie gedeckt.
Antonio trägt Laurella ins Schiffchen.	Laurella wird von Antonio ins Schiffchen getragen.
Wer haßt ihn?	Von wem wird er gehaßt?
Die Mutter rief die Tochter.	Die Tochter wurde von der Mutter gerufen.
Maria deckte den Tisch.	Der Tisch wurde von Maria gedeckt.
Kolumbus hat Amerika entdeckt.	Amerika ist von Kolumbus entdeckt worden.
Er hat die Bienen mit Farbe (paint) gezeichnet.	Die Bienen sind von ihm mit Farbe gezeichnet worden.
Durch den Gebrauch von Penicillin hat man schon manches Leben gerettet.	Schon manches Leben ist durch den Gebrauch von Penicillin gerettet worden.

* * *

Marie deckt gerade den Tisch. Wenn sie fertig ist, ist der Tisch gedeckt.—Als Gustav ins Wasser fiel, zog Paula ihn heraus. Als Gustav ins Wasser fiel, wurde er von Paula herausgezogen.—„Es wäre besser für mich", meinte Gustav, „wenn du mich nicht herausgezogen hättest." Und auch Gustavs Freunde meinten, es wäre besser für Gustav, wenn er nicht gerettet worden wäre.

Wir wissen nicht, wer das Feuer entdeckt hat. Niemand weiß, wann das Feuer entdeckt worden ist. Als Meyer auf die Welt kam, war das Feuer schon entdeckt.

Meyer wurde gestern von einem Auto überfahren (run over). Meyer ist gestern von einem Auto überfahren worden. Meyer soll gestern von einem Auto überfahren worden sein.

Die Mädchen in dieser Klasse arbeiten vom frühen Morgen bis zum späten Abend. In dieser Klasse wird viel gearbeitet.

Ein Ei. Ein gekochtes Ei. Ein nicht länger als vier Minuten gekochtes Ei. Ein Tisch. Ein gedeckter Tisch. Ein festlich gedeckter Tisch. Ein reich und festlich gedeckter Tisch.

Der Zeitsinn der Bienen

Der Mensch hat nicht im selben Sinne des Wortes einen Sinn für die Zeit, wie er einen Sinn für Farben oder für Wärme und Kälte hat. Der Leiter eines Warenhauses kann sein Auge sehr leicht dazu erziehen, Hunderte von Farben für Kleiderstoffe zu unterscheiden. Eine Mutter, die ihr Kind jeden Tag selber badet, wird sehr schnell ein genaues Gefühl dafür entwickeln, ob die Temperatur des Bades gerade richtig ist oder nicht. Nach einiger Übung wird sie sogar mit ziemlicher Genauigkeit auch ohne Thermometer sagen können, ob das Wasser dreißig (30) oder dreiunddreißig (33) Grad[1] (Zentigrad) warm ist. Aber dieselbe Mutter kann, ohne auf die Uhr zu sehen, nicht sagen, ob ihr Kind vor drei Stunden oder vor dreieinhalb Stunden zum letzten Mal gefüttert worden ist. Wir haben eben kein Organ, welches die Zeit registriert.

Ein und dasselbe Zeitintervall kommt uns manchmal kürzer und manchmal länger vor, als es in Wirklichkeit ist. Das Alter eines Menschen, die Art seiner Tätigkeit, sein Temperament und, wie wir sehen werden, physiologische Prozesse im Körper sind hier entscheidende Faktoren. Die Zeit zwischen zwei Weihnachtsfesten ist für die kleinen Neffen und Nichten viel länger als für die Tante, von der das Paket[2] mit der Wollweste und der elektrischen Eisenbahn nur darum im letzten Augenblick aufs Postamt gebracht wird, weil das Jahr für die würdige alte Dame so schnell vorbeigegangen ist. Und vier Wochen Ferien sind, wie Sie wissen, viel kürzer als vier Wochen Unterricht in der Kunst, in zwei Meter langen Sätzen das Subjekt zu finden—auch für den Lehrer.

Aber auch kurze Zeitintervalle können von uns ohne Instrumente (und dazu gehören Sonne und Sterne) nicht genau geschätzt werden. Es läßt sich experimentell beweisen, daß solche Schätzungen nur in höchst unvollkommener Weise gelingen. Es ist sehr unwahrscheinlich, daß alle Fehler dieser Art durch rein psychologische Faktoren erklärt werden können.

Daß aber wirklich auch physiologische Faktoren hier im Spiele sind, das ist erst von der modernen Biologie bewiesen worden.

Gewisse Insekten nämlich haben—wie von mehreren Beobachtern berichtet wurde—einen Zeitsinn, der mit unglaublicher Präzision,[3] und zwar ganz unabhängig von der Umwelt, arbeitet.

Die ersten Versuche über den Zeitsinn solcher Insekten sind mit Bienen
5 gemacht worden. Man stellte im Garten einen mit Zuckerwasser gefüllten Teller auf. Von den Bienen, die an diesen Teller flogen, wurden mehrere Dutzend mit Farbpünktchen gezeichnet. Diese Fütterung wurde mehrere Tage lang zu stets gleicher Tageszeit wiederholt, bis sich die Bienen an diese Zeit gewöhnt hatten und jeden Tag zur selben Stunde zum Futter-
10 platz kamen. Eines Tages wurde jedoch kein Futter gereicht. Dennoch kamen die Bienen zum Futterplatz und flogen über dem leeren Teller eifrig hin und her; und es war ganz gleich, ob man den Teller immer an denselben Platz oder jedesmal an einen andern Ort stellte.

Hier stellt sich nun die Frage: Woher wissen die Bienen, wann die
15 Stunde der Fütterung gekommen ist? Hunger kann sie schon darum nicht dazu treiben, zu einer bestimmten Stunde zum Futterplatz zu fliegen, weil sie den Zucker ja gar nicht fressen, sondern nach Hause tragen. (D. h. sie „fressen" ihn schon. Sie tragen ihn nämlich im Magen nach Hause und entleeren den Magen dann.) Der Stand der Sonne hilft ihnen auch nicht,
20 denn man hat Bienen in geschlossene Räume gebracht, die Tag und Nacht durch elektrisches Licht erleuchtet wurden. Aber selbst wenn während der Nacht gefüttert wurde, gelang es, die Bienen an eine bestimmte Futterzeit zu gewöhnen.

Dennoch war es höchst wahrscheinlich, daß Bienen die Zeit von einer
25 Fütterung zur anderen nicht einfach raten. Es ist experimentell bewiesen worden, daß der Zeitsinn der Bienen an den Vierundzwanzig-(24)-Stunden-Rhythmus gebunden ist. Man kann sie nur dann an eine bestimmte Futterzeit gewöhnen, wenn die Fütterung jeden Tag genau auf die gleiche Stunde fällt, und zwar ist es ganz gleich, ob man in freier Natur experimentiert
30 oder in Räumen, die Tag und Nacht erleuchtet sind.

Versuche der letzten Zeit haben das Problem, vor dem man hier anfangs stand, gelöst. Wir wissen heute, daß der Lebensrhythmus der Bienen derselbe ist wie der der Blumen, die sie besuchen. Der Honig wird nämlich in den Blumen meist nur zu ganz bestimmten Tagesstunden gebildet, und
35 zwar, und das ist wichtig, nicht bei allen Pflanzenarten zur selben Stunde. Die Erdbeere im Garten, die Kartoffel auf dem Acker, der Birnbaum auf

dem Felde und das Vergißmeinnicht auf der Wiese bilden den Honignektar in der Regel nicht zur selben Tageszeit. Nur wenn die Biene jede einzelne Blumen- und Obstbaumart ihrer Umgebung zur richtigen Zeit besucht, findet sie reichen Lohn für ihre Arbeit. Die biologische Bedeutung des an den Vierundzwanzig-Stunden-Rhythmus gebundenen Zeitsinns ist damit 5 erklärt. Es muß noch erwähnt werden, daß ähnliche Experimente auch mit anderen staatenbildenden Insekten gemacht worden sind und daß bei solchen Arten, die, wie die Bienen, gerne Blumen besuchen, der Vierundzwanzig-Stunden-Rhythmus ebenfalls beobachtet werden konnte.

Weitere Versuche brachten Klarheit über das „Organ" dieses Zeitsinnes. 10 Tiere nämlich, die mit Chloroform oder Äther behandelt[4] wurden, ließen sich dadurch in ihrem Rhythmus nicht stören, ein Zeichen dafür, daß ihr Zeitsinn physiologischer, nicht psychologischer Natur ist. Anders war es jedoch, wenn man etwas fütterte, was auf den Stoffwechsel wirkte. Euchinin,[5] das den Stoffwechsel verlangsamt,[5] hatte z. B. die Wirkung, daß die Tiere 15 vier Stunden zu spät an die Futterstelle kamen. Jodthyreoglubin, das den Stoffwechsel beschleunigt,[6] hatte die Wirkung, daß sie fünf Stunden zu früh ankamen. Der innere Rhythmus des Stoffwechsels ist also jene Uhr, die es den Bienen erlaubt, jede Blume zur richtigen Zeit zu besuchen.

NOTES. 1. Grad degrees. 2. Paket package. 3. Präzision precision. 4. behandelt treated. 5. Euchinin . . . verlangsamt euquinine, which retards metabolism. 6. Jodthyreoglubin . . . beschleunigt thyroiodine-globulin (an iodine-containing globulin in the thyroid gland), which accelerates metabolism.

BUILDING A PASSIVE VOCABULARY

abhängig ab off, hängen to hang, abhängig dependent on

das Alter alt old, das Alter the age

aufgestellt *here same as* gestellt

erleuchtet das Licht light, erleuchten to illuminate

gewöhnen gewöhnlich usual, customary, gewöhnen to accustom, adapt, adjust

im Freien frei free, unoccupied, vacant, im Freien in the open

mehrere mehr more, mehrere several

schätzen der Schatz the treasure, valued object, schätzen to treasure, value, estimate, geschätzt (*past part.*) estimated, die Schätzungen estimates, guesses

staatenbildend der Staat the state, bilden to form, found, establish, staatenbildend colonizing, social

der Stoffwechsel der Stoff the material, wechseln to change, der Stoffwechsel metabolism

die Tätigkeit tun to do, to act, die Tat the act, die Tätigkeit the activity

die Umwelt um around, die Welt the world, die Umwelt the surroundings, environment

unterscheiden scheiden to separate, unterscheiden to distinguish

das Warenhaus die Ware the merchandise, das Haus the house, das Warenhaus the house in which there is merchandise (for sale), the department store

die Wirkung wirken to work, effect, die Wirkung the effect, result

VOCABULARY

achten to regard
achten auf to pay attention to
der Acker, ¨ the (cultivated) field
aufpassen (*sep. prefix*) to pay attention to; take care of
baden to *bathe*
bedeuten to mean, signify
die Biene, –n the *bee*
die Birne, –n the *pear*
die Bohne, –n the *bean*
darum therefore; for the reason
das Dutzend, –e the *dozen*
ebenfalls likewise
die Eisenbahn, –en railway, railroad
entscheiden to decide, determine
entwickeln to develop
der Erbe, –n, –n the heir
die Erdbeere, –n the strawberry
erwähnen to mention
erziehen to educate; rear
die Ferien (*pl.*) the vacation
flach *flat*; shallow
der Honig the *honey*
der Körper, – the body
leiten to *lead*; direct
lohnen to reward, to pay
der Magen, – the stomach
der Mord, –e the *murder*
der Neffe, –n, –n the *nephew*
die Nichte, –n the *niece*
das Obst the fruit
die Post the mail; *post* office
die Regel, –n the rule
rein clear; pure
der Satz, ¨e the sentence
der Schaden, ¨ the harm, damage
schwimmen to *swim*
der Staat, –en the *state*
streichen to *stroke*
die Tante, –n the aunt
üben to practice; exercise
umgében to surround (*insep. prefix*)
die Ware, –n the merchandise, goods
Weihnachten Christmas
die Weste, –n the *vest*
wichtig important
die Wiese, –n the meadow
die Wolle the *wool*

die Würde, -n the dignity
zart tender, delicate
zeichnen to sketch; mark
der Zucker the *sugar*

IDIOMS

d. h. (das heißt) that is (i.e.)
erst recht more than ever
es geht nicht it can't be done

TEXT B

Psyche*

Es war an einem Vormittage im August, und die Sonne schien; aber das Wetter war stürmisch, der Wind kam hart aus Nordwest, und Wind und Flut[1] trieben die See in den breiten Meeresarm,[2] der zwischen zwei Deichen[2] von draußen bis an die Stadt reichte. Die Holzgebäude der beiden Badeflöße,[2] welche in einiger Entfernung voneinander nicht weit vom Ufer lagen, bewegten sich auf und ab. Der sonst so belebte Badeplatz war heute gänzlich leer. Nur dort vor dem Holzhäuschen, das auf dem Vorlande[2] neben dem Frauenfloß[2] lag, stand die knochige Gestalt der alten Badefrau. Die langen Bänder ihres großen Hutes flogen im Winde, den Rock hielt sie sich mit beiden Händen fest. Sie hatte nichts zu tun; die Handtücher der Damen und Kinder lagen drinnen im Hause ruhig in ihren Fächern. „Ich geh nach Haus", sagte sie bei sich selber; „es kommt niemand in dem Mordwetter."

Sie sah den Deich[2] entlang nach der Stadt hinab. Die Schafe auf dem Vorlande[2] hatten sich mit dem Rücken gegen den Wind gestellt; sonst war nichts zu sehen.—Doch nein! Dort auf dem Deiche kamen zwei Männer und stiegen dem Männerfloße[2] gegenüber an der Außenseite des Deiches herab; ihre Handtücher ließen sie über ihren Köpfen fliegen; ihre jugendlichen Stimmen, ihr helles Lachen konnte nicht zu der Alten dringen, denn der Wind nahm es ihnen von den Lippen.

„Hätten auch zu Haus bleiben können", brummte[3] die Alte, als sie die beiden in eine der Türen des Badefloßes hatte verschwinden sehen; „aber mir kann's gleich sein; ich geh' nach Haus! Es könnte nur e i n e kommen

---

*Theodor Storm, one of the best German authors of the nineteenth century, wrote *Psyche* in 1875. He based his tale on the story of "Cupid and Psyche" in *The Golden Ass*, by Apuleius, and on a newspaper account of the saving of a girl from drowning by a young man. A brief portion of "Cupid and Psyche" is retold in a later part of *Psyche*. The story presented here in an abbreviated form follows as closely as possible (that is, within the vocabulary limits of the Minimum Standard German Vocabulary) Storm's original version.

bei dem[4] Wetter, aber ihre Zeit ist schon vorbei; die Flut muß bald eine halbe Stunde stehen, und die, die kann immer kaum warten, bis das erste Wasser da ist."

Schon hatte sie die Tür des kleinen Hauses in der Hand, als sie bei einem 5 Blick, den sie noch zur Stadt hinüberwarf, mit beiden Händen ihren Hut festhielt. „Heilige Mutter Maria!" rief sie, „da kommt sie!"

Und wirklich, dort auf dem Deiche von der Stadt her kam ein junges Mädchen; und sie kam schnell trotz Wind und Wetter näher. Der flache Strohhut war ihr längst vom Kopfe gerissen, und sie trug ihn am Bande in 10 der Hand; ihr sonnenblondes Haar flog im Winde. Als sie die knochige Gestalt der Alten, die noch immer vor dem Holzhause stand, erkannt hatte, flog sie an der Seite des Deiches hinunter und dann über das Vorland zu ihr hinüber. „Kathi", rief sie, „Kathi, ich konnte nicht eher kommen; gut, daß du nicht nach Hause gegangen bist."

15 „Ja, ja", brummte[3] die Alte, „hätte ich das nur getan!"

„Kathi! Nicht brummen!" lachte das Mädchen und sah der Alten fast zärtlich in die Augen.

„Aber es geht ja doch nicht, Fräulein!" meinte noch einmal die Alte, indem sie dem Mädchen das blonde Haar von der Stirn zurückstrich.

20 „Aber es geht erst recht, Kathi! Heute gibt's hier weder kleine Kinder noch alte Tanten; ganz allein hab' ich heute das Reich, ich und über mir die Vögel in der Luft! Hurrah, Kathi, es wird eine Lust!"

„Aber, Kind, so sehen Sie doch nur, wie sich das Floß[2] auf und ab bewegt; der Weg dahin ist fußtief unter Wasser!"

25 Die junge Dame blickte zum Ufer hinab. „Freilich", sagte sie, lustig nickend, „ich muß mir Schuhe und Strümpfe in deinem Häuschen ausziehen."

Das Haus, in dem die beiden nun verschwanden, sah von außen nicht gerade freundlich aus. Aber innen war es doch ganz wohnlich. Der Tür gegenüber stand eine Ruhebank. Durch das kleine Fenster auf der einen 30 Seite schien die Mittagssonne, und der ganze Raum war daher warm und hell. Auf der anderen Seite stand der Tisch, an dem die älteren Damen nach dem Bade gewöhnlich eine Tasse Kaffee tranken, zu dem sie sich die Bohnen und den Zucker selber mitbrachten.

Aber heute waren die alten Damen zu Hause geblieben, und es war 35 niemand da, dem Kathi Kaffee hätte kochen können. Die Mutter der mutigen jungen Schwimmerin mußte das wohl gewußt haben, denn sie hatte

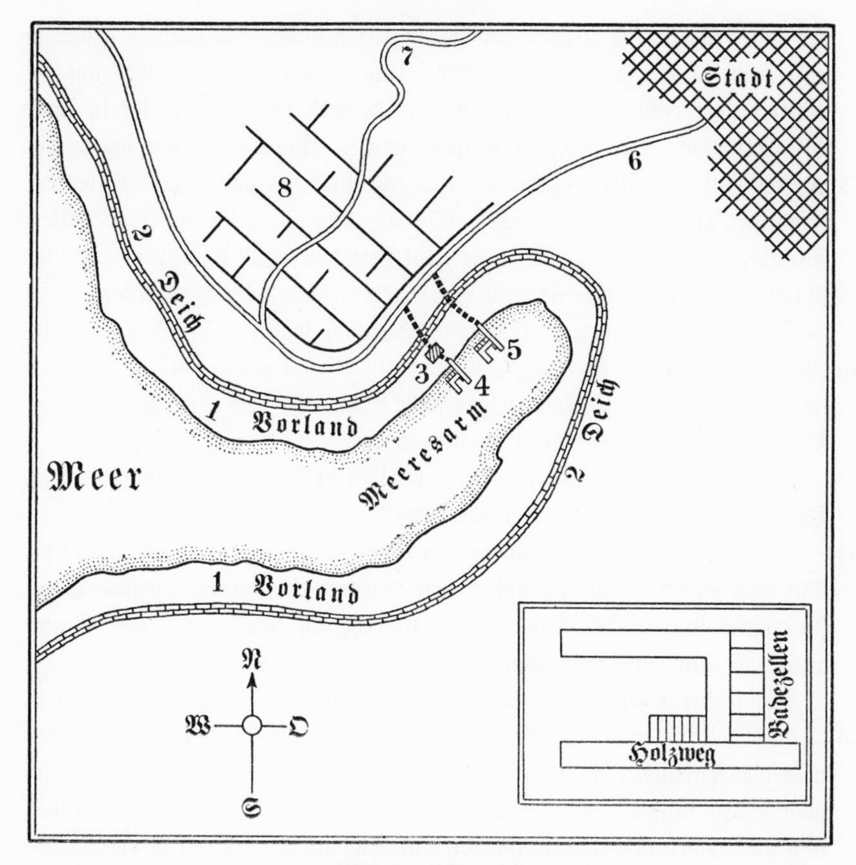

Plan for "Psyche"

1. Vorland land between the sea and the dike. 2. Deich dike. 3. Kathis Holzhaus. 4. Frauenfloß (Floß float) women's floating bathhouse. The floating bathhouses in our story are ⊔-shaped, and the swimmers confined their bathing to the area enclosed within the ⊔. Separate floats and the privacy of the enclosed space made nude bathing possible. Kathi feared that the girl would swim out of the enclosure and into the open and, on this day, dangerous ocean. For the plan of a floating bathhouse, see the lower right-hand corner of the map. 5. Männerfloß men's bathing float. 6. Direkter Weg zur Stadt. 7. Indirekter Weg zur Stadt. 8. Wassergraben ditch

ihrer Tochter Mokka und Zucker mitgegeben, damit Kathi, die zu arm war, um sich selber Kaffee kaufen zu können, doch noch ihr Täßchen bekam.

Kathi und die Mutter waren alte Freunde. Vor langer Zeit, als die Mutter noch ein Kind war, hatte Kathi für den Vater der Mutter, den Bürgermeister der Stadt, als Kindermädchen gearbeitet. „Mama", von

der das Fräulein die Freude am Baden geerbt hatte, war damals genau so wild gewesen wie heute die Tochter. Und so wie Kathi damals auf die Mutter aufgepaßt hatte, achtete sie jetzt darauf, daß die Tochter in ihrer Wildheit nichts tat, was ihr schaden konnte. Und das Baden bei diesem
5 Wetter hätte ihr schaden können. Um das Mädchen davon zurückzuhalten, erzählte Kathi daher etwas aus Mamas Jugend, denn in einer halben Stunde, das wußte sie, mußte die Flut zurückgehen, und wenn die Tochter so lange zuhörte, mußte sie nach Hause gehen, ohne gebadet zu haben.

Die Augen des jungen Mädchens glänzten, während die Alte erzählte.
10 „Weißt du, Kathi", sagte sie, „Mama muß reizend gewesen sein. Hätte ich sie so nur einmal sehen können!—Meine Mama ist noch reizend, und jung, Kathi! Ich glaub', sie könnt' noch heute von einer Mauer springen."

„Was das Fräulein für Gedanken hat! Aber freilich, damals gab's Tag für Tag etwas Neues mit dem Kindchen."

15 Sie hatte eben zu weiterem Erzählen die Hände aufs Knie gelegt, als die Tür von einem Windstoß aufgerissen wurde; ein vorbeifliegender Vogel stieß einen lauten Schrei aus; vom Ufer herauf konnte man das Wasser gegen das Floß schlagen hören.

Die leichte Gestalt des Mädchens stand plötzlich hoch vor der Alten.
20 „Kathi!" rief sie und hob böse den Finger; „nun merk' ich's erst, du wolltest mich hier festhalten, bis deine große Uhr eins schlüge und ich dann zu Mama nach Hause müßte! Aber diesmal, Kathi!"—Und schon war sie draußen und machte mit den kleinen Händen eine Schwimmbewegung in die Luft.

Die Alte war mit hinausgelaufen; aber sie sah ihr Spiel verloren. „Nur
25 um Himmels willen, Kind! Sie wollen doch heute nicht aus dem Floß hinausschwimmen?"

„Und warum nicht, Kathi? Du weißt ja, ich versteh's! Und ich sag' dir, es wird eine Lust!"

Und singend schritt sie über das grüne Vorland zum Ufer hinab, den
30 schönen Kopf dem Winde zugewandt.

Die Alte ging in ihr Häuschen zurück. Strümpfe und Schuhe des jungen Mädchens, die diese auf dem Boden hatte liegen lassen, legte sie unter die Ruhebank; dann stellte sie das Kaffeewasser auf und zündete in ihrem kleinen Ofen ein Feuer an. „Das Kind wird heute auch wohl eine Tasse
35 nehmen", sagte sie. Aber sie hatte doch keine Ruhe. Ein paarmal hatte sie schon den Kopf zur Tür hinausgesteckt; jetzt lief sie sogar an den Strand

hinab. Der Weg zum Badefloß war völlig unter Wasser, so daß das Floß ohne alle Verbindung mit dem Lande schien.—„Fräulein!" rief sie; „Fräulein!"

Es kam keine Antwort, aber ein Plätschern[5] kam aus dem Floß herauf. Und zufrieden nickend, ging die Alte wieder in ihr Haus. 5

[Fortsetzung folgt]

NOTES. 1. Flut flood tide, flood, water. 2. See plan, p. 217. 3. brummte muttered, mumbled. 4. dem this (miserable). 5. Plätschern splashing.

BUILDING A PASSIVE VOCABULARY

aussehen sehen to see, aussehen to look
ausziehen aus out, ziehen to pull, ausziehen to pull off, take off
das Band, die Bänder (*pl.*) binden to tie, das Band the ribbon, tie
belebt leben to live, belebt lively
die Entfernung fern far, distant, die Entfernung the distance
erkannt kennen to know, erkennen to recognize
der Gedanke denken to think, der Gedanke the thought
die Handtücher die Hand the hand, das Tuch the cloth, das Handtuch the hand towel
das Kindermädchen das Kind the child, das Mädchen the girl, das Kindermädchen the children's girl, *that is*, the nursemaid
knochig der Knochen the bone, knochig bony
längst lange long, längst long since
der Meeresarm das Meer the sea, der Arm the arm, der Meeresarm the inlet, bay
das Mordwetter der Mord the murder, das Wetter the weather, das Mordwetter the murderous, treacherous weather
die Ruhebank ruhen to rest, die Bank the bench, die Ruhebank sofa, couch
die Verbindung binden to bind, tie, *that is*, connect, die Verbindung the connection
der Windstoß der Wind the wind, stoßen to push, thrust, der Windstoß the gust of wind

GRAMMAR

128. The Passive Voice. The passive voice is formed by using the past participle of a given verb with the proper tense, person, and number of the auxiliary verb werden (*to be*): er wird gerufen *he is (being) called*, er wurde gerufen *he was (being) called.* In compound tenses werden itself requires, as in the active, the auxiliary sein; in these tenses the past participle of werden becomes worden, the ge-prefix being dropped: er ist gerufen worden *he has been called*, er war gerufen worden *he had been called.* (Note the position of the main verb.)

As in English, the direct object of a transitive verb in the active becomes the subject in the passive. The subject of the active becomes the agent in the passive.

English *by* is usually expressed by von when the agent is a person. The cause is expressed by durch; the instrument is expressed by mit.

Ich wurde von meinem Vater nach Hause gebracht. I was taken home by my father.

Die Stadt wurde durch Feuer vernichtet. The city was destroyed by fire.

Die Bienen wurden mit Farbpünktchen gezeichnet. The bees were marked with dots of paint.

129. Synopsis of treiben in the Passive (and of werden in the Active)

	Active of werden	**Passive of treiben**
Present	er wird	er wird getrieben
Past	er wurde	er wurde getrieben
Present Perfect	er ist geworden	er ist getrieben worden
Past Perfect	er war geworden	er war getrieben worden
Future	er wird werden	er wird getrieben werden

(Translation of passive forms: *he is being driven; he was being driven; he has been driven; he had been driven; he will be driven*)

The forms of the imaginative subjunctive, as might be expected, are:

Present time: ich würde gerufen, du würdest gerufen, I'd be called, you'd be called, and so on.

Past time: ich wäre gerufen worden, du wärest gerufen worden, I'd have been called, you'd have been called, and so on.

130. Apparent Passive. In § 85 it was explained that past participles may be used as attributive or predicate adjectives. When used predicatively, as in the example Die Tür war geschlossen, the student might mistakenly regard the phrase war geschlossen as passive because he translates both war geschlossen and wurde geschlossen by *was closed.* Die Tür war geschlossen (apparent passive) describes a state already existing: the door was closed (someone had previously closed it). Die Tür wurde geschlossen (passive) describes an action: someone was closing the door. (If you had to withdraw $10,000 from a bank, would you rather arrive at the bank when the door war geschlossen or when it wurde geschlossen?)

Examples of the passive and the apparent passive:

Passive	**Apparent Passive**
Der Brief wird gerade geschrieben.	Der Brief ist schon geschrieben.
The letter is just being written.	The letter is already written.
Die Äpfel wurden gerade gewaschen.	Die Äpfel waren schon gewaschen.
The apples were just being washed.	The apples were already washed.
Herr Meyer starb, und sein Haus wurde verkauft.	Gustav starb und war bald vergessen.
Mr. Meyer died, and his house was sold.	Gustav died and was soon forgotten.

131. Substitutions for the Passive. The passive in German is less frequent than in English. In its place German may use:

a. The active with man: Man sagte, daß . . . *It was said that . . .*

b. Reflexive constructions: Die Tür öffnete sich. *The door (was) opened.*

132. Impersonal Passive. All English passives have a subject. German may use passives with no subject or an indefinite es instead of a subject. This so-called impersonal passive cannot be translated literally but must be paraphrased:

Hier wird gearbeitet. People are working here, *or* Work is going on here.

Morgen wird geheiratet. Tomorrow a wedding will take place, *or* They are going to marry tomorrow.

Es wurde viel gesungen. There was much singing.

133. Participial Phrases. It was pointed out in §§ 49 and 85 that present and past participles may serve as attributive adjectives, as ein weinendes Kind, das versprochene Buch. Not infrequently in written German and particularly in science German this participle is preceded by its own object, prepositional phrase, or other qualifying element. As can be seen in the following examples, such participial phrases are usually best translated by using dependent clauses:

Ein **durch die Stadt fließender** Fluß . . . A river which flows through the city . . .

Die Bienen wurden durch einen **im Freien aufgestellten** Teller angelockt. The bees were attracted by a dish (which was) placed in the open.

Ein **mit Zuckerwasser gefüllter** Teller . . . A dish filled with sweetened water . . .

Die biologische Bedeutung des **an den Vierundzwanzig-Stunden-Rhythmus gebundenen** Zeitsinns ist damit erklärt. The biological importance of the sense of time which is connected with the twenty-four-hour rhythm is thus explained.

Erst später gab man dem neuen, **von Kolumbus entdeckten** Land den Namen Amerika. Not until later did they give the new land which was discovered by Columbus the name America.

Note this rule: If the noun does not follow the der-word, ein-word, or attributive adjective in its expected place, the student should always read on until he finds that noun following the participle and then go back and fill in the sentence with a dependent (adjective) clause.

134. Anticipative Pronouns. English may use the impersonal pronoun "it" to point to a following noun clause or infinitive phrase. Compare "He saw to *it* that I worked" and "*It* was senseless to think of marriage." German uses es in the same way, that is, as an anticipative pronoun.

Examples: Es tut mir leid, daß Sie nicht kommen können.
I am sorry that you cannot come.
Es war sinnlos, an Liebe und Ehe zu denken.
It was senseless to think of love and marriage.

Remember, however, that es before a preposition becomes da- (Cf. § 105).

Example: Er sah darauf, daß ich arbeitete.
He saw to it that I worked.

Frequently, the American reader feels such German pronoun substitutes to be superfluous. In such cases he should leave them untranslated.

Example: Sie entwickelt ein Gefühl dafür, ob das Wasser zu warm ist.
She develops a feeling as to whether the water is too warm.

Sometimes even the simple pronoun is felt to be superfluous. In such cases it, too, should be left untranslated:

Example: Ich verstehe es ja, daß du ihn liebst.
I understand, of course, that you love him.

Adverbs may be used in a similar manner. Sometimes they may be translated; at other times they should either be paraphrased or left out:

Example: Die Bienen kamen selbst dann, wenn . . .
The bees came even (then) when . . .
Hunger kann sie schon darum nicht treiben, weil sie den Honig nicht fressen.
Hunger cannot drive them [for the following reason] because they do not eat the honey.

Learn the principal parts of the following verbs:

schreiben	schrieb	hat geschrieben	schreibt	to write
entscheiden	entschied	hat entschieden	entscheidet	to decide
beißen	biß	hat gebissen	beißt	to bite
streichen	strich	hat gestrichen	streicht	to stroke
ziehen	zōg	hat gezōgen	zieht	to pull
erziehen	erzōg	hat erzōgen	erzieht	to educate
gewinnen	gewann	hat gewonnen	gewinnt	to win
schwimmen	schwamm	ist geschwommen	schwimmt	to swim
gēben	gāb	hat gegēben	gībt	to give
umgēben	umgāb	hat umgēben	umgībt	to surround

EXERCISES

I

A. Beantworten Sie folgende Fragen über Text A auf deutsch: 1. Wer kann sein Auge dazu erziehen, Hunderte von Farben zu unterscheiden? 2. Wer entwickelt bald ein Gefühl für die Temperatur des Badewassers? 3. Für wen ist die Zeit zwischen zwei Weihnachtsfesten zu kurz? 4. Wann bringt die Tante das Paket zur Post? 5. Was haben Sie lieber, vier Wochen Ferien oder vier Wochen Unterricht? 6. Was ist von der Biologie bewiesen worden? 7. Was stellte man im Garten auf? 8. Womit wurden die Bienen gezeichnet? 9. Was wurde zu stets gleicher Tageszeit wiederholt? 10. Was wurde eines Tages nicht gereicht? 11. Wohin tragen die Bienen den Honig? 12. Wodurch wurden die Räume erleuchtet? 13. Woran ist der Zeitsinn der Bienen gebunden? 14. Wann wird der Honig in den Blumen gebildet? 15. Womit sind ähnliche Experimente gemacht worden? 16. Was für eine Wirkung hatte Euchinin auf den Stoffwechsel?

B. Beantworten Sie folgende Fragen über Text B auf deutsch: 1. Wie war das Wetter an jenem Vormittage im August? 2. Woher kam der Wind? 3. Wohin trieben Wind und Flut die See? 4. Wie war sonst der Badeplatz? 5. Was hielt die alte Frau mit beiden Händen fest? 6. Wo grasten die Schafe? 7. Was ließen die jungen Männer über ihren Köpfen fliegen? 8. Wer kam von der Stadt her? 9. Wie war das Haar des Mädchens? 10. Wer brummte? 11. Wer hatte heute das Reich ganz allein? 12. Wie sah das Haus von innen aus? 13. Warum war der Raum warm und hell? 14. Für wen kochte die Alte sonst Kaffee? 15. Was war Kathi in ihrer Jugend gewesen? 16. Von wem hatte das Mädchen die große Freude am Baden geerbt? 17. Wovon begann die Alte zu erzählen? 18. Von wem wurde die Tür aufgemacht? 19. Warum sollte das Mädchen nicht aus dem Floß hinausschwimmen? 20. Wie ging sie über das grüne Vorland? 21. Wo hatte das Mädchen ihre Strümpfe und Schuhe liegen lassen? 22. Wohin legte Kathi sie? 23. Was zündete Kathi in ihrem Ofen an? 24. Wohin lief Kathi? 25. Was lag völlig unter Wasser? 26. War das Floß wirklich ohne alle Verbindung mit dem Lande? 27. Was rief Kathi? 28. Warum ging die Alte zufrieden nickend in ihr Haus zurück?

LESSON XX

II

Translate into German: 1. He was seen by three men. 2. The Rhine (Der Rhein) is loved by all Germans. 3. Last evening (Gestern abend) a song by Schubert was sung. 4. I love and am loved. 5. This stone was found in England. 6. She has never been kissed. 7. The windows are closed every evening at five o'clock. 8. The grass must be cut today. 9. Only two small children have been saved. 10. The most beautiful girls are not always found in the cities. 11. This cake must be eaten soon. 12. It was already eaten when we arrived. 13. Much coffee is drunk each year in Germany. 14. This book has been read by the entire class. 15. Mr. Meyer won the first prize. 16. The first prize was won by Mr. Meyer. 17. The carriage was drawn by two white horses 18. This egg was laid an hour ago (vor einer Stunde).

III

Translate into English:

der Bach	neidisch	auswendig	fassen
die Backe	die Menge	scheiden	der Fels
das Gegenteil	streng	schmecken	oben
klingeln	dick	die Gewalt	der Osten
die Gans	trocken	die Apfelsine	der Zufall
der Gast	die Sache	einsam	Freitag

IV

Translate into German:

stupid	the piece	eleven
dark	the peace	seven
the ice	to pour	to bark
to receive	usually	the bread
the fish	exactly	to flee
to continue	explain	the prince
to be sure	twelve	the spoon

V

Translate the following compounds and derivatives:

achten, die Achtung, aus Achtung gegen die Eltern, achte auf das Kind! Sturm und Regen nicht beachten; der Kartoffelacker; baden, das Badesalz; bedeuten, die Bedeutung, ein bedeutendes Werk, bedeutungslos, die Wortbedeutung; der Bienenhonig; die Birne, birnenförmig; entscheiden, die Entscheidung, unent-
5 schieden, ein entscheidender Augenblick, der Entscheidungskampf, mit großer Entschiedenheit sprechen; überentwickelt, unterentwickelt, die Entwicklung; erben, der Erbe, etwas von jemand erben, die Erbin; der Erzieher, die Erzieherin, ein schwer erziehbares Kind, vergiß deine gute Erziehung nicht! die Ferienreise, Weihnachtsferien, Sommerferien; der Mord, morden, der Mörder, der Selbst-
10 mord, mörderisches Feuer in der Schlacht; der Obstgarten, der Obstbaum; honigsüß; er ist ein guter Bergsteiger; mach die Ohren auf! die Begleitung; wählen, die Wahl; die Milchkuh; die Kühle, kühlen; das Ladenmädchen; mit dem Löffel rühren; Schulter an Schulter kämpfen; schwierig, die Schwierigkeit; selten, die Seltenheit; bei Lampenlicht arbeiten; der Marschbefehl; nebelgrau;
15 einen Strom überbrücken; das Stuhlbein; ein stumpfes Messer; das Eigelb; die Grenze, grenzen; ein hohler Baum; das Knäblein

VI

Give the following sentences in the past, present perfect, past perfect, and future: 1. Die Zeitung wird von der ganzen Familie gelesen. 2. Der Vogel wird von der Katze gefangen. 3. Der Ball wird in die Luft geworfen. 4. Das Buch wird von Frauen gern gelesen. 5. Fritzchen wird von seiner Mutter jeden Tag gebadet.

VII

Change to the passive: 1. Wir vergessen alles. 2. Columbus hat Amerika entdeckt. 3. Mein Vater hat diesen Baum gepflanzt. 4. Jedes Jahr besuchen viele Leute diese Kirche. 5. Seine Tante erzieht ihn.

VIII

Change to the active: 1. Das Problem wurde endlich von Herrn Müller gelöst. 2. Der Krug ist von August ins Haus gebracht worden. 3. Diese Arbeit wird schlecht bezahlt.* 4. Bist du gesehen worden?*

---

*Use *man* as the subject.

IX

Translate the following sentences into English: 1. Es wurde viel getrunken. 2. Hier wird Englisch gesprochen. 3. Am Sonntag wird nicht gespielt. 4. Es ist viel geredet aber wenig gesagt worden. 5. Viel wurde für die Armen nicht getan. 6. Es wurde laut gesungen. 7. Morgen wird gearbeitet. 8. Ein in Heidelberg wohnender Student verlor einmal sein Herz. 9. Die vielen während des Krieges gesungenen Lieder sind heute meist vergessen. 10. Sein mit Wein gefülltes Glas fiel ihm aus der Hand. 11. Das im letzten Jahre entdeckte Land wird im Laufe der nächsten Jahre schon vergessen werden. 12. Wir haben das im letzten Sommer verlorene und von uns schon fast vergessene Geld heute wieder gefunden. 13. Man behauptet, daß amerikanische Studenten nicht genug studieren.

X

Give the passive third person neuter singular in the present, past, present perfect, past perfect, and future of the following verbs:

fangen sagen beißen schließen empfangen lernen schreiben

LESSON XXI

TEXT A

Er meinte, es sei gar nicht so einfach, eine Geschichte für sein Buch zu schreiben, wie ich vielleicht glaube. Wenn die Geschichte nämlich zu schwer sei, dann werfe der Student das Buch in die Ecke. Wenn die Geschichte aber zu leicht sei, dann glaube der Student, das könne er schon, und gehe einfach
5 ins Bett, und im Bett lerne man den Dativ natürlich auch nicht.*

Er erzählte, es habe nicht lange gedauert, da sei der Mann nach Hause gekommen. Die Frau habe ihm alles erzählt. Dem Mann aber habe es gar nicht gefallen, daß der Strumpf mit dem Geld auf dem Weg zum Paradies gewesen sei. Er habe aber nichts gesagt, sondern nur sein Pferd geholt, und
10 nach kurzer Zeit habe er einen Mann am Wege sitzen sehen. Es sei Joseph gewesen, der mit dem Strumpf ins Paradies gewollt habe. Aber der Mann habe nicht den Strumpf mit dem Geld, sondern nur ein ehrliches Gesicht gesehen und habe Joseph gefragt, ob er einen Mann mit einem Strumpf gesehen habe. Joseph habe geantwortet, der sei gerade im Wald. Der
15 Bauer habe darauf Joseph gebeten, sein Pferd zu halten, und sei in den Wald gelaufen. Joseph aber sei mit dem Pferde verschwunden. (Cf. Lesson V.)

Der Redner stellte dann die Frage, ob die Maschine also doch die Schuld an unserer Not trage. Nein, meinte er, nicht die Maschine, sondern nur die Art und Weise, in der wir von der Maschine Gebrauch machten. Wir würfen
20 noch immer ein Produkt auf den Markt, ohne zu wissen, ob der Markt dieses Produkt aufnehmen könne. Es sei daher ganz natürlich, daß jeder Versuch, die Arbeitslosigkeit zu bekämpfen, erfolglos bleibe. Wenn wir jedem Arbeiter seine Arbeit geben wollten, müßten wir lernen, die Arbeit besser zu verteilen. Einen anderen Weg gebe es nicht; es sei der Weg zur Lösung des Problems.
25 (Cf. Lesson VI.)

Er schrieb, alle Zukunft müsse Gegenwart, alle Gegenwart Vergangenheit werden. Man könne daher auch in einer Grammatik leider nicht immer nur die Gegenwart gebrauchen. Die Sprache sei, wie ich sicher wisse, ganz wie das Leben: ein Verb habe wie der Mensch, von dem es etwas berichte,

---

*These passages are based upon earlier texts.

oft eine Vergangenheit und oft eine Zukunft. Und wie im Leben sei die Zukunft immer besser als die Vergangenheit. Die Zukunft im Deutschen sei nämlich leicht, die Vergangenheit schwer, und wenn ich die Grammatik dieser Lektion verstehen wolle, müsse ich in der kommenden Woche schwer arbeiten. Damit ich aber das Buch nicht wieder in die Ecke würfe, gebrauche er nur wenige Wörter. Und er hoffe, ich würde es ihm vergeben, wenn er wieder eine Liebesgeschichte erzähle.

Er nahm sogleich das Wort und sagte, ich solle den Mut nicht sinken lassen. Noch sei der Kampf nicht verloren. Ich hätte in meiner Rechnung einen Fehler gemacht und ihn einen Tag zu früh erwartet. Ich solle seinem Rate folgen und gleich wieder zurückkehren. Meinen Schatten werde er mir gerne wiedergeben. (Cf. Lesson XVI.)

Er sagte, er denke vor allem an seinen eigenen Vorteil. Andere Leute, die lieber ein Mädchen ins Unglück stürzten als ihre Seele verkauften, täten das zwar auch. Aber solche Leute seien nicht so ehrlich wie er. Ich solle ihm glauben, daß er zugleich an meinen Vorteil denke, wenn er mir noch einmal dringend rate, doch endlich zu unterschreiben. Unterschriebe ich nicht, so dürfe ich die Hoffnung, je wieder friedlich unter Menschen wohnen zu können, ruhig aufgeben. Einen Schattenlosen, das hätte ich erfahren, wolle niemand unter seinem Dach haben. Er verstehe ja, daß man sich nicht gern von etwas trenne, was man noch nie gesehen habe. Ich sei nicht der erste Fall dieser Art. Aber ich solle ihm glauben, daß bis jetzt noch jeder, der ihm einmal den Schatten verkauft habe, diesen Schatten auch wieder zurückgekauft habe. (Cf. Lesson XVIII.)

Sie fragte, ob ich viel von ihm wisse aus der Zeit, ehe sie ihn gekannt; ob ich nicht glaube, daß er glücklicher gewesen sei als jetzt. (G. Keller, „Sinngedicht")

Aus der Geschichte unsrer Sprache

Sie alle kennen wahrscheinlich die Geschichte vom Turmbau[1] zu Babel, jene altehrwürdige Erzählung des Alten Testaments, die davon berichtet, daß die Leute von Babylon[2] einst an einem Turm[1] bauten,[1] der bis an den Himmel reichen sollte, daß aber Gott, als er sah, wie das Volk ihn über seiner Arbeit vergaß, diesem Volk zur Strafe die Klarheit des Geistes nahm. Man entdeckte eines Tages in Babylon,[2] daß man sich nicht mehr verstand;

jeder glaubte, der andere rede eine fremde Sprache, und der Turm blieb daher ungebaut.[1]

Wie hinter vielen Berichten des Alten Testaments aus den Kindheitstagen der Menschheit, so verbirgt sich auch hinter den kindlich einfachen Worten 5 dieser Erzählung eine tiefe praktische Wahrheit. Bürger eines Staates, Angehörige eines Volkes, die den Turm ihrer Zivilisation höher und höher bauen wollen, müssen vor allem—und zwar in mehr als in einem Sinne—miteinander dieselbe Sprache reden. Wenn aber ein Volk das Wort „Liebe deinen Nächsten wie dich selbst!" vergißt und in einzelne Klassen zerfällt, die 10 sich untereinander hassen, sich nicht mehr verstehen, nicht mehr—symbolisch[3] gesprochen—dieselbe Sprache reden, dann ist es mit der Zivilisation eines solchen Volkes, ja mit seiner Existenz als Volk sehr bald zu Ende. Und wie bei den Babyloniern[2] kommt dies Ende gerade dann, wenn man sich auf dem Gipfel der Macht glaubt.

15 Diese tiefe symbolische Wahrheit der alten Erzählung hat man nicht immer erkannt. Man hat statt dessen sehr oft den Bericht buchstäblich genommen und geglaubt, Gott habe wirklich jeden einzelnen Babylonier, oder doch wenigstens jede einzelne Familie eine fremde, den andern gänzlich unbekannte Sprache reden lassen, so daß einer Englisch, ein anderer Deutsch 20 und ein dritter Russisch[4] gesprochen habe.

Aber unsere heutigen Sprachen sind gar nicht so alt, wie man vielleicht glauben möchte. Das Englische, das Sie sprechen, und das Deutsche, das Sie gerade lernen, haben nicht immer ihre heutige Form gehabt. Das moderne Englisch ist nicht einfach über Nacht entstanden oder eines Tages 25 auf Befehl des Königs von englischen Sprachlehrern „gemacht" worden. Das englische Volk und seine Sprache sind wie die Pflanzenarten Englands und die Kreidefelsen von Dover ein Produkt der Geschichte. Diese Felsen haben vor hunderttausend Jahren nicht so ausgesehen, wie sie heute aus-sehen; und ihre heutige Form ist das Resultat langsamer Entwicklung.

30 Auch Sprachen entwickeln und ändern sich langsam. Nicht nur werden von jeder Generation neue Wörter gebildet und alte Wörter vergessen, sondern auch die Aussprache der einzelnen Laute selber wird verändert, absichtlich oder unabsichtlich. Ebenso wie der junge Mann, der frisch vom Lande nach Oxford kommt, alles tut, was er kann, um den typischen[5] Akzent 35 des Oxford-Studenten anzunehmen und den ländlichen Akzent seines Dorfes zu verlieren, so haben die unteren Klassen eines Volkes immer danach

gestrebt, den Akzent und die Sprechweise der führenden Klassen anzunehmen. Der englische Bauer des zwölften Jahrhunderts trieb zwar richtige Schweine und Schafe auf den Markt, aber die normannischen Herren[6] des Landes, für die das Fleisch gebraten wurde, sagten nicht swine und sheep sondern pork und mutton. Und jeder, der zu den oberen „Vierhundert" gehörte oder gehören wollte, sagte daher auch pork und mutton. Und noch heute wird daher auch das bravste englische Schaf nur unter dem Namen mutton in die gute Gesellschaft aufgenommen. Und jeder Kellner in London wird zwar seinem Gast mit dem größten Vergnügen einen pork roast bringen, wird aber wahrscheinlich verächtlich lächeln, wenn jemand einen pig roast verlangen sollte. Man macht eben nicht gern einen Fehler, weder in der Aussprache der einzelnen Laute noch in der Wahl der Worte, und zwar nicht nur aus Liebe zu seiner Muttersprache, sondern auch darum, weil man von seinen lieben Nachbarn nicht nur nach seiner Kleidung und nach seinem Auto, sondern auch nach seiner Sprache beurteilt wird.

Aber trotz aller Arbeit, die sich die Eltern machen, ihre Kinder zu guten Sprechgewohnheiten zu erziehen, kommt der Sohn eines Tages doch nach Hause und sagt sump'n statt something, oder he ain't statt he isn't. Und wenn Papa und Mama auch die Hände über dem Kopf zusammenschlagen, eines Tages wird sich diese Aussprache oder dieser Fehler zum Schrecken der Eltern und Lehrer doch durchsetzen; ebenso wie es sich durchgesetzt hat, daß man das Wort light, das früher einmal wie das deutsche Wort „Licht" ausgesprochen wurde, heute ohne den ch-Laut ausspricht.

Die Veränderung, welche eine Sprache auf diese Art und Weise in zwei oder drei Generationen erfährt, ist natürlich unbedeutend. Aber in 400 oder 500 Jahren hat dieser für die Angehörigen eines Volkes fast unmerkliche Prozeß doch eine sehr merkliche Wirkung.

[Fortsetzung folgt]

NOTES. 1. Turm tower; bauen to build; ungebaut unbuilt. 2. Leute von Babylon, Babylon, Babyloniern inhabitants of Babylon, Babylon, Babylonians. 3. symbolisch symbolically, figuratively. 4. russisch Russian. 5. typischen typical. 6. normannischen Herren Norman lords.

BUILDING A PASSIVE VOCABULARY

altehrwürdig alt old, ehren to honor, würdig worthy, altehrwürdig venerable
Angehörige gehören belong to, Angehörige those belonging to; members
buchstäblich der Buchstabe the letter, buchstäblich literal(ly)
durchsetzen durch through, setzen to set, sich durchsetzen to prevail
erkannt kennen to know, erkennen to recognize
das Jahrhundert das Jahr the year, hundert hundred, das Jahrhundert the century
die Laute laut loud, der Laut the sound, die Laute the sounds
Nächsten (*acc.*) nah near, der Nächste the next, the one living next to you, neighbor
oberen *cf.* oben, ober upper
die Sprechgewohnheiten sprechen to speak, gewöhnlich usual, customary, habitual, die Sprechgewohnheiten the speech habits
unbekannte kennen to know, unbekannte unknown
verächtlich achten to regard, verachten to scorn, verächtlich scornfully

VOCABULARY

der Bauer, –n the farmer, peasant
braten to roast; fry
braun *brown*
der Buchstabe, –n, –n the letter (of the alphabet)
der Donner the *thunder*
das Eisen, – the *iron*
empor up, upwards; high
entstehen to originate
die Flamme, –n the *flame*
das Fleisch the meat
fremd strange; foreign
der Gipfel, – the peak; height
der Kellner, – the waiter
das Kinn, –e the *chin*
klagen to complain
die Kohle, –n the *coal*
die Kreide the chalk
praktisch *practical*
rauschen to roar; rustle
das Schwein, –e the *swine*, pig
der Sohn, ⸗e the *son*
die Strafe, –n the punishment; penalty, fine
streben to *strive*
die Treppe, –n the staircase; stair
das Vergnügen the pleasure, enjoyment
die Welle, –n the wave
zumachen (*sep. prefix*) to close, shut

IDIOMS

bald . . . bald now . . . now
dann und wann now and then
in Empfang nehmen to receive, take charge of
vor sich hinblicken to look aimlessly (dreamily)
was hast du? what is the matter?

TEXT B

Psyche

[Fortsetzung]

Auf dem ersten Floß[1] hatten indes die jungen Männer ihre Kleider abgeworfen und traten nun auf die offene Galerie hinaus, bereit, sich ins Meer zu stürzen.

Der größere mit dem dichten braunen Haar und den grauen hellblickenden Augen war ein junger Bildhauer[2] und erst vor einem Vierteljahr aus Rom in die nordische Hauptstadt, seinen Geburtsort, zurückgekehrt; vor einigen Tagen war er noch eine Strecke weiter nördlich, in diese kleine Stadt am Meer, gegangen, um endlich den Freund wiederzusehen, den jungen Baron von X, mit dem er im südlichen Deutschland zusammen studiert hatte.

Noch standen sie versunken in den Anblick der bewegten Wasserfläche. Ruhelos rollten die Wellen in nicht enden wollendem Wechsel über die Tiefe, wurden für einen kurzen Augenblick von der Sonne durchleuchtet und brachen sich dann, und andere rollten nach. Die Luft tönte von Sturm und Meeresrauschen. Eine starke Welle schlug eben an die eiserne Treppe, auf der die jungen Männer standen, und bedeckte sie mit ihrem Schaum.[3]

„Komm jetzt", rief der Baron, „und wie Meeresgötter wollen wir durch den grünen Kristall hindurchschießen."

Aber sein Freund, der Künstler, blickte in die Ferne und schien ihn nicht zu hören.

„Was hast du, Franz?"

„Dort! Vom Frauenfloß[1] her! Sieh doch!" Und er zeigte mit ausgestrecktem Arm auf die Wasserfläche.

Der andere stieß einen Laut des Schreckens aus. „Ein Weib!—Ein Kind!"

„So scheint es; aber keine Meeresgöttin!"

„Nein, nein; sie kämpft vergebens[4] mit den Wellen."

Der junge Baron wollte sich gerade ins Wasser stürzen, als ihn sein Freund mit schneller Hand zurückhielt.

„Du nicht, Ernst! Du weißt, dein Herz ist nicht sehr stark, und *einer* ist genug. Lauf zu der alten Badefrau und sag ihr, was zu sagen ist!"

Kaum war das letzte Wort gesprochen, so schlug das Wasser über dem Körper des Bildhauers[2] zusammen. Einen Augenblick später erschien der

Kopf des Schwimmers. Mit den kräftigen Armen die Wellen teilend, flog er dahin; nach einigen Schlägen stieg er mit der Brust über die Flut[5] empor, und seine hellen Blicke flogen über die Wasser.

Noch fern von ihm spielten die Wellen mit dem schönen sonnenblonden 5 Haar des Mädchens; zwei kleine Hände griffen zwar noch mit letzter Kraft durch die wild schäumende[3] See, aber auch mit ihnen spielten schon die Wellen. Ein Seevogel schoß dicht daneben in die Flut, stieg wieder hoch und flog, seinen scharfen Schrei ausstoßend, über die Wasserfläche dahin.

Die alte Frau Kathi, die eine Zeitlang vor ihrem kleinen Kohlenofen 10 gesessen und in die Flammen gesehen hatte, war doch wieder unruhig geworden. Der Sturm riß mit wachsender Stärke am Dache ihres Häuschens, dann und wann trug er von draußen aus der Luft einen Vogelschrei herein. Kathi hatte ihren Holzstuhl beiseitegeschoben und war wieder hinausgegangen, ja sie hatte ebenfalls ihre Schuhe ausgezogen, um zum Floß 15 hinüberzugehen, und stand jetzt dort, mit ihrer harten Hand bald an diese, bald an jene Badezelle[6] klopfend. Niemand antwortete. Ängstlich machte sie eine Türe nach der anderen auf und wieder zu. „Fräulein, ach liebes Fräulein, so antworten Sie mir doch!" rief sie mit klagender Stimme.

Aber es kam keine Antwort; nur das Rauschen der Wellen schlug 20 eintönig an ihr Ohr.

Als sie hilflos nach dem Land zurückblickte, sah sie einen Mann auf ihr Häuschen zulaufen, und gleich darauf hörte sie ihn rufen.—„Frau Kathi! Frau Kathi!" rief er durch den Wind hindurch.

„Hier! Um Gottes willen, hier!"—Und eilig lief die Alte ans Land 25 zurück. „Oh, mein Gott, Herr Baron, Sie sind es! Ach, das Kind, das Kind!"

Er faßte sie, ohne etwas zu sagen, an den Armen und zeigte mit der Hand auf die offene Wasserfläche.

„Ist das der andere Herr? Sucht er das Kind?"

30 Der junge Mann nickte.

„Guter Gott! Man soll nicht räsonieren![7] Ich räsonierte, Herr Baron, als ich Sie beide herauskommen sah! Man soll nicht räsonieren; nein, nie, niemals!"

Der Baron antwortete nicht; er sah mit scharfem Blick auf die Flut[5] 35 hinaus. Ein paar Augenblicke noch—weit von draußen her kam jetzt der Donner der offenen See—und er faßte wieder den Arm der Alten: „Jetzt,

Frau Kathi, da sehen Sie hin! Nun sucht er sie nicht mehr; er trägt sie schon in seinen Armen!"

Die Alte stieß einen lauten Schrei aus.

Da hob sich die Gestalt des Schwimmers mit der breiten Brust aus den schäumenden[3] Wellen, und bald darauf sah man ihn langsam, aber sicher am Ufer emporsteigen. In seinen Armen, an seiner Brust ruhte ein junger Körper von unaussprechlicher Schönheit, ein Mädchen mit den zarten Formen[8] des erwachenden Weibes; ein Bild der Psyche, wenn es je eins gegeben hatte. Aber der kleine Kopf war zurückgesunken; leblos hing der eine Arm herab.

Aus der Mittagshöhe des Himmels fiel der volle Sonnenschein auf die beiden Gestalten, deren Körper vom Wasser glänzten.

„Wie in den Tagen der Götter!" sagte leise der junge Baron, der atemlos diesem Geschehen zugesehen hatte.—„Aber jetzt, Frau Kathi, nehmen Sie das Kind in Empfang; ich laufe schnell zur Stadt und bringe einen Arzt; er könnte nötig sein!"

Noch ein paar kurze Befehle über das, was die alte Frau vornehmen[9] sollte, dann eilte er fort; nicht einmal den Namen des Mädchens hatte er erfahren.

Einige Minuten später lag drinnen im Hause die zarte Gestalt in ihrer ganzen Hilflosigkeit auf dem Ruhebette, bis zum Kinn von dem roten Umschlagetuch der Alten zugedeckt. Zitternd, ihr lautes Weinen niederkämpfend, stand diese vor ihr; sie hatte eben ein Handtuch genommen und wollte gerade mit dem jungen Körper alles vornehmen,[9] was ihr von den beiden Männern befohlen worden war.

„Kathi!"—Die jungen Lippen hatten es gerufen, und die jungen Augen blickten sie voll und lebenskräftig an. „Kathi, ich bin ja nicht ertrunken!"

Die Alte stürzte vor ihr nieder und bedeckte die Hände des Kindes mit ihren Küssen. „Ach, Fräulein, Herzenskindchen, was haben Sie uns für Angst gemacht! Wenn nun der liebe junge Herr nicht gekommen wäre! Und ich räsonierte,[7] als ich ihn aus der Stadt herauskommen sah!"

Das Mädchen legte mit angstvoller Bewegung ihr die Hand auf den Mund. „Um Gottes willen, Kathi, schweig! Ich will seinen Namen nicht wissen, nie!"

„Fräulein, ich weiß ihn ja selber nicht; ich habe den jungen Herrn heute zum ersten Male gesehen; er muß wohl ein Fremder sein."

Das junge Mädchen setzte sich auf und blickte unglücklich vor sich hin. „Kathi", sagte sie, „Kathi,—ich wollte, er wäre tot."

„Kind, Kind!" rief die Alte, „Sie vergessen sich!—Ach, Fräulein, der gute junge Mann; er hat ja doch auch sein Leben um Sie gewagt!"

5 „Sein Leben! Wirklich, sein Leben?—Ach, ich habe nicht daran gedacht!"

„Nun, Fräulein, hätten Sie nicht beide da ertrinken können?"

„Beide! Wir beide!"—Und sie schloß wie im Traum die Augen, aber dennoch sah sie das schöne Gesicht eines jungen Mannes, das in Angst und Zärtlichkeit auf sie herniederblickte.

[Fortsetzung folgt]

NOTES. 1. Cf. plan, Lesson XX. 2. Bildhauer sculptor. 3. Schaum, schäumend foam, foaming. 4. vergebens in vain. 5. Flut water. 6. Badezelle bathing cabin, dressing room. 7. räsonieren grumble. 8. Formen form (*singular in English*). 9. vornehmen to undertake, do.

BUILDING A PASSIVE VOCABULARY

der Anblick blicken to look, an on, at, der Anblick the sight, view

durchleuchtet durch through, leuchten *from* Licht; durchleuchten to illuminate, fill with light

eintönig ein one, der Ton the tone, eintönig monotonous(ly)

eiserne cf. das Eisen

entfernt fern far, distant, entfernt removed, far, distant

ertrinken, ertrunken (cf. trinken *and meaning of* er=, Lesson XXII) to drown, drowned

der Geburtsort geboren born, die Geburt the birth, der Ort the place, der Geburtsort the birthplace

Laut *here* cry

die Mittagshöhe der Mittag the midday, die Höhe (*from* hoch), the height, **die Mittagshöhe** the midday height(s)

das Umschlagetuch um around, schlagen to beat, *here* to throw, das Tuch the cloth, das Umschlagetuch the shawl

versunken *here* lost in thought

die Wasserfläche das Wasser the water, flach flat, plain, die Fläche the plain, surface, die Wasserfläche the surface of the water

GRAMMAR

135. Subjunctive of Indirect Discourse.

Direct Discourse	Indirect Discourse
Fritz said, "I am tired."	Fritz said (that) he was tired.
Fritz said, "I saw her."	Fritz said (that) he had seen her.

These examples reveal that when we shift from direct to indirect discourse in English we change (1) the verbatim quotation to a dependent clause without quotation marks; (2) the form of the person as the situation requires; (3) the tense from present to past or from past to past perfect.*

The shift in German from direct to indirect discourse follows steps one and two. The verb form, however, is changed from the indicative to a subjunctive. This change can be made in two ways: (A) by changing from the indicative to the forms of the imaginative subjunctive; (B) by changing from the indicative to a new set of subjunctive forms found only in indirect discourse.

A. *Shift from Indicative to Imaginative Subjunctive:*

Direct Discourse	Indirect Discourse
Hans sagte: „Du bist krank."	Hans sagte, ich wäre krank.
Hans sagte: „Du hast mein Buch."	Hans sagte, ich hätte sein Buch.
Hans sagte: „Fritz geht nach Berlin."	Hans sagte, Fritz ginge nach Berlin.
Hans sagte: „Du redest zu laut."	Hans sagte, ich redete zu laut.
Hans sagte: „Mutter war krank." Hans sagte: „Mutter ist krank gewesen."	Hans sagte, Mutter wäre krank gewesen.
Hans sagte: „Du hattest mein Buch."	Hans sagte, ich hätte sein Buch gehabt.
Hans sagte: „Du wirst mich nie wiedersehen."	Hans sagte, ich würde ihn nie wiedersehen.

*Usage varies in English.

From these examples the following rules may be derived: (1) The present indicative of direct discourse becomes present imaginative in indirect discourse; (2) Any past tense of direct discourse becomes past imaginative; (3) The forms ich werde, du wirſt, etc., of the future indicative become ich würde, du würdeſt, etc. in indirect discourse.

Since the imaginative subjunctive forms may always be used to express indirect discourse, those who wish to speak or to write German may use these forms exclusively.

Further examples follow:

Direct Discourse	Indirect Discourse
Der Kommiſſar ſagte ihm: „Der Präſident bleibt unſichtbar (invisible). Er reſidiert in den Bergen; und es iſt eine ungewöhnliche Ehre, wenn er Sie perſönlich begrüßt."	Der Kommiſſar ſagte ihm, daß der Präſident unſichtbar bliebe. Er reſi-dierte in den Bergen; und es wäre eine ungewöhnliche Ehre, wenn er mich perſönlich begrüßte.*

B. *Shift from Indicative to Indirect Discourse Subjunctive:*

In written German you will find another set of subjunctive forms used only in indirect discourse and preferred by many authors. This set is incomplete, having, except for ſein, no plural forms.

Direct Discourse	Indirect Discourse
Hans ſagte: „Du biſt krank."	Hans ſagte, ich ſei krank.
Hans ſagte: „Fritz hat mein Buch."	Hans ſagte, Fritz habe ſein Buch.
Hans ſagte: „Fritz geht nach Berlin."	Hans ſagte, Fritz gehe nach Berlin.
Hans ſagte: „Du darfſt kommen."	Hans ſagte, ich dürfe kommen.
Hans ſagte: „Mutter war krank."	Hans ſagte, Mutter ſei krank geweſen.
Hans ſagte: „Fritz hat mich geſehen."	Hans ſagte, Fritz habe ihn geſehen.
Hans ſagte: „Du wirſt mich nie wiederſehen."	Hans ſagte, ich werde ihn nie wieder-ſehen."

*Adapted from Hermann Kasack. Die Stadt hinter dem Strom, p. 32. (The verb forms are unchanged.)

To find the correct form of the indirect discourse subjunctive, observe the following three rules:

1. If the original statement was made in the *present*, use:

	haben	**ſein**	**werden**	**geben**	**ſagen**	**können**
ich	(habe)*	ſei	(werde)	(gebe)	(ſage)	könne
du	(habeſt)	ſeieſt	(werdeſt)	(gebeſt)	(ſageſt)	könneſt
er	habe	ſei	werde	gebe	ſage	könne
wir	—	ſeien	—	—	—	—
ihr	—	ſeiet	—	—	—	—
ſie	—	ſeien	—	—	—	—

2. If the original statement was made in *any past* tense (past, present perfect, past perfect, or historical present), use:

ich	(habe)		ſei	plus past participle
du	(habeſt)		ſeieſt	
er	habe		ſei	
		or		
wir	—		ſeien	
ihr	—		ſeiet	
ſie	—		ſeien	

3. If the original statement was made in the *future*, use:

ich	(werde)	plus infinitive
du	(werdeſt)	
er	werde	
wir	—	
ihr	—	
ſie	—	

C. *The Passive in Indirect Discourse:*

The shift from direct to indirect discourse in the passive may be made in two ways, as illustrated on the following page.

---

*The forms in parentheses occur mainly in literary style.

Direct	Indirect (See A above)	Indirect (See B above)
Er wird geliebt He is loved	Er würde geliebt	Er werde geliebt
Er wurde geliebt He was loved Er ist geliebt worden He has been loved.	Er wäre geliebt worden	Er sei geliebt worden

136. Influence of the Governing Verb. Since all indirect discourse is the restatement of someone's words, thoughts, or ideas, the governing verb is, of course, one of saying, thinking, believing, asking, reporting, and the like. One introductory or governing verb frequently introduces a series of indirect statements. When this verb is in the present tense, there is a growing tendency to use the indicative in the indirect statement:

Sie **sagt,** daß er recht **hat.** She says that he is right.

When the governing verb is first person singular present, the indicative must be used:

Ich **glaube,** daß ich krank **bin.** I believe that I am sick.

137. Indirect Commands. In changing imperative forms from direct to indirect discourse German may employ:

a. Infinitives:

Er befahl mir zu kommen. He commanded me to come.

b. Patterns using sollen plus the infinitive:

Er sagte, ich solle kommen. He said I was to come.
Er sagte, ich solle ihm glauben. He said I should believe him.

138. Omission of daß. In German the conjunction daß may be omitted when introducing indirect discourse, just as in English the conjunction *that* is frequently lacking. In such cases verb-second position is used:

Er sagte, { daß Otto in Berlin sei.
Otto sei in Berlin. }

139. Cardinal Numbers. The numbers from one to twelve were listed in § 102. Numbers above twelve are as follows:

13 dreizehn	30 dreißig
14 vierzehn	40 vierzig
15 fünfzehn	50 fünfzig
16 sechzehn	60 sechzig
17 siebzehn	70 siebzig
18 achtzehn	80 achtzig
19 neunzehn	90 neunzig
20 zwanzig	100 hundert

1000 tausend

Starting with 21, German uses the "four-and-twenty blackbirds" scheme: einundzwanzig, zweiundzwanzig, sechsunddreißig, achtundvierzig, neunundachtzig, and so on.

Numbers below one million are written as one word: hundertsiebzig, achthundertsiebenundvierzig, sechzehnhundertachtundvierzig, neunzehnhundertsiebzig, zwölfhundertfünfzehn.

140. Ordinal Numbers. These are formed by adding -te (from *second* to *nineteenth* inclusive) and -ste (from *twentieth* up) to the cardinals. Since they are attributive adjectives, they take the attributive adjective endings:

NOM. der zweite König, die zweite Königin, das zweite Kind
GEN. des vierten Königs, der vierten Königin, des vierten Kindes

Note the irregular forms:

the first der erste   the third der dritte   the eighth der achte

141. Fractions. Fractions are formed by adding the following suffixes to the cardinals:

a. -tel (contraction of Teil) from $\frac{1}{3}$ to $\frac{1}{19}$ inclusive: ein (das) Viertel, ein (das) Fünftel. Note the irregular forms $\frac{1}{3}$ ein (das) Drittel, $\frac{1}{8}$ ein (das) Achtel.

b. -stel from $\frac{1}{20}$ up; ein (das) Zwanzigstel, ein (das) Hundertstel.

Note that *a* (*the*) *half* is eine (die) Hälfte; the adjective *half* is halb (ein halbes Glas).

142. Time. Es ist (*It is*):

zwölf Uhr	12 o'clock	halb acht	7.30
ein Uhr	1 o'clock	zwanzig Minuten vor neun	8.40
zwei Uhr	2 o'clock	ein Viertel vor zehn *or* drei Viertel zehn	9.45
fünf Minuten nach drei	3.05	fünfzehn Minuten vor zehn	9.45
zehn Minuten nach vier	4.10	zehn Minuten vor elf	10.50
fünfzehn Minuten nach fünf	5.15	fünf Minuten vor zwölf	11.55
ein Viertel nach fünf	5.15	zwanzig Uhr fünfzehn	8.15 (P.M.)
zwanzig Minuten nach sechs	6.20		

Learn the principal parts of the following verbs:

schlāfen	schlief	hat geschlāfen	schläft	to sleep
brāten	**briet**	**hat gebrāten**	**brät**	**to roast**
stēhen	stand	hat gestanden	stēht	to stand
entstēhen	**entstand**	**ist entstanden**	**entstēht**	**to originate**

EXERCISES

I

A. Beantworten Sie folgende Fragen über Text A auf deutsch: 1. Wen vergaß das Volk? 2. Was nahm Gott dem Volk? 3. Was verbirgt sich hinter den kindlich einfachen Worten dieser Erzählung? 4. Womit ist es zu Ende, wenn ein Volk in einzelne Klassen zerfällt? 5. Wann kommt dieses Ende? 6. Was hat man nicht immer erkannt? 7. Was ist gar nicht so alt, wie man vielleicht glauben möchte? 8. Was ändert sich langsam? 9. Was tut der junge Mann, der frisch vom Lande nach Oxford kommt? 10. Was möchte er verlieren? 11. Wonach haben die unteren Klassen immer gestrebt? 12. Wonach wird man von seinen Nachbarn beurteilt?

B. Beantworten Sie folgende Fragen über Text B auf deutsch: 1. Wozu waren die jungen Männer bereit? 2. Wann war der junge Bildhauer aus Rom in die Hauptstadt zurückgekehrt? 3. Mit wem hatte er im südlichen Deutschland studiert? 4. Wovon tönte die Luft? 5. Wohin blickte der Künstler? 6. Wer wollte sich gerade ins Wasser stürzen? 7. Wer hielt den Baron zurück? 8. Womit spielten die Wellen? 9. Wie griffen die kleinen Hände durch die wild schäumende See? 10. Wo hatte Kathi eine Zeitlang gesessen? 11. Was riß mit wachsender Stärke am Dache des Häuschens? 12. Was trug der Wind von draußen herein? 13. Warum zog Kathi ebenfalls die Schuhe aus? 14. Wo klopfte sie? 15. Was rief Kathi? 16. Was schlug eintönig an ihr Ohr? 17. Wie blickte sie nach dem Lande zurück? 18. Wen sah sie auf ihr Häuschen zulaufen? 19. Wohin zeigte der Baron? 20. Wann hatte die Alte räsoniert? 21. Woher kam der Donner der offenen See? 22. Wer trug das Mädchen in seinen Armen? 23. Wie stieg der Schwimmer am Ufer empor? 24. Wie hing der eine Arm des Mädchens herab? 25. Was sagte der junge Baron? 26. Wer hatte atemlos diesem Geschehen zugesehen? 27. Wen wollte der Baron holen? 28. Was hatte der Baron nicht erfahren? 29. Wo lag das Mädchen? 30. Womit war sie zugedeckt? 31. Wer rief „Kathi"? 32. Wer war froh, daß das Fräulein gerettet worden war? 33. Was wollte das Fräulein nie erfahren? 34. Woran hatte das Fräulein nicht gedacht? 35. Was sah das Mädchen, als sie die Augen schloß?

II

Translate into German: 1. He said he had lost everything. 2. He asked them if (ob) they had enough money. 3. They claimed they had not eaten since Friday. 4. She believed she was dying. 5. He reported he had not been able to see them. 6. Mr. Schulz said they were his best friends. 7. He wrote that I could come now. 8. I know that I can do it. 9. He answered he was happy. 10. They wrote they were coming today. 11. That book was written two years ago. 12. If he were my father, I should help him. 13. If he were still living, he would be a very old man. 14. Not all flowers are planted in the spring. 15. Why did he say he had arrived in Hamburg? 16. I shall see you tomorrow. 17. How long have you been eating?

III

Translate into English:

begegnen	die Ehe	empfehlen	die Absicht	die Butter
biegen	der Eifer	entlang	der Teller	bedeuten
der Bleistift	einschlafen	die Familie	ähnlich	der Berg
schwierig	das Eis	fangen	allerdings	die Birne

IV

Translate into German:

false	to fill	the company	the fish
the bridge	the foot	healthy	the barrel
the bread	the guest	yesterday	nine
the grandchild	the present (time)	yellow	the straw
the pen	exactly	foreign	to bloom
ready	the business	the fox	the parents

V

Translate the following compounds and derivatives:

die Post, das Postamt, das Hauptpostamt; die Regel, die Regellosigkeit, die Spielregel; rein, die Reinheit, die Unreinheit, reinigen, zur Reinlichkeit erziehen, der Reiniger; üben, nicht mehr in der Übung sein; die schöne Umgebung dieser Stadt; Weihnachten, das Weihnachtsfest, das Weihnachtslied, der Weihnachts-5 baum, der Weihnachtsmann; wichtig, von großer Wichtigkeit; würdig, ehrwürdig; zart, die Zärtlichkeit, ein zartfühlender Mensch; zeichnen, der Zeichner, eine Handzeichnung; das Zeichen, ein Fragezeichen; der Zucker, zuckerkrank; der Zahnarzt; der Schaden, schädlich; streichen, der Strich; fremd, der Fremde, ein Fremder; achtzehnhundertachtundvierzig, neunzehnhunderteinundvierzig; 10 das Bächlein; trockene Blätter; auf den Busch klopfen; der Begleiter; die Dummheit; marschbereit; ein wertvolles Bild; der Knochen, knochig; der Koch; das Krankenbett; das Lämpchen; der Teelöffel; das Obst ist dieses Jahr früh reif geworden; die Reihe, reihen; breitschultrig; eine seltene Pflanze; die Einsamkeit; der Eisenbahnwagen; grenzenlos; das Taschenmesser; nebelig; 15 Ostafrika; Lesestoff

VI

Give the third person singular present and past subjunctive forms of the indirect discourse of the following verbs:

lernen	lachen	können	singen	machen	schlagen
zeigen	helfen	tun	geben	kommen	vorschlagen
schwimmen	fahren	tun können	reden	fliegen	fliehen

VII

Change the following quotations to indirect discourse, introducing each sentence with the words Er sagte (thus: „Ich habe mein

Buch verloren." Er sagte, er habe (hätte) sein Buch verloren.) 1. „Wir wollen durch den grünen Kristall hindurchschießen." 2. „Sie kämpft vergebens mit den Wellen." 3. „Dein Herz ist nicht sehr stark, und einer ist genug." 4. „Man soll nicht räsonieren." 5. „Ich bin ja nicht ertrunken." 6. „Ich will seinen Namen nicht wissen." 7. „Ich weiß ihn ja selber nicht." 8. „Ich habe den jungen Herrn heute zum ersten Male gesehen." 9. „Er muß wohl ein Fremder sein." 10. „Er hat ja doch auch sein Leben um Sie gewagt." 11. „Ich habe daran nicht gedacht." 12. „Meyer ist gestern von einem Auto überfahren worden." 13. „Meyer wurde gestern von einem Auto überfahren." 14. „Das Geld ist gefunden!" 15. „Du bist zu jung zum Heiraten." 16. „Wenn du willst, können wir morgen heiraten." 17. „Niemand hat den Frieden meines kleinen Königreiches je gestört." 18. „Ich ließ es dann meine erste Sorge sein, die Höhle etwas wohnlicher zu machen." 19. „Ich holte die für meine Arbeit notwendigen Instrumente in Deutschland, England oder Amerika." 20. „Ich machte meine Reise nach Moskau mitten im Winter." 21. „Es gelang mir, viel schneller über das Eis zu kommen, als ich erwartet hatte." 22. „Ich nahm also meine Pistole und schoß nach dem Zügel." 23. „Ich konnte meine Reise fortsetzen." 24. „Die anderen Häuser sind aus Holz und treiben zur Regenzeit wie Schiffe auf dem Wasser."

VIII

Translate into German:

the first book, the second book, a third book; the first man, the second man; the first murder, a fourth murder; the fifth flower; my sixth orange; the seventh sentence, the eighth sentence; the ninth example; the tenth day; the eleventh dog; the twelfth egg; the thirteenth [of] August, the fourteenth [of] September, the fifteenth [of] November, the sixteenth [of] December, the seventeenth [of] January; the eighteenth house; the twenty-first [of] March; the twenty-eighth [of] February; one fourth, one fifth, one third, one sixth, two sevenths

IX

Translate into English: 1. Dieses im Jahre siebzehnhundertneunzehn gedruckte Buch wird heute noch viel gelesen. 2. Diese Uhr hat mir meine vor etwa zehn Jahren gestorbene Tante geschenkt. 3. Heute ist die erst nach der Entdeckung Amerikas nach Deutschland gebrachte Kartoffel eine der wichtigsten Feldfrüchte. 4. Die mit Farbpünktchen gezeichneten Bienen kamen jeden Tag an den Futterplatz. 5. Diese in großen Tiefen lebenden Fische können nicht lebend an die Oberfläche (surface) gebracht werden.

X

Count in German by fives to one hundred; count by tens to one hundred.

LESSON XXII

TEXT A*

Ich würde mich sehr freuen, wenn Sie Weihnachten kommen könnten.—Wenn du deinen Mantel trügest, würdest du dich nicht erkälten.—Herr Meyer, Sie sehen gar nicht gut aus (aussehen to look). Ich würde an Ihrer Stelle einmal zum Arzt gehen. Vielleicht kann er Ihnen eine Medizin empfehlen, daß Sie abends besser einschlafen können.—Ich würde es niemals wagen, in seiner Gegenwart zu lachen.—Wir würden ja lieber mit der Eisenbahn fahren, aber das Auto ist billiger.—Sie würden mir und meiner Familie eine große Freude bereiten, wenn Sie mit Ihren Eltern auf ein paar Wochen zu uns kommen könnten.

Wenn man von jemandem sagen würde: er ist ein Dichter, aber er hat keine Gabe der Darstellung, so würde man ihm ganz gewiß den Rat geben, seine Arbeiten nicht drucken zu lassen; und man hätte sehr recht.

Wie wäre es, wenn wir uns heiraten würden?

Wenn du mich ernstlich bitten würdest, ich würde hingehen, und er würde mich nehmen.

In einer anderen Zeit würde mein Versuch nicht nötig sein.

An deiner Stelle würde ich sehen, daß ich Offizier würde.

Was würden wir geben, wenn wir zu ihnen zurückkönnten!

Wenn man ihn aus dem Graben (trench) ließe, würde er ohne Deckung (protection, cover) irgendwohin laufen.

Uns, den Soldaten in den Gräben (trenches), ist das Land unserer Jugend verloren. Und selbst wenn man es uns wiedergäbe, würden wir nicht wissen, was wir darin tun sollten. Wir würden in ihm sein und in ihm umgehen; wir würden uns erinnern und es lieben und bewegt sein von seinem Anblick. Aber es wäre das gleiche, wie wenn wir traurig werden vor dem Bild eines toten Kameraden (comrade). Wir würden nicht mehr verbunden sein mit ihm, wie wir es waren. Heute würden wir in dem Lande unserer Jugend umhergehen wie Reisende. Wir würden da sein; aber würden wir leben? (Aus „Im Westen nichts Neues", von Remarque).

---

*The sentences following the first paragraph were taken, with minor changes, from works of literature.

Und dennoch würden wir wieder auf sie schießen und sie auf uns, wenn sie frei wären.

„Wen würden Sie denn wohl an meiner Stelle entlassen (dismiss)? Sie würden sich also nicht entlassen, wenn Sie ich wären?" fragte er.

Das genügt mir. Meinem Freunde würde das nicht genügen.

Da sagt Pinneberg: „Ich habe eine große Bitte, Heilbutt." Heilbutt ist etwas erstaunt (surprised): „Ja? Natürlich, Pinneberg." Und Pinneberg: „Wenn Sie uns einmal besuchen würden?" Heilbutt ist noch erstaunter. „Ich habe nämlich meiner Frau so viel von Ihnen erzählt, und sie würde Sie gern einmal sehen. Wenn Sie einmal Zeit haben? Natürlich nur zu einem Butterbrot" (cold supper). Heilbutt lächelt wieder, aber es ist ein reizendes Lächeln: „Aber natürlich, Pinneberg. Ich wußte gar nicht, daß es Ihnen Freude machen würde. Ich komme gern einmal." (Aus „Kleiner Mann, was nun?" von Fallada)

Aus der Geschichte unsrer Sprache

[Fortsetzung]

Wenn Chaucer heute aus seinem Grabe aufstände, so würde er auch nicht einen mit normalem Tempo gesprochenen englischen Satz verstehen können. Auch würde kein Mensch auf den Gedanken kommen, daß er mit droughte (wie deutsch „druchte" ausgesprochen) unser modernes drought meinen könnte. Und wenn er in einen Laden ginge und soote win (mit stimmlosem, scharfem „s", langem „o" wie in „Strom", mit englischem „w" und langem „i" wie in „biegen") verlangte, so riete wohl auch der intelligenteste Verkäufer nicht, daß er damit „süßen Wein" meinte.

Einzig und allein die alte, seit Jahrhunderten kaum geänderte Orthographie des Englischen erlaubt es dem heutigen Leser, die Werke Chaucers nach kurzem Studium langsam zu lesen. Gehen wir aber noch weiter zurück, etwa in die Zeit um 900 nach Christo,[1] so ist es auch mit der uns bekannten Orthographie zu Ende; und der moderne Leser sieht sich plötzlich gezwungen, die englische Sprache der damaligen Zeit genau so zu lernen, als wäre sie eine Fremdsprache. Denn daß man für altenglisch cyning (künning), dagas und fremedon heute king, days und did sagt, das kann man wirklich nicht raten.

Aber woher kommt das Altenglische? Wie weit ist uns seine Geschichte bekannt? Denn wir dürfen ja wohl kaum erwarten, daß schon Adam und Eva im Paradies mit der Schlange[2] altenglisch gesprochen haben.

Nun, um 200 nach Christo war zwischen dem Altenglischen, dem Altdeutschen und dem Altskandinavischen[3] kein größerer Unterschied als heute zwischen den Dialekten Nord- und Südenglands. Wer damals Deutsch verstand, hat wahrscheinlich ohne Schwierigkeit Englisch verstehen können. Nicht das Englisch, das man heute spricht, sondern jenes alte „Englisch", das die Angeln[4] irgendwo auf dem Kontinent sprachen. „Deutsch" und „Englisch" waren damals wirklich nur Dialekte einer einzigen Sprache, der man den Namen „Urgermanisch", d. h. primitive Germanic gegeben hat. Urgermanisch ist sozusagen die Muttersprache: Englisch, Deutsch, Schwedisch, Dänisch, usw. sind Tochtersprachen. Die Mutter ist tot und längst vergessen, die Töchter leben noch.

Weil aber das heutige Englisch und das moderne Deutsch Töchter *einer* Mutter sind, darum gibt es auch in den beiden Sprachen noch eine große Zahl von Wörtern, die sich sehr ähnlich sind. Daß „Maus" und mouse, „sauer" und sour, „backen" und bake, „Schinken" und shank, „Hahn" und hen, „Haut" und hide miteinander verwandt sein müssen, obgleich sie nicht mehr alle dieselbe Bedeutung haben, ist leicht zu sehen. Auch daß „Fliege" und fly, „Zweig" und twig, „Daumen" und thumb, „Knopf" und knob irgendwie zusammenhängen müssen, läßt sich vielleicht noch erkennen. Nach einiger Übung wird man vielleicht auch noch auf den Gedanken kommen, daß der erste Teil des deutschen Wortes „Streichholz" mit englisch to strike verwandt ist. Daß aber englisch tinder mit deutsch „entzünden", englisch meat mit deutsch „Gemüse" und englisch crumple mit deutsch „krumm" zusammenhängt, das sieht man erst, wenn man ein Wörterbuch liest, das auf die Geschichte der einzelnen Wörter eingeht.

Natürlich darf man nun nicht glauben, daß jedes englische Wort, das einem deutschen Wort ähnlich ist, aus dem Urgermanischen in die Gegenwart gerettet worden ist. Beide Sprachen haben eine große Zahl von Wörtern aus dem Lateinischen[5] übernommen, „Keller" und „Literatur" zum Beispiel, aber auch „Tinte" und „Pult", die von tincta und pulpitum herkommen. Außerdem gibt es natürlich ganz gewöhnliche Wörter im Deutschen, deren „Verwandte" im Englischen ausgestorben sind, wie z. B. „billig" und „Heer".

Aber obgleich Deutsch und Englisch viele Wörter und Formen des alten Urgermanischen „vergessen" haben, so kann man doch durch Vergleich der Tochtersprachen miteinander noch ein genaues Bild der Muttersprache gewinnen. In jedem größeren Wörterbuch findet man heute hinter jedem

englischen oder deutschen Wort, das aus der Zeit des Urgermanischen in die Gegenwart gerettet worden ist, die Form und die Aussprache, die dieses Wort vor etwa zweitausend Jahren einmal gehabt hat. Man weiß also z. B., daß tooth und „Zahn" damals noch tanthaz hießen, daß day und
5 „Tag" noch dagaz lauteten[6] und daß man statt (I) have noch habaejo sagte.

Aber obgleich die Form habaejo, überhaupt die ganze urgermanische Sprache als solche, heute nicht mehr gesprochen wird, so sollte man doch vielleicht nicht einfach sagen, sie sei ausgestorben; denn von einer Bakterie, die sich teilt und deren Teile als selbständige Organismen weiterleben, kann
10 man ja auch nicht sagen, sie sterbe. Die Mutter lebt eben in den Töchtern weiter.

[Schluß folgt]

NOTES. 1. Christo Christ; vor Christo B.C.; nach Christo A.D. 2. Schlange snake, serpent. 3. Altskandinavisch Old Scandinavian. 4. Angeln Angles (a Germanic tribe that settled in England in the fifth century A.D.). 5. Lateinisch Latin. 6. lauteten sounded, were pronounced; were.

BUILDING A PASSIVE VOCABULARY

ausgesprochen, die Aussprache cf. Lesson XXI
bekannt (cf. kennen) known
ebenso just as
Jahrhundert cf. Lesson XXI
selbständig (cf. selbst stehen) independent
der Unterschied scheiden to separate, divide, der Unterschied the difference, distinction
der Vergleich gleich like, same, vergleichen to compare, *that is*, to see where things are alike (*or* unlike), der Vergleich the comparison
zusammenhängen zusammen together, hängen to hang, zusammenhängen to be connected, related

VOCABULARY

backen to *bake*
billig cheap
der Daumen, – the *thumb*
der Dichter, – the author, poet
entzünden to inflame
erwidern to reply
der Esel, – the donkey, *ass*
die Fliege, –n the *fly*
das Gemüse, – the vegetable
glatt smooth
das Grab, ⸚er the *grave*
der Graben, ⸚ the ditch, trench

der Hahn, ⸗e the rooster
die Haut, ⸗e the skin; *hide*
das Heer, –e the army
der Keller, – the *cellar*
der Knopf, ⸗e the button
krumm crooked
die Literatur, –en the *literature*
die Maus, ⸗e the *mouse*
der Offizier, –e the *officer*
das Pult, –e the desk
rund *round*
die Sahne the cream
sauer *sour*
der Schinken, – the ham
das Streichholz, ⸗er the match
die Tinte, –n the ink
träge idle; lazy
verwandt related
das Vieh the cattle
wider against
zahm *tame*
der Zweig, –e the *twig*, branch

IDIOMS

sich etwas gefallen lassen to put up with something; approve of something; *here* accept
usw. (und so weiter) etc. (and so forth)

TEXT B

Psyche

[Fortsetzung]

Die Alte hatte wieder das Tuch genommen und begann, ihr das lange Haar zu trocknen; manchmal strich sie leise mit ihrer harten Hand über die weiße Stirn des Mädchens.

„Kathi", begann diese wieder, „nein, nicht er, aber ich! Ich wollte, ich wäre tot! Kathi! Ich kann ihm nicht danken. Nie, niemals! O, wie unglücklich bin ich!" 5

„Nun", meinte Kathi, das junge Mädchen beruhigend, „Sie brauchen das ja auch nicht zu tun, Fräulein; Mama wird das ja alles schon besorgen."

„Mama!" rief das Mädchen.

„Mein Gott, Fräulein, hat Sie das erschreckt?" 10

Aber das Kind saß da, die nackten[1] Arme vor sich hingestreckt, in ihrer hilflosen Schönheit selbst für die Augen des armen alten Weibes ein bezaubernder[2] Anblick. „Mama!" rief sie wieder. „Ja, ja, Kathi, die würde es tun; und wenn ich sie noch soviel bäte, sie würde es dennoch tun.— Kathi, sie darf es nie erfahren; versprich es mir, Kathi!" Sie hatte die 15 Arme um den Hals der alten Frau gelegt, die neben ihr niedergekniet war.

„Ja, ja, Fräulein, wenn Sie nur ruhig werden, ich will schweigen wie das Grab."

„Nein, Kathi, sage: Bei Gott! daß du schweigen willst."

„Nun, Fräulein; bei Gott!—Ich hätt's auch ohnedies getan."

5 „Ich danke dir, alte Kathi! Aber es war noch einer da, nicht wahr?"

„Ja, Fräulein, es war—"

„Nein, nein, nicht seinen Namen, Kathi!" Und sie verschloß den Mund der Alten mit ihrer kleinen kalten Hand. „Sage nur, hat er mich erkannt, kann er mich erkannt haben?"

10 „Ich glaube nicht, Fräulein. Als Sie hier ankamen, war er mit dem anderen schon auf dem Männerfloß.[3] Nachher war er zu weit entfernt; auch ist er gleich zur Stadt zurückgegangen."

Das Mädchen nickte und legte sich auf die harte Ruhebank zurück, die Hände hinter den Kopf gelegt.

15 Die Alte war aufgestanden. „Ich komme gleich zurück", sagte sie; „ich geh' nur, um dem anderen Herrn zu sagen, daß es Ihnen wieder gut geht, und daß wir keinen Doktor brauchen."

Als die Alte nach einiger Zeit zurückkam, fand sie ihren jungen Gast schon völlig angekleidet, das Mädchen band sich gerade ein weißes Taschentuch um 20 den Kopf. Aber die gute Alte ließ sie nicht so fort; der Kaffee war ja noch heiß, und das Kind, da es so fror, ließ sich eine Tasse schon gefallen. Die Alte goß ihr selber ein, holte Zucker und Sahne und sagte: „Wenn das Fräulein warten will, können wir gleich zusammen gehen."

Aber das Fräulein wollte nicht auf dem geraden Wege nach der Stadt 25 zurück. Das Fräulein wollte den weiten Umweg durch die hinter dem Deich[3] liegenden Wiesen machen. Die Alte meinte zwar: „Um Gottes willen, Kind, wenn Sie eine solche Angst haben vor dem jungen Herrn, er wird gleich von dem Floß[3] herauskommen; wir warten nur ein Weilchen, dann ist er lange vor uns in der Stadt."

30 Aber das Fräulein wollte doch nicht.

„Nun", sagte die Alte, „so geh' ich mit Ihnen; bei mir zu Hause wartet keiner als mein Hinz, und der wartet auch nicht, der schläft unterm Ofen;—Sie können da nicht allein gehen, durch all das Vieh hindurch."

Aber das Fräulein wollte auch das nicht, sie wollte eben ganz allein gehen. 35 „Kathi, alte Kathi", sagte sie und strich mit ihrer kleinen Hand der alten Frau über die Stirn; „die Kühe tun mir nichts. Sie sind ja so zahm. Und dann bin ich ja auch ganz in Weiß; kein bißchen Rotes habe ich an mir!" Sie wandte[4] sich um[4] und ließ Kathi ihr weißes Sommerkleid sehen. „Da ist ja festes Land; ich laufe schnell hindurch; dann komme ich unbeobachtet von hinten in unseren Garten, und—siehst du, niemand hat mich gesehen als du, alte Kathi; und du—du hast mir versprochen, niemand etwas zu sagen."

Die Alte wollte noch etwas erwidern. Aber schon war das Mädchen zur Tür hinaus, und wie ein aufgeschreckter Vogel flog sie die Grasdecke des Deiches hinauf und ebenso an der anderen Seite wieder hinunter. Einen Augenblick stand sie still, als sei sie hier sicher. Die großen Augen blickten fast mehr als ernst über die grünen Wiesen, die sich endlos ihr zur Seite ausbreiteten. Es war nicht viel zu sehen dort; zwischen den silbrigen Wassergräben, die auf eine Strecke hinaus ihrem Auge sichtbar blieben, war nichts auf der weiten Fläche zu sehen als die glatten runden Kühe, die träge grasenden Schafe und Esel und die niedrigen Brücken, welche über die Gräben führten. Sie kannte das alles, sie hatte es oft gesehen. Und jetzt ging sie, die Stadt im Rücken lassend, auf dem engen Wege weiter, der zwischen einem Wassergraben zur Rechten[5] und dem Deich zur Linken[5] nach Südwesten führte. Da der Wind aus Nordwest kam, so war er hier noch viel stärker als an der Seeseite des Deiches. Einmal wurde der Strohhut, den sie auch jetzt in der Hand trug, ihr entrissen und gegen den Deich geworfen; ein paarmal mußte sie stehenbleiben, um sich das Taschentuch fester unter das Kinn zu binden. Dann blickte sie ängstlich hinter sich zurück, aber kein Mensch war zu sehen; nur über ihrem Kopf schoß manchmal ein Seevogel von draußen in das Land hinein.

Bald machte der Deich gegen Westen eine Biegung, und etwas später führte dann ein enger, grasbewachsener Weg über die Wassergräben in die Wiesen hinein. Als das Mädchen diese Stelle des Weges erreicht hatte, ging sie von Brücke zu Brücke über die Gräben zur Stadt. Von einer der Brücken erblickte sie nicht weit vom Deiche die Gestalt eines Mannes; fern, fast nur wie einen Schatten.

Erschrocken blieb sie stehen. Ihre geöffneten Lippen bewegten sich nicht, nur ihre dunklen Augen waren lebendig; sie folgten dem fernen Schatten, wie er langsam hinter den ersten Häusern der Stadt verschwand. Dann verließ sie die Brücke und ging wie[6] träumend weiter.

Hoch oben auf dem Deiche aber stand, unbeachtet von den jungen Augen, noch eine andere Gestalt und hob[7] sich wie eine große Silhouette von dem hellen Himmel ab[7]; die Silhouette einer weiblichen Gestalt, die oben in einem breiten Hute abschloß, wie ihn die Damenwelt vor etwa dreißig Jahren trug.

5 Dieser Hut stand so lange am Himmel, bis drunten auf den Wiesen das weiße Kleid verschwunden war.

[Fortsetzung folgt]

NOTES. 1. nackt bare. 2. bezaubernd charming, enchanting. 3. Männerfloß, Deich, Floß. See plan, Lesson XX. 4. wandte sich um turned around. 5. Rechten, Linken Either Seite or Hand is understood. 6. wie as if. 7. hob ab contrasted with.

BUILDING A PASSIVE VOCABULARY

der Anblick cf. Lesson XXI
ausbreiten breit broad, wide, ausbreiten to spread out
das bißchen beißen to bite, das Bißchen the little bite, ein bißchen a little bit
drunten da *plus* unten (*adv. to* unter) down there
ebenso likewise, in a similar manner
sichtbar sehen to see, sichtbar visible
das Taschentuch die Tasche the pocket, das Tuch the cloth, das Taschentuch the handkerchief
der Umweg um around, der Weg the way, der Umweg the detour, roundabout way
unbeachtet achten to regard, beachten to notice, heed, unbeachtet unnoticed
unten *adv. to* unter
weiblich das Weib the woman, weiblich womanly, feminine

143. The Future Imaginative Subjunctive (Sometimes Called the Conditional*). The present and past imaginative subjunctive was treated in Lesson XVIII. Since present forms (ich ginge, ich täte, ich stürbe) can be used with future meaning (cf. §§ 21 and 116), it was not necessary at that time to introduce the future forms of the imaginative subjunctive. There are times, however, where an author or speaker, in order to stress the futurity or prospective nature of some imagined situation, prefers to use the special future

*This treatment of the so-called conditional is based on its use in literary works.

forms of the imaginative subjunctive. These forms, which have *only future* meaning, are identical with the imaginative set of the future indirect discourse (see § 135, *A*): ich würde plus infinitive.* Thus:

Ich fühle, daß meine Kräfte wachsen würden, wenn du mit mir gingest. I feel that my powers would grow if you would go with me.

To express *future* time the present imaginative subjunctive and the würde-plus-infinitive forms may be used interchangeably, as long as the idea of futurity is not stressed:

Ich bleibe hier, denn in der Dunkelheit fände ich doch nicht den Weg durch den Wald; or Ich bleibe hier, denn in der Dunkelheit würde ich den Weg durch den Wald doch nicht finden. I shall remain here; for I should not be able to find my way through the forest in the darkness anyhow.

To express imagined situations in *present* time the forms with würde are not found in best literary usage. Example of correct form (present imaginative):

Wenn das Unglück nicht gekommen wäre, wäre heute manches anders. If the misfortune had not come (that is, if it weren't for the misfortune), many things would be different now.

144. Compound Adverbs. German uses many compound adverbs like dahin, daher, umher, herum, davon, hinzu, vorbei, and the like. The first element in such compounds is usually rather meaningless, and the sense of such compounds can therefore usually be derived from the latter element:

Er lief davon. He ran away. Er kam hinzu. He walked up (to a group). Er flog über das Wasser dahin. He flew across the water (away from the recent scene of action). Sie dürfen den Hund nicht frei herumlaufen lassen. You must not let the dog run around loose. Er blickte umher. He looked around. (Herum and umher both mean *around*).

*The forms würde plus past infinitive (second conditional) are not introduced because of the infrequency of their occurrence. In a count Professor B. Q. Morgan found that not one such form occurred in more than six thousand verbal forms,

145. Repetition of Prepositions. In expressions like er ging in das Haus hinein, er lief durch den Wald hindurch, aus . . . heraus, the adverbs hinein, hindurch, and heraus repeat the idea expressed by the preposition and are best left out in translation.

146. Ein=Words as Pronouns. When ein=words are used as pronouns, that is, when they do not modify a noun, they take strong endings:

Hier kann mich kein Mensch sehen. Hier kann mich keiner sehen. No one (no person) can see me here. Ich kann nur eines (eins) sagen. I can say only one thing.

147. Word Formation: The Prefix ver=. The syllable ver= is prefixed:

a. To nouns and adjectives to form verbs indicating that the quality expressed in the original noun or adjective is gained or transferred:

verarmen to grow poor
veralten to grow old *or* obsolete
verdummen to grow stupid *or* silly
vereinsamen to become isolated
vereisen to turn into ice
verändern to vary, change
verdeutschen to render (*or* translate) into German
veredeln to ennoble

b. To verbs to indicate completion of the activity or that the material is used up:

verbluten to bleed to death
verblühen to cease blooming, to wither
verbrennen to burn up *or* away
verhungern to die of hunger
verdecken to cover up
verbrauchen to use up

c. To verbs to express an error in the activity or to indicate that the effect is not desirable (note that most of these verbs are reflexive):

sich verlaufen to run the wrong way, to lose one's way
sich verschlafen to sleep too long
verführen to lead astray

148. Word Formation: The Prefix er=. The syllable er= is frequently prefixed to verbs to indicate the completion of the activity indicated in the verb:

erblicken to behold, discover
erreichen to reach, attain
ertöten to kill, exterminate
ergreifen to seize, take hold of
ertrinken to drown

Learn the principal parts of backen.

backen	backte	hat gebacken	bäckt	to bake

EXERCISES

I

A. Beantworten Sie folgende Fragen über Text A auf deutsch: 1. Wen würden wir nicht verstehen, wenn er heute aus seinem Grabe aufstände? 2. Wer würde das heutige Englisch nicht verstehen? 3. Wer würde auf den Gedanken kommen, daß er mit droughte unser modernes drought meinen könnte? 4. Was würden Sie bekommen, wenn Sie in einen Laden gingen und soote win verlangten? 5. Was erlaubt es dem heutigen Leser, die Werke Chaucers nach kurzem Studium langsam lesen zu können? 6. Was können wir von Adam und Eva kaum erwarten? 7. Zwischen welchen Sprachen war um 200 nach Christo kein großer Unterschied? 8. Mit welchem englischen Wort ist das deutsche Wort „Schinken" verwandt? 9. Wo kann man erfahren, ob ein englisches Wort mit einem deutschen Wort verwandt ist? 10. Aus welcher Sprache haben Deutsch und Englisch Wörter übernommen? 11. Wie kann man ein Bild des Urgermanischen gewinnen? 12. Wie wurde das deutsche Wort „Zahn" einmal ausgesprochen?

B. Beantworten Sie folgende Fragen über Text B auf deutsch: 1. Was machte die Alte mit dem Tuch? 2. Wie war die Stirn des Mädchens? 3. Wer ist unglücklich? 4. Wer könnte dem jungen Mann danken, wenn das Fräulein es nicht kann? 5. Wer würde es bestimmt tun, wenn sie etwas von der Rettung erführe? 6. Was darf die Mutter des Mädchens nie erfahren? 7. Wie will Kathi schweigen? 8. Womit verschloß das Fräulein den Mund der Alten? 9. Wo war der junge Bildhauer, als das Mädchen ankam? 10. Wer von den beiden Männern ging gleich zur Stadt zurück? 11. Wem wollte Kathi sagen, daß es dem Fräulein wieder gut ginge? 12. Was band das Mädchen sich um den Kopf? 13. Wie war der Kaffee? 14. Wer ließ sich eine Tasse gefallen? 15. Wer goß den Kaffee ein? 16. Was hätte das Fräulein tun müssen, wenn die Alte mit ihr zur Stadt zurückgegangen wäre? 17. Welchen Weg wollte das Fräulein machen? 18. Vor wem hatte das Mädchen Angst? 19. Wo lag Hinz? 20. Warum meinte die Alte, das Fräulein solle nicht durch die Wiesen gehen? 21. Wie zeigte sie Kathi ihr Kleid? 22. Wie wissen wir, daß hinter dem Hause der Mutter ein Garten war? 23. Wie flog das Mädchen die Grasdecke des Deiches hinauf? 24. Was konnte das Fräulein auf den Wiesen sehen? 25. Wie waren die Kühe? 26. Woher kam der Wind? 27. Was wurde ihr einmal entrissen? 28. Wie trug sie ihren Strohhut? 29. Warum mußte sie ein paarmal stehenbleiben? 30. Wie blickte sie hinter sich zurück? 31. Womit war der Weg bewachsen, der zwischen den Gräben in die Wiesen hineinführte? 32. Was erblickte das Mädchen nicht weit vom Deiche, als sie das Ende des Weges erreicht hatte? 33. Wer stand hoch oben auf dem Deiche? 34. Wann hatte Kathi den Hut gekauft, den sie auf dem Kopf trug? 35. Wie lange blieb sie auf dem Deiche stehen?

II

Translate the following sentences into German: 1. He is getting old. 2. He will go with you tomorrow. 3. He would see them tomorrow if he were there. 4. Hans cannot come out (heraus); he is just being bathed. 5. She is getting more and more beautiful. 6. She will help you with (bei) your work. 7. She would probably come if everything were ready. 8. She is often sent (*use* schicken) to Berlin. 9. What would you do if you had two thousand marks (Mark)? 10. If I had more money I would buy a house. 11. He would not travel (fahren) to England in winter. 12. I should like to stay longer, but I must be in Hamburg tomorrow. 13. Would you visit Munich (München) if you were to take (machen) a trip to Germany?

III

Translate into English:

trösten	das Messer	der Preis	gelb
der Stoff	die Gabel	die Schlacht	gering
streng	schwach	selten	gestern
die Mauer	der Schmerz	setzen	glatt
messen	notwendig	der Schaden	gesund
der Löffel	der Nachbar	scharf	der Käse

IV

Translate into German:

seven	the tea	to quarrel
seventeen	to divide	the chair
seventy	Saturday	the cup
satisfied	the state	the plate
the goal	the star	the tree trunk
to open	the knee	ill
to close	proud	the orange
to return	to disturb (interrupt)	to fetch

V

Translate the following compounds and derivatives:

Einen Rundgang durch die Stadt machen, eine Rundreise durch Europa machen; Kellner, ich nehme Erdbeeren mit Schlagsahne; grasende Viehherden; widersprich mir nicht! du sollst mir nicht immer Widerworte geben; der Bäckerladen, der Kuchenbäcker; die Halsentzündung, Lungenentzündung; das erste Frühgemüse; er ist unnahbar; der Schweinebraten; es donnert und blitzt; das Pferdefleisch; 5 der Fremdenhaß; die Braunkohle, der Kohlenbaron, die Kohlenförderung (output) ist gestiegen, die Kohlenpreise sind gefallen; Einbruch ist strafbar; der Weg verengt sich; auf vereisten Straßen ist das Autofahren gefährlich; man muß sich einmal ganz klarmachen, daß . . .; von diesem Bilde mußt du eine Vergrößerung machen lassen; verjüngt und mit frischem Mut aus den Ferien wiederkommen; 10 nur noch verkohlte Knochen waren von ihm übriggeblieben; verbilligen, verbessern, verdünnen, verkürzen, verdoppeln, verbrauchen; er hat sein ganzes Geld verspielt; er vertrinkt alles, was er verdient; versalzen; sich versprechen; erfrieren, erfüllen, ergänzen, erhärten, erkämpfen, erlernen; der Waldbach; das Bad, das Badezimmer; der Birnbaum; felsenfest; die Hohlheit; das Eichenholz; körperlicher 15 Schmerz; die Kuhmilch; mit Flugpost; die Selbstmörderin; etwas Wichtiges

VI

Translate the following idioms: 1. Fritz ist jetzt auf dem Lande. 2. Mit einem Male wurde es wieder hell. 3. Sagen Sie es, bitte, noch einmal. 4. Wollen Sie nicht Platz nehmen? 5. Er hat jedenfalls genug für die erste Reise. 6. Wir würden ihn heute abend empfangen können. 7. Beim ersten Wort schon wurde er über und über rot. 8. Ich will vor allem mit ihrer Mutter reden. 9. Wir sind ihn endlich los.

VII

Make up five sentences in the prospective future using the conditional in the main clause.

VIII

Make up five sentences in which you use quotations, and then rewrite the same sentences in indirect-discourse subjunctive.

IX

Change the following indirect-discourse sentences into the indicative: 1. Er sagte, er habe die ganze Nacht gearbeitet. 2. Er schrieb, daß die Gefahr zu groß sei und daß er nicht mehr fliege. 3. Er meinte, er sei mir nicht im Wege. 4. Er sagte, ich solle nicht vom Dache fallen. 5. Sie sagte, es gehe ihr besser. 6. Du schriebst, du hättest ihn gesehen. 7. Ich lachte und sagte, es wäre mir sehr angenehm. 8. Die Biene sagte zu ihrer Freundin, sie würde selten Honig in den Taschen der Menschen finden. 9. Er behauptete, Fritz sei nicht gekommen.

X

Translate into English: 1. Nun schien die Sonne auf den vor der Tür liegenden, über Nacht gefallenen Schnee, und bald lief das Wasser ins Haus. 2. Ein großer Teil der in den ägyptischen Königsgräbern gefundenen Schätze ist heute im Britischen Museum. 3. Als Kolumbus Amerika entdeckte, waren die gegen Ende des zehnten Jahrhunderts von isländischen Wikingern gemachten Fahrten schon längst vergessen.

LESSON XXIII

TEXT A

Aus der Geschichte unsrer Sprache

[Schluß]

Mit dem Urgermanischen ist jedoch die Geschichte des Englischen und des Deutschen noch nicht zu Ende. Auch diese in den Jahrhunderten vor und nach Christo[1] gesprochene Sprache war nur ein Dialekt, ein Zweig eines großen Baumes, nur die „Tochter"sprache einer noch älteren „Mutter"=sprache. 5

Es kann nämlich kein Zufall sein, daß in jedem englischen Wörterbuche die Wörter

*p*aternal durch *f*atherly,
*p*lain durch *f*lat or level country

und noch viele andere Wörter unter dem Buchstaben *p*, die das Englische 10 aus dem Lateinischen[2] übernommen hat, durch Wörter mit einem *f* im Wortanfang erklärt werden. Es muß doch einen Grund haben, daß

*d*entist	etwas mit	*t*ooth	und	„Zahn",
*d*ouble	etwas mit	*t*wo	und	„zwei",
*d*ecade	etwas mit	*t*en	und	„zehn" 15

zu tun hat, daß also viele lateinische Wörter mit *d* durch englische Wörter mit *t* und deutsche Wörter mit „z" übersetzt werden.

Nun, haben nicht viele englische Wörter mit *d*, wie deep, daughter, death, dream, drive, drink, door, deutsche „Verwandte", die alle mit einem „t" anfangen? Wenn also neben vielen englischen Wörtern mit *t* im 20 Wortanfang lateinische Wörter mit *d* stehen, dann müssen eben Lateinisch und Englisch auch miteinander verwandt sein.

Wirklich wissen wir heute und haben die Beweise dafür, daß das Urgermanische, die Mutter des Englischen und des Deutschen, selber die Tochter einer Mutter war, die außerdem noch viele andere solche „Töchter" hatte, 25 nämlich Lateinisch,[2] Griechisch,[3] Persisch, Keltisch[3] und andere. Ja, fast alle Sprachen, die heute in Europa und Westasien[4] gesprochen werden, sind

Zweige eines einzigen Baumes, Tochtersprachen einer einzigen Muttersprache, der man in England den Namen *Indo-European* und in Deutschland den Namen Indogermanisch gegeben hat.

Die Menschen, welche dieses Indogermanische einmal sprachen, heißen nach ihrer Sprache Indogermanen.[5] Der Streit um die Heimat der Indogermanen ist zwar immer noch nicht abgeschlossen; aber man sucht diese Heimat heute mit einiger Sicherheit in den weiten Steppen,[6] die sich südlich vom Ural[7] von Osteuropa bis nach Asien hin ausstrecken. Früher hat man diese Heimat im inneren Asiens oder in Nordeuropa gesucht.

Warum die Indogermanen nicht in ihrer Heimat blieben, weiß man nicht. Vielleicht zwangen lange Zeiten großer Trockenheit einen Teil des Volkes, sich fern von der Heimat neues Land zu suchen. Sicher ist, daß Indogermanische Stämme im zweiten Jahrtausend vor Christo bis nach Indien,[8] Persien, Griechenland und Italien[8] vordrangen. Sicher ist auch, daß Indogermanen sich von der Donau[9] langsam nach Thüringen[10] und von da weiter nach Norden vorschoben.

Jeder der abziehenden Stämme nahm seine Sprache, das Indogermanische, mit in die neue Heimat, deren Bewohner man mit Waffengewalt unterwarf. Die Unterworfenen nahmen dann im Laufe der Zeit die Sprache der neuen Herren an, vermischten sich aber bald mit ihnen und bildeten so ein neues Volk, dessen Sprache ihren Indogermanischen Charakter nie ganz verlor. In Nordeuropa trafen die Indogermanen auf ein Volk vom Typ[11] der Cromagnonleute[11] und aus der Vermischung dieses Volkes mit den Indogermanen sind die Germanen entstanden.

Im germanischen Nordeuropa entwickelte sich langsam das Urgermanische. Ein reines, streng geregeltes Urgermanisch hat es sicher nie gegeben. Aber die germanischen Stämme haben sich untereinander verstehen können, auch wenn jeder von ihnen nur einen urgermanischen Dialekt sprach.

Im Laufe der Völkerwanderung,[12] die noch in den letzten Jahrhunderten vor Christo begann, verließen viele Germanen ihre Heimat. Angeln[13] und Sachsen[13] zogen nach England. Die Vandalen[14] zogen bis nach Nordafrika. Erst gegen sechshundert nach Christo kommt Europa langsam wieder zur Ruhe. Indessen aber haben die neuentstandenen Völker ihre alte Sprache schon so stark verändert, daß man von nun an nicht mehr von Germanisch, sondern nur noch von Altenglisch oder Altdeutsch reden kann.

Noch heute aber erkennt ein geschultes Auge mit Leichtigkeit die Verwandtschaft der neuentstandenen Sprachen mit der indogermanischen Ursprache. Noch heute kann man beweisen, daß das „st" in „Nest" identisch[15] ist mit dem *s* und dem *t* in sit, weil „Nest" früher „Sitzplatz" hieß. Noch heute kann man zeigen, daß eat zum lateinischen edo gehört und daß das *t* oder das *d* von eat oder von edo identisch[15] ist mit dem *t* und dem *d* in tooth und dentist, weil Zahn ursprünglich „der Essende" hieß. 5

Vom Englischen oder vom Deutschen aus führt so eine gerade Linie über das Urgermanische in das Indogermanische. Von da ab aber verliert sich diese Linie im Dunkel der Vergangenheit.

NOTES. 1. vor Christo B.C., nach Christo A.D. 2. Lateinisch Latin. 3. Griechisch, Persisch, Keltisch Greek, Persian, Celtic (Keltic). 4. Asien Asia. 5. Indogermanen Indo-Europeans. 6. Die Steppen The (Russian) Steppes. 7. Ural Urals (mountain system in Russia). 8. Indien, Persien, Griechenland, Italien India, Persia, Greece, Italy. 9. Donau Danube. 10. Thüringen Thuringia (state in central Germany). 11. Typ der Cromagnonleute of the type of the Cro-Magnon race. 12. Völkerwanderung (great) migration of peoples, nations. 13. Angeln, Sachsen Angles, Saxons. 14. Vandalen Vandals. 15. identisch identical.

BUILDING A PASSIVE VOCABULARY

Bewohner wohnen to dwell, live, bewohnen to live in, inhabit, die Bewohner the inhabitants

die Heimat das Heim the home, die Heimat the home, native place

Jahrhundert, Jahrtausend das Jahr the year, hundert hundred, Jahrhundert century, tausend thousand, Jahrtausend millennium, thousand years

loslösen lösen *from* los loose, loslösen to sever, free, release

unterwerfen, die Unterworfenen unter under, down, werfen to throw, unterwerfen to subject, subdue, subjugate, die Unterworfenen the ones defeated, subdued, the vanquished

die Verwandtschaft verwandt related, die Verwandtschaft the relationship

VOCABULARY

das Datum, *pl.* die Daten the *date*
gelten to be valid, worth, of value
die Großmutter, ⸚ the *grandmother*
der Kaiser, – the emperor
die Kusine, –n the *cousin* (female)
lehnen to *lean*
der Prinz, –en, –en the *prince*
die Schwester, –n the *sister*
übersetzen to translate
der Vetter, –n the cousin (*male*)
die Waffe, –n the *weapon*
der Zeuge, –n, –n the witness

TEXT B

Psyche

[Fortsetzung]

Es war indessen wieder Winter geworden.—Der erste Schein des Dezember-Morgenrotes stand am Himmel und warf sein warmes Licht in das Halbdunkel einer Künstlerwerkstatt. Abgüsse antiker Bilderwerke und einzelne Modelle[1] von des Künstlers eigener Hand standen überall umher.
5 Aber alles warf noch tiefe Schatten.

Jetzt hörte man von draußen Schritte, und gleich darauf wurde die Eingangstür geöffnet. Der Künstler selbst war es, der jetzt in seine Werkstatt trat, ein schlanker, jugendlicher Mann mit grauen, hellblickenden Augen und dunklem braunem Haar. Doch weder fremde noch eigene Werke
10 reizten seinen Blick. Er ging, ohne sie anzusehen, an ihnen vorbei und griff nach einem offenen Briefe, der vor ihm auf einem Tische lag und der, nach dem Datum zu urteilen, schon einige Tage alt war. Dann warf er sich in einen daneben stehenden Lehnstuhl und begann zu lesen. Aber nur an einer bestimmten Stelle des Briefes, die er schon mehr als einmal gelesen
15 hatte, hingen seine Augen.

„Du zweifelst wohl nicht daran", so las er heute wieder, „daß ich mein Versprechen treu gehalten habe. Weder vor Göttern noch vor Menschen habe ich Deine Tat erwähnt. Sogar das Verlangen, den Namen der Geretteten zu erfahren oder sie kennenzulernen, habe ich in mir ertötet. Ja,
20 selbst als sie mir eines Tages so nahe war, daß ich nur über eine Gartenmauer hätte blicken brauchen, um sie zu sehen, bin ich, obgleich ich mich dazu zwingen mußte, pflichttreu vorbeigegangen.—Auch auf der anderen Seite hat niemand das Schweigen gebrochen, und selbst der Mund unserer alten Badefrau, außer Dir und mir der einzige Augenzeuge der Rettung, muß
25 durch irgendwelche geheime Kraft verschlossen sein.—Und dennoch, ich weiß, wen Du gerettet hast.

Es gibt eine sehr junge Dame in unserer Stadt, wagemutig wie ein Knabe und zart wie eine Blume. Obgleich sie erst mit dem letzten Frühling aus dem Klassenzimmer ans Tageslicht gekommen ist, mag doch schon
30 mancher junge Mann in warmer Sommernacht davon geträumt haben, sie im Winter auf einem Feste für sich gewinnen zu können. Aber das blonde Götterkind erschien auf keinem Feste, nicht einmal auf dem Ball, den die alte

Bürgermeisterin, ihre Großmutter, für die Offiziere vom Regiment Prinz August am Geburtstag des Kaisers gab. Nur Alltagsmenschenkinder mit erhitzten Gesichtern, keines Künstlerauges würdig, waren zu sehen. Nur im engsten Kreise,[2] zu dem ich leider nicht gehöre, soll sie zu erblicken sein; ja schon seit dem Spätsommer soll sie das Haus und den Garten ihrer Mutter nicht mehr verlassen haben; und eine gewisse sehr jugendliche mutige Schwimmerin ist seit jenem Tage nicht wieder auf dem Badeplatz gesehen worden.

Geredet wird viel darüber. Einige meinen, sie sei irgendeinem entfernten Verwandten, einem Vetter, versprochen, der das Schwimmen seiner Kusine nicht leiden könne, und der nun plötzlich seine[3] Rechte geltend mache.[3] Andere sagen einfach, sie sei—verliebt.

Nein, nein, fürchte nicht, daß ich den Namen nenne! Ich kenne Dich ja. Die Wirklichkeit mit ihrem kalten Licht soll deine Träume nicht durchbrechen. So seid ihr beide sicher, Du in Deinem Künstlertraum und sie in ihrer heiligen Jungfräulichkeit,[4] die Du mir übrigens—o unerklärlicher Widerspruch des Menschenherzens!—mit fast eigennützigem[5] Eifer zu bewachen scheinst."

Er las nicht weiter, er hatte den Brief aus der Hand fallen lassen. Er stand auf und, in Gedanken versunken, ergriff er einen auf dem Tische liegenden Tonklumpen,[6] dann auch bald eins der Modellierhölzchen,[7] die dicht daneben lagen.

„Was erzählt doch der Dichter von Psyche?—‚Psyche, das arme leichtgläubige Königskind, hatte auf ihre neidischen Schwestern gehört: Der Geliebte, der nur in dunkler Nacht sie besuche, sei ein Ungeheuer.[8] Nach dem Rate der Schwestern war sie mit brennender Lampe und scharfer Waffe an das Bett des Schlafenden getreten und erkannte, zitternd vor unsagbarer Freude, den schönsten aller Götter. Aber die Lampe schwankte[9] in der kleinen Hand, ein Tropfen heißen Öls erweckte[9] den Schlafenden, und mit harten Worten für die Geliebte erhob sich der Gott in die Luft und flog davon. Als im leeren Luftraum ihr Auge ihn verlor, da hörte sie den nahen Strom rauschen; da sprang sie auf und stürzte sich hinein; ihr zartes Leben sollte untergehen in den kalten Wassern.

Doch der Gott des Stromes, fürchtend den mächtigeren Gott, trug sie auf seinen Armen empor und legte sie auf die blühenden Blumen des Ufers.'—O, süße Psyche, ich hätte dich an keinen Gott zurückgegeben!"

Nur in seinem Inneren, unhörbar hatte er alle diese Worte gesprochen.— Draußen am Himmel war das Morgenrot verschwunden, und dem schönen Aufgang war ein grauer Tag gefolgt. Nur auf dem Gesicht des Künstlers selber schien der Glanz des frühen Lichtes zurückgeblieben zu sein. Aber von 5 den farbenreichen Bildern, die vor seinem inneren Auge vorbeigezogen waren, sah ihn, wie um Gestaltung bittend, das eine Bild nur an.—Und seine Hände hatten nicht geruht; schon war aus dem formlosen Tonklumpen[6] ein zarter Mädchenkopf erkennbar, schon sah man die geschlossenen Augen und den kleinen, halb geöffneten Mund.

10 Die Mittagshelle des Wintertages war heraufgezogen; da klopfte es von draußen mit leisem Finger an die Tür. Eine alte Frau trat ein. „Aber Franz, willst du denn gar kein Frühstück?"

„Mutter, du!"—Er war aufgesprungen und hatte eilig ein neben ihm liegendes Tuch über das junge Werk geworfen.

15 „Soll ich's nicht sehen, Franz? Hast du ein neues Werk begonnen? Du bist ja sonst nicht so geheimnisvoll."

„Ja, Mutter, und diesmal, fühl' ich's, ist's das rechte.—Aber darum— noch nicht sehen. Auch du nicht, meine liebe alte Mutter!"

Der Sohn hatte den Arm um sie gelegt. So führte er sie aus seiner 20 Werkstatt, während sie zärtlich nickend zu ihm aufblickte, und bald traten die beiden in das freundliche Wohnzimmer, wo seit langem der Frühstückstisch für ihn bereitstand.

[Schluß folgt]

NOTES. 1. Abgüsse ... Modelle casts of ancient statues and single models. 2. Kreise circle(s). 3. seine ... mache *literally*, is making his rights valid, is asserting his rights. 4. Jungfräulichkeit virginity. 5. eigennützig selfish. 6. Tonklumpen lump of clay. 7. Modellierhölzchen modeling tools. 8. Ungeheuer monster. 9. schwankte ... erweckte wavered in her small hand, a drop of hot oil awakened.

BUILDING A PASSIVE VOCABULARY

Alltagsmenschenkinder everyday, common mortals

bewachen wach wake, awake, wachen to watch, guard, bewachen to guard

die Eingangstür ein (*as prefix in separable compounds means* in), gang *from* gehen, die Tür the door, die Eingangstür the entrance, door through which one enters

erhitzt heiß hot, die Hitze the heat, erhitzen to heat, erhitzt heated, hot

erkennbar erkennen to recognize, erkennbar recognizable
der Geburtstag geboren born, die Geburt the birth, der Tag the day, der Geburtstag the birthday
das Geheimnis, geheimnisvoll geheim secret, das Geheimnis the secret, geheimnisvoll mysterious
die Geliebte lieben to love, die Geliebte the beloved
die Künstlerwerkstatt die Kunst the art, der Künstler the artist, das Werk the work, Statt place (*stead*), die Werkstatt the workshop, die Künstlerwerkstatt the artist's studio
der Lehnstuhl lehnen to lean, die Lehne the back (of a chair), armrest, der Stuhl the chair, der Lehnstuhl armchair
leichtgläubig leicht light, easy, glauben to believe, leichtgläubig credulous
verliebt lieben to love, verliebt in love
versunken lost, buried
wagemutig wagen to dare, der Mut the courage, wagemutig daring, courageous, venturesome
die Werkstatt *cf.* Künstlerwerkstatt
der Widerspruch wider against, sprechen to speak, der Widerspruch the contradiction

GRAMMAR

149. Word Order. The following suggestions should prove helpful to students who wish to read German correctly and with ease:

a. Look first for the subject (which is in the nominative case). In verb-second position the subject as a rule immediately precedes or follows the inflected verb:

Im Frühling arbeitet **Kurzhals** immer auf dem Felde. **Kurzhals** arbeitet im Frühling immer auf dem Felde.

In verb-first position the subject is usually found immediately following the verb:

Gehen **Sie** heute in die Stadt?

In verb-last position the subject follows the relative pronoun or subordinating conjunction:

Die Maschine ist nicht nur ein Feind des Arbeiters, den **sie** auf die Straße wirft, . . . Außer ihrer Freundin sieht kein Mensch, daß **der Hut** schon ein Jahr alt ist.

Sometimes the relative pronoun itself is the subject:

Ein Arbeiter, **der** nichts verdient . . .

b. Find the inflected verb form in verb-first, verb-second, or verb-last position and look to the end of the clause for separable prefixes, participles, and infinitives:

Er fährt heute nach Hause zurück.
Er ist heute nach Hause zurückgefahren.
Er will heute nach Hause zurückfahren.

c. Find the objects, if any, direct and indirect. The indirect object precedes the direct object, except when the direct object is a personal pronoun:

Friedrich gibt der Frau das Geld.
Friedrich gibt ihr das Geld.
Friedrich gibt es ihr.

d. Locate the adverbial elements, which are usually arranged in the following order: time, place, manner (or time, manner, place):

Kurzhals hat gestern auf dem Felde eifrig gearbeitet.
Kurzhals arbeitet im Frühling eifrig auf dem Felde.

e. See if there are negatives (nicht *not*, nie *never*) in the sentence. These negatives modify either

(1) The verb (and therefore the entire clause) and stand as near the end of the sentence as possible: Ich kann heute leider nicht gehen; or

(2) A particular element of the clause and immediately precede that element: Nicht jeder kann Goethe in seiner Muttersprache lesen.

f. Remember that most of the foregoing rules are flexible and vary chiefly according to this principle:

The most important elements of a German sentence are found at the beginning and at the end. As stated in § 6, any sentence element may stand at the beginning in a declarative sentence except, of course, the inflected verb. (In English the subject is usually the first element.) The remaining elements are arranged in such a manner that the more important elements tend toward the end. For that reason prefixes of separable compounds, infinitives, past participles, and negatives are found at or near the end. In a broader sense the specific idea which completes the verb may be considered to be a part of the verb—a separable prefix, as it were; and that part which completes the verbal idea will usually be found at the end of a clause in the position of a separable prefix:

Seit Februar fährt er jeden Morgen mit seinem Auto in die Stadt. Verbal idea: in die Stadt fahren

Die Schwalben arbeiteten unter den Dächern der langen Häuserreihe an ihren Nestern. Verbal idea: arbeiteten an ihren Nestern

Damals hatten ihre Eltern etwa eine halbe Stunde vor der Stadt ein großes Gut. Verbal idea: hatten ein großes Gut

Ich warf das Geld dem Grauen schnell vor die Füße. Verbal idea: warf vor die Füße

Er wurde sehr bald nach dem Tode seines Vaters Offizier. Verbal idea: wurde Offizier. (Cf. the position in English: *He became an officer very soon after the death of his father.*)

150. Word Formation: The Prefix ur=. Ur= means very old or original and is prefixed to nouns:

der Urwald the virgin forest
die Urheimat the original home
der Urgroßvater the great-grandfather
die Urbewohner the original inhabitants, aborigines

Learn the principal parts of gelten:

helfen	half	hat geholfen	hilft	to help
gelten	galt	hat gegolten	gilt	to be worth

EXERCISES

I

A. Beantworten Sie folgende Fragen über Text A auf deutsch: 1. Womit ist die Geschichte des Englischen nicht zu Ende? 2. Von welcher Sprache war das Urgermanische ein Dialekt? 3. Was sind die deutschen „Verwandten" für deep, daughter, drive, thin, thick, thief, thing, three und thumb? 4. Wofür haben wir Beweise? 5. Nennen Sie vier Schwestersprachen des Urgermanischen. 6. Zu welcher Sprachfamilie gehören fast alle Sprachen, die heute in Europa gesprochen werden? 7. Wie nennt man das Volk, das einmal Indogermanisch sprach? 8. Wo sucht man heute die Urheimat dieses Volkes? 9. Wo hat man sie früher gesucht? 10. Warum blieben die Indogermanen nicht in ihrer Heimat? 11. Welche Sprache nahmen die abziehenden Stämme mit in die neue Heimat? 12. Wer wurde mit Waffengewalt unterworfen? 13. Was hat die Sprache der neuen Völker nie verloren? 14. Auf welches Volk trafen die Indogermanen in Nordeuropa? 15. Wo entwickelte sich langsam das Urgermanische? 16. Wann kam Europa langsam wieder zur Ruhe? 17. Welche Sprache wurde um das Jahr siebenhundert (nach Christo) in England gesprochen?

B. Beantworten Sie folgende Fragen über Text B auf deutsch: 1. Woher wissen wir, daß es noch früh am Tage war? 2. Woher kamen die Schritte? 3. Wer trat in die Werkstatt? 4. Was für Augen hatte der junge Mann? 5. Wonach griff er? 6. Wer hatte sein Versprechen gehalten? 7. Welche Tat hatte der Baron nicht erwähnt? 8. Wer war wagemutig wie ein Knabe? 9. Wer gab den Ball? 10. Wann wurde der Ball gegeben? 11. Seit wann hatte die Heldin unsrer Geschichte das Haus ihrer Mutter nicht verlassen? 12. Wie oft ging sie jetzt schwimmen? 13. Was meinten einige? 14. Was sagten andere? 15. Was sollte des Künstlers Träume nicht durchbrechen? 16. Was ließ der Künstler aus der Hand fallen? 17. Wo lag der Tonklumpen? 18. Wer war ein Königskind? 19. Was hatten die Schwestern gesagt? 20. Wann wurde Psyche von ihrem Geliebten besucht? 21. Wen erkannte Psyche? 22. Was erweckte den Schlafenden? 23. Was konnte Psyche rauschen hören? 24. Was tat sie darauf? 25. Wen fürchtete der Stromgott? 26. Was sagte der Künstler? 27. Was war dem schönen Sonnenaufgang gefolgt? 28. Was war schon aus dem formlosen Tonklumpen erkennbar? 29. Wen sollte das neue Werk darstellen? 30. Wer trat nun herein? 31. Was warf Franz über das neue Werk? 32. Was lag für Franz auf dem Tisch bereit?

II

Übersetzen Sie folgende Sätze ins Deutsche: 1. Will he be able to eat by (bis) Wednesday? 2. Are you ill? 3. When are we going?

4. Today we want to work hard. 5. The book I should like to buy is not expensive. 6. We knew him well. 7. We are not happy but sad. 8. I can stay no longer, for I must read thirty-five pages before I go to (zu *or* ins) bed. 9. May I ask why you are going? 10. He claims to have lost much more money than he ever had. 11. Are you not the lady whose hat fell into the water? 12. He gave my friend Marie a ring. 13. He gave it [the ring] to my friend. 14. He gave her the ring. 15. He has already given it to her. 16. If we may use a pencil, we shall be able to write faster tomorrow. 17. Did you see my new knife? 18. We have been studying German about seven or eight months. 19. I know you have not forgotten me. 20. He must have done it. 21. He wrote you he had fallen from a horse. 22. I have never heard her sing. 23. She claimed she could speak English well. (*Verbal idea:* to speak English.) 24. Every morning August drove the only sheep of the family into the forest. 25. I have been looking the whole day, but I cannot find my money.

III

Übersetzen Sie folgende Wörter:

gering	lehren	die Bohne	die Beere	der Laden
entlang	leiten	braten	das Geschäft	die Lampe
der Enkel	begegnen	brav	das Heft	der Marsch
Juni	begleiten	der Brunnen	das Gemüse	stolz
der Leib	bilden	bedeuten	der Kuchen	wirken

IV

Übersetzen Sie folgende Wörter:

the brother	to pay	perfect
May	the tooth	completely
the mouse	twenty	the vest
the punishment	thirty	to weigh
to strike	important	neither . . . nor
the wall	round	the straw
the root	the salt	at the same time

V

Übersetzen Sie folgende Zusammensetzungen, Wortbildungen und Redensarten:

Wir wohnen in der Kaiserstraße; Deutschland war früher ein Kaiserreich; die deutsche Kaiserkrone, die kaiserlichen Prinzen; in vielen Eisenbahnwagen haben die Sitzplätze rechts und links eine Armlehne; für manche Zwecke gebraucht man gern einen Stuhl ohne Rückenlehne; man muß sich nicht gegen eine Wand lehnen, solange die Farbe (paint) noch naß (wet) ist; der Kronprinz; und dann heiratete der Prinz die Prinzessin, und sie lebten glücklich bis an ihr Ende; schwesterliche Liebe; ein vom Englischen ins Deutsche übersetztes Buch; das Tragen von Schußwaffen ist nicht erlaubt; jemand bewaffnen, jemanden entwaffnen, bewaffnet oder unbewaffnet sein, leicht- oder schwerbewaffnet sein; der Waffenstillstand wurde am 11. November unterzeichnet (signed); der Tierarzt, eine Kinderärztin; für oder gegen jemanden zeugen; seine Tat zeugt von Mut; ein gutes Zeugnis in der Schule bekommen; jemand nicht achten, sondern verachten; mehrere Brücken verbinden die beiden Stadtteile; die Eisenbahnverbindung zwischen den beiden Städten ist schlecht; die Zeit verging wie im Fluge; ihm sind zwei Finger erfroren; einem Arbeiter den Lohn erhöhen; ein Buch aus dem Urtext übersetzen, die Urgeschichte der Menschheit, der Urstamm, der Urzustand; der Donner, der Tag, Donnerstag; das Flachland; körperliche Kraft; die Krankheit; der Brudermord; zuckerig

VI

Conjugate in the present tense:

finden	verlieren	müssen	lachen
abstoßen	fahren	arbeiten können	schlafen

VII

Give a synopsis in the third person singular indicative of the following verbs (thus: er hilft, er half, er hat geholfen, er hatte geholfen, er wird helfen):

machen	schweigen	mögen	halten	halten dürfen
gehen	schwimmen	kaufen	dürfen	aufstehen

VIII

Translate the following sentences containing participial phrases:
1. Die etwa zwei Eisenbahnstunden westlich von Nürnberg liegende Stadt Rothenburg hat heute noch eine schöne alte Stadtmauer. 2. Durch genaue Beobachtung der zum Futterplatz kommenden Bienen läßt sich beweisen, daß staatenbildende Insekten einen mit erstaunlicher (astonishing) Präzision arbeitenden Zeitsinn haben. 3. Trotzdem Fische während ihres ganzen Lebens nicht aufhören (cease, stop) zu wachsen, ist eine genaue Bestimmung des von einem einzelnen Fisch erreichten Alters (age) mit den größten Schwierigkeiten verbunden. 4. Die höchsten Eierpreise werden nicht etwa für frische Eier bezahlt, sondern für die vor vielen Millionen von Jahren gelegten Eier der heute ausgestorbenen Dinosaurier.

LESSON XXIV

TEXT A*

Scheiden. Scheiden ist sozusagen das Gegenteil von „zusammengehören" oder von „zusammenbringen". Eheleute, die nicht mehr zusammenleben wollen, lassen sich daher scheiden. Ihn nennt man dann einen geschiedenen Mann und sie eine geschiedene Frau. Beide aber müssen früher oder später aus dem Leben scheiden. Frauen leben meist länger als Männer. Und daher steht dann eines Tages in der Zeitung: „Mein heißgeliebter Mann, unser guter, treusorgender Vater, unser lieber Großvater, Bruder und Onkel ist nach langem, schwerem Leiden in Frieden verschieden. Die Beerdigung findet am Freitag statt (stattfinden to take place).—Die trauernden Hinterbliebenen."

Am Grabe nimmt die Frau weinend für immer Abschied. Sie ist inzwischen vernünftiger geworden und beurteilt viele Dinge jetzt anders als früher—auch ihren verschiedenen Mann. Den Nachbarn entgeht (entgehen to escape) der Unterschied zwischen ihrem früheren und ihrem jetzigen Urteil nicht; und wirklich sind die beiden Urteile so verschieden, daß man die Verschiedenheit einfach nicht übersehen kann. Die Nachbarn aber sagen: „Jetzt ist es zu spät. Sie hätte früher Wichtiges von Unwichtigem unterscheiden lernen sollen. Denn nur ihre geringe Unterscheidungsgabe hat das Unglück über sie gebracht. Es ist nun einmal so, daß sich in der Ehe sehr oft Menschen von ganz verschiedenartigem Charakter zusammenfinden, und daher kommen dann und wann auch einmal Meinungsverschiedenheiten vor. Man muß dafür sorgen, daß sie nicht zu einer Scheidewand werden, die das Zusammenleben unmöglich macht.

Der Schatz. Ein Schatz ist immer etwas Wertvolles. Und daher nennt ein junger Mann, der seine Freundin für einen Schatz hält, der sie mit

---

*From the few examples in this Text A the student can gain an idea of the vast number of words which can be formed from the one thousand words introduced in this book. The importance of reading intelligently for context and not for single words will at once become apparent from this text. The Passive Vocabulary, which has purposely been kept small, should not be consulted until the student has made a serious attempt to understand the text without its aid.

anderen Worten also schätzt, diese Freundin oft kurz—und manchmal mit Recht—„Schätzchen". „Schätzen" heißt also soviel wie „das Wertvolle oder den Wert in einer Sache erkennen." Dabei kommt es oft vor, daß man eine Sache unter- oder überschätzt. Besonders überschätzen sich die Menschen gerne selbst und leiden dann an Selbstüberschätzung. Wer reif und ver- 5 nünftig ist und sich während eines langen Lebens einen reichen Schatz von Erfahrungen hat sammeln können, macht selten einen solchen Fehler.

Manche indische (Indian) Fürsten hatten Edelsteine (precious stones) von unschätzbarem Wert.—Eisen, Silber, Kohlen, Gold und Petroleum sind Bodenschätze (Boden ground).—Staaten hatten früher oft einen 10 Staatsschatz. Heute haben sie meist nur Schulden.

Die Sache. Der Weihnachtsmann bringt den Kindern Spielsachen. Für die Kleinen ist das beim Weihnachtsfest die Hauptsache. Wenn sich ein Reicher ein Auto kauft, so ist der Preis Nebensache. Für einen Armen ist er die Hauptsache. Nebensächliche Dinge soll man nicht wichtig nehmen. Eine 15 gute Kritik soll sich von allem Persönlichen fernhalten und nur die Sache oder das Objekt selbst beurteilen. Mit anderen Worten: eine Kritik soll sachlich, nicht unsachlich sein. Wir alle sollten nach strenger Sachlichkeit in unseren Urteilen streben.—Daß du ihm Hilfe versprochen hast, ist eine Tatsache (fact); daß du dein Versprechen erfüllst, ist Ehrensache. 20

BUILDING A PASSIVE VOCABULARY

scheiden der Abschied the leave, farewell, geschieden divorced, unterscheiden to distinguish (between), der Unterschied the difference, verschieden different, verschieden (*as past part. in Text A*) passed away, die Verschiedenheit the difference

die Sache die Hauptsache the main, chief thing, die Nebensache the thing of minor, *or* less importance, side issue, subordinate matter, sachlich, objective, die Sachlichkeit the objectivity

VOCABULARY

die Bahn, -en the railroad; road
die Bank, -en the *bank*
der Koffer, - the trunk, suitcase
loben to praise
die Mühle, -n the *mill*
der Ruhm the fame, glory
senden to *send*
der Regenschirm, -e the umbrella
der Sonnenschirm, -e the parasol
der Zug, ⸗e the train; procession

TEXT B

Psyche

[Schluß]

Es war Winter gewesen und Frühling geworden; aber auch der und der halbe Sommer waren schon dahingegangen; die Linden auf der breiten Mühlenstraße in der Hauptstadt verloren schon einzelne Blätter. Statt der Natur, die hier so früh schon ihre Schönheit zurückzog, hatte die Kunst ihre Schätze ausgebreitet. Es war das Jahr der Kunstausstellung; die Türen des Akademiegebäudes gegenüber der Stadtbank hatten schon seit einigen Wochen dem Publikum[1] offengestanden.

Unter den Werken der Bildhauerkunst[2] war es besonders eine Marmorgruppe[3] in halber Lebensgröße, welche bei jung und alt großes Interesse hervorrief. Ein junger Stromgott, an abfallendem Ufer emporsteigend, hielt eine reizende Mädchengestalt auf seinen Armen. Trotz des zurückgesunkenen Hauptes und der geschlossenen Augen der letzteren sah man die Menschen leise an das Bild herantreten, als ob sie in jedem Augenblick den ersten neuerwachten Atemzug in der jungen Brust erwarten müßten. „Die Rettung der Psyche" stand hinter der Nummer des Werkes im Katalog.

Der Name des noch jungen Künstlers ging von Mund zu Mund; stets stand eine Menge von Bewunderern um das Werk herum, die nicht müde wurden, die Gruppe zu loben.

Aber wie es so oft geschieht, nachdem man genug bewundert hatte, entdeckte der eine oder der andere dann auch wohl etwas, was ihm nicht gefiel. Besonders das Herabhängen des einen Armes der Psyche fand man zu naturalistisch.[4]

„Aber, ihr Männer, könnt ihr denn gar nicht sehen?" rief eine hellblickende Dame, die, vor dem Kunstwerk stehend, eben ein solches Urteil hörte; „dieser schöne Arm ist eine Reminiszenz! Glauben Sie mir, das da hat seine lebendige Geschichte, die Gruppe[3] ist ein Denkmal[5]; vielleicht . . ."

„Auf dem Grabe einer Liebe?"

„Vielleicht! Wer weiß!"

„Aber dann wären wir ja mit aller Kritik[6] am Ende!"

„Ich dächte, ja!"

Indessen stand der Künstler selber vor dem Fenster seiner Werkstatt und blickte durch die Bäume ins Feld hinaus. Es stand jetzt kein Wintermorgenrot am Horizont; der Himmel war eintönig weiß von der Mittagssonne des Spätsommers.

In seinen Gedanken wiederholte sich ein Gespräch, das er in den letzten Tagen mit seiner Mutter gehabt hatte. „Du solltest ein wenig reisen, Franz", hatte sie gesagt; „du bist ermüdet von der Arbeit."—„Ja, ja, Mutter", hatte er erwidert, „es mag sein."—„Und ich hoffe, du fängst nicht nach deiner Art gleich etwas Neues an."—„Meinst du? Aber mir ist im Gegenteil, es wäre vielleicht das Beste."—Fast ein wenig böse war die Mutter geworden. „Was redest du denn, Franz! Du widersprichst dir selbst."—„Sorge nicht, Mutter! Ich kann nichts Neues machen."—Es war ein so seltsamer Ton gewesen, womit er das gesprochen; die kleine Frau hatte sich an seinen Arm gehangen: „Aber mein Sohn, du suchst mir etwas zu verbergen!"—Und liebevoll zu ihr niederblickend, hatte er erwidert: „Für wen, als für dich, Mutter, habe ich zuerst das Tuch von meiner Psyche aufgehoben? Laß auch dies hier in meiner Brust noch eine kurze Zeit bedeckt, so lange nur, bis ich weiß, ob es Gestalt gewinnen kann. Wenn nicht . . ." Er hatte den Satz nicht beendet; aber die beiden Arme der Mutter hatten den großen Mann umfangen. „Vergiß es nicht, daß du noch immer unter meinem Herzen liegst!"—Ein paar Tränen[7] hatte sie sich abgetrocknet; dann aber hatten ihre Augen ganz mutig zu ihm aufgeblickt. „Aber du mußt dennoch reisen, Franz! Dein Freund da unten an der Nordsee hat eine fröhliche Natur; eine Woche bei ihm täte dir gut; er hat dich ja schon wieder dringend gebeten, ihn doch zu besuchen."

Der Sohn hatte nicht geantwortet, er hatte es vor plötzlichem gewaltigem Herzklopfen nicht gekonnt; aber noch am selben Tage hatte er einen Brief an seinen Freund gesandt.

Die Antwort darauf konnte er heute schon erwarten. Und jetzt wurde die Tür geöffnet. Da war der Brief. Die großen, geraden Buchstaben ließen keinen Zweifel: er war von Ernst!

„Ich wußte wohl", so schrieb der junge Baron, „daß Du kommen würdest.—Seitdem Dein Bild[8] die Stille Deiner Werkstatt verlassen hat, wächst in Dir das Verlangen, sie, Deine Gerettete, wiederzusehen. Nun streckst Du nach der Lebendigen Deine Arme aus; das ist so natürlich, daß jeder Arzt es Dir vorausgesagt hätte.

Deine Frage, ob Du unerkannt ihr würdest nahen können, ob die Gewalt der Wellen ihr damals tief genug die hellen Augen geschlossen hat,—diese Frage kann ich nicht beantworten.

Dein Zimmer und Freundeshände sind für Dich bereit. Aber Franz— und jetzt höre mich ruhig an!—die Rettung einer gewissen jungen Dame
5 durch einen fremden Künstler ist hier inzwischen doch bekannt geworden; wie, das weiß ich nicht, denn die alte Bade-Kathi sieht mir nicht aus wie eine Schwätzerin.[9] Aber die Leute wissen es, wissen es wirklich; sie reden davon, alle und überall; nur Deinen Namen weiß man nicht.

Hundert Hände griffen nach Deinem schönen Schmetterling[10]; und da
10 ist er dann einfach davongeflogen; wohin, das kann ich Dir nicht sagen."

Schon längere Zeit hatte die Mutter vor dem Lesenden gestanden und ihm in das heiße Gesicht geblickt. Jetzt wandte er ihr langsam seine Augen zu.

„Ich werde meine Psyche von der Ausstellung zurückziehen", sagte er
15 traurig, „und dann, Mutter, reise ich; aber nicht nach der Stadt an der Nordsee."

Die Sonne stand am folgenden Tage noch nicht hoch am Himmel, als der junge Künstler schon unter den Linden der Hauptstadt dem Akademiegebäude zueilte.

20 So viel war sicher, er wollte fort, wollte ganz mit sich allein sein; kein Sohn einer Mutter, kein Freund eines Freundes. Er dachte an den Schwarzwald, in dessen Schatten er sich einmal mit seinem Freunde einen Sommermonat lang verloren. Seine Koffer hatte er schon zur Bahn bringen lassen; aber ehe er mit dem Mittagszug nach Süden fuhr, wollte er noch
25 einmal seine Psyche sehen und dann einem diensteifrigen Freunde alles überlassen, was zur Zurückziehung des Werkes nötig war.

Die Räume des Akademiegebäudes waren zwar schon offen, aber die gewöhnliche Stunde des Besuches war noch nicht gekommen; in den unteren Räumen, wo die Werke der Bildhauerkunst aufgestellt waren, schien noch
30 alles leer.

Und doch war der junge Bildhauer nicht der erste, der in die unteren Räume trat. Mit leisem Schritt war ein früher Besucher in den letzten der drei Räume getreten, gerade als der Künstler die große Tür des Haupteingangs hinter sich schloß. Auch er ging mit leisem Tritt, als fürchte er, das
35 Echo zu wecken,[11] das nur leicht in diesen Räumen schlief.

Sein eigenes Werk war im letzten Raum aufgestellt. Es schien ihm plötzlich, als könne die Gruppe in dieser lautlosen Stille nicht toter Marmor[3] geblieben sein, ja fast, als müsse er durch die offene Tür das Atmen des schönen Steines hören können.

Da schlug von dort ein leiser Klagelaut ihm an das Ohr; schnell war er in die Tür getreten; aber er kam nicht weiter. Dort an einer der großen Säulen,[12] welche hier die Decke tragen, lehnte ein Mädchen, wie in sich zusammenbrechend, und sah mit aufgerissenen Augen auf seine Marmorgruppe; ein kleiner Sonnenschirm, ein Sommerhut lagen am Boden neben ihr.

Nun wandte sie den Kopf und ihre Augen trafen sich. Es war nur wie ein Blitz, der zwischen ihnen aufleuchtete; aber das schöne, ihm zugewandte Mädchengesicht war von einem Ausdruck des Schreckens wie versteinert. Den schlanken Körper wie zur Flucht gebogen, und doch mit niederhängenden Armen, stand sie da; nur ihre Augen irrten jetzt umher, als ob sie einen Ausgang suchten.

Aber dort in der Tür, die allein zur Freiheit führte, stand er, dem—seit wie lange schon!—selbst ihre Gedanken zu entfliehen strebten; zwar, wie sie selbst, noch immer unbeweglich, aber seine Arme waren nach ihr ausgestreckt.

Noch einmal wagte sie, ihn anzublicken; dann, wie ein ratloses Kind, verbarg sie das Gesicht in ihren Händen; all ihr Mut hatte sie verlassen.

„Psyche, süße Psyche!"—Und an beiden Händen hielt er sie gefangen.

Sie bog den Kopf zurück; ihre Augen schlossen sich wie untergehende Sterne. Er ließ sie nicht; er hob sie auf seine Arme; er bog den Mund zu ihrem kleinen Ohre nieder, und leise, aber mit einer Stimme, die vor übergroßer Freude zitterte, sprach er, was er einst nur fern von ihr gedacht: „Nun laß ich dich nicht mehr; ich gebe dich an keinen Gott heraus!"

Seine Augen ruhten auf dem süßen Gesicht, das sie noch immer mit geschlossenen Augen ihm entgegenhielt.[13] Nun aber schlug sie die Augen leise auf; erst noch ein wenig zurückhaltend, dann immer vertrauender blickte sie ihn an, und immer sonniger wurde der Ausdruck ihres lieblichen Gesichtes.

Wie lange er sie so an seiner Brust gehalten?—Wer könnte es sagen!—Ein Vogel, der von draußen aus den Lindenbäumen gegen die Fenster flog, brachte den ersten Laut der Außenwelt zu ihren Ohren.

„Aber du!" sagte er—und es war, als wenn er plötzlich mit Verwunderung sie ansah—„wie bist du nur hierhergekommen?"

„Das da", sagte sie, „ich mußte es allein sehen, ehe die andern mit mir kamen. Mich trieb eine Angst—nein, frag mich nicht! Ich weiß nicht was! Aber hier hab' ich mich sehr gefürchtet."

„Welche andern?" fragte er.

5 „Die mit mir sind: mein Onkel und meine Mutter. Ich war mit ihnen oben in den anderen Räumen; ganz heimlich bin ich ihnen fortgelaufen. Aber", rief sie lachend, „wie heißt du denn? Ich weiß nicht eimal deinen Namen!"

„Ja, rat einmal!"

10 „Nein, rate du zuerst!"

„Ich, was soll ich raten?"

„Was du raten sollst? Als ob ich keinen Namen hätte!"

„Aber den kenne ich ja längst!" Er strich das blonde Haar ihr von der Stirn. „Sieh nur hin! Das bist du ja! Und glaub es nur, ich habe jeden 15 Tag zu dir gesprochen in all der langen, langen Zeit."

Von dunklem Rot übergossen legte sie die Hände um seinen Hals und ließ ihn tief in ihre Augen blicken. „O, welch ein Glück, daß du der Künstler bist!"

Mit beiden Armen umfing er die Geliebte und küßte zum ersten Male den 20 jungen Mund.—Dann aber sagten sie sich ganz leise, als seien es Geheimnisse, die selbst die steinernen Gestalten um sie her nicht wissen dürften, ihre Namen; und er konnte es nicht verstehen, daß sie „Maria" hieß.

Es war ihm, als höre er in weiter Ferne das Wellenrauschen der Nordsee. Und auch die Geliebte schien er mit sich dahin gezogen zu haben; denn sie 25 wandte plötzlich den Kopf zu ihm empor und sagte: „Aber du, die alte Bade-Kathi muß doch mit zu unserer Hochzeit!"[14]

Da löste sich die Stille in ein frohes Lachen des Glücks; am Himmel draußen stand in vollem Glanze die Sonne, noch immer die Sonne Homers,[15] und schien wieder einmal auf ein junges aufblühendes Menschenpaar.

NOTES. 1. Publikum public. 2. Bildhauer sculptor. 3. Marmor, marble; Gruppe, group; Marmorgruppe, marble group, statue. 4. naturalistisch naturalistic. 5. Denkmal monument, memorial. 6. Kritik criticism. 7. Tränen tears. 8. Bild work of art, statue. 9. Schwätzerin gossip. 10. Schmetterling butterfly. 11. wecken awaken. 12. Säulen pillars. 13. entgegenhielt turned to. 14. Hochzeit wedding. 15. Homers of Homer.

LESSON XXIV

BUILDING A PASSIVE VOCABULARY

anhören zuhören
aufblühen sich blühend öffnen, aufblühend promising
aufleuchtete (cf. **Licht**) flashed
der Ausdruck aus *Latin* ex, drücken to press, der Ausdruck the expression
der Ausgang aus *Latin* ex, gang *from* gehen to go, der Ausgang the exit
ausgebreitet aus out, breit broad, wide, ausbreiten to spread out
die Ausstellung aus *Latin* ex, stellen to place, put, die Ausstellung the exhibition, exposition
die Bewunderer, bewundert das Wunder the wonder, bewundern to admire, die Bewunderer the admirers, bewundert admired
der Eingang cf. Lesson XXIII
eintönig cf. Lesson XXI
die Flucht *noun in verb-noun pair to* fliehen
die Geheimnisse cf. Lesson XXIII
das Gespräch sprechen to speak, talk, das Gespräch the conversation
heimlich geheim secret, heimlich secretly, quietly
das Interesse interessant interesting, das Interesse the interest
inzwischen indessen
Klagelaut cf. **Laut**
die Kunstausstellung cf. Ausstellung
längst (*from* **lang**) long ago, long since
der Laut cf. Lesson XXI
löste sich lösen solve, dissolve
nahen nah close, nahen to approach
seltsam selten seldom, seltsam strange
sieht aus, aussehen to look, appear
umfangen, umfing um around, fangen to catch, umfangen to embrace
unerkannt cf. Lesson XXI
Verwunderung (cf. das Wunder) surprise
vorausgesagt, voraussagen voraus in advance, sagen to say, voraussagen to say in advance, to predict
die Werkstatt cf. Lesson XXIII
widersprichst cf. Lesson XXIII (wider is an inseparable prefix)
zurückziehen, die Zurückziehung zurück back, ziehen to pull, draw, zurückziehen to withdraw
zusammenbrechend zusammen together, brechen to break, zusammenbrechen to collapse

Learn the principal parts of senden:

wenden	wandte (wendete)	hat gewandt (gewendet)	to turn
senden	sandte (sendete)	hat gesandt (gesendet)	to send

EXERCISES

I

Beantworten Sie folgende Fragen über Text B auf deutsch: 1. Was verloren die Linden schon? 2. Was hatte die Kunst ausgebreitet? 3. Wer hielt eine reizende Mädchengestalt auf seinen Armen? 4. Wie traten die Menschen an das Bild heran? 5. Wie hieß die Marmorgruppe? 6. Was fand man an dem Bild zu naturalistisch? 7. Wo stand indessen der Künstler? 8. Wohin blickte er? 9. Mit wem hatte er in den letzten Tagen ein Gespräch gehabt? 10. Was hatte seine Mutter ihm gesagt? 11. Wer konnte jetzt nichts Neues machen? 12. Für wen hatte der Künstler zuerst das Tuch von seiner Psyche aufgehoben? 13. Wie blickte die Mutter zu ihrem Sohn hinauf? 14. Wo wohnte der Baron? 15. Worum hatte der Baron seinen Freund gebeten? 16. Warum antwortete der Künstler seiner Mutter nicht? 17. Wann hatte Franz einen Brief an seinen Freund gesandt? 18. Wann konnte er seine Antwort erwarten? 19. Woher wußte Franz, daß der Brief, der jetzt kam, von seinem Freunde war? 20. Was wußte der Baron? 21. Nach wem streckte der Künstler nun die Arme aus? 22. Was hatte Franz den Baron gefragt? 23. Was war in der kleinen Nordseestadt für Franz bereit? 24. Was ist in der Stadt inzwischen bekannt geworden? 25. Was wußten die Leute noch nicht? 26. Was wollte der Künstler von der Ausstellung zurückziehen? 27. Wie hatte der Brief auf ihn gewirkt? 28. Wann eilte Franz dem Akademiegebäude zu? 29. Mit wem wollte er reisen? 30. Woran dachte er? 31. Mit wem war er einmal einen Monat lang im Schwarzwald gewesen? 32. Was hatte er schon zur Bahn bringen lassen? 33. Wohin wollte er fahren? 34. Wann sollte der Zug abfahren? 35. Warum wollte er ins Akademiegebäude hineingehen? 36. Warum war in den Kunsträumen noch alles leer? 37. Wer war in den letzten der drei Räume getreten? 38. In welchem Raum war des Künstlers Werk aufgestellt? 39. Was schlug ihm ans Ohr? 40. Was lag auf dem Boden? 41. Was suchten die Augen des Mädchens? 42. Wie viele Türen führten zur Freiheit? 43. Wo verbarg das Mädchen ihr Gesicht?

44. Wessen Stimme zitterte? 45. Warum war das Mädchen allein in diesen Raum gekommen? 46. Wer war mit dem Mädchen gekommen? 47. Was sollte das Mädchen raten? 48. Wie sagten die beiden sich ihre Namen? 49. Warum konnte Franz nicht verstehen, daß das Mädchen Maria hieß? 50. Wer sollte mit zu der Hochzeit? 51. Wie war das Wetter draußen? 52. Worauf schien die Sonne?

II

Übersetzen Sie folgende Wörter:

durchaus	der Haufe	der Honig
darum	herrlich	klingeln
je deutlicher, desto besser	freilich	der Knochen
drucken	das Fach	notwendig
der Durst	erwähnen	die Reihe
brav	flach	rühren
die Grenze	ewig	der Tee
die Gunst	hohl	der Stoff

III

Übersetzen Sie folgende Wörter:

the bush	the loss	the sugar	to smell
thick	to hurt	the nut	envious
thousand	the weather	to test	the shoulder
proud	the root	the point	to disturb
to instruct	the dignity	the fool	the cow
to compose	the condition	the stove	the horse

IV

Übersetzen Sie folgende Wortbildungen, Zusammensetzungen und Redensarten:

der Befehlshaber eines Heeres; er ist ein guter Bergsteiger; der Bleistiftspitzer (instrument); der Messerschärfer (instrument); auf jedem Schlachtschiff gebraucht man einen Entfernungsmesser; der Hundefänger; die Musiklehrerin; die Kaiserin, die Fürstin; die Bäuerin; der Träumer, umhergehen wie ein Träumender; lohnende Arbeit finden; Gott ist allwissend; eine unbedeutende 5 Kleinigkeit; ein unerwarteter Besuch; ein nie aufgeklärtes Unglück; etwas

Gewesenes; eine unverkäufliche Ware; ein unvergeßlicher Abend; ein sehr achtbarer Bürger; das Glück unsrer Jugend ist unwiederbringlich verloren; in unermeßlicher Ferne; eine unbeweisbare Behauptung; eine unerfüllbare Forderung; die unverkennbaren Zeichen des herannahenden Alters (age); sich durch
5 einen künstlichen Bart unkenntlich machen; absichtlich; eine grünliche Farbe; rötliches Haar; göttliche Weisheit; erfolglose Wiederbelebungsversuche an einem Ertrunkenen machen; zu keiner Entscheidung kommen können; Einführung in die Psychologie; die Wegkrümmung; die Heiligsprechung der Jeanne d'Arc; langlebig; kampflustig; milchig; wollig; stumpfnäsig; nebelig; die Mathematik
10 glaubt nicht mehr an die Unendlichkeit des Raumes; seine kalten Hände erwärmen; nur für Erwachsene; einen Berg ersteigen; sich unnötig das Leben erschweren; er hat sich gestern erschossen; mit erneuter Kraft an die Arbeit gehen; ein vernichtendes Artilleriefeuer; die Abendsonne vergoldete den Gipfel des Berges; Tinte verfließt auf schlechtem Papier; eine Erinnerung aus verflossenen Tagen;
15 sein trauriges Ende hat seinen Ruhm nicht verdunkelt; erfrieren; ein Bienlein; die Eisenbahnbrücke

SELECTED POEMS

Mein

Du bist mein, ich bin dein,
Des[1] sollst du gewiß sein.
Du bist verschlossen
In meinem Herzen.
Verloren ist das Schlüsselein,[2]
Du mußt immer drinnen[3] sein.

—**Anonymous**

NOTES. 1. **Des = dessen** 2. **das Schlüsselein** small key. 3. **drinnen = darin.**

Heidenröslein[1]

Sah ein Knab' ein Röslein stehn,
Röslein auf der Heiden,
War so jung und morgenschön,
Lief er schnell, es nah zu sehn,
Sah's mit vielen Freuden.
Röslein, Röslein, Röslein rot,
Röslein auf der Heiden.

Knabe sprach: „Ich breche dich,
Röslein auf der Heiden!"
Röslein sprach: „Ich steche dich,
Daß du ewig denkst an mich,
Und ich will's nicht leiden."
Röslein, Röslein, Röslein rot,
Röslein auf der Heiden.

Und der wilde Knabe brach
's Röslein auf der Heiden;
Röslein wehrte sich[2] und stach,
Half ihm doch kein Weh und Ach,[3]
Mußt' es eben leiden.
Röslein, Röslein, Röslein rot,
Röslein auf der Heiden.

—**Goethe (1749–1832)**

NOTES. 1. **Heidenröslein** little rose on the heath. 2. **sich wehren** to defend oneself. 3. **Weh und Ach** cries of pain.

Gefunden

Ich ging im Walde
So für mich hin,[1]
Und nichts zu suchen,
Das war mein Sinn.

Im Schatten sah ich
Ein Blümchen stehn,
Wie Sterne leuchtend,[2]
Wie Äuglein schön.

Ich wollt' es brechen,
Da sagt' es fein:
„Soll ich zum Welken[3]
Gebrochen sein?"

Ich grub's mit allen
Den Würzlein aus,
Zum Garten trug ich's
Am hübschen[4] Haus.

Und pflanzt' es wieder
Am stillen Ort:
Nun zweigt es immer
Und blüht[5] so fort.

—Goethe

NOTES. 1. **So für mich hin: vor sich hingehen** just to walk along, stroll. 2. **leuchten** to shine. 3. **welken** to wither, wilt. 4. **hübsch** pretty. 5. **blühen** to bloom, blossom.

Es war ein alter König

Es war ein alter König,
Sein Herz war schwer, sein Haupt war grau;
Der arme alte König,
Er nahm eine junge Frau.

Es war ein schöner Page,
Blond war sein Haupt, leicht war sein Sinn;
Er trug die seidne[1] Schleppe[2]
Der jungen Königin.

Kennst du das alte Liedchen?
Es klingt so süß, es klingt[3] so trüb[4]!
Sie mußten beide sterben,
Sie hatten sich viel zu lieb.

—Heine (1797–1856)

NOTES. 1. **seidne** silken. 2. **die Schleppe** train (of dress). 3. **klingen** to sound. 4. **trüb** sad.

Wenn ich ein Vöglein[1] wär'

Wenn ich ein Vöglein wär',
Und auch zwei Flügel[2] hätt',
Flög' ich zu dir.
Weil's aber nicht kann sein,
Bleib' ich allhier.[3]

Bin ich gleich[4] weit von dir,
Bin ich doch im Schlaf bei dir,
Und red' mit dir.
Wenn ich erwachen[5] tu',
Bin ich allein.

Es vergeht[6] kein' Stund' in der Nacht,
Da nicht mein Herz erwacht,
Und an dich gedenkt,
Daß du mir viel tausendmal
Dein Herz geschenkt.

—Volkslied

NOTES. 1. **Das Vöglein = kleiner Vogel.** 2. **der Flügel** wing. 3. **allhier = hier** 4. **gleich = obgleich.** 5. **erwachen = wach werden.** 6. **vergehen** to pass.

Der Gast

Das Kind ist krank zum Sterben,
Die Lampe gibt trägen[1] Schein,
Die Mutter spricht: „Mir ist es,
Als wären wir nicht allein."

Der Vater sucht[2] zu lächeln,
Doch im Herzen pocht's[3] ihm bang[4];
Stiller wird's und stiller—
Die Nacht ist gar zu lang.

Nun scheint der Tag ins Fenster,
Die Vögel singen so klar;
Die beiden wußten lange,
Wer der Gast gewesen war.

—Fontane (1819–1898)

NOTES. 1. **träg(e)** dull, weak. 2. **sucht = versucht.** 3. **pochen** to pound. 4. **bang** (in) fear, dread.

Erlkönig[1]

Wer reitet so spät durch Nacht und Wind?
Es ist der Vater mit seinem Kind;
Er hat den Knaben wohl in dem Arm,
Er faßt ihn sicher, er hält ihn warm.

„Mein Sohn, was birgst[2] du so bang[3] dein Gesicht?" —
„Siehst, Vater, du den Erlkönig nicht?
Den Erlenkönig mit Kron' und Schweif[4]?" —
„Mein Sohn, es ist ein Nebelstreif.[5]" —

„Du liebes Kind, komm, geh' mit mir!
Gar schöne Spiele spiel' ich mit dir;
Manch bunte Blumen sind an dem Strand;
Meine Mutter hat manch gülden Gewand.[6]" —

„Mein Vater, mein Vater, und hörest du nicht,
Was Erlenkönig mir leise verspricht?" —
„Sei ruhig, bleibe ruhig, mein Kind;
In dürren[7] Blättern säuselt[8] der Wind." —

„Willst, feiner Knabe, du mit mir gehn?
Meine Töchter sollen dich warten[9] schön;
Meine Töchter führen den nächtlichen Reihn[10]
Und wiegen[11] und tanzen und singen dich ein.[11]" —

„Mein Vater, mein Vater, und siehst du nicht dort
Erlkönigs Töchter am düstern[12] Ort?" —
„Mein Sohn, mein Sohn, ich seh' es genau:
Es scheinen die alten Weiden[13] so grau." —

„Ich liebe dich, mich reizt deine schöne Gestalt;
Und bist du nicht willig,[14] so brauch' ich Gewalt!" ·
„Mein Vater, mein Vater, jetzt faßt er mich an!
Erlkönig hat mir ein Leids getan[15]!" —

Dem Vater grauset's,[16] er reitet geschwind,[17]
Er hält in den Armen das ächzende[18] Kind,
Erreicht den Hof mit Müh' und Not[19];
In seinen Armen das Kind war tot.

—Goethe

NOTES. 1. **Erlkönig** king of elves. 2. **bergen = verbergen.** 3. **bang** (in) fear. 4. **der Schweif** train. 5. **der Streif** streak, strip, patch. 6. **gülden Gewand** golden attire, raiment. 7. **dürr** dry, dead. 8. **säuseln** to rustle. 9. **warten** to attend, wait on. 10. **der nächtliche Reihen** nocturnal dance. 11. **wiegen . . . ein** rock you and dance you and sing you to sleep. 12. **düstern** dark. 13. **die Weide** willow. 14. **willig** willing. 15. **ein Leids tun** to harm. 16. **grausen** to shudder. 17. **geschwind** fast. 18. **ächzen** to moan, groan. 19. **mit Müh' und Not** with great difficulty.

APPENDIX I

Translations of Compounds and Derivatives

Translations of the most difficult compounds and derivatives in Exercise V of Lessons VIII, X–XXIII and Exercise IV of Lesson XXIV.

VIII

gefahrlos without danger, safe; die Windstille calm; der Augenblickserfolg momentary success; die Haustür *specifically* front door; das Handtuch towel; der Kopfarbeiter the head or brain or mental worker; der Machthaber ruler

X

die Stellung position; der Wortwechsel exchange of words, argument; ungerade not straight, crooked, odd; die Sonnenuhr sundial; der Reiseführer travel leader, guide; der Notfall case of emergency; das Muttergottesbild Madonna; die Menschwerdung Gottes war ein Wunder God's becoming a man was a miracle; das Hänschen little Hans; die Meinung opinion; die Verwandlung change, transformation; die Führung conduct, guidance, management, command; rede nicht beim Essen! don't talk while eating; er fiel beim Einsteigen ins Wasser while boarding (the ship) he fell into the water

XI

er fiel kopfüber ins Wasser he fell headfirst into the water; augenblicklich momentarily; unbeschreiblich schön indescribably beautiful; ein zusammenlegbares Bett a collapsible (folding) bed, cot; fraglich questionable, doubtful; dieses Kleid ist nicht käuflich this dress is not (buyable) for sale; unabwendbar inevitable; Hildegard traf Paul beim Wasserholen Hildegard met Paul while getting water

XII

das Taschentuch handkerchief; das Gesellschaftsspiel the party game

XIII

ein vielsagender Blick a very expressive or significant look or glance

XIV

die Heilsarmee Salvation Army; die Unschuld innocence

XV

die Baumart kind (species) of tree; der Befehlshaber one having command, commanding officer; die Brennbarkeit combustibility, inflammability; die Ehescheidung (marriage separation) divorce; ehelos unmarried, single; meterlang meter long

XVI

die Gewalttat deed, act of violence; herbeiholen bring here, go for; die Jahrhundertfeier century celebration, centennial; der Einzelkampf single combat

XVII

das Narrenhaus (fools' house) madhouse; amtlich official

XVIII

arbeitslos werden, das heißt brotlos werden to become unemployed means to become breadless; die Hausschuhe slippers; breitstirnig having a broad forehead

XIX

der Darsteller representer, actor; druckfertig ready to print (for the press); eine Erkältung haben to have a cold; zerfallen to fall to pieces, disintegrate, decompose

XX

Sturm und Regen nicht beachten to disregard storm and rain der Entscheidungskampf decisive battle; mit großer Entschiedenheit sprechen to speak with great decisiveness, firmness, determination; der Selbstmord suicide; einen Strom überbrücken to bridge a large river; das Eigelb egg yolk

XXI

die Regellosigkeit irregularity, disorderliness; nicht mehr in der Übung sein to be out of practice; ein zartfühlender Mensch a sensitive person; ein Fragezeichen a question mark; zuckerkrank diabetic; auf den Busch klopfen to beat around the bush

XXII

einen Rundgang durch die Stadt machen to take a sightseeing tour of the city; eine Rundreise tour; die Schlagsahne whipping cream; widersprich mir nicht! don't contradict me; du sollst mir nicht immer Widerworte geben you must not always contradict me; die Halsentzündung sore (inflammation of the) throat; Lungenentzündung pneumonia; unnahbar unapproachable, inaccessible; auf vereisten Straßen on icy streets; verjüngt und mit frischem Mut aus den Ferien wiederkommen to return from the vacation rejuvenated and with fresh (courage) spirits

XXIII

ein Stuhl ohne Rückenlehne a chair without a back; Schußwaffen (shooting weapons) firearms; der Waffenstillstand armistice

XXIV

der Befehlshaber commanding officer; der Entfernungsmesser range finder; etwas Gewesenes something that has been; unwiederbringlich irretrievably (*adv.*); unverkennbar unmistakable; sich durch einen künstlichen Bart unkenntlich machen to make oneself unrecognizable by means of an artificial beard; Einführung introduction; die Heiligsprechung canonization; Tinte verfließt auf schlechtem Papier ink spreads on poor paper; verflossen former, past

APPENDIX II*

Grammatical Paradigms

PERSONAL PRONOUNS

SINGULAR

	1st Pers.	2d Pers.	3d Pers. Masc.	3d Pers. Fem.	3d Pers. Neut.	3d Pers. Reflex.
NOM.	ich	du	er	sie	es	——
GEN.	——	——	——	——	——	——
DAT.	mir	dir	ihm	ihr	ihm	sich
ACC.	mich	dich	ihn	sie	es	sich

PLURAL

	1st Pers.	2d Pers.	3d Pers. (All Genders)	Polite Form	3d Pers. Reflex.
NOM.	wir	ihr	sie	Sie	——
GEN.	——	——	——	——	——
DAT.	uns	euch	ihnen	Ihnen	sich
ACC.	uns	euch	sie	Sie	sich

INDEFINITE PRONOUNS

SINGULAR

NOM.	man	niemand	jemand
GEN.	——	niemands	jemands
DAT.	einem	niemand(em)	jemand(em)
ACC.	einen	niemand(en)	jemand(en)

INTERROGATIVE PRONOUNS AND ADJECTIVES

SINGULAR

	M. F.	N.	M.	F.	N.
NOM.	wer	was	welcher	welche	welches
GEN.	wessen	——	(welches)	(welcher)	(welches)
DAT.	wem	——	welchem	welcher	welchem
ACC.	wen	was	welchen	welche	welches

PLURAL

			M.F.N.
NOM.	——	——	welche
GEN.	——	——	(welcher)
DAT.	——	——	welchen
ACC.	——	——	welche

was für +

NOM.	ein	eine	ein
GEN.	——	——	——
DAT.	einem	einer	einem
ACC.	einen	eine	ein

NOM.	Männer
GEN.	
DAT.	Männern
ACC.	Männer

(or any other noun in its proper case)

*Words in parentheses are rarely used. Endings in parentheses represent both optional and nonoptional variations.

APPENDIX II

Wer asks for persons only.

Was asks for things only.

Welcher, Welche, and **Welches** ask for specification of the following noun (which may be understood) and is declined like dieser.

Was für is indeclinable. It means *What kind of* and precedes either the indefinite article or a plural noun without article.

der-WORDS

SINGULAR

	M.	F.	N.	M.	F.	N.	M.	F.	N.
NOM.	der	die	das	dieser	diese	dieses	jeder	jede	jedes
GEN.	des	der	des	dieses	dieser	dieses	jedes	jeder	jedes
DAT.	dem	der	dem	diesem	dieser	diesem	jedem	jeder	jedem
ACC.	den	die	das	diesen	diese	dieses	jeden	jede	jedes

PLURAL

	M.F.N.	M.F.N.	M.F.N.
NOM.	die	diese	alle
GEN.	der	dieser	aller
DAT.	den	diesen	allen
ACC.	die	diese	alle

ein-WORDS

SINGULAR

	M.	F.	N.	M.	F.	N.	M.	F.	N.
NOM.	ein	eine	ein	kein	keine	kein	unser	unsere	unser
GEN.	eines	einer	eines	keines	keiner	keines	unseres	unserer	unseres
DAT.	einem	einer	einem	keinem	keiner	keinem	unserem	unserer	unserem
ACC.	einen	eine	ein	keinen	keine	kein	unseren	unsere	unser

PLURAL

				M.F.N.	M.F.N.
NOM.	——	——	——	keine	unsere
GEN.	——	——	——	keiner	unserer
DAT.	——	——	——	keinen	unseren
ACC.	——	——	——	keine	unsere

RELATIVE PRONOUNS

SINGULAR

	M.	F.	N.	M.	F.	N.	M.F.	N.
Nom.	der	die	das	welcher	welche	welches	wer	was
Gen.	dessen	deren	dessen	——	——	——	wessen	——
Dat.	dem	der	dem	welchem	welcher	welchem	wem	——
Acc.	den	die	das	welchen	welche	welches	wen	was

PLURAL

	M.F.N.	M.F.N.
Nom.	die	welche
Gen.	deren	——
Dat.	denen	welchen
Acc.	die	welche

NOUNS AND THEIR DECLENSION

TABLE OF ENDINGS

	Class 1	Class 2	Class 3	Class 4
SINGULAR				
Nom.	——	——	——	——
Gen.	s	(e)s	(e)s	(e)n
Dat.	——	(e)	(e)	(e)n
Acc.	——	——	——	(e)n
PLURAL				
Nom.	—, ¨	-e, ¨e	¨er	(e)n
Gen.	—, ¨	-e, ¨e	¨er	(e)n
Dat.	-n, ¨n	-en, ¨en	¨ern	(e)n
Acc.	—, ¨	-e, ¨e	¨er	(e)n

PARADIGMS TO CLASS 1

[See also §§ 88--90]

SINGULAR

der Wagen	der Vogel	das Mädchen
des Wagens	des Vogels	des Mädchens
dem Wagen	dem Vogel	dem Mädchen
den Wagen	den Vogel	das Mädchen
das Fenster	die Mutter	die Tochter
des Fensters	der Mutter	der Tochter
dem Fenster	der Mutter	der Tochter
das Fenster	die Mutter	die Tochter

PLURAL

die Wagen	die Vögel	die Mädchen
der Wagen	der Vögel	der Mädchen
den Wagen	den Vögeln	den Mädchen
die Wagen	die Vögel	die Mädchen
die Fenſter	die Mütter	die Töchter
der Fenſter	der Mütter	der Töchter
den Fenſtern	den Müttern	den Töchtern
die Fenſter	die Mütter	die Töchter

PARADIGMS TO CLASS 2

[See also § 94]

SINGULAR

der Tag	der Baum	die Wand	das Wort
des Tages	des Baumes	der Wand	des Wortes
dem Tag(e)	dem Baum(e)	der Wand	dem Wort(e)
den Tag	den Baum	die Wand	das Wort

PLURAL

die Tage	die Bäume	die Wände	die Worte
der Tage	der Bäume	der Wände	der Worte
den Tagen	den Bäumen	den Wänden	den Worten
die Tage	die Bäume	die Wände	die Worte

NOTE. Masculine nouns of this class may or may not take umlaut. Feminine nouns of this class always take umlaut. Neuter nouns of this class never take umlaut.

PARADIGMS TO CLASS 3

[See also § 103]

SINGULAR	PLURAL	SINGULAR	PLURAL
der Mann	die Männer	das Haus	die Häuſer
des Mannes	der Männer	des Hauſes	der Häuſer
dem Mann(e)	den Männern	dem Haus(e)	den Häuſern
den Mann	die Männer	das Haus	die Häuſer

PARADIGMS TO CLASS 4

[See also § 109]

SINGULAR

die Dame	die Frau	der Menſch	der Knabe
der Dame	der Frau	des Menſchen	des Knaben
der Dame	der Frau	dem Menſchen	dem Knaben
die Dame	die Frau	den Menſchen	den Knaben

der Staat	das Auge	das Bett
des Staates	des Auges	des Bettes
dem Staat(e)	dem Auge	dem Bett(e)
den Staat	das Auge	das Bett

PLURAL

die Damen	die Frauen	die Menschen	die Knaben
der Damen	der Frauen	der Menschen	der Knaben
den Damen	den Frauen	den Menschen	den Knaben
die Damen	die Frauen	die Menschen	die Knaben

die Staaten	die Augen	die Betten
der Staaten	der Augen	der Betten
den Staaten	den Augen	den Betten
die Staaten	die Augen	die Betten

Like **der Staat** are declined

der Doktor, -s, -en; der Schmerz, -es, -en;
der Nachbar, -s, -n; der Bauer, -s, -n; der See, -s, -n.

Like **das Bett** and **das Auge** are declined

das Ohr das Hemd das Ende

Irregular in the singular are the following:

das Herz	der Herr
des Herzens	des Herrn
dem Herzen	dem Herrn
das Herz	den Herrn

ADJECTIVES

ADJECTIVE ENDINGS

	Strong Endings				Weak Endings			
	Singular			Plural (*all genders*)	Singular			Plural (*all genders*)
	Masc.	*Fem.*	*Neut.*		*Masc.*	*Fem.*	*Neut.*	
Nom.	er	e	es	e	e	e	e	en
Gen.	en	er	en	er	en	en	en	en
Dat.	em	er	em	en	en	en	en	en
Acc.	en	e	es	e	en	e	e	en

APPENDIX II

PARADIGMS

SINGULAR

NOM.	alter Mann	alte Frau	altes Haus
GEN.	alten Mannes	alter Frau	alten Hauſes
DAT.	altem Mann(e)	alter Frau	altem Haus(e)
ACC.	alten Mann	alte Frau	altes Haus

PLURAL

NOM.	alte Männer	alte Frauen	alte Häuſer
GEN.	alter Männer	alter Frauen	alter Häuſer
DAT.	alten Männern	alten Frauen	alten Häuſern
ACC.	alte Männer	alte Frauen	alte Häuſer

SINGULAR

NOM.	der alte Mann	die alte Frau	das alte Haus
GEN.	des alten Mannes	der alten Frau	des alten Hauſes
DAT.	dem alten Mann(e)	der alten Frau	dem alten Haus(e)
ACC.	den alten Mann	die alte Frau	das alte Haus

PLURAL

NOM.	die alten Männer	die alten Frauen	die alten Häuſer
GEN.	der alten Männer	der alten Frauen	der alten Häuſer
DAT.	den alten Männern	den alten Frauen	den alten Häuſern
ACC.	die alten Männer	die alten Frauen	die alten Häuſer

SINGULAR

NOM.	kein alter Mann	keine alte Frau	kein altes Haus
GEN.	keines alten Mannes	keiner alten Frau	keines alten Hauſes
DAT.	keinem alten Mann(e)	keiner alten Frau	keinem alten Haus(e)
ACC.	keinen alten Mann	keine alte Frau	kein altes Haus

PLURAL

NOM.	keine alten Männer	keine alten Frauen	keine alten Häuſer
GEN.	keiner alten Männer	keiner alten Frauen	keiner alten Häuſer
DAT.	keinen alten Männern	keinen alten Frauen	keinen alten Häuſern
ACC.	keine alten Männer	keine alten Frauen	keine alten Häuſer

THE CARDINAL NUMERALS

1 eins	6 sechs	11 elf	16 sechzehn
2 zwei	7 sieben	12 zwölf	17 siebzehn
3 drei	8 acht	13 dreizehn	18 achtzehn
4 vier	9 neun	14 vierzehn	19 neunzehn
5 fünf	10 zehn	15 fünfzehn	20 zwanzig

21 einundzwanzig	40 vierzig	100 hundert
22 zweiundzwanzig	50 fünfzig	101 hunderteins
23 dreiundzwanzig	60 sechzig	102 hundertzwei
30 dreißig	70 siebzig	111 hundertelf
31 einunddreißig	80 achtzig	121 hunderteinundzwanzig
32 zweiunddreißig	90 neunzig	135 hundertfünfunddreißig

199 hundertneunundneunzig	1001 tausendeins
200 zweihundert	1009 tausendneun
201 zweihunderteins	2000 zweitausend
267 zweihundertsiebenundsechzig	6843 sechstausendachthundertdreiundvierzig
300 dreihundert	100,000 hunderttausend
1000 tausend	1,000,000 eine Million

0 Null

0,34 Null Komma drei vier

THE ORDINAL NUMERALS

All ordinals are adjectives. Since uninflected forms do not occur, either the proper strong or the proper weak ending must be added to the forms of the following table:

1 erst-	8 acht-	20 zwanzigst-
2 zweit-	9 neunt-	23 dreiundzwanzigst-
3 dritt-	10 zehnt-	98 achtundneunzigst-
4 viert-	11 elft-	100 hundertst-
5 fünft-	12 zwölft-	101 hundertunderst-
6 sechst-	13 dreizehnt-	102 hundertundzweit-
7 sieb(en)t-	19 neunzehnt-	1000 tausendst-

THE FRACTIONAL NUMERALS

Fractional numerals are neuter nouns of the first class. The denominator is formed by adding **-el** to the corresponding ordinal. An exception is **die Hälfte.**

$\frac{1}{2}$ die Hälfte, ein halb-	$\frac{9}{10}$ neun Zehntel
$\frac{1}{3}$ ein Drittel	$\frac{3}{11}$ drei Elftel
$\frac{1}{4}$ ein Viertel	$\frac{6}{100}$ sechs Hundertstel
$\frac{2}{5}$ zwei Fünftel	$\frac{7}{1000}$ sieben Tausendstel

VERBS

sein	haben	werden

INDICATIVE

PRESENT

sein	haben	werden
ich bin	habe	werde
du bist	hast	wirst
er ist	hat	wird
wir sind	haben	werden
ihr seid	habt	werdet
sie sind	haben	werden

PAST

sein	haben	werden
ich war	hatte	wurde
du warst	hattest	wurdest
er war	hatte	wurde
wir waren	hatten	wurden
ihr wart	hattet	wurdet
sie waren	hatten	wurden

PRESENT PERFECT

sein	haben	werden
ich bin gewesen	habe gehabt	bin geworden
du bist gewesen	hast gehabt	bist geworden
er ist gewesen	hat gehabt	ist geworden
wir sind gewesen	haben gehabt	sind geworden
ihr seid gewesen	habt gehabt	seid geworden
sie sind gewesen	haben gehabt	sind geworden

PAST PERFECT

sein	haben	werden
ich war gewesen	hatte gehabt	war geworden
du warst gewesen	hattest gehabt	warst geworden
er war gewesen	hatte gehabt	war geworden

wir waren gewesen	hatten gehabt	waren geworden
ihr wart gewesen	hattet gehabt	wart geworden
sie waren gewesen	hatten gehabt	waren geworden

FUTURE

ich werde sein	werde haben	werde werden
du wirst sein	wirst haben	wirst werden
er wird sein	wird haben	wird werden
wir werden sein	werden haben	werden werden
ihr werdet sein	werdet haben	werdet werden
sie werden sein	werden haben	werden werden

FUTURE PERFECT

ich werde gewesen sein	werde gehabt haben	werde geworden sein

IMAGINATIVE SUBJUNCTIVE

PRESENT TIME

ich wäre	hätte	würde
du wärest	hättest	würdest
er wäre	hätte	würde
wir wären	hätten	würden
ihr wäret	hättet	würdet
sie wären	hätten	würden

PAST TIME

ich wäre gewesen	hätte gehabt	wäre geworden
du wärest gewesen	hättest gehabt	wärest geworden
er wäre gewesen	hätte gehabt	wäre geworden
wir wären gewesen	hätten gehabt	wären geworden
ihr wäret gewesen	hättet gehabt	wäret geworden
sie wären gewesen	hätten gehabt	wären geworden

FUTURE TIME

ich würde sein	würde haben	würde werden
du würdest sein	würdest haben	würdest werden
er würde sein	würde haben	würde werden

wir würden sein	würden haben	würden werden
ihr würdet sein	würdet haben	würdet werden
sie würden sein	würden haben	würden werden

SUBJUNCTIVE OF INDIRECT DISCOURSE

[Cf. 135]

PRESENT

ich sei	(habe)	(werde)
du seiest	(habest)	(werdest)
er sei	habe	werde
wir seien	——	——
ihr seiet	——	——
sie seien	——	——

PAST

ich sei gewesen	(habe gehabt)	sei geworden
du seiest gewesen	(habest gehabt)	seiest geworden
er sei gewesen	habe gehabt	sei geworden
wir seien gewesen	—— ——	seien geworden
ihr seiet gewesen	—— ——	seiet geworden
sie seien gewesen	—— ——	seien geworden

FUTURE

ich (werde sein)	(werde haben)	(werde werden)
du (werdest sein)	(werdest haben)	(werdest werden)
er werde sein	werde haben	werde werden
wir —— ——	—— ——	—— ——
ihr —— ——	—— ——	—— ——
sie —— ——	—— ——	—— ——

The Modals

INFINITIVE

können	wollen	mögen	sollen	dürfen	müssen

INDICATIVE

PRESENT

ich kann	will	mag	soll	darf	muß
du kannst	willst	magst	sollst	darfst	mußt
er kann	will	mag	soll	darf	muß
wir können	wollen	mögen	sollen	dürfen	müssen
ihr könnt	wollt	mögt	sollt	dürft	müßt
sie können	wollen	mögen	sollen	dürfen	müssen

PAST

ich konnte	wollte	mochte	sollte	durfte	mußte
du konntest	wolltest	mochtest	solltest	durftest	mußtest
er konnte	wollte	mochte	sollte	durfte	mußte
wir konnten	wollten	mochten	sollten	durften	mußten
ihr konntet	wolltet	mochtet	solltet	durftet	mußtet
sie konnten	wollten	mochten	sollten	durften	mußten

PRESENT PERFECT

ich habe
du hast
er hat
wir haben
ihr habt
sie haben

+ *either* { dependent infinitive + { können, wollen, mögen, sollen, dürfen, müssen } *or* { with dependent infinitive understood { gekonnt, gewollt, gemocht, gesollt, gedurft, gemußt }

PAST PERFECT

ich hatte
du hattest
er hatte
wir hatten
ihr hattet
sie hatten

+ *either* { dependent infinitive + { können, wollen, mögen, sollen, dürfen, müssen } *or* { with dependent infinitive understood { gekonnt, gewollt, gemocht, gesollt, gedurft, gemußt }

PAST PARTICIPLE

können	wollen	mögen	sollen	dürfen	müssen
gekonnt	gewollt	gemocht	gesollt	gedurft	gemußt

APPENDIX II

FUTURE

ich werde du wirst er wird wir werden ihr werdet sie werden	+ infinitive +	können	wollen	mögen	sollen	dürfen	müssen

FUTURE PERFECT

The future perfect is never used with the dependent infinitive expressed, and so the only forms which may occur are these:

ich werde gekonnt haben	ich werde gewollt haben	*etc.*
du wirst gekonnt haben	du wirst gewollt haben	*etc.*
etc.	*etc.*	

IMAGINATIVE SUBJUNCTIVE

PRESENT TIME

ich	könnte	wollte	möchte	sollte	dürfte	müßte
du	könntest	wolltest	möchtest	solltest	dürftest	müßtest
er	könnte	wollte	möchte	sollte	dürfte	müßte
wir	könnten	wollten	möchten	sollten	dürften	müßten
ihr	könntet	wolltet	möchtet	solltet	dürftet	müßtet
sie	könnten	wollten	möchten	sollten	dürften	müßten

PAST TIME

ich hätte du hättest er hätte wir hätten ihr hättet sie hätten	+ *either*	dependent infinitive +	können wollen mögen sollen dürfen müssen	*or* with dependent infinitive understood	gekonnt gewollt gemocht gesollt gedurft gemußt

FUTURE TIME

ich würde du würdest er würde wir würden ihr würdet sie würden	+ infinitive +	können	wollen	mögen	sollen	dürfen	müssen

SUBJUNCTIVE OF INDIRECT DISCOURSE

[Cf. § 135]

PRESENT

ich	könne	wolle	möge	solle	dürfe	müsse
du	könnest	wollest	mögest	sollest	dürfest	müssest
er	könne	wolle	möge	solle	dürfe	müsse
wir	——	——	——	——	——	——
ihr	——	——	——	——	——	——
sie	——	——	——	——	——	——

PAST

ich (habe)
du (habest)
er habe

wir ——
ihr ——
sie ——

+ *either* { dependent infinitive + { können, wollen, mögen, sollen, dürfen, müssen } *or* { with dependent infinitive understood { gekonnt, gewollt, gemocht, gesollt, gedurft, gemußt }

FUTURE

ich (werde)
du (werdest)
er werde

wir ——
ihr ——
sie ——

+ infinitive + können wollen mögen sollen dürfen müssen

The Strong Verb

In order to conjugate a strong verb, one has to know its principal parts. In the following table **schlagen** is taken as an example. Its principal parts are **schlagen, schlug, hat geschlagen, schlägt.**

ACTIVE	PASSIVE
PRESENT INFINITIVE	
schlagen	geschlagen werden
PAST INFINITIVE	
geschlagen haben	geschlagen worden sein

APPENDIX II

PRESENT PARTICIPLE

ſchlagend	——

INDICATIVE

PRESENT

ich ſchlage	ich werde geſchlagen
du ſchlägſt	du wirſt geſchlagen
er ſchlägt	er wird geſchlagen
wir ſchlagen	wir werden geſchlagen
ihr ſchlagt	ihr werdet geſchlagen
ſie ſchlagen	ſie werden geſchlagen

PAST

ich ſchlug	ich wurde geſchlagen
du ſchlugſt	du wurdeſt geſchlagen
er ſchlug	er wurde geſchlagen
wir ſchlugen	wir wurden geſchlagen
ihr ſchlugt	ihr wurdet geſchlagen
ſie ſchlugen	ſie wurden geſchlagen

PRESENT PERFECT

ich habe geſchlagen	ich bin geſchlagen worden
du haſt geſchlagen	du biſt geſchlagen worden
er hat geſchlagen	er iſt geſchlagen worden
wir haben geſchlagen	wir ſind geſchlagen worden
ihr habt geſchlagen	ihr ſeid geſchlagen worden
ſie haben geſchlagen	ſie ſind geſchlagen worden

PAST PERFECT

ich hatte geſchlagen	ich war geſchlagen worden
du hatteſt geſchlagen	du warſt geſchlagen worden
er hatte geſchlagen	er war geſchlagen worden
wir hatten geſchlagen	wir waren geſchlagen worden
ihr hattet geſchlagen	ihr wart geſchlagen worden
ſie hatten geſchlagen	ſie waren geſchlagen worden

FUTURE

ich werde schlagen	ich werde geschlagen werden
du wirst schlagen	du wirst geschlagen werden
er wird schlagen	er wird geschlagen werden
wir werden schlagen	wir werden geschlagen werden
ihr werdet schlagen	ihr werdet geschlagen werden
sie werden schlagen	sie werden geschlagen werden

FUTURE PERFECT

ich werde geschlagen haben	ich werde geschlagen worden sein
etc.	*etc.*

IMAGINATIVE SUBJUNCTIVE

PRESENT TIME

ACTIVE	PASSIVE
ich schlüge	ich würde geschlagen
du schlügest	du würdest geschlagen
er schlüge	er würde geschlagen
wir schlügen	wir würden geschlagen
ihr schlüget	ihr würdet geschlagen
sie schlügen	sie würden geschlagen

PAST TIME

ich hätte geschlagen	ich wäre geschlagen worden
du hättest geschlagen	du wärest geschlagen worden
er hätte geschlagen	er wäre geschlagen worden
wir hätten geschlagen	wir wären geschlagen worden
ihr hättet geschlagen	ihr wäret geschlagen worden
sie hätten geschlagen	sie wären geschlagen worden

FUTURE TIME

ich würde schlagen	ich würde geschlagen werden
du würdest schlagen	du würdest geschlagen werden
er würde schlagen	er würde geschlagen werden
wir würden schlagen	wir würden geschlagen werden
ihr würdet schlagen	ihr würdet geschlagen werden
sie würden schlagen	sie würden geschlagen werden

APPENDIX II

SUBJUNCTIVE OF INDIRECT DISCOURSE

[Cf. § 135]

ACTIVE	PASSIVE
PRESENT	
ich (schlage)	ich (werde geschlagen)
du (schlagest)	du (werdest geschlagen)
er schlage	er werde geschlagen
wir ——	wir —— ——
ihr ——	ihr —— ——
sie ——	sie —— ——
PAST	
ich (habe geschlagen)	ich sei geschlagen worden
du (habest geschlagen)	du seiest geschlagen worden
er habe geschlagen	er sei geschlagen worden
wir —— ——	wir seien geschlagen worden
ihr —— ——	ihr seiet geschlagen worden
sie —— ——	sie seien geschlagen worden
FUTURE	
ich (werde schlagen)	ich (werde geschlagen werden)
du (werdest schlagen)	du (werdest geschlagen werden)
er werde schlagen	er werde geschlagen werden
wir —— ——	wir —— —— ——
ihr —— ——	ihr —— —— ——
sie —— ——	sie —— —— ——

The Weak Verb

ACTIVE	PASSIVE
PRESENT INFINITIVE	
lieben	geliebt werden
PAST INFINITIVE	
geliebt haben	geliebt worden sein
PRESENT PARTICIPLE	
liebend	——

INDICATIVE

PRESENT

ich liebe
du liebst
er liebt

wir lieben
ihr liebt
sie lieben

ich werde geliebt
du wirst geliebt
er wird geliebt

wir werden geliebt
ihr werdet geliebt
sie werden geliebt

PAST

ich liebte
du liebtest
er liebte

wir liebten
ihr liebtet
sie liebten

ich wurde geliebt
du wurdest geliebt
er wurde geliebt

wir wurden geliebt
ihr wurdet geliebt
sie wurden geliebt

PRESENT PERFECT

ich habe geliebt
du hast geliebt
etc.

ich bin geliebt worden
du bist geliebt worden
etc.

PAST PERFECT

ich hatte geliebt
du hattest geliebt
etc.

ich war geliebt worden
du warst geliebt worden
etc.

FUTURE

ich werde lieben
du wirst lieben
etc.

ich werde geliebt werden
du wirst geliebt werden
etc.

FUTURE PERFECT

ich werde geliebt haben
du wirst geliebt haben
etc.

ich werde geliebt worden sein
du wirst geliebt worden sein
etc.

APPENDIX II

IMAGINATIVE SUBJUNCTIVE

ACTIVE	PASSIVE
PRESENT TIME	
ich liebte	ich würde geliebt
du liebtest	du würdest geliebt
etc.	*etc.*
PAST TIME	
ich hätte geliebt	ich wäre geliebt worden
du hättest geliebt	du wärest geliebt worden
etc.	*etc.*
FUTURE TIME	
ich würde lieben	ich würde geliebt werden
du würdest lieben	du würdest geliebt werden
etc.	*etc.*

SUBJUNCTIVE OF INDIRECT DISCOURSE

Endings exactly like those of **schlagen**

PRINCIPAL PARTS OF STRONG AND WEAK VERBS WITH VOWEL CHANGE

Infinitive	Past	Auxiliary, Past Participle	Third Person Singular	Meaning
anfangen	fing an	hat angefangen	fängt an	to begin
ankommen	kam an	ist angekommen	kommt an	to arrive
backen	backte	hat gebacken	bäckt	to bake
befehlen	befahl	hat befohlen	befiehlt	to command
beginnen	begann	hat begonnen	beginnt	to begin
beißen	biß	hat gebissen	beißt	to bite
bekommen	bekam	hat bekommen	bekommt	to receive, get
beweisen	bewies	hat bewiesen	beweist	to prove
biegen	bog	hat gebogen	biegt	to bend
binden	band	hat gebunden	bindet	to tie
bitten	bat	hat gebeten	bittet	to ask
bleiben	blieb	ist geblieben	bleibt	to stay
braten	briet	hat gebraten	brät	to roast
brechen	brach	hat gebrochen	bricht	to break
brennen	brannte	hat gebrannt	brennt	to burn

bringen	brachte	hat gebracht	bringt	to bring
denken	dachte	hat gedacht	denkt	to think
dringen	drang	iſt gedrungen	dringt	to penetrate
einſchlafen	ſchlief ein	iſt eingeſchlafen	ſchläft ein	to go to sleep
empfangen	empfing	hat empfangen	empfängt	to receive
empfehlen	empfahl	hat empfohlen	empfiehlt	to recommend
empfinden	empfand	hat empfunden	empfindet	to feel
entſcheiden	entſchied	hat entſchieden	entſcheidet	to decide
entſchließen	entſchloß	hat entſchloſſen	entſchließt	to decide
entſtehen	entſtand	iſt entſtanden	entſteht	to originate
erfahren	erfuhr	hat erfahren	erfährt	to learn
erziehen	erzog	hat erzogen	erzieht	to educate
eſſen	aß	hat gegeſſen	ißt	to eat
fahren	fuhr	iſt gefahren	fährt	to travel
fallen	fiel	iſt gefallen	fällt	to fall
fangen	fing	hat gefangen	fängt	to catch
finden	fand	hat gefunden	findet	to find
fliegen	flog	iſt geflogen	fliegt	to fly
fliehen	floh	iſt geflohen	flieht	to flee
fließen	floß	iſt gefloſſen	fließt	to flow
freſſen	fraß	hat gefreſſen	frißt	to eat (*of animals*)
frieren	fror	hat gefroren	friert	to freeze
geben	gab	hat gegeben	gibt	to give
gefallen	gefiel	hat gefallen	gefällt	to please
gehen	ging	iſt gegangen	geht	to go
gelingen	gelang	iſt gelungen	gelingt	to succeed
gelten	galt	hat gegolten	gilt	to be worth
genießen	genoß	hat genoſſen	genießt	to enjoy
geſchehen	geſchah	iſt geſchehen	geſchieht	to happen
gewinnen	gewann	hat gewonnen	gewinnt	to win
gießen	goß	hat gegoſſen	gießt	to pour
graben	grub	hat gegraben	gräbt	to dig
greifen	griff	hat gegriffen	greift	to grasp
halten	hielt	hat gehalten	hält	to hold
hängen	hing	hat gehangen	hängt	to hang
heben	hob	hat gehoben	hebt	to lift
heißen	hieß	hat geheißen	heißt	to be called
helfen	half	hat geholfen	hilft	to help
kennen	kannte	hat gekannt	kennt	to know

kommen	kam	ist gekommen	kommt	to come
lassen	ließ	hat gelassen	läßt	to let
laufen	lief	ist gelaufen	läuft	to run
leiden	litt	hat gelitten	leidet	to suffer
lesen	las	hat gelesen	liest	to read
liegen	lag	hat gelegen	liegt	to lie
messen	maß	hat gemessen	mißt	to measure
nehmen	nahm	hat genommen	nimmt	to take
nennen	nannte	hat genannt	nennt	to name
raten	riet	hat geraten	rät	to advise
reißen	riß	hat gerissen	reißt	to tear
reiten	ritt	ist geritten	reitet	to ride
riechen	roch	hat gerochen	riecht	to smell
rufen	rief	hat gerufen	ruft	to call
scheiden	schied	hat geschieden	scheidet	to separate
scheinen	schien	hat geschienen	scheint	to shine
schieben	schob	hat geschoben	schiebt	to shove
schießen	schoß	hat geschossen	schießt	to shoot
schlafen	schlief	hat geschlafen	schläft	to sleep
schlagen	schlug	hat geschlagen	schlägt	to hit
schließen	schloß	hat geschlossen	schließt	to close
schneiden	schnitt	hat geschnitten	schneidet	to cut
schreiben	schrieb	hat geschrieben	schreibt	to write
schreien	schrie	hat geschrie(e)n	schreit	to cry
schreiten	schritt	ist geschritten	schreitet	to stride
schweigen	schwieg	hat geschwiegen	schweigt	to be silent
schwimmen	schwamm	ist geschwommen	schwimmt	to swim
schwinden	schwand	ist geschwunden	schwindet	to disappear
sehen	sah	hat gesehen	sieht	to see
sein	war	ist gewesen	ist	to be
senden	sandte	hat gesandt	sendet	to send
singen	sang	hat gesungen	singt	to sing
sinken	sank	ist gesunken	sinkt	to sink
sitzen	saß	hat gesessen	sitzt	to sit
sprechen	sprach	hat gesprochen	spricht	to speak
springen	sprang	ist gesprungen	springt	to spring
stechen	stach	hat gestochen	sticht	to sting
stehen	stand	hat gestanden	steht	to stand
steigen	stieg	ist gestiegen	steigt	to climb

sterben	starb	ist gestorben	stirbt	to die
stoßen	stieß	hat gestoßen	stößt	to push
streichen	strich	hat gestrichen	streicht	to stroke
streiten	stritt	hat gestritten	streitet	to quarrel
tragen	trug	hat getragen	trägt	to carry
treffen	traf	hat getroffen	trifft	to hit
treiben	trieb	hat getrieben	treibt	to drive
treten	trat	ist getreten	tritt	to step
trinken	trank	hat getrunken	trinkt	to drink
tun	tat	hat getan	tut	to do
umgeben	umgab	hat umgeben	umgibt	to surround
verbergen	verbarg	hat verborgen	verbirgt	to hide
vergessen	vergaß	hat vergessen	vergißt	to forget
verlieren	verlor	hat verloren	verliert	to lose
verschwinden	verschwand	ist verschwunden	verschwindet	to disappear
versprechen	versprach	hat versprochen	verspricht	to promise
verstehen	verstand	hat verstanden	versteht	to understand
vorkommen	kam vor	ist vorgekommen	kommt vor	to happen
vorschlagen	schlug vor	hat vorgeschlagen	schlägt vor	to suggest
vorziehen	zog vor	hat vorgezogen	zieht vor	to prefer
wachsen	wuchs	ist gewachsen	wächst	to grow
wenden	wandte	hat gewandt	wendet	to turn
werden	wurde	ist geworden	wird	to become
werfen	warf	hat geworfen	wirft	to throw
wiegen	wog	hat gewogen	wiegt	to weigh
wissen	wußte	hat gewußt	weiß	to know
ziehen	zog	hat gezogen	zieht	to pull
ziehen	zog	ist gezogen	zieht	to move
zwingen	zwang	hat gezwungen	zwingt	to force

APPENDIX III

Review Lists of Words

These lists are for the convenience of students and teachers.

LESSONS I–III

aber	einfach	das Kleid	der Preis	viel
alle	erfahren	kommen	rechnen	viele
alles	fahren	können	recht	wach
allein	fast	kosten	reden	die Wand
alt	finden	lachen	die Reise	warten
an	fragen	lang	rot	warum
atmen	die Frau	laufen	sagen	was
auch	das Fräulein	legen	schlafen	das Wasser
auf	für	leider	der Schnee	weiß
auswendig	die Gans	leise	schon	wenn
bei	gar	lesen	schön	wer
bekommen	gebrauchen	das Mädchen	schreiben	werden
beobachten	gehen	man	schwer	wie
berichten	das Geld	die Mark	sehen	wieder
bestimmt	gewinnen	mehr	sein	wissen
das Bett	das Glas	meinen	sitzen	die Woche
beweisen	glauben	mögen	so	wohnen
bleiben	gut	müssen	sollen	wollen
der Bleistift	das Haar	nach	spät	das Wunder
brauchen	haben	natürlich	still	zahlen
bringen	der Herr	neben	das Stück	zeigen
das Buch	heute	neidisch	tun	die Zeitung
da	hier	nein	über	zu
dann	hoffen	nicht	übrigens	zufrieden
das	holen	nichts	die Uhr	zurück
denken	hören	noch	um	zwar
deutsch	immer	nun	und	zwischen
dicht	interessant	nur	das Urteil	
dünn	die Jugend	ob	vergessen	
dürfen	jung	oder	verstehen	
ein	kein	das Papier	versuchen	

LESSONS I–V

der Abend
aber
alle
allein
alles
also
alt
an
antworten
der Apfel
die Arbeit
arbeiten
arm
atmen
auch
auf
aus
außerdem
auswendig
bei
beißen
bekommen
beobachten
berichten
bestimmt
das Bett
beweisen
bleiben
der Bleistift
brauchen
bringen
das Buch
da
danken
dann
das
daß
dauern
denken
denn
deutsch
dicht
dieser
doch
dünn
dürfen
die Ecke
ehrlich
ein
einfach
eng
die Erbse
die Erde
erfahren
erzählen
essen
etwas
fahren
fast
das Feld
finden
fragen
die Frau
das Fräulein
der Freund
frisch
der Frühling
für
die Gans
ganz
gar
geben
gehen
gebrauchen
gefallen
der Gefallen
gehören
das Geld
genug
gerade
gern
das Geschäft
die Geschichte
das Gesicht
gewinnen
das Glas
glauben
gleich
glücklich
gut
das Haar
haben
halb
die Hälfte
halten
das Haus
der Held
der Herbst
der Herr
heute
heute abend
hier
hinter
der Hof
hoffen
holen
hören
hungrig
immer
in
interessant
ja
das Jahr
jeder
jemand
jener
die Jugend
jung
die Kartoffel
kaufen
kaum
kein
kennen
die Klasse
das Kleid
kommen
können
kosten
der Krieg
kurz
lachen
lang(e)
lassen
laufen
legen
leicht
leider
leise
lernen
lesen
lieben
liegen
machen
das Mädchen
man
mancher
der Mann
die Mark
mehr
meinen
mit
mögen
müssen
nach
nah
natürlich
neben
nehmen
neidisch
nein
nicht
nichts
noch
nun
nur
ob
oder
oft
ohne
das Papier
das Pferd
pflanzen
der Preis
rechnen
recht

reden
reisen
die Reise
riechen
riechen nach
rot
sagen
schlafen
der Schnee
schon
schön
schreiben
schwer
sehen
sein
seit
seitdem

sitzen
so
solcher
sollen
spät
spielen
stehen
still
der Strumpf
das Stück
der Student
studieren
der Teil
teilen
tun
über
übrigens

die Uhr
um
und
unter
das Urteil
vergessen
verlieren
verschwinden
verstehen
versuchen
viel
viele
vielleicht
von
vor
wach
wachsen

der Wald
die Wand
wann
warten
warum
was
das Wasser
der Weg
weinen
weiß
welcher
wenn
wer
werden
werfen
wie
wieder

wissen
wo
die Woche
wohin
wohnen
wollen
das Wunder
zahlen
zeigen
die Zeit
die Zeitung
zu
zufrieden
zurück
zwar
zwischen

LESSONS I–VIII

ab
der Abend
aber
alle
allein
alles
als
also
alt
an
ander
anders
antworten
der Apfel
die Arbeit
arbeiten
arm

die Art
atmen
auch
auf
das Auge
der Augenblick
aus
außer
außerdem
auswendig
die Bank
begegnen
behaupten
bei
beißen
bekommen
beobachten

berichten
besser
bestimmt
das Bett
beweisen
bezahlen
das Bild
binden
bis
bitten
blau
bleiben
der Bleistift
blicken
das Blut
der Boden
brauchen

brechen
bringen
das Buch
da
daher
damit
danken
dann
das
daß
dauern
denken
denn
derselbe
deutsch
dicht
dieser

doch
das Dorf
dünn
durch
dürfen
die Ecke
ehe
ehrlich
ein
einander
einfach
das Ende
endlich
eng
der Enkel
die Erbse
die Erde

erfahren
der Erfolg
ernst
erwarten
erzählen
essen
etwas
das Fach
fahren
der Fall
die Farbe
fast
der Feind
das Feld
das Fenster
fern
finden
der Fisch
fließen
folgen
fortsetzen
fragen
die Frau
das Fräulein
der Freund
frisch
früh
der Frühling
führen
für
fürchten
die Gans
ganz
gar
geben
gebrauchen

die Gefahr
gefallen
  der Gefallen
die Gegenwart
gehen
gehören
das Geld
genug
gerade
gern
das Geschäft
die Geschichte
das Gesicht
gewinnen
das Glas
glauben
gleich
glücklich
grün
grüßen
gut
das Haar
haben
der Hafen
halb
  die Hälfte
halten
die Hand
hart
das Haus
heben
heilig
heiß
der Held
helfen
hell

her
der Herbst
der Herr
das Herz
heute
hier
hin
hindern
hinter
der Hof
hoffen
holen
hören
hungrig
der Hut
immer
in
innen
interessant
ja
das Jahr
jeder
je . . . desto
jemand
jener
jetzt
die Jugend
jung
die Kartoffel
kaufen
kaum
kein
kennen
das Kind
die Klasse
das Kleid

klein
kommen
können
der Kopf
kosten
die Kraft
der Krieg
kurz
küssen
lachen
das Land
lang(e)
lassen
laufen
legen
leicht
leider
leise
lernen
lesen
lieben
liegen
los
-los
die Lösung
machen
die Macht
das Mädchen
man
mancher
der Mann
die Mark
der Markt
das Meer
mehr
meinen

der Mensch
mit
mögen
möglich
der Mond
morgen
  der Morgen
müssen
die Mutter
nach
die Nacht
nah
der Name
nämlich
natürlich
neben
nehmen
neidisch
nein
nennen
neu
nicht
nichts
noch
die Not
nun
nur
ob
obgleich
oder
öffnen
oft
ohne
das Papier
das Pferd
pflanzen

der Platz
plötzlich
der Preis
rechnen
recht
reden
reisen
die Reise
reizen
retten
richtig
riechen
riechen nach
der Rock
rot
der Rücken
sagen
scheinen
schenken
schieben
das Schiff
schlafen
schlagen
schlank
der Schnee
schnell
schon
schön
schreiben
schreien
die Schuld
schuldig
schwarz
schwer
sehen
sein
seit
seitdem
die Seite
selber
sinken
sitzen
so
solcher
sollen
sondern
die Sonne
sonst
spät
spielen
sprechen
springen
stehen
steigen
stellen
still
stoßen
die Straße
strecken
der Strumpf
das Stück
der Student
studieren
stürzen
suchen
der Tag
der Teil
teilen
tief
töten
tragen
treffen
treiben
trennen
treten
trotz
der Trotz
das Tuch
tun
die Tür
über
übrigens
die Uhr
um
und
unter
das Urteil
der Vater
verbergen
verdienen
vergessen
verkaufen
verlieren
verschwinden
verstehen
versuchen
verwandeln
viel
viele
vielleicht
von
vor
wach
wachsen
während
der Wald
die Wand
wann
warten
warum
was
das Wasser
wechseln
weder ... noch
der Weg
weil
weinen
die Weise
weiß
weit
welcher
wenden
wenn
wer
werden
werfen
wie
wieder
der Wind
wissen
wo
die Woche
wohin
wohnen
wollen
das Wort
das Wunder
zahlen
zeigen
die Zeit
die Zeitung
ziehen
zu
zufrieden
die Zukunft
zurück
zusammen
zwar
zwingen
zwischen

LESSONS I–XII

ab
der Abend
aber
ach
alle
allein
alles
als
also
alt
an
ander
anders
anfangen
ankommen

anstatt
antworten
der Apfel
der April
die Arbeit
arbeiten
arm
der Arm
die Art
der Arzt
atmen
auch
auf
das Auge
der Augenblick
der August
aus
außer
außerdem
auswendig
die Bank
der Bart
begegnen
behaupten
bei
beißen
bekommen
beobachten
berichten
besser
bestimmt
besuchen
das Bett
beweisen
bezahlen
das Bild
binden
bis
bitten
blau
bleiben
der Bleistift
blicken
das Blut
der Boden
böse
brauchen
brechen
bringen
der Brunnen
die Brust
das Buch
die Butter
der Charakter
da
daher
damit
danken
dann
das
daß
dauern
denken
denn
derselbe
deutlich
deutsch
der Dezember
dicht
dienen
der Dienstag
dieser
doch
der Donnerstag
das Dorf
drücken
dünn
durch
dürfen
eben
die Ecke
ehe
die Ehe
ehrlich
eigen
ein
einander
einfach
einzeln
einzig
das Eis
empfangen
das Ende
endlich
eng
der Enkel
entschließen
die Erbse
die Erde
erfahren
der Erfolg
erinnern an
sich erinnern an
erklären
ernst
erst
erwarten
erzählen
essen
etwa
etwas
ewig
das Fach
fahren
der Fall
fallen
die Familie
die Farbe
das Faß
fast
der Februar
fein
der Feind
das Feld
das Fenster
fern
fertig
fest
finden
der Fisch
fließen
folgen
fortsetzen
fragen
die Frau
das Fräulein
frei
der Freitag
fressen
sich freuen
der Freund
frisch
froh
früh

der Frühling
führen
für
fürchten
die Gans
ganz
gar
geben
gebrauchen
die Gefahr
gefallen
  der Gefallen
gegen
das Gegenteil
gegenüber
die Gegenwart
gehen
gehören
das Geld
genau
genug
gerade
gern
das Geschäft
die Geschichte
die Gesellschaft
das Gesicht
gewinnen
gewöhnlich
das Glas
glauben
gleich
glücklich
der Gott
greifen
groß

grün
der Grund
grüßen
gut
das Haar
haben
der Hafen
halb
  die Hälfte
halten
die Hand
hart
hassen
das Haus
heben
heilig
heiraten
heiß
heißen
der Held
helfen
hell
her
der Herbst
der Herr
das Herz
heute
hier
der Himmel
hin
hindern
hinter
hoch
der Hof
hoffen
holen

hören
hungrig
der Hut
immer
in
innen
interessant
irgend
ja
das Jahr
der Januar
jeder
je . . . desto
jemand
jener
jetzt
die Jugend
der Juli
jung
der Juni
der Kaffee
kalt
die Kartoffel
kaufen
kaum
kein
kennen
das Kind
die Kirche
klar
die Klasse
das Kleid
klein
kommen
können
der Kopf

kosten
die Kraft
der Krieg
die Krone
der Kuchen
kurz
küssen
lächeln
lachen
das Land
lang(e)
langsam
lassen
laufen
laut
leben
legen
leicht
leider
leise
lernen
lesen
letzt
lieben
liegen
die Linie
los
-los
die Lösung
der Löwe
die Luft
machen
die Macht
das Mädchen
der Mai
das Mal

man
mancher
der Mann
der Mantel
die Mark
der Markt
der März
das Meer
mehr
meinen
meist
der Meister
der Mensch
merken
mit
der Mittwoch
mögen
möglich
der Monat
der Mond
der Montag
morgen
der Morgen
der Mund
müssen
der Mut
die Mutter
nach
nachdem
die Nacht
nah
der Name
nämlich
die Nase
natürlich
neben

nehmen
neidisch
nein
nennen
neu
nicht
nichts
nicken
nie
niemand
noch
die Not
nötig
der November
nun
nur
ob
obgleich
oder
öffnen
oft
ohne
der Oktober
der Onkel
das Papier
die Person
der Pfennig
das Pferd
pflanzen
die Pflicht
der Platz
plötzlich
der Preis
rechnen
recht
reden

der Regen
reisen
die Reise
reizen
retten
richtig
riechen
der Rock
rot
der Rücken
rufen
ruhen
die Sache
sagen
der Samstag
das Schaf
scheinen
schenken
schicken
schieben
schießen
das Schiff
schlafen
schlagen
schlank
schließen
der Schmerz
der Schnee
schnell
schon
schön
der Schreck(en)
schreiben
schreien
die Schuld
schuldig

schwarz
schweigen
schwer
der See
die See
sehen
sehr
sein
seit
seitdem
die Seite
selber
der September
der Sieg
sinken
sitzen
so
soeben
sogar
sogleich
solcher
sollen
sondern
der Sonnabend
die Sonne
der Sonntag
sonst
spät
spielen
spitz
sprechen
springen
die Stadt
stark
statt
stehen

steigen
der Stein
stellen
sterben
still
die Stimme
stoßen
die Straße
strecken
der Strumpf
das Stück
der Student
studieren
die Stunde
der Sturm
stürzen
suchen
der Tag
die Tasche
die Tasse
der Teil
teilen
tief
der Tisch
die Tochter
töten
tragen
trauen
treffen
treiben
trennen
treten
trinken
trösten
trotz
der Trotz

das Tuch
tun
die Tür
über
überhaupt
übrigens
die Uhr
um
und
unter
das Urteil
der Vater
verbergen
verdienen
die Vergangenheit
vergessen
verkaufen
verlangen
verlieren
die Vernunft
verschwinden
versprechen
verstehen
versuchen
verwandeln
viel
viele
vielleicht
vollkommen
von
vor
vorbei
vorher
wach
wachsen
wagen
während
der Wald
die Wand
wann
warm
warten
warum
was
das Wasser
wechseln
weder . . . noch
der Weg
das Weib
weil
der Wein
weinen
die Weise
weiß
weit
welcher
wenden
wenig
wenn
wer
werden
werfen
wie
wieder
wiederholen
wild
der Wind
der Winter
wirken
wirklich
wissen
wo
die Woche
wohin
wohnen
wollen
das Wort
das Wunder
wünschen
zahlen
zählen
zeigen
die Zeit
die Zeitung
ziehen
zittern
zu
zufrieden
zuhören
die Zukunft
zurück
zusammen
zwar
zwingen
zwischen

GERMAN-ENGLISH VOCABULARY

This vocabulary aims to be complete with the following exceptions: words given in footnotes; words alike or very similar in both languages, e.g., **Thermometer, Intervall, Temperatur, Psychologie**; inflected forms, e.g., **geholfen, kälter;** compounds whose meanings may be understood when the component parts are known, e.g., **die Nordsee, der Sommerhut, abstoßen**; and some words occurring only in Exercise V of lessons beginning with Lesson VI.

Accents indicate the place of the *main* accent. Two accents on one word indicate that either syllable may be stressed without changing the meaning or the function of that word. The asterisk after words with two accents indicates a difference in function or meaning between the two possible accentuations, a discussion of which is beyond the scope of this book.

ab off; down; away
der Abend -s, -e evening
aber but, however; why (*cf.* § *22*)
abgeben. *See* **geben**
abhängig. *See* **hängen**
der Abschied. *See* **scheiden**
abschließen. *See* **schließen**
die Absicht —, -en intention; **ab′sicht′lich** intentional; **un′absichtlich** unintentional
absteigen. *See* **steigen**
abwechselnd. *See* **wechseln**
abwenden. *See* **wenden**
ach oh! ah! alas!
acht eight
achten to regard; **achten auf** to pay attention to; **achtlos** inattentive, absentminded, heedless(ly); **außer Acht lassen** to leave out of consideration; **un′beach′tet** unobserved; **verachten** to despise, scorn; **verächtlich** contemptuously, scornfully
achtzehn eighteen
achtzig eighty
der Acker -s, ⁓ field, tilled land
ähnlich similar
alle all; **ein Alltagsmenschenkind** a common mortal
allein′ alone; but
allerdings′ to be sure
allerlei. *See* **-erlei**
alles everything
der Allmächtige. *See* **die Macht**
als than; when; as; but
also therefore; thus; so; then; well (*cf.* § *22*)
alt old; **das Alter** age; **altehr′würdig** venerable. (*Cf.* **ehren** *and* **die Würde**)
das Amt -es, ⁓er office; duty
an on; at; near; of; for; to; in
der Anblick. *See* **blicken**
ander other, different; **ändern** to change; **anders** different; **verändern** to change; **die Veränderung** change
anfangen (fing an, angefangen, fängt an) to begin, start; do; **der Anfang** beginning; **anfangs** in the beginning
angehen. *See* **gehen**
der Angehörige. *See* **gehören**
angenehm agreeable, pleasant; **un′angenehm** disagreeable, unpleasant
das Angesicht. *See* **das Gesicht**
die Angst —, ⁓e anxiety; fear; **ängstlich** anxious, afraid
anhören. *See* **zuhören**
ankleiden. *See* **das Kleid**
ankommen (kam an, angekommen, kommt an) to arrive. *Cf. also* **kommen**

annehmen. *See* **nehmen**
ansehen. *See* **sehen**
antworten to answer; **die Antwort** answer; **beantworten** to answer, give answer to
anziehen. *See* **ziehen**
anzünden (*sep. prefix*) to light, ignite
der Apfel -s, ⸚ apple; **der Apfelkuchen** apple tart; **der Apfelwein** cider
die Apfelsi'ne —, -n orange
der April' -s April
arbeiten to work; **die Arbeit** work; **der Ar'beitge'ber** employer; **der Ar'beitneh'mer** employee; **arbeitslos** unemployed; **die Arbeitslosigkeit** unemployment
arm poor
der Arm -es, -e arm
die Art —, -en manner; sort, kind; **auf diese Art und Weise** in this way and manner
der Arzt -es, ⸚e physician
der Atem, der Atemzug. *See* **atmen**
atemlos. *See* **atmen**
atmen to breathe; **der Atem** breath; **atemlos** breathless; **der Atemzug** breath
auch too, also; either; even; **(auch wenn.** *See* **wenn)**
auf on, up, upon; at; to; in; open; out; for; **auf und ab** up and down, back and forth
aufblühen. *See* **blühen**
die Aufgabe —, -en lesson, assignment; duty, task
der Aufgang. *See* **gehen**
aufmachen (*sep. prefix*) to open
aufnehmen to take up, absorb. *See* **nehmen**
aufpassen (*sep. prefix*) to pay attention to; take care of
aufschlagen. *See* **schlagen**
aufschließen. *See* **schließen**
aufspringen. *See* **springen**
aufstehen. *See* **stehen**
das Auge -s, -n eye
der Augenblick -s, -e moment
der August' -s August
aus out of, from; of; for
ausbreiten. *See* **breit**
der Ausdruck. *See* **drücken**
ausdrücken. *See* **drücken**
der Ausgang. *See* **gehen**
ausgeben. *See* **geben**
ausruhen. *See* **ruhen**
ausschließen. *See* **schließen**
aussehen. *See* **sehen**
die Aussprache. *See* **sprechen**
aussprechen. *See* **sprechen**
außen outside; **draußen** out of doors
außer besides; except for; out of; outside of
au'ßerdem' moreover, besides
au'ßeror'dentlich* extraordinary
die Ausstellung. *See* **stellen**
ausstoßen. *See* **stoßen**
auswendig (learn *or* know) by heart
ausziehen. *See* **ziehen**

der Bach -es, ⸚e brook
die Backe —, -n cheek; **rotbäckig** red-cheeked
backen (backte, gebacken, bäckt) to bake
badelustig. *See* **die Lust**
baden to bathe
die Bahn —, -en railroad; road
bald soon; **bald . . . bald** now . . . now; **sobald** as soon as
das Band. *See* **binden**
die Bank —, -en bank
die Bank —, ⸚e bench
der Bart -es, ⸚e beard
der Bauer -s, -n farmer, peasant
der Baum -es, ⸚e tree
beant'worten. *See* **antworten**
bedecken. *See* **decken**
bedeuten to mean, signify; **die bedeutung** meaning, importance; **un'bedeutend** unimportant, insignificant
beenden. *See* **das Ende**

die Beer'digung. *See* **die Erde**
die Beere —, –n berry
befehlen (befahl, befohlen, befiehlt) to command
begegnen (*w. dat.*) to meet, encounter
beginnen (begann, begonnen, beginnt) to begin
beglei'ten to accompany; **der Beglei'ter** companion
begrüßen. *See* **grüßen**
behalten. *See* **halten**
behaupten to affirm, assert; **die Behauptung** assertion, claim
bei at; with; by; near; in; **beim** + *inf.* while . . . -ing; **beim Aufstehen** while arising
beide both; two
das Bein –es, –e leg
beiseite. *See* **die Seite**
das Beispiel –s, –e example; **zum Beispiel (z. B.)** for example
beißen (biß, gebissen, beißt) to bite; **der Biß** bite; **beißend** bitingly, sarcastically; **das bißchen** little bit
bekämpfen. *See* **der Kampf**
bekannt. *See* **kennen**
bekommen (bekam, bekommen, bekommt) to get, receive
belebt. *See* **leben**
bellen to bark
beo'bachten to observe, watch; **der Beobachter** observer; **unbeobachtet** unobserved, unnoticed
bereit' ready, prepared; **un'vor'bereitet** unprepared
der Berg –es, –e mountain
berichten to report
beruhigend. *See* **ruhen**
beschreiben. *See* **schreiben**
besonder, besonders. *See* **sonder**
besorgen. *See* **sorgen**
besser better; **verbessern** to correct, improve
bestimmt' definitely; certainly; made (for); **un'bestimmt** indefinite, vague, uncertain
besuchen to visit; **der Besuch** visit; **der Besucher** visitor
das Bett –es, –en bed
beur'teilen. *See* **das Urteil**
bewachen. *See* **wach**
bewegen (bewog, bewogen, bewegt) to move, budge; **beweglich** movable; agile; stormy; **die Bewegung** movement, motion; **unbeweglich** motionless
beweisen (bewies, bewiesen, beweist) to prove; **der Beweis** proof, evidence; **zum Beweise** as evidence
der Bewohner. *See* **wohnen**
bewundern, der Bewunderer, die Bewunderung. *See* **das Wunder**
bezahlen to pay
biegen (bog, gebogen, biegt) to bend, turn; **die Biegung** bend
die Biene —, –n bee
das Bild –es, –er picture
bilden to form, shape; educate
billig cheap
binden (band, gebunden, bindet) to bind, tie; **das Band** ribbon, tie, bond; **die Verbindung** connection; **verbunden** connected, united
der Birnbaum. *See* **die Birne**
die Birne —, –n pear; **der Birnbaum** pear tree
bis to, up to; until; **bis zu** until
das bißchen. *See* **beißen**
bitten (bat, gebeten, bittet (um)) to beg (for), ask (for); **die Bitte** request
das Blatt –es, ⸚er leaf; sheet
blau blue
bleiben (blieb, geblieben, bleibt) to stay, remain; **der Hinterblie'bene** survivor; **(steh'enbleiben** [*sep. prefix*]. *See* **stehen)**
der Bleistift –s, –e pencil
blicken to look, glance; **der Anblick** sight; view; **der Blick** look, glance; **erblicken** to see, catch sight of
der Blitz –es, –e lightning

blühen to bloom; **aufblühend** promising, budding
die Blume —, -n flower
das Blut -es blood; **blutig** bloody
der Boden -s, ¨ ground; bottom; floor
die Bohne —, -n bean
böse angry; bad
braten (briet, gebraten, brät) to roast, fry
brauchen to need; use; **brauchbar** useful; **un'brauch'bar** useless
braun brown
brav good, well-behaved
brechen (brach, gebrochen, bricht) to break; **zerbrechen** to break to pieces, shatter, smash
breit broad; **ausbreiten** to spread, extend
brennen (brannte, gebrannt, brennt) to burn
der Brief -es, -e letter
bringen (brachte, gebracht, bringt) to bring; take
das Brot -es, -e bread
die Brücke —, -n bridge
der Bruder -s, ¨ brother
der Brunnen -s, — well; fountain
die Brust —, ¨e breast, chest
das Buch -es, ¨er book
der Buchstabe -n, -n letter (of the alphabet); **buch'stäblich** literally
der Bürger -s, — citizen
der Busch -es, ¨e bush
die Butter — butter

der Charak'ter -s, -te're character

da there; since; then; (*Cf.* §§ *22*, *105*); **davon** away
das Dach -es, ¨er roof
da'her'* therefore
damals then, at that time; **damalig** of that time
die Dame —, -n lady
damit' so that, in order that (*conj.*); with it (*cf.* § *105*)
danken (*w. dat.*) to thank; **dankbar** thankful, grateful; **danke schön** thank you
dann then; **dann und wann** now and then, at intervals
darstellen (*sep. prefix*) to present, represent; **die Darstellung** presentation
da'rum'* therefore; for the reason
das the; that
daß (*conj.*) that
das Datum -s, *pl.* **Daten** date
dauern to last; take (time); **dauernd** constantly
der Daumen -s, — thumb
decken to cover; set (table); **bedecken** to cover; **die Decke** ceiling, cover, blanket; **entdecken** to discover
denken (dachte, gedacht, denkt) to think; **denken an** to think of; **sich denken** imagine; **der Gedanke** thought
denn (*conj.*) for. (*Cf.* § *22*)
dennoch nevertheless
deutlich clear, plain
deutsch German; **Deutschland** Germany
der Dezem'ber -s December
dicht thick; close
der Dichter -s, — author, poet
dick thick, fat
der Dieb -es, -e thief
dienen (*w. dat.*) to serve; **der Diener** servant; **der Dienst** service; **diensteifrig** zealous, helpful
der Dienstag -s, -e Tuesday
dieser this; the latter
diesmal. *See* **Mal**
das Ding -es, -e thing
doch yet, however, but (sometimes coordinating conjunction). (*Cf.* § *22*)
der Doktor -s, -to'ren doctor
der Donner -s thunder
der Donnerstag -s, -e Thursday
doppelt double

das Dorf -es, ⸚er town, village
dort there; **dortig** of that place (*or* town *or* locality)
draußen. *See* **außen**
drei three
dreißig thirty
dreizehn thirteen
dringen (drang, gedrungen, dringt) to enter by force, penetrate; **vordringen** to advance, push on; **dringend** urgent
drinnen. *See* **innen**
der Druck. *See* **drücken**
drucken to print
drücken to press, squeeze; **der Ausdruck** expression; **ausdrücken** to express; **der Druck** pressure; **unterdrü'cken** to suppress
dumm stupid, "dumb"
dunkel dark, obscure; **die Dunkelheit** darkness; **im Dunkeln** in the dark
dünn thin
durch through; by
durch'aus' thoroughly; absolutely; **durchaus' nicht** not in any way, not for any reason
durchleu'chten. *See* **das Licht**
durchsetzen. *See* **setzen**
dürfen (durfte, gedurft, darf) to be permitted to, may
der Durst -es thirst; **durstig** thirsty
das Dutzend -s, -e dozen

eben even; level; flat; just now; simply (*cf.* § *22*); **e'benso** just as, likewise; **soe'ben** just now
e'benfalls likewise
ebenso. *See* **eben**
die Ecke —, -n corner
edel noble; lofty
ehe before
die Ehe —, -n marriage
die Ehre —, -n honor; **ehrlos** dishonorable; **verehren** to honor
ehrlich honest; **die Ehrlichkeit** honesty
das Ei -s, -er egg
die Eiche —, -n oak
der Eifer -s zeal, ardor, eagerness; **eifrig** zealous, eager
eigen own
eilen to hasten, hurry; **die Eile** haste, hurry, speed; **eilig** hasty, quick
ein, eine, ein a, an; one; in (when prefixed to verb); **einheitlich** unified
einan'der one another, each other
einfach simple; simply
einfinden. *See* **finden**
der Eingang. *See* **gehen**
einheitlich. *See* **ein**
einige a few, some
einmal. *See* **Mal.** (*Cf.* § *22*)
einsam lonesome; solitary
einschlafen (schlief ein, eingeschlafen, schläft ein) to go to sleep
einschließen. *See* **schließen**
einst once, formerly
einsteigen. *See* **steigen**
eintönig. *See* **der Ton**
eintreten. *See* **treten**
einzeln single, individual; **der Einzelne** individual
einzig only, sole; unique; single
das Eis -es ice
das Eisen -s, — iron; **eisern** iron, of iron
die Eisenbahn —, -en railroad; train
eisern. *See* **das Eisen**
die Eltern parents
empfangen (empfing, empfangen, empfängt) to receive; der **Empfang** reception
empfehlen (empfahl, empfohlen, empfiehlt) to recommend; **die Empfehlung** recommendation
empfinden (empfand, empfunden, empfindet) to feel; perceive
empor' up, upwards; high
das Ende -s, -n end, close; **beenden** to finish; **endlich** finally; **endlos** endless; **am Ende** after all

eng narrow
England, -s England
der Enkel -s, — grandson; grandchild; **die Enkelin** granddaughter
entdecken. *See* **decken**
entfernen. *See* **fern**
entfernt. *See* **fern**
entfliehen. *See* **fliehen**
entlang along
entleeren. *See* **leer**
entreißen. *See* **reißen**
entscheiden (entschied, entschieden, entscheidet) to decide, determine; **entscheidend** decisive
sich entschließen (entschloß, entschlossen, entschließt) to decide; **der Entschluß** decision, resolve
der Entschluß. *See* **entschließen**
entstehen (entstand, entstanden, entsteht) to originate
ent'weder . . . oder either . . . or
entwickeln to develop; **die Entwicklung** development
entzünden to inflame
der Erbe -n, -n heir; **erben** to inherit
erblicken. *See* **blicken**
die Erbse —, -n pea
die Erdbeere —, -n strawberry
die Erde —, -n earth, ground; **die Beer'digung** burial, interment
erfahren (erfuhr, erfahren, erfährt) to find out, learn; **die Erfahrung** experience; **un'erfahren** inexperienced
der Erfolg' -s, -e success; result; **erfolglos** unsuccessful
die Erfüllung. *See* **füllen**
ergreifen. *See* **greifen**
sich erheben. *See* **heben**
sich erhellen. *See* **hell**
erhitzen. *See* **heiß**
erinnern an to remind of; **sich erinnern an** to remember
sich erkälten to catch cold
erkennen (erkannte, erkannt, erkennt) to recognize **erkennbar** recognizable; **unerkannt** unrecognized
erklären to explain; declare; **un'erklärlich** inexplicable
erlauben to allow, permit
-erlei kinds of; **allerlei** all kinds of
erleuchten. *See* **das Licht**
ermüden. *See* **müde**
ernst serious, earnest; **ernstlich** earnest(ly), serious(ly)
erreichen. *See* **reichen**
erscheinen. *See* **scheinen**
erschreckt. *See* **der Schreck**
erschrocken. *See* **der Schreck**
erst first; at first; not until; only; **zuerst'** at first; **erst recht** more than ever
ertöten. *See* **töten**
ertrinken. *See* **trinken**
erwachen. *See* **wach**
erwähnen to mention
erwarten to await; expect; **die Erwartung** expectation, anticipation
erwidern to reply
erzählen to relate, tell; **die Erzählung** story
erziehen (erzog, erzogen, erzieht) to educate; rear
der Esel -s, — donkey; ass
essen (aß, gegessen, ißt) to eat; **eßbar** edible
etwa about; perhaps
etwas something; somewhat; anything; some; **so etwas** something of the kind
ewig eternal; **die Ewigkeit** eternity

das Fach -es, ⸚er subject; drawer
fahren (fuhr, gefahren, fährt) to ride; drive; go; **die Fahrt** ride; trip, journey
der Fall -es, ⸚e case; **jedenfalls, auf jeden Fall** in any case, at any rate
fallen (fiel, gefallen, fällt) to fall; **zerfallen** to fall (to pieces); **ins**

Wort *or* **in die Rede fallen** to interrupt; **überfal'len** to overtake; surprise; invade
falsch false; forged
die Fami'lie —, -n family
fangen (fing, gefangen, fängt) to catch
die Farbe —, -n color; paint; **farblos** colorless
das Farbpünktchen. *See* **die Farbe** *and* **der Punkt**
das Faß -es, ⸚er barrel, cask; **das Fäßchen** little barrel, keg
fassen to seize; contain
fast almost
der Februar -s February
die Feder —, -n pen; feather; spring; **der Federzug** (**die Feder** pen, **der Zug** (*from* **ziehen**) stroke)
fehlen to miss; be lacking (to)
der Fehler -s, — mistake, error
feiern to celebrate
fein fine; excellent; neat(ly)
der Feind -es, -e enemy
das Feld -es, -er field
der Felsen (der Fels) -s, — rock
das Fenster -s, — window
die Ferien (*pl.*) vacation
fern far, distant; **entfernen** to remove; **entfernt** removed, distant; die **Entfernung** distance; **die Ferne** distance
sich fernhalten von. *See* **halten**
fertig ready; finished
fest firm, solid; fast
das Fest -es, -e feast, festival; **festlich** festive(ly)
das Feuer -s, — fire; **feurig** fiery
finden (fand, gefunden, findet) to find; **einfinden** to arrive; appear
der Finger -s, — finger
der Fisch -es, -e fish; **das Fischerdorf** fishing village
flach flat; shallow; **die Fläche** surface; **die Wasserfläche** surface of the water
die Flamme —, -n flame
das Fleisch -es meat
die Fliege —, -n fly
fliegen (flog, geflogen, fliegt) to fly; **der Flug** flight
fliehen (floh, geflohen, flieht) to flee; **entfliehen** to escape; **die Flucht** flight
fließen (floß, geflossen, fließt) to flow, run; **der Fluß** river
die Flucht. *See* **fliehen**
der Flug. *See* **fliegen**
der Fluß. *See* **fließen**
folgen (*w. dat.*) to follow
fordern to demand; challenge
fördern to further, advance; bring out
die Form —, -en form, shape; figure; **formen** to mould, shape, fashion; **formlos** formless, shapeless
fort away; gone; on
fortsetzen (*sep. prefix*) to continue; **die Fortsetzung** continuation
fragen to ask; **die Frage** question; **fragen nach** to ask for
die Frau —, -en woman; wife; **Frau** Mrs.
das Fräulein -s, — young lady; **Fräulein** Miss
frei free; vacant; **die Freiheit** freedom; **im Freien** in the open air
freilich certainly, to be sure
der Freitag -s, -e Friday
fremd strange; foreign; **der Fremde** stranger; foreigner; **die Fremdsprache** (**fremd** foreign; **die Sprache** language)
fressen (fraß, gefressen, frißt) (*of animals*) to eat
die Freude —, -n joy, pleasure
sich freuen to be glad; **sich auf etwas freuen** to be happy in anticipation of something
der Freund -es, -e friend; **die Freundin** girl *or* woman friend; **freundlich** friendly, kind, pleasantly; **un'freundlich** unfriendly

der Friede(n) -ns, -n peace; **friedlich** peaceful
frieren (fror, gefroren, friert) to freeze; to feel cold
frisch fresh
froh glad, happy, joyful; **fröhlich** happy, gay, merry
die Frucht —, ⸚e fruit
früh early; **früher** earlier, sooner, formerly
der Frühling -s, -e spring
das Frühstück -s, -e breakfast
der Fuchs -es, ⸚e fox
fühlen to feel; touch; **das Gefühl** feeling
führen to lead, guide
füllen to fill; **die Erfüllung** fulfillment; **die Fülle** fullness
fünf five
fünfzehn fifteen
fünfzig fifty
für for
fürchten to fear; **sich fürchten vor** to be afraid of
der Fürst -en, -en prince; sovereign
der Fuß -es, ⸚e foot
das Futter -s fodder, feed; **füttern** to feed

die Gabe. *See* **geben**
die Gabel —, -n fork
die Gans —, ⸚e goose
ganz whole, entire; very; quite; just; **gänzlich** entirely, completely; **ganz gleich** regardless
gar *strengthens or emphasizes*; very; **gar' nicht** not at all; **gar' nichts** nothing at all
der Garten -s, ⸚ garden; **Gartenhaus** (garden) summer house
der Gast -es, ⸚e guest
das Gebäu'de -s, — building
geben (gab, gegeben, gibt) to give; **abgeben** to deliver, hand over (in); **ausgeben** to give out, spend; **vergeben** to forgive; **die Gabe** gift; **der Geber** giver, donor; **es gibt** there is, there are
gebo'ren born
gebrau'chen to use
der Geburts'ort. *See* **der Ort**
der Geburts'tag. *See* **der Tag**
der Gedan'ke. *See* **denken**
die Gefahr' —, -en danger; **gefährlich** dangerous
gefal'len (gefiel, gefallen, gefällt) (*w. dat.*) to please; **der Gefallen** favor
das Gefühl'. *See* **fühlen**
ge'gen against, toward; in comparison with; in return for
der Ge'genstand -s, ⸚e object
das Ge'genteil -s, -e opposite; **im Gegenteil** on the contrary
gegenü'ber (*w. dat.*) opposite; as compared with
die Ge'genwart — presence; present time
geheim' secret; **geheimnisvoll** mysterious; **das Geheim'nis** secret; **heimlich** secret
gehen (ging, gegangen, geht) to go; walk; **der Aufgang** going up, rising, rise; **der Ausgang** exit; **der Eingang** entrance; **untergehen** to sink; fall; perish; set; **vergehen** to slip past, fail; **es geht mir gut** I am well; **es geht Sie nichts an** that is none of your business; **was die Zeit angeht** as far as time (*or* the tense) is concerned
gehö'ren (*w. dat.*) to belong to; **der An'gehörige** relative; member
der Geist -es, -er spirit; ghost; mind
gelb yellow
das Geld -es, -er money
geliebt, der Geliebte. *See* **lieben**
gelin'gen (gelang, gelungen, gelingt) (*impers.*, *w. dat.*) to succeed; **es gelingt mir** I succeed
gelten (galt, gegolten, gilt) to be valid, to be worth, to be of value

gemein' mean, common; general
das Gemü'se -s, — vegetable
genau' exact, precise; **die Genauigkeit** exactness, precision
genie'ßen (genoß, genossen, genießt) to enjoy
genug' enough; **genügen** to suffice, be sufficient
gera'de straight; just; exactly
geregelt. *See* **die Regel**
der Gerettete. *See* **retten**
gering' slight; inferior
gern gladly, willingly; **gern** (*plus verb*) to like to; **gern essen** to like to eat; **un'gern** unwillingly
das Geschäft' -s, -e business; deal; store; affair
gescheh'en (geschah, geschehen, geschieht) to happen, take place
das Geschenk'. *See* **schenken**
die Geschich'te —, -n story; history
geschieden. *See* **scheiden**
das Geschrei'. *See* **schreien**
geschult'. *See* **die Schule**
die Gesell'schaft —, -en company; party; society; **gesell'schaftlich** social
das Gesicht' -s, -er face; das **An'gesicht** face, countenance
das Gespräch'. *See* **sprechen**
die Gestalt' —, -en form, figure; **die Gestal'tung** formation
gestat'ten to allow, permit
ge'stern yesterday
gesund' healthy, sound
die Gewalt'—, -en power, force; violence
gewin'nen (gewann, gewonnen, gewinnt) to win; **der Gewinn'** winning, gain, profit
gewiß' certain, sure; **die Gewißheit** certainty
sich gewöhnen an. *See* **gewöhnlich**
gewöhn'lich usual, customary; **ungewöhnlich** unusual; **die Gewohnheit** habit, custom; **die Sprechgewohnheit** speech habit; **die Gewöhnung** adaptation, adjustment; **sich gewöhnen an** to accustom, adapt oneself to
gießen (goß, gegossen, gießt) to pour; cast
der Gipfel -s, — peak; height
glänzen to glisten, shine, glitter, gleam; **der Glanz** luster, splendor; **glänzend** glittering, shining, brilliant
das Glas -es, ⸚er glass; **das Gläschen** small glass
glatt smooth
glauben to believe; **glauben an** to believe in; **der Glaube** belief, faith; **leicht'gläubig** credulous, gullible; **un'gläubig** incredulous, unbelieving; **unglaub'lich** unbelievable
gleich like; same; immediately; equal(ly); regardless, immaterial, no matter; **gleichzeitig** at the same time; **der Vergleich** comparison; **es ist mir gleich** it is all the same to me; **ganz gleich** regardless, all the same
das Glied -es, -er limb; member; **das Mitglied** member
das Glück. *See* **glücklich**
glücklich happy; safely; **das Glück** happiness, luck; fate; fortune; **das Un'glück** misfortune, bad luck, unhappiness; **un'glücklich** unhappy; **Glück haben** to be fortunate; **zum Glück** luckily
das Gold -es gold
der Gott -es, ⸚er god; **die Göttin** goddess
das Grab. *See* **der Graben**
der Graben -s, ⸚ ditch, trench; **graben** to dig; **das Grab** grave
der Graf -en, -en count; **die Gräfin** countess
das Gras -es, ⸚er grass
grau gray
greifen (griff, gegriffen, greift) to seize, grasp; **greifen nach** reach for
die Grenze —, -n limit, boundary

groß great, large; tall; **die Größe** greatness, size
die Großmutter —, ⁻̈ grandmother; **der Großvater** grandfather
grün green; **grünlich** greenish
der Grund -es, ⁻̈e ground; cause; reason; bottom; depths; **gründen** to found, establish; **grundlos** groundless, without foundation
grüßen to greet; wave; **begrüßen** to greet; **der Gruß** greeting
die Gunst —, ⁻̈e favor
gut good; well; **die Güte** kindness, goodness; **es geht mir gut** I am well; **es geht ihr gut** she is well
das Gut -es, ⁻̈er estate; goods

das Haar -es, -e hair
haben (hatte, gehabt, hat) to have
der Hafen -s ,⁻̈ harbor, port; **der Hafenarbeiter** dock worker
der Hahn -es, ⁻̈e rooster
halb half; **die Hälfte** half
der Hals -es, ⁻̈e throat; neck
halten (hielt, gehalten, hält) to hold; think, regard (as); stop; **behalten** to keep; **sich fernhalten von** to keep out of the way of, steer clear of, avoid; **halten für** to consider, take to be; **halten von** to think of
die Hand —, ⁻̈e hand
das Handtuch. *See* **das Tuch**
hängen (hing, gehangen, hängt) to hang; **abhängig** dependent; **unabhängig** independent; **zusammenhängen** hang together, connect
hart hard; harsh; rough
hartherzig. *See* **das Herz**
hassen to hate
der Haufe(n) -ns, -n heap, pile; crowd
das Haupt -es, ⁻̈er head; chief
die Hauptstraße. *See* **die Straße**
das Haus -es, ⁻̈er house; **das Häuschen** small house; **der Nachhau'seweg** road (way) home; **nach Hause gehen** to go home; **zu Hause sein** to be at home
die Haut —, ⁻̈e skin; hide
heben (hob, gehoben, hebt) to lift, raise; **sich erheben** to arise
das Heer -es, -e army
das Heft -es, -e notebook
die Heide —, -n heath
das Heil -es happiness; salvation; welfare; **das Un'heil** evil, harm, misfortune
heilig holy, sacred
das Heim -es, -e home; **die Heimat** home
heimlich. *See* **geheim**
heiraten to marry
heiß hot; fervent(ly); passionate(ly); **erhitzen** to heat, grow warm; **die Hitze** heat
heißen (hieß, geheißen, heißt) to be called; call; command; mean; **das heißt** that is to say
der Held -en, -en hero; **die Heldin** heroine
helfen (half, geholfen, hilft) to help; **die Hilfe** help, aid; **hilflos** helpless; **die Hilflosigkeit** helplessness
hell clear, merry; bright, light; **die Helle** brightness; **sich erhellen** to clear up
das Hemd -es, -en shirt
her toward the speaker *or* scene of action; ago; *often not translated*
herbei' here; hither
der Herbst -es, -e autumn
die Herde —, -n herd
der Herr -n, -en gentleman; master; Lord; sir; **Herr** Mr.
herrlich excellent, splendid
hervor' forth, out
das Herz -ens, -en heart; **das Herzenskindchen** darling; **hartherzig** hardhearted
heute today; **heutig** present-day, today's; **heute abend** this evening; **heute morgen** this morning

hier here
die Hilfe. *See* **helfen**
hilflos. *See* **helfen**
die Hilflosigkeit. *See* **helfen**
der Himmel -s, — sky; heaven; **himmlisch** heavenly
hin away from the speaker *or* scene of action; there; gone; **hin und her** back and forth
hindern to hinder, prevent; **verhindern** to prevent
hinter behind
der Hinterbliebene. *See* **bleiben**
hinzu' besides, in addition; there
die Hitze. *See* **heiß**
hoch (hoh-) high; tall; **die Höhe** height(s)
der Hof -es, ⸚e court; farm; yard; **höflich** courteous, polite; **der Kirchhof** churchyard, cemetery; **die Höflichkeit** politeness; die **Un'höflichkeit** rudeness, impoliteness
hoffen to hope; **die Hoffnung** hope; **hoffnungslos** past (all) hope
die Hoffnung, hoffnungslos. *See* **hoffen**
höflich. *See* **der Hof**
die Höflichkeit. *See* **der Hof**
die Höhe. *See* **hoch**
hohl hollow; **die Höhle** cave
holen to fetch, bring, get
das Holz -es, ⸚er wood; **das Un'terholz** underbrush
der **Honig -s** honey
hören to hear; **hören auf** to listen to; **der Hörer** receiver; auditor; **unhör'bar** inaudible
die Hose —, -n trousers
der Hund -es, -e dog, hound
hundert hundred
hungrig hungry; **verhungern** to starve to death
der Hut -es, ⸚e hat

immer always; **immer bes'ser** better and better; **immer wie'der** again and again; **im'mer noch (noch immer)** still
in in; into
indem' while; by (*cf.* § *127*)
indes' (indes'sen) meanwhile; nevertheless
innen inside, within; **in seinem Inneren** in his inner self; to himself; **vor seinem inneren Auge** in his mind's eye; **drinnen** inside, within
interessant' interesting; **das Interes'se** interest
inzwi'schen. *See* **zwischen**
irgend- (ein) any (old); some; **irgendwelche** some kind of; **irgendwie** somehow; **irgendwo** somewhere; **irgendwoher** somewhere (or other)
irren to err; stray, wander

ja yes; *often used as a flavoring particle* (*cf.* § *22*); **jawohl'** yes indeed
jagen to hunt; chase; der **Jäger** hunter
das Jahr -es, -e year; **das Jahrhun'dert** century; **das Jahrtausend** millennium
der Januar -s January
jawohl'. *See* **ja**
je ever; always
je . . . desto the . . . the
jeder each, every; any; **jedenfalls** at any rate
jedoch' however
jemand somebody, someone; anyone
jener that; the former
jetzt now; **jetzig** present
die Jugend — youth; **jugendlich** youthful
der Juli -s July
jung young; **jung'verhei'ratet** (*from* **heiraten**) recently married
der Juni -s June

der Kaffee -s coffee

der Kaiser -s, — emperor; kaiser
kalt cold; **die Kälte** cold
der Kampf -es, ¨e combat, battle; struggle; **kämpfen** to fight; **bekämpfen** to combat
die Karte —, -n card; ticket; map
die Kartof'fel —, -n potato
der Käse -s cheese
die Katze —, -n cat
kaufen to buy; **der Käufer** purchaser, buyer
kaum scarcely
kein no, not any
der Keller -s, — cellar
der Kellner -s, — waiter
kennen (kannte, gekannt, kennt) to know (by acquaintance); **bekannt** known, acquainted; **die Kenntnis** knowledge; **un'bekannt** unknown; **(kennenlernen.** *See* **lernen)**
das Kind -es, -er child; darling; **das Kindchen** small child; dear one; darling; **die Kindheit** childhood; **kindlich** childlike; **das Kindermädchen** nursemaid
das Kinn -es, -e chin
die Kirche —, -n church
der Kirchhof. *See* **der Hof**
klagen to complain, lament
klar clear, plain; **die Klarheit** clearness, clarity
die Klasse —, -n class
das Kleid -es, -er dress; **ankleiden** to dress; **die Kleider** the clothes; **das Kleidchen** little dress, fine, pretty dress; **die Kleidung** clothing, dress
klein small, little; **die Kleinigkeit** trifle
klingeln to ring
klopfen to knock, beat; pound
der Knabe -n, -n boy; youth
das Knie -(e)s, -(e) knee
der Knochen -s, — bone; **knochig** bony; *in compounds*, -boned
der Knopf -es, ¨e button
kochen to cook; boil
der Koffer -s, — trunk; suitcase
die Kohle —, -n coal
kommen (kam, gekommen, kommt) to come; get; **es kommt darauf an** it depends; **vor'wärtskommen** to get ahead; **zusammenkommen** to meet, assemble
der König -s, -e king
das Königreich. *See* **das Reich**
können (konnte, gekonnt, kann) to be able, can
der Kopf -es, ¨e head
das Kopftuch. *See* **das Tuch**
der Körper -s, — body
kosten to cost
die Kraft —, ¨e force, power, strength; **kräftig** powerful, strong
krank ill, sick; **das Krankenhaus** hospital
die Kreide — chalk
der Krieg -es, -e war
die Krone —, -n crown
der Krug -es, ¨e pitcher; jug
krumm crooked
der Kuchen -s, — cake
die Kuh —, ¨e cow
kühl cool
die Kunst —, ¨e art; skill; **der Künstler** artist
kurz short, brief
die Kusi'ne —, -n cousin (female)
küssen to kiss

lächeln to smile
lachen to laugh; **das Lachen** laughter
der Laden -s, ¨ store, shop
die Lampe —, -n lamp
das Land -es, ¨er land, country; **ländlich** rustic, country-like; **auf das Land gehen** to go to the country; **auf dem Lande sein** to be in the country
lang (lange) long; for a long time; **die Länge** length; **längst** long

since, long ago; **lange her** long ago; **solange** as long as
langsam slow
längst. *See* **lang**
lassen (ließ, gelassen, läßt) to let; make, cause; **verlassen** to leave, desert
laufen (lief, gelaufen, läuft) to run; **der Lauf** course, run
laut loud, noisy; **der Laut** sound; **lautlos** without a sound, silent
leben to live; **belebt′** lively; **das Leben** life; **leben′dig** alive, lively; **leblos** lifeless
le′benskräftig. *See* **leben** *and* **die Kraft**
leer empty, vacant; **entleeren** to empty
legen to lay, place, put; **nie′derlegen** to lay down; **sich nie′derlegen** to lie down
lehnen to lean; **der Lehnstuhl** armchair
lehren to teach; **der Lehrer** teacher; **die Lehrerin** female teacher
der Leib -es, -er body; waist
leicht easy; light; graceful; slender; **die Leichtigkeit** ease
leichtgläubig. *See* **glauben**
leiden (litt, gelitten, leidet) to suffer, bear, tolerate; **das Leid** grief, sorrow, wrong
leider unfortunately
leid tun: es tut mir leid I am sorry
leise soft, gentle; slight(ly)
leiten to lead; direct; **der Leiter** leader, manager
lernen to learn; **kennenlernen** (*sep. prefix*) to make the acquaintance of
lesen (las, gelesen, liest) to read; **der Leser** reader
letzt last; **zuletzt** at last
leuchten. *See* **das Licht**
die Leute people
das Licht -es, -er light; **leuchten** to emit light, gleam; **durchleuch′ten** to illuminate, fill with light; **erleuchten** to illuminate
lieben to love; **lieb** dear; **die Liebe** love; **lieblich** lovely; **geliebt** beloved; **der Geliebte** the beloved, loved one, sweetheart, darling; **verliebt** in love; **liebhaben** to be fond of
lieber rather
das Lied -es, -er song
liegen (lag, gelegen, liegt) to lie; be situated
die Linde —, -n linden (tree)
die Linie —, -n line
link left; **links** to the left
die Lippe —, -n lip
die Literatur′ —, -en literature
loben to praise
der Löffel -s, — spoon
lohnen to reward; pay
los loose; **loswerden** to get rid of
-los -less
die Lösung —, -en solution; **lösen** to dissolve, solve, release
der Löwe -n, -n lion
die Luft —, ⸚e air; **der Luftraum** space
die Lust —, ⸚e desire; pleasure; **lustig** gay, merry; **badelustig** liking to bathe

machen to make; do; put
die Macht —, ⸚e might, power, force; **mächtig** mighty; **der Allmächtige** the Almighty; **die Ohnmacht** faint
das Mädchen -s, — girl
der Magen -s, — stomach
das Mahl -es, -e meal; **die Mahlzeit —, -en** meal
der Mai -s May
das Mal -es, -e time (instance); **manchmal** sometimes; **einmal** once (just once) (*cf.* § *22*); **auf ein′mal** suddenly; **mit einem Male** suddenly; **nicht′ einmal** not even; **noch einmal** again; **diesmal** this

time; **zum ersten Mal** for the first time

man one

mancher many a; **manchmal** sometimes

der Mann -es, ⸚er man; husband; **das Männchen** little man; **Männchen** darling; **männlich** manly, masculine

der Mantel -s, ⸚ coat cloak, mantle

die Mark — mark (coin)

der Markt -es, ⸚e market

der Marsch -es, ⸚e march

der März -es March

die Mauer —, -n (outside) wall

das Maul -es, ⸚er mouth (of animal)

die Maus -, ⸚e mouse

das Meer -es, -e ocean, sea; **der Meeresarm** bay, inlet

mehr more; **mehrere** several; **nicht mehr** no longer

meinen to think; mean; say; **die Meinung** opinion; **nach meiner Meinung** in my opinion

meist most; usually; **meistens** usually

der Meister -s, — master

die Menge —, -n quantity; number(s); crowd

der Mensch -en, -en human being, person; **die Menschheit** mankind; **menschlich** human

merken to mark, note; **merklich** noticeable; **unmerk'lich** imperceptible

messen (maß, gemessen, mißt) to measure

das Messer -s, — knife

das (*or* **der**) **Meter -s, —** meter

die Milch — milk

mischen to mix; **vermischen** to intermix, intermingle; **die Vermischung** mixture, intermixture; crossing (of races)

mit with; along

der Mittag. *See* **die Mitte**

die Mitte — middle, center; **mitten in** in the middle of; **der Mittag** midday, noon; **der Vor'mittag** forenoon, morning

der Mittwoch -s Wednesday

möchte. *See* **mögen** *and* *§ 122*

mögen (mochte, gemocht, mag) to want to, like to; may

möglich possible; **die Möglichkeit** possibility; **un'mög'lich*** impossible

der Monat -s, -e month

der Mond -es, -e moon

der Montag -s, -e Monday

der Mord -es, -e murder; **der Mörder** murderer

der Morgen -s, — morning; **morgen** tomorrow; **morgen früh** tomorrow morning

müde tired; **ermüden** to tire

die Mühle —, -n mill

der Mund -es, -e mouth

die Musik' — music

müssen (mußte, gemußt, muß) to be obliged to, compelled to, have to, must

der Mut -es courage; **mutig** bold, courageous

die Mutter —, ⸚ mother; **das Mütterchen** little mother, old lady

die Muttersprache. *See* **sprechen**

nach to; toward; after; according to; at; **nach und nach** little by little

der Nachbar -n, -n neighbor; **die Nachbarin** female neighbor

nachdem' after (*conj.*)

der Nachhau'seweg. *See* **das Haus**

nach'her'* afterwards

nächst, der Nächste. *See* **nah**

die Nacht —, ⸚e night

nah close, near by; **die Nähe** vicinity, proximity; **nächst** next; nearest; **der Nächste** neighbor; **nahen** to approach

der Name -ns, -n name; **nämlich** namely, you see

nämlich. *See* **der Name**
der Narr -en, -en fool
die Nase —, -n nose
natür'lich naturally; **ü'bernatürlich** supernatural
der Nebel -s, — fog, mist
neben next to, beside
die Nebensache. *See* **die Sache**
der Neffe -n, -n nephew
nehmen (nahm, genommen, nimmt) to take; **annehmen** to accept, assume; **aufnehmen** to take up, absorb; accept, receive; **(Platz nehmen.** *See* **der Platz)**
neidisch jealous, envious; **neidisch auf** jealous of, envious of; **der Neid** jealousy, envy
nein no
nennen (nannte, genannt, nennt) to name, call
das Nest -es, -er nest
neu new
neuerwachen. *See* **wach**
neun nine
neunzehn nineteen
neunzig ninety
nicht not; **nicht einmal.** *See* **das Mal**; **nicht mehr.** *See* **mehr**; **nicht wahr.** *See* **wahr**
die Nichte —, -n niece
nichts nothing
nichts'sagend. *See* **sagen**
nicken to nod
nie, niemals never; **(noch nie.** *See* **noch)**
nieder low; mean; down; **niedrig** low
niedergeschlagen. *See* **schlagen**
niemand nobody, no one
noch still, yet; even; only; very; ever; (*Cf.* § *22*); **noch' einmal** again; **noch nicht** not yet; **noch nie'** never before; **noch im'mer, im'mer noch.** *See* **immer (weder . . . noch.** *See* **weder)**
der Norden -s north; **nordisch** northern; **nördlich** northern, to the north
die Not —, ⸚e need, want; distress; **der Notfall** case of need, emergency
nötig necessary
not'wendig necessary; **die Not'wen'digkeit** necessity
der Novem'ber -s November
die Nummer —, -n number
nun now; well; then; (*Cf.* § *22*)
nur only
die Nuß —, ⸚e nut

ob whether; if
oben above; upstairs; **ober** upper
obgleich' although
das Obst -es fruit
oder or
der Ofen -s, ⸚ stove, oven
offen. *See* **öffnen**
die Offenheit. *See* **öffnen**
der Offizier' -s, -e officer
öffnen to open; **offen** open; **ungeöffnet** unopened; **die Offenheit** openness, frankness
oft often
ohne without; **ohne zu sagen** without saying; **ohne zu wachsen** without growing
die Ohnmacht. *See* **die Macht**
das Ohr -es, -en ear
der Okto'ber -s October
der Onkel -s, — uncle
der Ort -es, -e (⸚er) place; town; **der Geburts'ort** (*from* **geboren**) birthplace
der Osten -s east; **ost-, öst-** east-; **östlich** eastern
das Paar -es, -e pair; couple; **ein paar** a few; **ein paarmal** a few times
das Papier -s, -e paper
die Person' —, -en person; **persön'lich** personally
der Pfarrer -s, — clergyman, minister, priest
der Pfennig -s, -e penny

das Pferd -es, -e horse
pflanzen to plant; **die Pflanze** plant; **die Pflanzenwelt** vegetable kingdom
die Pflicht —, -en duty
der Platz -es, ⸚e place; room; **das Plätzchen** little place, room; **Platz nehmen** (*like sep. prefix*) to sit down
plötzlich suddenly
die Post — mail; post office
praktisch practical
der Preis -es, -e prize; price
der Prinz -en, -en prince
prüfen to test, examine; **die Prüfung** test, examination
das Pult -es, -e desk
der Punkt -es, -e point; period, dot; **das Pünktchen** little dot

raten (riet, geraten, rät) to advise; guess; **der Rat** advice, counsel; **ratlos** helpless
das Rathaus -es, ⸚er city hall
rauchen to smoke
der Raum -es, ⸚e room; space
rauschen to roar; rustle
rechnen to figure; **die Rechnung** bill, account, reckoning, figuring; **rechnen auf** to count on
recht right(-hand); proper, correct; **rechts** to the right
das Recht -es, -e right; **un'recht** wrong; **das Un'recht** injustice; **es ist mir recht** it is all right with me; **mit gutem Recht** rightly; **recht haben** to be right
reden to talk, speak; **die Rede** speech; conversation; **in die Rede fallen** to interrupt; **der Redner** speaker; **überre'den** to persuade
die Regel —, -n rule; **geregelt** regulated, bound by rules
der Regen -s rain; **regnen** to rain; **die Regenzeit** rainy season
der Regenschirm. *See* **der Schirm**
regnen. *See* **der Regen**
reich rich
das Reich -es, -e realm; **empire**; **das Königreich** kingdom
reichen to reach; extend; hand (to); suffice; provide, offer; **errei'chen** to reach, attain; **un'erreich'bar** unattainable; **überreich'en** to hand to, deliver
reif ripe; mature
die Reihe —, -n row, rank; series
rein clear; pure
die Reise —, -n trip; **reisen** to travel; **der Reisende** traveler
reißen (riß, gerissen, reißt) to tear; **entreißen** to tear away; **zerreißen** to tear to pieces, break
reiten (ritt, geritten, reitet) to ride (horseback)
reizen to irritate; charm; **reizend** charming
retten to save; **die Rettung** saving, rescue, escape; **der Gerettete** the (one) rescued
richtig correct, right, accurate
riechen (roch, gerochen, riecht) to smell; **riechen nach** to smell of
der Ring -es, -e ring
der Rock -es, ⸚e coat; skirt
die Rose —, -n rose
rot red
rot'bäckig. *See* **die Backe**
der Rücken -s, — back; **der Rückenwind** tail wind
rufen (rief, gerufen, ruft) to call; shout
ruhen to rest; **ausruhen** to rest, relax; **beruhigend** soothing, reassuring; **die Ruhe** rest, peace, calm; **ruhig** peaceful, calm; *frequently a flavoring particle meaning* simply, perfectly, all right, *etc.* (*cf.* § *22*); **ruhelos** restless; **un'ruhig** restless
der Ruhm -es fame, glory; **rühmen** to praise
rühren to stir, move
rund round

die Sache —, -n thing; affair; **die Nebensache** secondary consideration; **sachlich** objective; **die Sachlichkeit** objectivity; **unsachlich** subjective

sagen to say; tell; **nichts'sagend (nichtssagende Worte)** empty, meaningless (words); **unsag'bar** unspeakable, inexpressible

die Sahne — cream

das Salz -es salt

sammeln to collect, gather; **die Sammlung** collection; **beim Sammeln** while collecting

der Samstag -s, -e Saturday

der Satz -es, ⸗e sentence

sauer sour

die Schachtel —, -n box, carton

der Schaden -s, ⸗ harm, damage; **es ist schade** it is too bad

das Schaf -es, -e sheep

scharf sharp; **die Schärfe** sharpness

der Schatten -s, — shade; shadow; **schattenlos** shadowless; **die Schattenlosigkeit** shadowlessness, absence of a shadow

der Schatz -es, ⸗e treasure; beloved, sweetheart; **schätzen** to value, estimate; **die Schätzung** estimate, evaluation; **unschätz'bar** inestimable, priceless

scheiden (schied, geschieden, scheidet) to separate, part; **der Ab'schied** departure, farewell; **geschieden** divorced; **sich scheiden lassen** to sue for a divorce; **unterschei'den** to distinguish, discriminate, differentiate; **der Unterschied** distinction, difference; **verscheiden** to pass away, die; **verschieden** different; **verschie'denartig** of a different kind *or* character; **die Verschiedenheit** difference

scheinen (schien, geschienen, scheint) to shine; seem; **erscheinen** to seem, appear; **der Schein** shine, light, gleam

schenken to present with, bestow, give; **das Geschenk** gift

schicken to send

schieben (schob, geschoben, schiebt) to shove, push; (put off)

schießen (schoß, geschossen, schießt) to shoot; **der Schuß** shot

das Schiff -es, -e ship, boat; **das Schiffchen** the little boat

der Schinken -s, — ham

der Schirm -es, -e protection; **der Regenschirm** umbrella; **der Sonnenschirm** parasol

die Schlacht —, -en battle

schlafen (schlief, geschlafen, schläft) to sleep; **schlafen gehen** to go to sleep; **das Schläfchen** nap, snooze; **der Schlafende** the sleeper, the one sleeping

schlagen (schlug, geschlagen, schlägt) to beat, strike; **der Schlag** blow, stroke; **aufschlagen** to open; **niedergeschlagen** dejected, despondent, depressed

schlank slender

schlecht bad; wicked

schließen (schloß, geschlossen, schließt) to close; lock; conclude; **abschließen** to finish, end, conclude; **aufschließen** to unlock; **ausschließen** to exclude (lock out); **einschließen** to lock in; **schließlich** finally; **der Schluß** close, end, conclusion; **verschließen** to lock up

der Schluß. *See* **schließen**

schmecken to taste

der Schmerz -es, -en pain; grief; **schmerzen** to ache; **schmerzend** painful

der Schnee -s snow

schneiden (schnitt, geschnitten, schneidet) to cut

schnell fast, quick

schon already; as early (soon) as; *often used as flavoring particle* (*cf.* § *22*); all right; very; even; etc.

schön beautiful; handsome; fine; **die Schönheit** beauty
der Schreck(en) -s, -en fright, horror, shock; **erschrecken** to frighten; **erschrecken (erschrak, erschrocken, erschrickt)** to be frightened; **schrecklich** terrible, frightful
schreiben (schrieb, geschrieben, schreibt) to write; **beschreiben** to describe; **unbeschreib'lich** indescribable; **unterschrei'ben** to sign; **die Un'terschrift** signature
schreien (schrie, geschrie(e)n, schreit) to cry, shout; **das Geschrei** cry, shout(ing); noise; **der Schrei** cry, scream
schreiten (schritt, geschritten, schreitet) to step, pace, walk; **der Schritt** step, pace
der Schritt. *See* **schreiten**
der Schuh -es, -e shoe
die Schuld —, -en guilt, blame; debt; fault; **schuld** guilty, to blame; **die Un'schuld** innocence; **un'schuldig** innocent
die Schule —, -n school; **geschult** schooled, trained; **der Schüler** schoolboy
die Schulter —, -n shoulder
der Schuß. *See* **schießen**
schwach weak, feeble
schwarz black
schweigen (schwieg, geschwiegen, schweigt) to be silent
das Schwein -es, -e swine, pig
schwer difficult, hard; heavy
die Schwester —, -n sister
schwierig difficult; **die Schwierigkeit** difficulty
schwimmen (schwamm, geschwommen, schwimmt) to swim; float; **der Schwimmer** swimmer; **die Schwimmerin** female swimmer
sechs six
sechzehn sixteen
sechzig sixty
die See —, -n sea, ocean; **der See -s, -n** lake
die Seele —, -n soul
sehen (sah, gesehen, sieht) to see; look; **ansehen** to look at, watch; **aussehen** to look, appear; **überse'hen** to overlook; **zusehen** watch; **sichtbar** visible; **vor'sichtig** careful, cautious; **die Vorsehung** Providence
sehr very
sein (war, gewesen, ist) to be
seit for; since; **seitdem'** since that time; *as conj.*, since
die Seite —, -n side; page; **beiseite** aside
selb- same; -self (*cf.* § *112*); **dersel'be** the same
selbst even; -self (*cf.* § *112*)
selb'ständig. *See* **stehen**
selten seldom, rare; **seltsam** strange, peculiar
senden (sandte, gesandt, sendet) to send
der Septem'ber -s September
setzen to set, place, put; **sich setzen** to sit down; **sich durch'setzen** to prevail, win out
sicher safe; certain(ly); steady; sure; definite(ly); **die Sicherheit** certainty; **un'sicher** uncertain, unsteady
sichtbar. *See* **sehen**
sieben seven
siebzehn seventeen
siebzig seventy
der Sieg -es, -e victory; **der Sieger** victor
das Silber silver; **silbrig** silverlike
silbrig. *See* **das Silber**
singen (sang, gesungen, singt) to sing
sinken (sank, gesunken, sinkt) to sink; **versunken** lost in thought
der Sinn -es, -e sense; mind; **sinnlos** senseless, mad, foolish

sitzen (saß, gesessen, sitzt) to sit
so so; thus; as; in this manner; in such a way; well; just as; **so ein** such a; **sobald.** *See* **bald; soviel.** *See* **viel**
soe'ben. *See* **eben**
sogar' even; as a matter of fact
sogleich' immediately, at once
der Sohn -es, ⸗e son
solcher such
der Soldat' -en, -en soldier
sollen to be obliged to; to be to; to be said to; ought to; to be supposed to
der Sommer -s, — summer
sonder- special . . .; **besonder** special; **beson'ders** especially; **son'derbar** peculiar, strange
sondern but
der Sonnabend -s, -e Saturday
die Sonne —, -n sun; **sonnig** sunny, radiant; **der Sonnenaufgang** sunrise
der Sonnenaufgang. *See* **Sonne**
der Sonnenschirm. *See* **der Schirm**
der Sonntag -s, -e Sunday
sonst otherwise; usual; **sonst noch etwas** anything (something) else
sorgen to care; worry; **besorgen** to take care of; **die Sorge** care, worry
soviel. *See* **viel**
spät late
spielen to play; **das Spiel** play; game
spitz pointed, acute; **die Spitze** point, top
die Sprache. *See* **sprechen**
sprachlos. *See* **sprechen**
sprechen (sprach, gesprochen, spricht) to speak; say; **die Aussprache** pronunciation; **aussprechen** to pronounce, utter; **das Gesprä'ch** conversation; **die Muttersprache** mother tongue; **die Sprache** language, speech; **sprachlos** speechless; **unaussprech'lich** inexpressible; **der Wi'derspruch** contradiction; **widerspre'chen** to contradict, to talk back to
springen (sprang, gesprungen, springt) to spring, jump; **aufspringen** to jump up; fly open; **zerspringen** to burst
der Staat -es, -en state; **staatenbildend (der Staat, bilden)** colonizing
die Stadt —, ⸗e city, town; **das Städtchen** small city
der Stamm -es, ⸗e stem, trunk; tribe, race
der Stand. *See* **stehen**
stark strong; heavy; stout; hard; **die Stärke** strength
statt (anstatt') instead of; **statt zu geben** instead of giving; **die Werkstatt** workshop **(Statt** = stead = place)
stechen (stach, gestochen, sticht) to prick, pierce, sting
stecken to stick; put (in pocket); pin
stehen (stand, gestanden, steht) to stand; **aufstehen** to stand up, get up, arise; **selb'ständig** independent; **der Stand** position, booth; **stehenbleiben** (*sep. prefix*) to stop
steigen (stieg, gestiegen, steigt) to climb; mount; rise; **absteigen** dismount; **einsteigen** step, get in
der Stein -es, -e stone, rock; **steinern** of stone; **versteinert** petrified, turned to stone
stellen to place, put, set; **die Stelle** position, place; **die Ausstellung** exhibition, show; **die Stellung** position; **auf der Stelle** at once
sterben (starb, gestorben, stirbt) to die
der Stern -es, -e star
stets always
still still, quiet; **die Stille** stillness, quiet, silence
die Stimme —, -n voice; **stimmlos** voiceless

die Stirn —, -en forehead
der Stoff -es, -e material; cloth
der Stoffwechsel. *See* **wechseln**
stolz proud; **der Stolz** pride
stören to disturb; interrupt
stoßen (stieß, gestoßen, stößt) to push, thrust; **ausstoßen** to exclude; eject; scream, emit, utter, let out; **der Windstoß** gust of wind
die Strafe —, -n punishment, fine, penalty
der Strand -es, -e strand, beach
die Straße —, -n street; **die Hauptstraße** highway, main street
streben to strive
strecken to stretch; extend; **die Strecke** stretch, distance, little way
streichen (strich, gestrichen, streicht) to stroke
das Streichholz -es, ⸚er match
streiten (stritt, gestritten, streitet) to dispute, quarrel
streng severe, strict, stern; **die Strenge** severity, sternness
das Stroh -es straw
der Strom -es, ⸚e large river; current; torrent
der Strumpf -es, ⸚e stocking
das Stück -es, -e piece
der Student′ -en, -en student; **studie′ren** to study (attend a university or college); **das Stu′dium** study
der Stuhl -es, ⸚e chair
stumpf dull, blunt
die Stunde —, -n hour; lesson
der Sturm -es, ⸚e storm; **stürmen** to storm; **stürmisch** stormy, emotional
stürzen to rush; tumble; throw. cast
suchen to seek; **die Suche** search
der Süden -s south; **süd-** south-; **südlich** southern, to the south
die Sünde —, -n sin
süß sweet; **die Süße** sweetness; **das Süßwasser** fresh water

der Tag -es, -e day; **täglich** daily; **der Geburts′tag** (*from* **geboren**) birthday; **ans Tageslicht bringen, fördern** to bring to light (out)
die Tanne —, -n fir (tree)
die Tante —, -n aunt
die Tasche —, -n pocket
das Taschentuch. *See* **das Tuch**
die Tasse —, -n cup; **das Täßchen** small cup
die Tat. *See* **tun**
die Tätigkeit. *See* **tun**
der Tau -s dew
tausend thousand
der Tee -s tea
teilen to divide; share; **der Teil** part, share; **verteilen** to distribute; **das Ge′genteil** contrary, opposite; **im Ge′genteil** on the contrary
der Teller -s, — plate
teuer dear; expensive
der Teufel -s, — devil
tief deep; low; **die Tiefe** depth(s)
das Tier -es, -e animal; **die Tierwelt** animal kingdom
die Tinte —, -n ink
der Tisch -es, -e table
die Tochter —, ⸚ daughter
der Tod. *See* **töten**
der Ton -es, ⸚e sound; **tönen** to sound, resound, ring; **eintönig** monotonous
töten to kill; **ertöten** to kill; stifle; **der Tod** death; **tot** dead; **todmüde** dead tired
träge idle; lazy
tragen (trug, getragen, trägt) to carry, bear; wear
trauen to marry (join in wedlock); trust; **vertrauen** to confide, entrust, trust
trauern to grieve, mourn; **traurig** sad; **die Traurigkeit** sadness
träumen to dream; **der Traum** dream
traurig. *See* **trauern**

treffen (traf, getroffen, trifft) to hit; meet

treiben (trieb, getrieben, treibt) to drive; set in motion; drift

trennen to separate; **sich trennen von** to part with; **die Trennung** separation

die Treppe —, -n staircase; stair

treten (trat, getreten, tritt) to step, walk; **ein'treten** to step in, enter; occur; **der Tritt** step

treu true, faithful

trinken (trank, getrunken, trinkt) to drink; **ertrinken** to drown

der Tritt. *See* **treten**

trocken dry; **trocknen** to dry; **die Trockenheit** dryness, drought

trösten to console; **der Trost** consolation, comfort; **trostlos** disconsolate, cheerless; **untröst'lich** inconsolable, disconsolate

der Trotz -es spite; obstinacy; haughtiness; **trotz** in spite of; **trotzen** to defy; **trotzig** defiant, scornful, obstinate; **trotz'dem** (*adv.*) in spite of it, nevertheless; **trotzdem'** (*conj.*) though; **der Trotzkopf** stubborn person

das Tuch -es, ⸗er cloth; **das Handtuch** towel; **das Kopftuch** scarf; **das Taschentuch** handkerchief; **das Umschlagetuch** scarf, shawl

tun (tat, getan, tut) to do; act; **tun, als ob** act as if, **die Tat** deed, act; **die Tätigkeit** activity

die Tür —, -en door

üben to practice, exercise; **die Übung** exercise, practice

über over, above; about; on; **über und über** all over, thoroughly

ü'berall' everywhere

überfal'len. *See* **fallen**

überhaupt' at all; on the whole; as a matter of fact

ü'bernatürlich. *See* **natürlich**

überre'den. *See* **reden**

überrei'chen. *See* **reichen**

überse'hen. *See* **sehen**

überset'zen to translate

übrigens by the way

die Übung. *See* **üben**

das Ufer -s, — shore, bank

Uhr o'clock; **die Uhr** clock, watch

um at; around, about; for; **um zu** in order to; **umfan'gen** to encircle, embrace **(um . . . willen.** *See* **willen)**

umge'ben to surround; **die Umge'bung** surroundings

das Um'schlagetuch. *See* **das Tuch**

der Um'weg. *See* **der Weg**

die Um'welt. *See* **die Welt**

un'abhängig. *See* **hängen**

un'absichtlich. *See* **die Absicht**

un'angenehm. *See* **angenehm**

unaussprech'lich. *See* **sprechen**

un'beach'tet. *See* **achten**

un'bedeutend. *See* **bedeuten**

un'bekannt. *See* **kennen**

unbeobachtet. *See* **beobachten**

unbeschreib'lich. *See* **schreiben**

un'bestimmt. *See* **bestimmt**

un'beweglich. *See* **bewegen**

un'brauch'bar. *See* **brauchen**

und and

un'erfahren. *See* **erfahren**

un'erkannt'. *See* **erkennen**

un'erklär'lich. *See* **erklären**

unerreich'bar. *See* **reichen**

un'freundlich. *See* **der Freund**

un'geöff'net. *See* **öffnen**

un'gern. *See* **gern**

un'gewöhnlich. *See* **gewöhnlich**

un'gläubig. *See* **glauben**

unglaub'lich. *See* **glauben**

das Un'glück. *See* **glücklich**

un'glücklich. *See* **glücklich**

das Un'heil. *See* **das Heil**

die Un'höflichkeit. *See* **der Hof**

unhör'bar. *See* **hören**

unmerk'lich. *See* **merken**

un'mög'lich. *See* **möglich**

un'recht. *See* **das Recht**
das Un'recht. *See* **das Recht**
un'ruhig. *See* **ruhen**
un'sachlich. *See* **die Sache**
unsag'bar. *See* **sagen**
unschätz'bar. *See* **der Schatz**
die Un'schuld. *See* **die Schuld**
un'schuldig. *See* **die Schuld**
un'sicher. *See* **sicher**
unten. *See* **unter**
unter under, below; among; down; low; **unten** below
unterdrück'en. *See* **drücken**
un'tergehen. *See* **gehen**
das Un'terholz. *See* **das Holz**
unterrich'ten to instruct; inform; **der Un'terricht** instruction
unterschei'den. *See* **scheiden**
der Un'terschied. *See* **scheiden**
unterschrei'ben. *See* **schreiben**
die Un'terschrift. *See* **schreiben**
unterwer'fen. *See* **werfen**
untröst'lich. *See* **trösten**
un'verdient'. *See* **verdienen**
die Un'vernunft. *See* **die Vernunft**
un'vernünftig. *See* **die Vernunft**
un'verständlich. *See* **verstehen**
un'vollkommen. *See* **vollkommen**
un'vor'bereitet. *See* **bereit**
un'wahrscheinlich. *See* **wahrscheinlich**
un'weise. *See* **weise**
un'wichtig. *See* **wichtig**
un'wirklich. *See* **wirklich**
unzäh'lig. *See* **zählen**
un'zufrieden. *See* **zufrieden**
der Ur'sprung -s, ⸚e origin; **ursprüng'lich** originally
das Urteil -s, -e judgment; opinion; slogan; **beur'teilen** to judge; **urteilen** to judge

der Vater -s, ⸚ father; **väterlich** fatherly
verächtlich. *See* **achten**
verändern. *See* **ander**
die Veränderung. *See* **ander**
verbergen (verbarg, verborgen, verbirgt) to hide, conceal; **verbergen vor** to conceal from
verbessern. *See* **besser**
die Verbindung. *See* **binden**
verbunden. *See* **binden**
verdienen to earn; **un'verdient'** unearned, undeserved
verehren. *See* **die Ehre**
der Verein -s, -e club, organization
verfassen to write, compose; **der Verfasser** author
die Vergangenheit — past
vergeben. *See* **geben**
vergehen. *See* **gehen**
vergessen (vergaß, vergessen, vergißt) to forget
der Vergleich. *See* **gleich**
das Vergnügen -s pleasure, enjoyment
verhindern. *See* **hindern**
verhungern. *See* **hungrig**
verkaufen to sell; **der Verkäufer** salesman, clerk, merchant, dealer
verlangen to demand, require; desire
verlassen. *See* **lassen**
verliebt. *See* **lieben**
verlieren (verlor, verloren, verliert) to lose; waste; **verloren** forlorn
der Verlust -s, -e loss
vermischen, die Vermischung. *See* **mischen**
die Vernunft' reason (mind); senses; **vernünf'tig** reasonable, sensible; rational; **die Un'vernunft** lack of reason, unreasonableness; **un'vernünftig** irrational; **vernunft'los** senseless
verscheiden. *See* **scheiden**
verschieden. *See* **scheiden**
verschiedenartig. *See* **scheiden**
die Verschiedenheit. *See* **scheiden**
verschließen. *See* **schließen**
verschwinden (verschwand, verschwunden, verschwindet) to disappear

versprechen (versprach, versprochen, verspricht) to promise

verständlich. *See* **verstehen**

verstehen (verstand, verstanden, versteht) to understand; **verständlich** clear, intelligible; **un'verständlich** incomprehensible

versteinert. *See* **der Stein**

versuchen to try, attempt; **der Versuch** attempt, experiment

versunken. *See* **sinken**

verteilen. *See* **teilen**

vertrauen. *See* **trauen**

verwandeln to transform, change; **die Verwandlung** transformation

verwandt related; **der Verwandte** relative; **die Verwandtschaft** relationship

die Verwunderung. *See* **das Wunder**

der Vetter -s, -n cousin (male)

das Vieh -s cattle

viel much; **viele** many; **soviel** as much as

vielleicht' perhaps

vier four

vierzehn fourteen

vierzig forty

der Vogel -s, ¨ bird

das Volk -es, ¨er people; nation

voll full, filled; **völlig** completely

voll'kom'men* complete, perfect; **un'vollkommen** imperfect, incomplete

voll'ständig complete; **die Voll'ständigkeit** completeness

von of; from; by; about

vor before, in front of; from; to; with; on account of; ago; **vorn** in front; **vor allem** above all; **vor einer Woche** a week ago

vor'aus'* ahead, in advance; **voraus'sagen** to predict

vorbei' past, by; gone

vordringen. *See* **dringen**

vor'her'* before, previously

vorkommen (kam vor, vorgekommen, kommt vor) to occur, happen; come forward; seem

der Vor'mittag. *See* **die Mitte**

vorn. *See* **vor**

vorschlagen (schlug vor, vorgeschlagen, schlägt vor) to suggest, propose; move

die Vorsehung. *See* **sehen**

vor'sichtig. *See* **sehen**

der Vor'teil -s, -e advantage

vor'wärtskommen. *See* **kommen**

vorziehen (zog vor, vorgezogen, zieht vor) to prefer; pull out

wach awake; **bewachen** to guard; **erwachen** to awaken; **neuerwachen** newly awakened

wachsen (wuchs, gewachsen, wächst) to grow

die Waffe —, -n weapon; **die Waffengewalt** force of arms

wagen to dare, venture; risk; **wagemutig** courageous, venturesome

der Wagen -s, — wagon, carriage, car

wählen to choose, select; elect; **die Wahl** choice, selection

wahr true, real; **wahrhaf'tig** truly; **die Wahrheit** truth; **nicht wahr?** isn't that so?

während while, during

die Wahrheit. *See* **wahr**

wahr'scheinlich probable, likely; **un'wahrscheinlich** improbable, unlikely

der Wald -es, ¨er forest

die Wand —, ¨e wall

wann when

die Ware —, -n merchandise, goods; **das Warenhaus** department store

warm warm; **die Wärme** warmth

warten to wait; **warten auf** to wait for

-wärts -ward, -wards; **aufwärts** upward

warum' why

was what, whatever; that; **was für ein** what sort of

das Wasser -s, — water
die Wasserfläche. *See* **flach**
wechseln to change; to exchange; **ab'wechselnd** changing off, alternately; **der Stoffwechsel** metabolism
weder . . . noch neither . . . nor
weg away, off; gone
der Weg -es, -e way; road; path; **der Um'weg** roundabout way, detour; **sich auf den Weg machen** to set out
weh'tun (tat weh, weh getan, tut weh) to hurt, pain; **es tut mir weh** it hurts me
das Weib -es, -er woman; wife; **weiblich** feminine
Weih'nachten Christmas; **der Weihnachtsmann** Santa Claus
weil because, since
das Weilchen. *See* **die Weile**
die Weile — while, space of time; **das Weilchen** little while
der Wein -es, -e wine
weinen to cry, weep
weise wise, prudent; **unweise** unwise
die Weise —, -n manner, way
weiß white
weit far, distant; wide; large; expansive; **weiter** farther, further; on; **weitergehen** to continue; **weiterreden** to go on talking; **und so weiter (u. s. w., usw.)** and so forth, etc.
welcher which, what
die Welle —, -n wave
die Welt —, -en world; **die Umwelt** surroundings, environment
wenden (wandte, gewandt, wendet) to turn; **abwenden** to turn away, divert
wenig few, little; **wenige** few; **ein wenig** a little; **wenigstens** at least
wenn when, whenever; if; **wenn auch** *or* **auch wenn** although, even if
wer who; whoever
werden (wurde, geworden, wird) to become; get. (*See § 124 and § 128*)
werfen (warf, geworfen, wirft) to throw; **unterwer'fen** to subject, subjugate, subdue
das Werk -es, -e work
die Werkstatt. *See* **statt**
der Wert -es, -e value, worth; **wertvoll** valuable
das Wesen -s, — being; creature; essence
die Weste —, -n vest
der Westen -s west; **südwesten** southwest
das Wetter -s weather
wichtig important; **unwichtig** unimportant
wider against
widerspre'chen. *See* **sprechen**
der Wi'derspruch. *See* **sprechen**
wie as; **how**; like; *sometimes* as if
wieder again; **auf Wie'dersehen** good-by
wiederho'len to repeat
wiegen (wog, gewogen, wiegt) to weigh
die Wiese —, -n meadow
wild wild; **die Wildheit** wildness
der Wille. *See* **wollen**
willen: **um . . . willen** for the sake of
der Wind -es, -e wind, breeze
der Windstoß. *See* **stoßen**
der Winter -s, — winter
wirken to work; effect; be; **die Wirkung** result, effect
wirklich real, genuine; **unwirklich** unreal; **die Wirklichkeit** reality
die Wirkung. *See* **wirken**
der Wirt -es, -e innkeeper, landlord
wissen (wußte, gewußt, weiß) to know
wo where; **wo'her'*** whence; **wo'hin'*** whither, to what place. (*Cf.* § *106*)
die Woche —, -n week; **eine Woche lang** for a week
wohl well; no doubt (*cf.* § *22*)

wohnen to dwell, live; **der Bewohner** inhabitant; **wohnlich** habitable, snug, cozy; **die Wohnung** home, dwelling

die Wolke —, -n cloud

die Wolle — wool

wollen to want to, wish; to be about to; **der Wille** will, wish, intention

das Wort -es, -e *or* **⸚er** word; **wortlos** wordless, silent(ly); **das Wörterbuch** dictionary; **der Wortwechsel** exchange of words, argument

das Wunder -s, — wonder, miracle; **bewundern** to admire; **der Bewunderer** admirer; **die Bewunderung** admiration; **sich wundern** to be surprised; **die Verwunderung** surprise, amazement

wünschen to wish, desire; **der Wunsch** wish

die Würde dignity; **würdig** worthy

die Wurzel —, -n root

zahlen to pay

zählen to count, number; **die Zahl** number; **unzäh'lig** countless

zahm tame

der Zahn -es, ⸚e tooth

zart tender, delicate; **zärtlich** tender, affectionate; **die Zärtlichkeit** tenderness

das Zeichen -s, — sign, signal

zeichnen to sketch; mark

zeigen to show

die Zeit —, -en time; **eine Zeitlang** for a time

die Zeitung —, -en newspaper

zerbrechen. *See* **brechen**

zerfallen. *See* **fallen**

zerreißen. *See* **reißen**

zerspringen. *See* **springen**

der Zeuge -n, -n witness

die Ziege —, -n goat

ziehen (zog, gezogen, zieht) to pull, draw; move; make; derive; **anziehen** to put on, dress; **ausziehen** to take off, (*refl.*) to undress; **zurückziehen** to withdraw

das Ziel -es, -e aim, goal, destination

ziemlich rather; considerable

das Zimmer -s, — room

zittern to tremble, shake

zu to; at; for; in; too

der Zucker -s sugar

zuerst'. *See* **erst**

der Zu'fall -s, ⸚e chance; accident

zufrie'den satisfied, contented; **un'zufrieden** discontented, dissatisfied

der Zug -es, ⸚e train; procession

zugleich' at the same time

zu'hören (*sep. prefix*) to listen

die Zu'kunft — future

zuletzt'. *See* **letzt**

zu'machen (*sep. prefix*) to close, shut

zunächst' first of all; at first

zurück' back

zurück'kehren (*sep. prefix*) to turn back, return

zurückziehen. *See* **ziehen**

zusam'men together; **zusammenbrechen** to collapse

zusammenhängen. *See* **hängen**

zusammenkommen. *See* **kommen**

zusehen. *See* **sehen**

der Zu'stand -es, ⸚e condition

zwanzig twenty

zwar granted; of course; to be sure; *often* **zwar** *introduces an elaboration of a preceding statement*

der Zweck -es, -e purpose; use

zwei two

der Zweifel -s, — doubt; **zweifellos** beyond a doubt, certainly

der Zweig -es, -e twig, branch

zwingen (zwang, gezwungen, zwingt) to force, compel

zwischen between; **inzwi'schen** meanwhile, in the meantime

zwölf twelve

ENGLISH-GERMAN VOCABULARY

able: be able to **können (konnte, gekonnt, kann)**
about **ungefähr**
advice **der Rat -es** (*no pl.*); advise **raten (riet, hat geraten, rät)**
afraid: be afraid (of) **sich fürchten (vor** (*dat.*))
after (*prep.*) **nach** (*dat.*)
again **wieder**
against (*prep.*) **gegen** (*acc.*)
ago: two years ago **vor zwei Jahren**
allow **erlauben**
almost **fast**
alone **allein**
already **schon**
although **obgleich**
always **immer**
answer **antworten**
apple **der Apfel -s, ¨**
arm **der Arm -es, -e**
arrive **ankommen (kam an, ist angekommen, kommt an)**
as soon as **sobald (als** *or* **wie), sowie**
ask (request), ask for **bitten (bat, hat gebeten, bittet) um** (*acc.*)
ask (question) **fragen**; ask about **fragen nach** (*dat.*)
autumn **der Herbst -es, -e**
away **weg**

back **zurück**
bad **böse, schlecht**
barrel **das Faß -es, ¨er**
bathe **baden**
be **sein (war, ist gewesen, ist)**; I am to **ich soll**; he is to **er soll**; be able. *See* able, can
beard **der Bart -es, ¨e**
beat **schlagen (schlug, hat geschlagen, schlägt)**
beautiful **schön**
because **weil**
become **werden (wurde, ist geworden, wird)**
bed **das Bett -es, -en**; go to bed **zu Bett (ins Bett) gehen**
before (*conj.*) **ehe, bevor**
begin **beginnen (begann, hat begonnen, beginnt), anfangen (fing an, hat angefangen, fängt an)**
believe **glauben** (*w. dat. of person*); to believe in **glauben an** (*w. acc.*)
belong to **gehören** (*w. dat.*)
bench **die Bank —, ¨e**
best **best-** (*cf.* **gut**; §§ *95, 96, 97*)
better **besser** (*cf.* **gut**; §§ *95, 96, 97*)
between **zwischen** (*dat. or acc.*)
big **groß ¨er, ¨t**
bird **der Vogel -s, ¨**
bite **beißen (biß, hat gebissen, beißt)**
black **schwarz ¨er, ¨est**
blood **das Blut -es**
blue **blau**
book **das Buch -es, ¨er**
bread **das Brot -es** (*no pl.*)
break **brechen (brach, hat gebrochen, bricht)**
breathe **atmen**
bridge **die Brücke —, -n**
bright **hell**
bring **bringen (brachte, hat gebracht, bringt)**
brother **der Bruder -s, ¨**
building **das Gebäude -s, —**
business **das Geschäft -es, -e**
but **aber, sondern.** *See* § *38*
buy **kaufen**
by (*prep.*) (*means or agent*) **von** (*dat.*)

cake **der Kuchen -s, —**
called, to be **heißen (hieß, hat geheißen, heißt)**

can, be able **können (konnte, hat gekonnt, kann)**
carriage **der Wagen -s, —**
cast **werfen (warf, hat geworfen, wirft)**
catch **fangen (fing, hat gefangen, fängt)**
charming **reizend**
child **das Kind -es, -er**
church **die Kirche —, -en**
citizen **der Bürger -s, —**
city **die Stadt —, ⸚e**
claim **behaupten**
class **die Klasse —, -n**
clear **klar**
clock **die Uhr —, -en**
close **schließen (schloß, hat geschlossen, schließt)**
coat **der Rock -es, ⸚e**
coffee **der Kaffee -s**
cold **kalt, ⸚er, ⸚est**
color **die Farbe —, -n**
come **kommen (kam, ist gekommen, kommt)**
console **trösten**
contented **zufrieden**
corner **die Ecke —, -n**
cost **kosten**
could. *See* can, able
count **zählen**; count on **rechnen auf** (*acc.*)
country **das Land -es, ⸚er**; in the country **auf dem Lande**; to the country **auf das Land**
couple: a couple (a few) **ein paar**
cry **schreien (schrie, hat geschrie(e)n, schreit)**
cup **die Tasse —, -n**
cut **schneiden (schnitt, hat geschnitten, schneidet)**

danger **die Gefahr —, -en**
dark **dunkel**
day **der Tag -es, -e**
deep **tief**
defiance **der Trotz -es** (*no pl.*)
definite(ly) **bestimmt**
devil **der Teufel -s, —**
dictionary **das Wörterbuch -es, ⸚er**
die **sterben (starb, ist gestorben, stirbt)**
difficult **schwer**
disappear **verschwinden (verschwand, ist verschwunden, verschwindet)**
do **machen, tun (tat, hat getan, tut)**
door **die Tür —, -en**
double **doppelt**
down **herunter**
draw **ziehen (zog, hat gezogen, zieht)**
dress **das Kleid -es, -er**
drink **trinken (trank, hat getrunken, trinkt)**
drive **treiben (trieb, hat getrieben, treibt)**

early **früh**
earn **verdienen**
earth **die Erde —**
easy **leicht**
eat **essen (aß, hat gegessen, ißt)**; eaten (up) **aufgegessen**
egg **das Ei -es, -er**
eight **acht**
eighteen **achtzehn**
enjoy **genießen (genoß, hat genossen, genießt)**
England **England**
English **Englisch, englisch**
enough **genug**
entire **ganz**
even (*adv.*) **sogar, selbst**
evening **der Abend -s, -e**; in the evening **abends**; one evening **eines Abends**; this evening **heute abend**
ever **je**
every **jeder**
everything **alles**
everywhere **überall**
examine **prüfen**
example **das Beispiel -s, -e**
expect **erwarten**
expensive **teuer**
explain **erklären**

face **das Gesicht –es, –er**
fall **fallen (fiel, ist gefallen, fällt)**; *from a horse* **stürzen**
family **die Familie —, –n**
farm **der Hof –es, ⸗e**
fast **schnell**
father **der Vater –s, ⸗**
fetch **holen**
few **wenig**
find **finden (fand, hat gefunden, findet)**
find out **erfahren (erfuhr, hat erfahren, erfährt)**
finger **der Finger –s, —**
first **erst**
five **fünf**
flower **die Blume, —, –n**
for (*prep.*) **für** (*acc.*); (*conj.*) **denn**
forest **der Wald –es, ⸗er**
forget **vergessen (vergaß, hat vergessen, vergißt)**
four **vier**
Friday **Freitag**
friend **der Freund –es, –e; die Freundin —, –nen**
front: in front of **vor** (*dat. or acc.*)
fruit **die Frucht —, ⸗e; das Obst –es** (*no pl.*)

garden **der Garten –s, ⸗**
gentleman **der Herr –n, –en**
German (*adj.*) **deutsch**; German (person) **der, die Deutsche**; German (language) **Deutsch**
Germany **Deutschland –s**
get (receive) **bekommen (bekam, hat bekommen, bekommt)**; get (fetch) **holen**; get (become) **werden (wurde, ist geworden, wird)**
girl **das Mädchen –s, —**
give **geben (gab, hat gegeben, gibt)**
glass **das Glas –es, ⸗er**; a glass of water **ein Glas Wasser**
go **gehen (ging, ist gegangen, geht)**
goat **die Ziege —, –n**
good **gut, besser, best**
goose **die Gans —, ⸗e**
grandson **der Enkel –s, —**; granddaughter **die Enkelin —, –nen**
granted **zwar**
grass **das Gras –es, ⸗er**
green **grün**
grow **wachsen (wuchs, ist gewachsen, wächst)**
guest **der Gast –es, ⸗e**

hair **das Haar –es, –e**
hand **die Hand —, ⸗e**
happy **glücklich**; to be happy **sich freuen**
harbor **der Hafen –s, ⸗**
hard **schwer**
hat **der Hut –es, ⸗e**
hate **hassen**
haughtiness **der Trotz –es**
have **haben (hatte, hat gehabt, hat)**; have to (obligation) **müssen (mußte, hat gemußt, muß)**
he **er**; he who **wer**
head **der Kopf –es, ⸗e**
hear **hören**
heart: by heart **auswendig**
heavy **schwer**; heavily **schwer**
help **helfen (half, hat geholfen, hilft)** (*w. dat.*)
here **hier**
hero **der Held –en, –en**
hide **verbergen (verbarg, hat verborgen, verbirgt)**
history **die Geschichte —, –n**
hold **halten (hielt, hat gehalten, hält)**
holy **heilig**
home: be at home **zu Hause sein**; go home **nach Hause gehen**
honest **ehrlich**
hope **hoffen**
horse **das Pferd –es, –e**; to fall from one's horse **vom Pferde stürzen**
hot **heiß**
house **das Haus –es, ⸗er**
how **wie**
husband **der Mann –es, ⸗er**

I **ich**
ice **das Eis -es**
if **wenn**
ignite **anzünden**
ill **krank ¨er, ¨st**
immediately **sogleich**
in, into **in** (*cf.* § *28*)
intention **die Absicht —, -en**
interesting **interessant**
it *masc.* **er,** *fem.* **sie,** *neut.* **es**

jealous (envious) **neidisch**
July **Juli -s**
jump **springen (sprang, ist gesprungen, springt)**
just (*adv. of time*) **gerade**

kaiser **der Kaiser -s, —**
kiss **küssen**
knife **das Messer -s, —**
know **kennen, wissen.** *See* § *66*

lady **die Dame —, -n**
language **die Sprache —, -n**
large **groß ¨er, ¨t**
last **dauern;** (*adj.*) **letzt**
late **spät**
laugh **lachen**
lay **legen**
lead **führen**
learn **lernen**
left **links**
less **weniger**
let **lassen (ließ, hat gelassen, läßt)**
letter **der Brief -es, -e**
lie **liegen (lag, hat gelegen, liegt)**
like **mögen (mochte, hat gemocht, mag);** I like to read **ich lese gern;** I like to play **ich spiele gern**
line **die Linie —, -n**
listen **zuhören**
little **klein; wenig**
live (be alive) **leben;** (dwell) **wohnen**
long **lang(e) ¨er, ¨st**
look for **suchen**
lose **verlieren (verlor, hat verloren, verliert)**

loud **laut**
love **lieben**
lovely **lieblich**

make **machen**
man **der Mann -es, ¨er**
many **viele**
March **März -es**
marry **heiraten**
may (*permission*) **dürfen (durfte, hat gedurft, darf);** (*possibility*) **können (konnte, hat gekonnt, kann)**
measure **messen (maß, hat gemessen, mißt)**
meet **treffen (traf, hat getroffen, trifft)**
milk **die Milch —**
mistake **der Fehler -s, —**
mix **mischen**
money **das Geld -es**
month **der Monat -s, -e**
moon **der Mond -es, -e**
more **mehr**
more and more **immer** + *compar.*
morning **der Morgen -s, —;** in the morning **morgens**
mother **die Mutter —, ¨**
move **ziehen (zog, ist gezogen, zieht)**
Mr. **Herr;** Mrs. **Frau**
much **viel**
must **müssen (mußte, hat gemußt, muß)**
my **mein**
myself (*cf.* §§ *112*, *44*)

narrow **eng**
natural **natürlich**
need **brauchen**
nephew **der Neffe -n, -n**
never **nie**
new **neu**
newspaper **die Zeitung —, -en**
next **nächst;** next to **neben** (*dat. or acc.*)
niece **die Nichte —, -n**
night **die Nacht —, ¨e**
no *adj.* **kein;** *adv.* **nein**

noble **edel**
not **nicht**
nothing **nichts**
now **jetzt, nun**

observe **beobachten**
obstinacy **der Trotz -es** (*no pl.*)
o'clock **Uhr**
of **von** (*cf.* § *35*)
of course **zwar**
often **oft**
old **alt ¨er, ¨est**
on (upon) **auf** (*dat. or acc.*)
only **nur**
or **oder**
other **ander**
otherwise **sonst**
ought to *subjunctive of* **sollen**
out of **aus** (*dat.*)
own **eigen**

page **die Seite —, -n**
paper **das Papier -s, -e; die Zeitung —, -en**
pay **zahlen**
pay for **bezahlen**
pea **die Erbse —, -n**
peace **der Friede(n) -ns**
pen **die Feder —, -n**
pencil **der Bleistift -s, -e;** use a pencil **mit Bleistift schreiben**
penny **der Pfennig -s, -e**
permitted: to be permitted **dürfen (durfte, hat gedurft, darf)**
physician **der Arzt -es, ¨e**
picture **das Bild -es, -er**
piece **das Stück -es, -e**
plant **pflanzen**
play **spielen**
please **gefallen (gefiel, hat gefallen, gefällt)** (*w. dat.*)
pocket **die Tasche —, -n**
poor **arm ¨er, ¨st**
possible **möglich**
potato **die Kartoffel —, -n**
presence **die Gegenwart —,** (*no pl.*)
present **das Geschenk -s, -e;** (time) **die Gegenwart —** (*no pl.*)
press **drücken**
price **der Preis -es, -e**
prize **der Preis -es, -e**
probably **wahrscheinlich**
program **das Programm -es, -e**
proud **stolz**
prove **beweisen (bewies, hat bewiesen, beweist)**
push **stoßen (stieß, hat gestoßen, stößt)**

rain **der Regen -s**
rather **ziemlich**
read **lesen (las, hat gelesen, liest)**
ready (complete) **fertig;** (prepared) **bereit**
receive **erhalten (erhielt, hat erhalten, erhält)**
red **rot ¨er, ¨est**
remain **bleiben (blieb, ist geblieben, bleibt)**
remind (of) **erinnern (an** (*acc.*)**)**
report **berichten**
return **zurückkehren**
ride (on a horse) **reiten (ritt, ist geritten, reitet)**
right: it is all right with me **es ist mir recht**
ring **der Ring -es, -e**
rock **der Stein -es, -e**
roof **das Dach -es, ¨er**
room **das Zimmer -s, —**
rose **die Rose —, -n**
run **laufen (lief, ist gelaufen, läuft)**

sacred **heilig**
sad **traurig**
satisfied **zufrieden**
Saturday **Samstag, Sonnabend**
save **retten**
say **sagen**
scarcely **kaum**
sea **die See —, -n; das Meer -es, -e**
see **sehen (sah, hat gesehen, sieht)**
send **schicken**

sentence **der Satz -es, ⸚e**
seven **sieben**
shall (*cf.* § *124*)
share **teilen**
she **sie**
sheep **das Schaf -es, -e**
ship **das Schiff -es, -e**
short **kurz ⸚er, ⸚est**
shove off **abstoßen (stieß ab, hat** *or* **ist abgestoßen, stößt ab)**
show **zeigen**
silent, to be **schweigen (schwieg, hat geschwiegen, schweigt)**
simple **einfach**
since (*prep.*) **seit** (*dat.*)
sing **singen (sang, hat gesungen, singt)**
sit **sitzen (saß, hat gesessen, sitzt)**
sit down **Platz nehmen**
six **sechs**
sleep **schlafen (schlief, hat geschlafen, schläft)**
slender **schlank**
small **klein**
smell **riechen (roch, hat gerochen, riecht)**
smile **lächeln**
snow **der Schnee -s**
so **so**
softly **leise**
someone **jemand**
something **etwas**
song **das Lied -es, -er**
soon **bald, früh**
speak **sprechen (sprach, hat gesprochen, spricht); reden**
spring **der Frühling -s**
stand **stehen (stand, hat gestanden, steht)**
star **der Stern -es, -e**
stay **bleiben (blieb, ist geblieben, bleibt)**
step out **hinaustreten (trat hinaus, ist hinausgetreten, tritt hinaus)**
still **noch, noch immer**
stone **der Stein -es, -e**
story **die Geschichte —, -n**
straight **gerade**
street **die Straße —, -n**
student **der Student -en, -en**
study **lernen, studieren**
success **der Erfolg -es, -e**
suddenly **plötzlich**
summer **der Sommer -s, —**
sun **die Sonne —, -n**
Sunday **Sonntag**; on Sundays **Sonntags**
sure: to be sure **zwar**
swim **schwimmen (schwamm, hat geschwommen, schwimmt)**

take **nehmen (nahm, hat genommen, nimmt)**
talk **sprechen (sprach, hat gesprochen, spricht), reden**
ten **zehn**
test **prüfen**
than **als**
thank **danken** (*dat.*)
that (*conj.*) **daß**; (*rel. pron.*: *cf.* §§ *30*, *91*); (*pron. adj.*: *cf.* § *31*); *see footnote, p. 55*
then **da; dann**
there **da, dort**
these **diese** (*cf.* § *91*)
they **sie**
thick **dicht**
thin **dünn**
thing **die Sache —, -n**
think **denken (dachte, hat gedacht, denkt)**; think of **denken an** (*acc.*)
this **dies-** (*Cf.* § *31 and footnote, p. 55*)
thirty-five **fünfunddreißig**
thousand **tausend**
three **drei**
throw **werfen (warf, hat geworfen, wirft)**
time **die Zeit**
to (*prep.*) **nach** (*dat.*), **zu** (*dat.*)
today **heute**
together **zusammen**
tomorrow **morgen**
too (also) **auch; too** (much) **zu (viel)**
travel **reisen**

tree **der Baum -es, ⁼e**
trip **die Reise —, -n**
trust **trauen, vertrauen**
try **versuchen**
Tuesday **Dienstag**
two **zwei**

uncle **der Onkel -s, —**
understand **verstehen (verstand, hat verstanden, versteht)**
unfortunately **leider**
unhappy **unglücklich**
up **-auf (hinauf, herauf)**
use **gebrauchen**

very **sehr**
visit **besuchen**
voice **die Stimme —, -n**

wait **warten**
wall **die Wand —, ⁼e**
want to **wollen (wollte, hat gewollt, will)**
war **der Krieg -es, -e**
watch *noun*: **die Uhr —, -en**; *verb*: **beobachten**
water **das Wasser -s, —**
wear **tragen (trug, hat getragen, trägt)**
Wednesday **Mittwoch**
we **wir**
week **die Woche —, -n**
weigh **wiegen (wog, hat gewogen, wiegt)**
well **gut**
what **was** (*cf.* § *106*)
when **als; wenn; wann**; (*Cf.* § *65*)
whenever **wenn**
where **wo**
which **welch-**
while (*conj.*) **während**
white **weiß**
who **wer**
whole **ganz**
whose **wessen** (*cf.* §§ *36, 91*)
why **warum**
wife **die Frau —, -en**
will (*cf.* § *124*)
win **gewinnen (gewann, hat gewonnen, gewinnt)**
wind **der Wind -es, -e**
window **das Fenster -s, —**
wine **der Wein -es, -e**
winter **der Winter -s, —**
wish **wünschen**
with **mit** (*dat.*)
without **ohne** (*acc.*)
woman **die Frau —, -en**
wonder: no wonder **kein Wunder**
word **das Wort -es, ⁼er**
work die **Arbeit —, -en**
work **arbeiten**
write **schreiben (schrieb, hat geschrieben, schreibt)**

year **das Jahr -es, -e**
yes **ja**
yesterday **gestern**
yet: not yet **noch nicht**
you **du, ihr, Sie**
young **jung ⁼er, ⁼st**
your **dein, euer, Ihr**

INDEX

Unless otherwise indicated, numbers preceding the colon refer to sections; the numbers following the colon refer to pages.

I J K L M N O P Q 0 6 9 8 7 6 5 4

PRINTED IN THE UNITED STATES OF AMERICA